The Serpent's Plumes

SUNY series, Trans-Indigenous Decolonial Critiques
———————
Arturo Arias, editor

The Serpent's Plumes

Contemporary Nahua Flowered Words
in Movement

ADAM W. COON

Cover Credit: *Universo de las hilanderas* (Universe of Women Spinners; created in 2010, innovative mix of designs and threads from traditional embroidery) by Eneida Hernández. Courtesy of Eneida Hernández.

Published by State University of New York Press, Albany

© 2024 State University of New York

All rights reserved

Printed in the United States of America

No part of this book may be used or reproduced in any manner whatsoever without written permission. No part of this book may be stored in a retrieval system or transmitted in any form or by any means including electronic, electrostatic, magnetic tape, mechanical, photocopying, recording, or otherwise without the prior permission in writing of the publisher.

For information, contact State University of New York Press, Albany, NY
www.sunypress.edu

Library of Congress Cataloging-in-Publication Data

Name: Coon, Adam W., author.
Title: The serpent's plumes : contemporary Nahua flowered words in movement / Adam W. Coon.
Description: Albany : State University of New York Press, 2024. | Series: SUNY series, trans-indigenous decolonial critiques | Includes bibliographical references and index.
Identifiers: LCCN 2023042659 | ISBN 9781438497778 (hardcover : alk. paper) | ISBN 9781438497792 (ebook) | ISBN 9781438497785 (pbk. : alk. paper)
Subjects: LCSH: Nahuatl literature—History and criticism. | Decolonization in literature. | Nahuatl language. | Nahua philosophy. | Nahuas—Intellectual life.
Classification: LCC PM4068 .C66 2024 | DDC 897/.45209—dc23/eng/20240228
LC record available at https://lccn.loc.gov/2023042659

10 9 8 7 6 5 4 3 2 1

To GrandKathie, Grandma Coon, and Tonana Vero,
tlauel nimechijlamiki

Contents

ACKNOWLEDGMENTS ix

INTRODUCTION
The Serpent's Quills, Keyboards, and Touchscreens: Writing, Not Being Written 1

CHAPTER ONE
More Mexican Because We Speak Mexican: Natalio Hernández Transgressing the Borders of Nationalist Discourse 37

CHAPTER TWO
Ritual Shouts of the Forgotten: Anti-colonial Protest in Martín Tonalmeyotl's *Tlalkatsajtsilistle* 79

CHAPTER THREE
Grinding Words: Ethel Xochitiotzin Pérez's Subversion of Nahua and Nation-State Patriarchy in *Tlaoxtika in tlajtoli* 115

CHAPTER FOUR
Words of Water: Fluid Nahua Identities in Judith Santopietro's *Palabras de agua* 159

CHAPTER FIVE
Redressing the Eagle and Feathered Serpent: Mardonio Carballo's Trans-Indigenous Dialogues and Descolonizing *Contrapunteo* 181

CHAPTER SIX
Nahuatl Language and Territory as Coping Strategies in Ateri Miyawatl's *Neijmantototsintle* (2018) and *Tsintatak* (2020) 223

CONCLUSION
Slinging Xochitlajtoli at Dams: A Prismatic Project(ion) of
Contemporary Nahua Literature   257

NOTES   267

BIBLIOGRAPHY   305

INDEX   333

Acknowledgments

This book is a tequio of countless contributions from broad networks of authors, activists, family, friends, colleagues, and administrators. I feel a great responsibility to share these networks with care and respect. This genre of acknowledgments cannot do justice to what should include flowered necklaces, fuertes abrazos, and music. I express my deepest gratitude to Nahua artists throughout Northern Abiayala for their inspiration to press forward with this project, our yolotl-felt discussions, and the hospitality I received in their homes.

I express my appreciation to the Luna family in San Bernardino, California, for the conversations two decades ago that introduced me to the Nahuatl language and a Nahua family history of active participation in forming what many call Mexico and the United States today.

To Natalio Hernández and Bertha Serrano for welcoming me to your home and inviting me to participate in community projects in Tepeko. Noiknij Natalio, your words "nochi ika pamitl" often come to mind as inspiration, to follow the lines of the furrows, to move carefully step by step in the completion of any project.

To Tonana Vero, Totataj Manuel, Armando Hernández, Tonana Florentina, Eneida Hernández, and Marcelina Cruz Osorio, for receiving me in your Huastecan homes like family. I will forever treasure the experiences we have shared.

While completing this book, I have been a guest on Anishinaabe, Dakota, and Nahua lands. Although this study focuses on Nahuas, there are numerous intersections among Indigenous experiences across Turtle Island and Anahuac. It is my hope that this study approaches those spaces with tlatlepanitalistli, with respect, and foregrounds Native knowledge production within a wide conception of what constitutes territory. I thank the many Native students at the University of Minnesota Morris for their insights from discussions inside and outside the classroom.

To Arturo Arias, editor of the series Trans-Indigenous Decolonial Critiques, for his support through the different stages of this project, from its beginnings to now. Thank you for being the best mentor one could possibly hope for through the challenging times that inevitably arise in taking up the task of writing a book. With expertise and camaraderie, you took the time, above and beyond expectations, to give detailed comments and overall moral support. I am indebted to you for the invaluable discussions we have had and for believing in this project. Maltyox!

I thank the editors and staff at State University of New York Press who have made possible the series Trans-Indigenous Decolonial Critiques and the production of this book. I am humbled for this text to be included alongside titles from brilliant scholars such as Víctor Montejo and Mikel Ruiz. Thank you, James Peltz and Rebecca Colesworthy, for leading the editorial process. I express my appreciation to the three anonymous reviewers who gave exceptional feedback that strengthened the manuscript.

To the outstanding colleagues who guided this project. I express my deepest gratitude to Luis Cárcamo Huechante, who has been there with me through difficult moments. Thank you for your support and for being such a wonderful mentor. Thank you for always reminding me of the ethical implications of our work and leading me to pay attention to often overlooked elements such as the complexities of sound. Chaltu mai peñi. To Shannon Speed, for your unwavering encouragement through the Native American and Indigenous Studies program and for introducing me to Indigenous intellectuals from throughout Abiayala. To Héctor Domínguez Ruvalcaba, for discussions that led me to explore more deeply the theme of migration and to question the traditional depictions of Indigenous Nations in Mexico. To Jossianna Arroyo, for your support for this study since my first semester at The University of Texas Austin. To Kelly McDonough for being a volunteer mentor, a fount of moral support, and an all-around amazing person. To Jill Robbins for championing this project since we first met at the KFLC in 2008 and for your invaluable guidance. I would like to acknowledge James Cox for his support that led to the publication of an earlier version of the first chapter of this project in *The Oxford Handbook of Indigenous American Literature*. Portions of chapter 1 were published as "Ixtlamatiliztli / Knowledge with the Face: Intellectual Migrations and Colonial Displacements in Natalio Hernández's *Xochikoskatl*," in *The Oxford Handbook of Indigenous American Literature*, ed. James H. Cox and Daniel Heath Justice (Oxford, 2014), pp. 215–33. Thank you to Emil' Keme for leading the publication of an earlier chapter of this project, and for profound discussions about Abiayala.

I thank the Abiayala Working Group within the Native American and Indigenous Studies Association (NAISA) for inspiring panels and roundtables, feedback, and a nurturing network that centers on the ethical implications of the work we do. NAISA is a caring professional organization where kinship ties are formed while doing rigorous academic work. I thank the remarkable colleagues with whom I have had the opportunity to collaborate through the working group, and for the privilege to serve with Emiliana Cruz. I thank the Otros Saberes section of the Latin American Studies Association for their encouragement, and for creating a warm, compassionate space within what can be an overwhelmingly large organization. Thank you to Rosalva Aída Hernández Castillo, Mariana Mora, Angela Stuesse, Sandra J. Gutiérrez, Rocío del Pilar Moreno Badajoz, Emma Cervone, Diana Negrín, Genner Llanes-Ortiz, Vasun Jairath, and Alejandro Cerda.

I thank the team at the Briggs Library at the University of Minnesota Morris: LeAnn Dean, Angela Vetsch, Sandra Kill, Peter Bremer, and Naomi Skulan. Thank you to the archivists at the Archivo General de la Nación in Mexico City and the community archivists of libraries in the Huasteca and Tlaxcala. Thank you to Makiko Legate, Cindy Poppe, Jayne Hacker, and Michelle Blake in the Humanities Division Office for the behind-the-scenes work to make this research possible. Thank you, Alisande Allaben, Roger Wareham, John Hamerlinck, and the Grants Development Office, for your guidance.

I thank the Fulbright Program and FLAS for support of this project. I express appreciation for the broad array of funding provided by the University of Minnesota through the Grant-in-Aid program, the Institute of Advanced Study, the Imagine Fund, and the Global Programs and Strategy Alliance. From the Dean's Office on the Morris campus, I received Faculty Research Enhancement Funds and a sabbatical. I would like to acknowledge the University of Texas Austin Department of Spanish and Portuguese, Native American and Indigenous Studies, LLILAS, the Center for Mexican American Studies, and the Mellon Sawyer faculty seminar for direction from the faculty of these programs and for grants that made this research financially possible. While completing these acknowledgments, my colleague Emily Bruce shared an essential read, Emily Callaci's article "On Acknowledgments." Callaci signals that in the listing of fellowships what often goes unacknowledged is how grants are a "rare privilege" that should be widely available on a global scale. We should do everything possible to create grant programs both accessible to and directed by scholars from throughout Abiayala and beyond.

Thank you to the Nahua scholars Sabina de la Cruz, Ofelia Cruz Morales, Abelardo de la Cruz, Delfina de la Cruz, Eduardo de la Cruz, Victoriano Teposteko, and to John Sullivan, for introducing me to Huastecan Nahuatl and opening up the possibility to travel to the Huasteca and join a network of Nahua artists, professors, and community members. I thank you for letting me know that I had a home away from home with you. Thank you to the Nahua youth in Tepeko for your insights and the privilege to work with you in the community, especially Heydi, Edgar, Yazmin, and Pati. To Noé and Gustavo Zapoteco Sideño for receiving me in your home and for our conversations. I would like to acknowledge the wonderful people throughout Mexico who helped me during my travels: Eneida Hernández, Lucina Martínez, Tonana Gonzala, Tokomalej Aminda, Tokompaj Goyo, Totataj Alejandro Olguin, Tonana Juanita Olguin, Citlalli H. Xochitiotzin, Ethel Xochitiotzin Pérez, Refugio Nava Nava, Juan Hernández Ramírez, Justyna Olko, La familia Adán, Humberto Iglesias, Carmen Flores Cisneros, Jonathan Amith, Mili Mauricio, Fabiola Carrillo Tieco, Raquel Bronstein, René Esteban Trinidad, Juan Hernández Ramírez, Leticia Aparicio, Zabyna Mora, Mardonio Carballo, Ateri Miyawatl, Martín Tonalmeyotl, Judith Santopietro, Yankuik Metztli, Crispín Amador Ramírez, Ixchel Sáenz, Paulina Josh, José Antonio Flores Farfán, Arturo Gómez Martínez, Pedro Martínez Escamilla, Yolanda Matías García, Rosa Alba Tepole Quiahua, Dixie Lee Sullivan, Ildefonso Maya, Refugio Miranda San Román, Sixto Cabrera González, Christopher Woolley, Sarah Kress, Ramón Tepole González, Tirso Bautista Cárdenas, Betel Ortiz, Beti, Teo, Armandotsij, Mimi, and Diego.

There are at least thirty variants of the Nahuatl language. I speak Nahuatl from the Huasteca Veracruzana. I express my appreciation to authors from multiple regions for helping me understand the nuances among different variants. That said, I take responsibility for any mistakes in these shifts across the myriad complexities of the Nahuatl language.

I thank colleagues who gave feedback on drafts and lifted my spirits through writing in parallel. To Thomas Genova for your sage advice and New Jersey humor. To the American Indian and Indigenous Studies Workshop at the University of Minnesota. To Jean O'Brien, E. Ornelas, Kaylen James, Katrina Phillips, and Meredith McCoy. I thank Tiffany D. Creegan Miller, Hannah Burdette, David Tavárez, Emily Bruce, Cristina

Ortiz, liz Thompson, Elliot James, Stacey Aronson, Mary Jo Mayne, Julie Eckerle, Julia Dabbs, Kevin Whalen, Bradley Deane, Miriam Gieske, and Nic McPhee. To colleagues at the University of Minnesota Institute of Advanced Study. To Jimmy Patiño, Jennifer Gunn, Robert Allen Warrior, Hanna Takemoto, Kathryn Nuernberger, Carrie Oelberger, Elana Shever, Ioana Vartolomei Pribiag, Fernando Burga, Miguel Castañeda, Camila Gavin, and David Melendez. To accountability and support groups through the National Center for Faculty Development & Diversity Program, and for University of Minnesota Morris funding that allowed me to participate.

I express appreciation to my undergraduate research assistants. Clara Martínez Zuviria went above and beyond expectations in giving professional-quality feedback as we reviewed the manuscript. She is probably more familiar with this book now than anyone. I also thank Estella Acevedo, Isa Schomberg, and Brandi Kloss.

Thank you to the many other colleagues and friends who helped make this project possible: Raúl Olmo Fregoso Bailón, Alejandra Ramírez, Jacinta Toribio, Jesús Alberto Flores, Jennifer Gómez Menjívar, Gloria Elizabeth Chacón, Paul M. Worley, Rita M. Palacios, Gabe Desrosiers, Arturo Gómez Martínez, Constantina Bautista Nava, Beatriz Cuahutle Bautista, Werner Hernández, Wenceslao Herrera Coyac, Ricardo Zúñiga, Yumiko Tokumoto, José Manuel Gallardo, Ailenne Mendoza, Charles Hale, Katie Arens, Sarah Buchanan, Sergio Romero, René Carrasco, Ignacio Carvajal Regidor, Anne Martínez, Margarita Huayhua, Gabriela Polit, Stephanie Wood, Rodrigo Lopes de Barros, Monica Detrick, Magnus Pharao Hansen, David Shook, Susan Zakaib, Giovanni B'atz, Gabriela Spears-Rico, Ulises Juan Zevallos-Aguilar, Daniela Sevilla, Carlos Amador, Nicolás Emilfork, Dan Olson, Amy Olen, Joseph Pierce, Rebecca Thompson, Janet Schrunk Ericksen, Peh Ng, J. Wesley Flinn, Becca Gercken, Jason Ramsey, Windy Roberts, Tammy Berberi, Athena Kildegaard, Benjamín Narváez, Lisa Bevevino, and James Wojtaszek. I thank Isabel Dulfano and Deyanira Ariza-Velasco for inspiring me to become a professor and embark on this project.

I express my deepest gratitude to my family. This would have been impossible without your unwavering love and support. Thank you, Dad, for your feedback and wise counsel always. To my brothers Christopher, Jonathan, and Jeremy, for their amazing example. To Marce, Chloe, and Benjamin, for your support in this long journey with all its highs and lows. To the friends, family, and caretakers who stepped in and helped us when there were more diapers, hospital visits, and life surprises than we could have ever handled on our own. Thank you for your many prayers and love.

Three foundations in my life passed on during this time. They made all the difference in this project, with hugs and ánimo through tough moments. Thank you, Mom, for your exemplary grit in facing challenges. (How many mothers compete in marathons and climb Kilimanjaro past retirement age after surviving a life-threatening infection?) To Grandma Coon for listening attentively to this project's developments. To Tonana Vero for your wisdom and teaching me to laugh through adversity. Tlaskamati miak, nimechiknelia iuan nochipa nimechijlamikis. Las quiero mucho. To everyone who has made a difference in this journey, thank you.

Introduction

The Serpent's Quills, Keyboards, and Touchscreens

Writing, Not Being Written

> La serpiente es un símbolo para los pueblos de Mesoamérica. . . . Cuando uno escucha Quetzalcoatl piensa de inmediato en "La Serpiente Emplumada"; en el pasado glorioso de México, pasado que, de tan glorioso, nos estorba. Por eso preferí,—preferimos—hablar de los pueblos indígenas vivos, de *Las Plumas de la Serpiente* que siguen dotando a nuestro país de rostros y posibilidades múltiples.
>
> (The serpent is a symbol for the nations of Mesoamerica. . . . When someone hears Quetzalcoatl, they think immediately of "The Plumed Serpent"; of the glorious past of Mexico, a past so glorious it gets in our way. That is why I preferred,—we preferred—to speak about the living Indigenous nations, of *The Serpent's Plumes* who continue to endow our country with multiple faces and possibilities.)
>
> —Mardonio Carballo, *Las Plumas de la Serpiente* (2012)

"It's so pretty! How difficult is it to learn Nahuatl?" Nahua writer, activist, and television/radio host Mardonio Carballo tires of hearing this remark.[1] Although seemingly positive on the surface, calling Nahuatl "pretty" falls into recycled tropes that treat Indigenous languages like a romanticized antique veneer smeared on Mexican nationalist sentiments, rather than a source for meaningful contributions to present-day society.[2] Carballo responds that Nahuatl can be just as beautiful or ugly as any language. "How difficult is it?" belies the assumption that Nahuatl, the most spoken Native language in Mexico, is somehow rudimentary and easy to acquire. That view emerges in the erroneous use of *dialecto*, heard in the commonplace statement "Indians speak dialects, not languages," to suggest a fictitious deficiency of complex grammar, lexicon, or writing. In 2004, Carballo wrote to renowned Mexican news reporter Carmen Aristegui to protest references to Indigenous languages as *dialectos* on her radio program. She subsequently invited him to correct such misrepresentations and share Native perspectives with her audience. This exchange led to the creation of the radio short series *Las Plumas de la Serpiente* (The Serpent's Plumes), and *Las Plumas* endures nearly two decades later.

What is at stake in this battle over terminology? Carballo's defense of the language points to Nahuatl's importance in struggles that extend far beyond linguistic representation alone. Language is territory. In a broad sense of the term, territory encompasses an intersectional blend of acoustic, linguistic, visual, epistemic, and topographic spaces. Intimating that Nahuas failed to develop their linguistic skills mirrors a pernicious view that they also did not, and have not, sufficiently developed the lands on which they live. Within this settler colonialist framework, much as Castilian[3] displaces Nahuatl, transnational companies and nation-state-sponsored squatters who purportedly better exploit the "real estate" displace Nahuas. This study analyzes how Nahua writers use bilingual Nahuatl-Spanish xochitlajtoli (flowered words / sentences / discourse / language),[4] or "well-cultivated language," written from the 1980s to the present, to defend territory in a wide sense of the term.[5] Xochitlajtoli's invocation of a fruition situated within Nahua lands and audiovisual spaces insists upon a nexus among speech, the people, and what Marisol de la Cadena calls "other-than-humans" (*Earth Beings* xx). I understand Nahua territory as both archive and repertoire engaged in recording and performing languages, histories, and wor(l)dings at odds with nation-state-sponsored land appropriation and renderings of who constitutes sanctioned citizenry.[6]

I draw on Nahua perspectives as a decolonizing theoretical framework to argue that Nahua writers deploy unique worldviews, namely ixtlamatilistli (knowledge with the face, which highlights the value of personal experiences), yoltlajlamikilistli (knowledge with the heart, which underscores the importance of an affective intelligence), and tlaixpan (that which is in front, which expresses a view of the past as in front of a subject, as opposed to behind—as *past* and *pasado* suggest in English and Castilian). I use these concepts to dismantle the narrative frame of "vanquished Indians," found in Mexican nationalist discourse and its championing of a pervasively procrustean form of "Modernity."[7] While paradoxically upholding Indigenous symbols as fundamental to Mexico's origins, state-sponsored nationalist discourse considers only *mestizo* subjects as full-fledged citizens. Their partial Native ascendancy makes them natural heirs to the land, but "progress" is contingent upon the distance removed from that Native past.[8] However, Nahua artists represent dynamic knowledge production against a backdrop of official history that depicts them as antiquated. The views of ixtlamatilistli, yoltlajlamikilistli, and tlaixpan are key in Nahua struggles and effectively challenge those who attempt to marginalize Native knowledge production. Yet, this is not a reactive response to colonial practices.[9] It constitutes a conscientious effort in which, through this Nahua lens, these authors offer remedies and healing from the deep wounds of colonialism. Their literature speaks to Nahuas and Native Nations throughout Abiayala (the Americas)[10] and on a global scale, as well as to a public at large that perhaps unwittingly perpetuates and benefits from colonial practices.

Contemporary Xochitlajkuiloanij / Flowered Authors (Re)write, (Re)right, and (Re)rite

The authors addressed in this study similarly debunk the myth of their disappearance by insisting on their status as knowledge producers. I explore the writings and cultural production of contemporary Nahua xochitlajkuiloanij (the writers of xochitlajtoli) Natalio Hernández, Martín Tonalmeyotl, Ethel Xochitiotzin, Judith Santopietro, Mardonio Carballo, and Ateri Miyawatl. Taken together, these authors provide a panorama of contemporary Nahua literary production. This study is not an exhaustive account of Nahua writing, as there are numerous authors whose works should be analyzed in depth.[11] I focus on these six writers because they represent a range of ages, places of origin, and gender identities. In this sense *The Serpent's Plumes* resembles Cherokee literary scholar Daniel Heath Justice's approach toward Cherokee literary traditions in *Our Fire Survives the Storm* (2006). He brings to the forefront a dynamic interplay of authors' cultural expressions and understandings as "an analytical beginning, not an end point of discussion" (20–21). Reflecting the extensive corpus of contemporary publications, all authors in this study underscore the importance of contemporary Nahua knowledge production. And, while they differ in their approaches and how they articulate ixtlamatilistli, yoltlajlamikilistli, and tlaixpan, they emphasize the importance of territory in its multiple permutations across land, airwaves, visual media, and the internet.

Often translated as "poetry," the polysynthetic incorporation of xochitl (flower) in these authors' xochitlajtoli (flowered words) carries greater meaning than the word *poetry* would suggest. Xochitl resembles what Paul M. Worley and Rita M. Palacios identify in the Maya concept ts'íib as "an alternative to understanding 'writing' that does not stand in opposition to alphabetic writing but rather fully encompasses it, placing it alongside of and in dialogue with a number of other forms of recording knowledge" (*Unwriting Maya Literature* 3). Xochi—figuratively and quite literally—projects a trans-genre mixture of poetry, narrative, ceremony, textiles, and other forms of expression, a wider conception of what constitutes a text or an archive. Flowers make natural dyes for the scribbling thread on text(iles). The land itself constitutes a text read for imminent dangers and events, while acting as a mnemonic scape for a community's history. This is even more salient when one considers that the primordial flower in Nahuatl is maize, and xochitlajtoli can also signify "words of maize," encompassing a wide arc of ceremonial expression centered on this sacred food. These words and Native spaces move toward a broader formulation beyond the narrow expression of written texts and accentuate carefully cultivated reflections.

Contemporary xochitlajtoli shifts away from the Mexican nationalist nostalgic gaze fixed on ancient Pre-Columbian *flor y canto* (flower and song) and iconography.[12] In the epigraph to this introduction, Mardonio Carballo reworks the trite nation-state appropriated symbol of the Mesoamerican deity of wind and learning, Quetzalcoatl (*La Serpiente Emplumada* or "The Plumed Serpent"). Official state and tourist discourses have so over(ab)used Pre-Columbian figures that, when not reappropriated by Nahua authors, they have become an impediment and play to the continual relegation of Nahuas to exotic relics.[13] The complex symbol of the Serpent's Plumes (capitalized like a proper name) breaks with stereotypical portrayals by riffing off Quetzalcoatl to "hablar de los pueblos indígenas vivos, de *Las Plumas de la Serpiente* que siguen dotando a nuestro país de rostros y posibilidades múltiples" (speak about the living Indigenous nations, of *The Serpent's Plumes* who continue to endow our country with a multiplicity of faces and possibilities; 7). The Serpent's Plumes point to Nahua specificities—in other words actual Nahuas of "flesh and blood" as Carballo describes on his program—by alluding to Carballo's small Huastecan hometown of Maguey Maguaquite. Maguaquite (*bothrops asper*; mauakijtli in Nahuatl), also called *nauyaca* (four noses, because it appears to have four nasal passages), is the most feared snake in that region due to its powerful venom. The creative strength of Nahua publications is suggested by the image of the snake itself, whose elongated shape resembles a writing instrument as well as a tongue. Although a seemingly small shift, "Serpent's Plumes" plays on the word *pluma* (feather) in Castilian, which can mean "pen" and underscores Nahuas' creative production in the present. While wielding this pen, Nahuas publish and broadcast through a wide array of media such as books, progressive rock, rap, film, social media, podcasts, radio, and television (to mention only a few). Carballo named his film production studio Nauyaca Producciones, referring to the symbol of the Maguaquite and echoing the word Nahua. Analyzed in the fifth chapter, his book of xochitlajtoli-laden lyric essays *Las Plumas de la Serpiente* is based on a collection of radio shorts from his eponymous program on Carmen Aristegui's news site. The figure of the serpent accentuates the capacity to defend and attack, which subverts the insidious depiction of Nahuas as vanquished victims. They write—text, tweet, post, perform, publish, and broadcast—as opposed to being written. To borrow from Native American studies scholar Cutcha Risling-Baldy (Hupa, Yurok, Karuk) and Indigenous education scholar Linda Tuhiwai Smith (Māori), these authors *(re)write, (re)right*, and *(re)rite* Indigenous epistemologies (Risling-Baldy 7–8; see also Tuhiwai Smith, *Decolonizing Methodologies*). The Serpent's Plumes serve as a central metaphor throughout this study of xochitlajtoli.

Contemporary Nahua knowledge production is absent in the public imaginary. Quetzalcoatl, Moctezuma, Malinche, Cuauhtemoc, Mexihco-Tenochtitlan . . . these figures and places come to many people's minds when they think of Nahuas, more popularly known as Aztecs or Mexicas.[14] Mexicas founded the altepetl (city-state) of Mexihco-Tenochtitlan, the Centro Histórico of present-day Mexico City, and dominated the surrounding regions—reaching as far as Central Abiayala (Central America)—into the early sixteenth century. They speak Nahuatl,[15] like numerous other altepemeh (city-states). While *Mexica* denotes people from the area of Mexihco-Tenochtitlan and most likely derives from the name of an early leader, *Nahua* refers to all who speak Nahuatl or arguably those who have an ancestral connection to the language. Nahuatl derives from a verb meaning "to sound clearly" and has loaned numerous words to English and Castilian.¹⁶ Yet, despite being the most widely spoken Indigenous language in Mexico, popular understanding of it is anything but clear. References to Nahuas in Mexico's past abound on money, in museums, within murals, national flags, names, surnames, video games, street signs, and toponyms like *Mexico* itself. They are understood to have once *been* glorious, howbeit with their culture no longer having relevance. Calling Nahuas "Aztecs," a term even sixteenth-century Mexicas would have considered anachronistic, reflects the tendency to relegate them to a distant past and obscures their complexities.¹⁷ Many, both in Mexico and on an international scale, are unaware that there are millions of Nahuas today.¹⁸ According to Mexican nationalist discourse, Nahuas cleared the ground for the country predestined to emerge in the nineteenth century (Tarica xxii–xxiii). This narrative of antiquity teaches that Spanish invaders conquered the Mexicas, and Nahuas subsequently disappeared, leaving mere vestiges of their once awe-inspiring apotheosis to be reincarnated as a mystic trope in the construction of the modern Mexican Republic.

How Nahua writers represent themselves offers a radically different account. Nonetheless, pervasive nationalist discourse steeped in colonial practices often drowns out their voices. That discourse dismisses Native knowledge production as straggling superstition, exploits Native populations deemed to be cheap manual labor, and racializes them as an inferior group destined to penury. Nahua authors dismantle such myths regarding themselves and other Native Nations; they signal the intricate linguistic and social landscapes surrounding them. As explored in detail within this study, language plays a key role in this struggle, in ways that go well beyond a revisionist history. These writers articulate a decolonizing framework from perspectives grounded in their language and lived experiences.

This study is not an ethnography. Readers will not find *the* Nahua perspective here. *Nahua* refracts into multiple meanings, spaces, and ideas. Authors pull influences from a wide gamut of regions, experiences, and publications. Within this multivocality, the perspectives of ixtlamatilistli (knowledge with the face), yoltlajlamikilistli (knowledge with the heart), and tlaixpan (that which is in front, or the past in front) are read into a dynamic literary and artistic arena to imagine a world that engages genuinely with Nahua voices, with all their nuances and diverse viewpoints. I deploy these perspectives to analyze Nahua literature, but they can also function as frameworks to examine other contexts, both Indigenous and non-Indigenous. Nahuas observe instead of being observed, and they write instead of being conscripted into ethnography or what literary scholar Gloria Elizabeth Chacón calls "tributary knowledge" (46). Their perspectives fundamentally challenge broad colonial brushstrokes that paint them as incapable of offering solutions for the present (discounting their experiential knowledge), overly emotional and unqualified to lead (viewing affective intelligence as weakness and collectivity as precluding individual thought), and confined to a distant past (rather than recognizing the past as in front). In fact, if there is an ethnography present here, it is the work of these authors who flip the imperial gaze and conduct critical ethnographies of the societies and urban spaces surrounding them.

What is the importance of this literature? Who reads it?[19] Nahuas have asked themselves these same questions, often self-critically. The stakes are high in this endeavor. Literary scholar Arturo Arias describes the ethical commitment that these authors feel toward their communities ("Tramas y dramas de la descolonización" 202). They negotiate this responsibility along with their insertion into a literary and academic intelligentsia that hesitates to grant them full membership. Academic and political spheres often view them as too ensconced in communalism to think independently.[20] Otherwise, if Native intellectuals appear independent, these same spheres of influence deem them distanced from their communities and too "tainted" by foreign ideas to represent their people properly.[21] As Anishinaabe Irish literary scholar Kelly S. McDonough indicates, these debates and the association of terms like *intellectual* with an embrace of Western Modernity and betrayal of one's Native heritage have led some Nahua writers like Gustavo Zapoteco Sideño to reject being called "intellectuals" altogether (*The Learned Ones* 7). McDonough observes how the public bias against Native writing manifests itself when people swear that Nahuas, at least "real Nahuas," do not write (5). Such an assertion is symptomatic of the pervasive view that Native people are un(der)developed in all aspects, evidenced by the false assumption that they speak an illiterate "dialect" devoid of complex grammar (5). Numerous scholars in Native American and Indigenous studies attest that Western ideologues consider the combination of *Nahua* or *Native* with *intellectual* to be an oxymoron.[22] Particularly one sees in Nahua literature the potential to imagine spaces of empowerment and shift t(r)opographic encroachments on Nahua realities. The defense of acoustic, linguistic, visual, epistemic, and topographic spaces is interwoven, although the recognition of that intersectionality is understudied in academia.

My attention to territory is inspired by a roundtable of Nahua scholars at the Otros Saberes Congress of the Latin American Studies Association

(LASA) in Boston in 2019. While a longer panel at the congress offered simultaneous interpretation into Castilian and English, we also organized a preconference presentation in which participants spoke in Nahuatl without translation. The intent was not to exclude audience members who did not speak Nahuatl, but rather to invite them to listen attentively and recognize the performative importance of filling acoustic spaces with Native languages. In the Q&A, many in attendance commented on how not everyone in the audience could understand, and that challenged academics' desire to know everything. One attendee then remarked that language was all fine, but "Where are the politics? What about land rights?" Nahua scholars Sabina de la Cruz, Bety Martínez, Eduardo de la Cruz, and Abelardo de la Cruz responded that you cannot dissociate language from the defense of the land and its political implications. Language is not "merely cultural." Western frameworks categorize and subcategorize concepts into separate disciplines and themes to the extent that methodologies of comparative studies and intersectionality are needed to remedy that tendency. The intersection of different types of territory was obvious to the Nahua researchers.

The title *The Serpent's Plumes: Contemporary Nahua Flowered Words in Movement* emphasizes how authors' xochitlajtoli confronts the Mexican nation-state's appropriations of Nahua symbols, such as the Plumed Serpent, in dynamic ways (*movement* referring to both authors' migration to urban centers and Nahua perspectives in which the word for movement can signify walking, philosophy, and life). In its departure from the mock plumage of pervasive stereotypes, Carballo's metaphor of the serpent's feathers features the experiences of Nahua migrants. Many have had to migrate (in a figurative sense "fly") to Mexico City, as in the case of Carballo, or to other countries, principally the United States and Canada. This movement defies common stereotypes regarding Indigenous peoples, namely notions of fixedness and isolation. Nahuas network with people transnationally. Each "feather" or Native personal experience featured on Carballo's program adds another ink-dipped quill to a panoply of shared suffering and synchronicities. Carballo's own life reflects this. He relocated in his teens from the Huasteca Veracruzana to Mexico City to complete his secondary education. Nearly all published Nahua artists have had similar experiences of migrating from smaller communities to urban settings. Their negotiation among these different places is central to present-day Nahua literature and reflects how their efforts join a panorama of Indigenous struggles on a continental and global scale.

Note that in the epigraph to this introduction Carballo writes in Castilian rather than Nahuatl. The play on language with "las Plumas de la Serpiente" only works in Castilian, although it connects with distinctive cultural symbols in Nahuatl and Carballo's home community. While Nahuatl plays a key role, some authors like Carballo write mostly in Spanish or a sort of Spanahuatl, or hybridization of the two languages. In part this is because it reflects the reality of many Nahuas, especially those who have relocated to urban areas. Writing in Castilian also allows Carballo to reach a wider audience. Much like in Northern Abiayala, Native Nations in Mexico have appropriated the colonizers' language and Indigenized it in unique ways as we see with Spanahuatl. Within this language, it is important to observe a distinct conception of what constitutes territory. You can leave your family's lands (tikisa), but you do not leave them in the sense of abandoning or leaving them behind (tijkaua, from which the verb to denote forgetting is derived). The territory moves with a person in a perennial reciprocal relationship, akin to one's mother not ceasing to be a mother when a child moves away. Our Earth Mother (Totlalnantsij) here is still Our Earth Mother elsewhere. The perspectives of ixtlamatilistli, yoltlajlamikilistli, and tlaixpan are tightly bound up with this relationship, intertwined with the knowledges gained from close interaction with those landscapes (ixtlamatilistli), the affective connection to them (yoltlajlamikilistli), and a reciprocity with their history in front (tlaixpan), much like relatives commune with their deceased loved ones.

Tendencies within Nahua and Native Studies

Previous studies, with notable exceptions such as Kelly McDonough's *The Learned Ones*, tend to offer overviews of Nahua literary works and read them in translation. *The Serpent's Plumes* closely analyzes this artistic production in the Nahuatl language. Without engaging with the texts in Nahuatl, we miss the aforementioned perspectives on decoloniality vis-à-vis language use that are more poignant in Native language texts. The Castilian versions are not exact replications, and it is pressing to analyze these texts in/on their own terms. *The Serpent's Plumes* brings Nahuatl to the forefront, both in methodology and within the works themselves. My approach reads between the Nahuatl and Castilian to elucidate critical perspectives articulated through this translingual literature.[23] Certain meanings, often with subversive implications, are lost or hidden in translation. Concurrently, there are messages in the Castilian that do not appear in the Nahuatl. Self-translation serves as a strategy for marking these differences and highlighting Native concepts within the interstices of rough translations. For example, Mardonio Carballo's essay collection *Las Plumas de la Serpiente* contains abundant code-switching plays between Nahuatl and Spanish that are not fully understood without reading both languages.

These authors' works form part of larger projects to *strengthen* (kiyolchikaua) use of Nahuatl (as opposed to "revitalize" it).[24] Natalio Hernández has led the Fundación Macuilxochitl, an organization that joined choirs from Mexico City and the Huasteca to sing bilingual compositions. Ethel Xochitiotzin is a professor of Nahuatl in Tlaxcala. Martín Tonalmeyotl, Judith Santopietro, and Mardonio Carballo are influencers who promote the language on social media. Santopietro created the *libro cartonero* publishing house Iguanazul for Indigenous authors. Tonalmeyotl and Miyawatl help fellow authors publish in anthologies, editorial series, and newspapers. It is important to recognize their works as part of these wider efforts.

In *The Learned Ones*, McDonough observes this commitment in contemporary Nahua authors Luz Jiménez and Ildefonso Maya. She offers an extensive analysis of Nahua literary production and highlights a continuity of intellectual history, from the sixteenth century to the present, contrary to the typical depiction of their knowledge production as having fallen into a Dark Age after the Spanish invasion. She argues that Nahua intellectual tradition was suppressed and that, despite this marginalization, texts from the colonial era to the present attest to a continuous tradition. McDonough signals how Nahuas redefine what it means to be an intellectual. She uses ixtlamatilistli (literally, "knowledge with the face") as a key approach in her analysis of Nahua literature. I build on this excellent work by focusing on contemporary authors in order to underscore that these writers do not always need to be linked to the Pre-Columbian or early colonial period.

The Serpent's Plumes enters a critical conversation within recent Indigenous studies publications. Especially with UNESCO's declaration that 2019 was the Year of Indigenous Languages, and a subsequent declaration that 2022–2032 is the Decade of Indigenous Languages, there has been a surge in studies on Native literatures.[25] Arturo Arias's first two volumes of *Recovering Footprints* (vol. 1, 2017; vol. 2, 2018) examine contemporary Maya literature, and the forthcoming third volume will address literatures, including Nahuatl, throughout Mesoamerica. Arias's work shifts effectively from global Native studies to analyzing specific Mesoamerican contexts. It resists the temptation to create macronarratives, while at the same time tracing similarities, alliances, and dialogues across a wide berth of Indigenous literary production. *Recovering Footprints* does so by reading narratives found in what Arias describes as the "marginality of marginality" (vol. 1, 51). Arias argues that contemporary written Indigenous narratives reenact aspects of Indigenous epistemologies, what Mayas call "cosmovisión" or "cosmocimiento" (33). He concludes the first volume of *Recovering Footprints* stating that his main goal is to develop an analysis based on Maya terms for these narratives, and the development of this terminology is an ongoing process (224–25). I take up Arias's invitation to develop those terms within a Nahua context with this study's framework based on Nahua perspectives by analyzing xochitlajtoli and seeking to avoid overarching narratives distanced from specificities.

In this vein, *The Serpent's Plumes* resembles Keme's *Le Maya Q'atzij / Our Maya World* (2021) and Worley and Palacios's *Unwriting Maya Literature* (2019). Keme offers a critical analysis of ten contemporary Maya authors' articulation of their Native rights and cultural identities. He signals decolonizing strategies in Maya poetics to interrogate "the structures of colonial power while also vindicating the complexity that the Maya world represents through their works" (9). Keme uses Q'atzij, the K'iche' term for "our word" or "our tongue," to denote contemporary Maya poetry and signal a broader conception than "literature" in Western paradigms. This term stresses "the value of the 'word' as a carrier of knowledge and wisdom in the creation of the universe and humanity" (9). In *Unwriting Maya Literature*, Worley and Palacios argue, in a related manner, that the Maya ts'íib encompasses myriad ways of recording knowledge. They affirm with this term that "Eurocentric models of literary criticism can only partially account for what happens in these works and that they must be understood as literary works within the context of their own traditions that fall outside of the Western tradition" (9). While *The Serpent's Plumes* focuses on texts written with Latin graphemes, it also opens to a wider consideration of what constitutes a text with the term xochitlajtoli. Xochi- appears in multiple settings and genres, continually referenced within written texts, such as the xochikali (flowered house or ceremonial house) and xochitlatsotsontli (flowered music or ceremonial refrains). The xochikoskatl (flowered necklace) is present in ceremonial spaces; it is also the title of Natalio Hernández's first book and Mardonio

Carballo's program on Radio UNAM. Additionally, xochi- appears in xochitlajtsontli (flowered embroidery), xochitlajkuiloani (flowered writer or poet/novelist), xochitekitl/xochitlachijchiualistli (flowered work, the task of tying ceremonial flowers), xochikuikatl (flowered song or maize song), and Chikomexochitl (Seven Flower, the sacred life force of maize). This study addresses how contemporary Nahua texts intersect with a multiplicity of spaces and media.

McDonough, Arias, Keme, Palacios, and Worley share the goal of using Indigenous frameworks as a methodology for their study of Indigenous literature, principally Maya cultural production. *The Serpent's Plumes* seeks to develop a similar framework to read contemporary xochitlajtoli. These studies, and others like them in Latin American and Native studies,[26] aim to rewrite the "universal" literary canon. *The Serpent's Plumes* builds on this important work by confronting language barriers—not only between Castilian and English but also among the numerous languages spoken in Abiayala—that hinder trans-Indigenous and transnational discussions.[27] In part due to this divide within Native American and Indigenous studies, it is more common for scholars from the US and Canada to dialogue with colleagues in Aotearoa (New Zealand) and Australia than with neighboring scholars in Southern Abiayala. By addressing race and ethnicity within Abiayala, *The Serpent's Plumes* considers the lived experiences of Native peoples in Mexico and the US who unsettle and complicate the meanings of *Latinx* and *Chicanx*. This analysis of contemporary Nahua authors' works is of particular interest to comparative literary studies in placing new authors into dialogue with wider literary production to, as Gayatri Chakravorty Spivak argues, "take the languages of the Southern Hemisphere as active cultural media rather than as objects of cultural study by the sanctioned ignorance of the metropolitan migrant" (*Death of a Discipline* 9). Nahua literary production heeds Spivak's calls for a "fostering not only of national literatures of the global South but also of the writing of countless indigenous languages in the world that were programmed to vanish when the maps were made" (15).

From Southern Californahuas to the Huasteca Veracruzana: Networks and Methodologies

Above all, the most significant aim of this project is to collaborate with Nahuas as colleagues and full-fledged knowledge producers. As opposed to entering communities with a foreign model (i.e., Western theoretical frameworks and pedagogies), I have sought in my fieldwork to promulgate and work closely with Nahua-run programs. In conducting this research, I was affiliated as an instructor and advisor with the Macuilxochitl Cultural Foundation, directed by Natalio Hernández from 2009 until its final year in 2019. Since 2012, I have collaborated on projects with the organization Xochiojtli (Flowered Path), directed by Eneida Hernández and Natalio Hernández. Initiated in 2012, this organization has assumed and amplified the goals of the Macuilxochitl Cultural Foundation. Both Macuilxochitl and Xochiojtli have aided youth in the Huastecan community of Tepeko (Lomas del Dorado, Ixhuatlán de Madero, Veracruz), and Xochiojtli plans to create a cultural center there. A central component of contemporary Nahua literature and these efforts is to promote respect for Nahua ceremonies. The texts I study are intertwined with the goal to help Nahuatl-speaking youth and are more fully understood with participation in programs led by Nahua authors. Such projects correlate with the theoretical basis of my research in which Indigenous knowledges should be met on their own terms and in their own language.

The roots of this study or tekipamitl, "work-furrow," began nearly two decades ago while I was living in Southern California. There, my Nahua friends Benjamin and Freddy Luna spoke Nahuatl at home. They told stories about their family members' active roles in society. For example, their grandparents fought in the Mexican Revolution. The subsequent move to Southern California was a deliberate decision in which they developed a transnational network of kinship. While Benjamin and Freddy communicated in Nahuatl among themselves, they spoke only Castilian outside the home. They avoided doing so publicly out of fear of oppression for speaking what others disparagingly called a *dialecto*. My experiences with their family instilled in me a determination to understand Nahua communities' diverse self-representations.

Nahuas are no distant Other; they work, create, and intervene in English-dominated areas. Nahuas constitute a significant population whose presence is obscured within Mexico and the US. I began learning Nahuatl in Southern California. In 2008 I had the opportunity to study at a summer language immersion course in Oapan, Guerrero. In 2009 this program moved to the Instituto de Docencia e Investigación Etnológica de Zacatecas (IDIEZ) at the University of Zacatecas. Nahua professors from the Huasteca Veracruzana teach the classes there. In both Veracruz and Guerrero, numerous Nahuas had long-term ties with relatives in the US.

Their perspectives elucidate the complexities of US Latinx communities, a category to which they are ascribed instead of Native, although they would not necessarily consider themselves Latinx or Hispanic.[28] Even in the small community of Morris, Minnesota, where I live, there are Nahua families.

"Axnijneki ninauatis pampa san nisaniloa nauatl *cuatrapeado*" (I don't want to speak Nahuatl because the Nahuatl I use is broken), the father of a teenage student explained to me in Tepeko in 2010. I heard this self-deprecation many times thereafter, always with the Castilian loanword *cuatrapeado*—a word that carries connotations of speaking senselessly like an animal (from *cuatro* + *pies*, four-footed). Such is the product of systemic discrimination over centuries against Native languages and cultural practices. Parents who have experienced this marginalization frequently avoid teaching their children Nahuatl in the hope that they evade a similar fate. In Tepeko, children of some migrants return speaking more English than Castilian (and no Nahuatl). Interactions with them, as well as depictions privileging English within mass media, motivate children in the community to want to learn English.

Natalio Hernández is from Tepeko and—with the aim of uprooting discriminatory practices and strengthening use of the Nahuatl language—he developed the novel idea of an annual bilingual Nahuatl-English summer course for high school students. When Hernández asked if I could impart this course in 2010, it was the last thing I wanted. Why have a gringo from the US teach the colonial language? He explained that most children did not want to speak Nahuatl, but all desired to learn English. The colonizer's language could serve as a *gancho* or hook to draw them into the course and teach that Nahuatl is just as important. Hernández led the formation of curriculum for this course based on a mix of methodologies from student-centered communicative techniques and approaches gleaned from a key text in the formation of Nahua pedagogical perspectives, Paulo Freire's *Pedagogy of the Oppressed* (1968). My experience with the Nahuatl-English course exposed the far-reaching effects of English in both linguicide and epistemicide. With television and internet widely available, this process is ever accelerating.

"Namaj nikita kena ipatij nauatlajtoli uan axmelauak tlen techijluiaj koyomej" (Now I see that Nahuatl is valuable and what the "coyotes" tell us isn't true), Norberto said in one of the class sessions. Koyomej, "coyotes," refers to people who persecute Indigenous communities, and who promote the idea that Nahuatl is synonymous with backwardness and unintelligence. Normally reticent to speak the language, Norberto changed his perspective after studying contemporary Nahua cultural production. Class activities included some of the literary texts explored in the present study and a special presentation by Nahua medical doctor Enrique Ramírez. Becoming acquainted with an accomplished doctor who values his Nahua upbringing was a life-changing experience for students. They began to question stereotypes regarding Native Nations and to criticize the bullying of classmates who admit they are Nahua. The successes of the course confirm the powerful effect (and affect) that ethically minded teaching and cultural production led by Nahuas can have. These experiences were the principal influence that guided me to analyze this cultural production in greater detail and also formed the key network, principally through Natalio Hernández, that resulted in meeting dozens of Nahua authors throughout Mexico.

Given the linguistic discrimination against Nahuatl, why write this study in English?[29] Would it not be more appropriate to publish in Nahuatl or Castilian? In the synopsis in Castilian of their English-language academic publication *Unwriting Maya Literature*, Worley and Palacios ask these same questions. Despite the contradictions within an academia that demands publications in English, they aver that inner critiques intervene in dominant scholarly paradigms from Latin American, Mexican, and Mesoamerican studies. The fact that the English hegemony reaches into Tepeko in the Huasteca Veracruzana underscores, somewhat ironically, the exigency of publications in English to combat that very hegemony. Worley and Palacios state, "[A]lthough we cite and attribute the authorship of ideas that are not ours throughout the book, we consider it more than necessary to indicate that the key concept, the backbone, of our study is not a new concept or ours; neither is it an academic neologism with copyright: the authorship and authority of *ts'iib* pertains to Maya nations" (my trans.; 4). The same can be said of the Nahua perspectives that serve as the crux of the present study.

Nahua Methodologies and Intellectual Rights

This study has its theoretical footing within the Nahuatl language itself. In contemporary Nahua cultural production in Mexico, the perspectives connected to ixtlamatilistli (knowledge with the face), yoltlajlamikilistli (knowledge/remembrance with the heart), and tlaixpan (altar / that which is in front) continually emerge. One of the main roots of this methodology derives from a weekly exercise led by Nahua artist Eneida Hernández in the Huastecan Nahua community of Tepeko. Called "Tijxochiyotisej tlajtoli" / "Hacer florecer la palabra" (Making the Word Flourish), the regular meeting entailed community members discussing words or phrases at length for an hour or more. Out of these dialogues came thoughts on the meanings and historic importance of ixtlamatilistli, yoltlajlamikilistli, and tlaixpan. The terms used to identify these perspectives can vary among the thirty Nahuatl variants (or *dialects* in the proper meaning of the word), but the concepts behind them are cross-regional. These same perspectives are readily apparent within contemporary Nahua literature and serve as a lens to delve deeper into them. Using Native categories for textual analysis of their own literary production offers innovative theoretical and aesthetic approaches to challenges across Abiayala.

A significant shift, especially within the last decade, calls for studies centered on Indigenous methodologies.[30] What are the implications of this move? Osage literary scholar Robert Warrior asserted at a talk at the University of Minnesota that it comes down to a question of whom you cite ("The Finest Men We Have Ever Seen").[31] He critiques the incessant need to quote "untouchable" Western intellectuals such as Alexander Humboldt and Thomas Jefferson when Native intellectuals expressed similar ideas. Kanaka Maoli scholar Lisa Kahaleole Hall analyzes at length this pressure to cite Euro-American scholars while Native intellectuals' ideas are left uncited or plagiarized.[32] On his media programs, Carballo addresses numerous forms of plagiarism, from foreign companies copying Native textile designs to the appropriation of the Mesoamerican scientific discovery of maize cultivation.[33] Land acknowledgments imply that Native peoples were and *are* here, and should carry with them earnest engagement with their present speaking, thinking, and theorizing. This study seeks to answer this call to *cite*, *site*, and *center* Native perspectives.

Although Nahua artists do not explicitly postulate concepts like ixtlamatilistli, yoltlajlamikilistli, and tlaixpan as theory in a Western propositional sense, they offer alternative perspectives that should be set in critical dialogue with mainstream theoretical frameworks. These views constitute a philosophy, in Nahuatl nemilistli (way of life / walking / feeling / thinking), articulated in practice and based on personal experiences and on an affective connection with one's knowledge production—a way of life key to healthy kinship and communities. In short, rather than suggesting that Nahuas seek to reach the upper echelons of Western philosophy, "philosophy" carries a great significance for Nahuas since their views traditionally have been excluded from the field. Both Natalio Hernández and Miguel León Portilla address how many people view *philosophy* and *Nahua* as incommensurate. León Portilla met resistance when he wrote his dissertation, later published as *La filosofía náhuatl* (Nahuatl Philosophy, 1956). Now in its tenth edition, this work helped open a space for Nahua perspectives to be taken seriously. His analysis of the ixtlamatini (one who knows wisdom with the face) as philosopher resembles contemporary iterations of ixtlamatilistli.

From contemporary Nahua xochitlajtoli-flowered words emerges a mode of reading tied to ixtlamatilistli. This deep reading heeds what Robert Warrior describes as a dynamic process between what the writer means to write and what readers interpret, and the experiences both bring to this encounter (*The People and the Word* xiv–xv). Nahuas expand the notion of what constitutes ixtli / face-text. Xochitlajtoli serves as a means to experience these contexts, and, in this sense, it offers a degree of experiential knowledge. In the Huasteca Veracruzana, such knowledge would be more often referred to as tlajlamikilistli (knowledge/remembrance) and tlachialistli (observation, perception, foresight). In contemporary Nahuatl, the concepts of ueuejtlajtoli (old/wise words) and ueuejtlakamej (old/wise people) link to a distinct view in which elders with their wealth of lived knowledges are intellectuals. In their movement and migration toward urban centers, Nahua artists highlight their communities' lived knowledges. They propose a remapping in which, instead of receiving from the North, Nahua communities transit knowledge globally to prioritize their perspectives taken lightly by society writ large. The emphasis on the eyes in Nahua literary production highlights an ability to observe among these movements and underscores ixtlamatilistli.[34] This ocular focus breaks with stereotypical representations of Indigenous peoples as made for manual labor and incapable of critical analysis.

The related concept of yoltlajlamikilistli (knowledge/remembrance with the heart) accentuates an affective intelligence in which cognition is "conjugated" with emotions (Natalio Hernández, *Semanca huitzitzilin* 11–15). *Conjugated* suggests a nexus between cognition and affect, and signals that this perspective is codified in the language itself. Yolotl (heart / corn seed) integrates into verbs as an adverb (such as ni**jyol**mati, "I know with my heart [as a medium or tool]," and nimo**yol**nojnotsa, "I inner-dialogue with my heart"). Additional terms that connect with yoltlajlamikilistli are yolchikaualistli (strength of heart) and kuali iyolo (a good heart). In fact, *yol* so commonly appears in texts that it is often dropped in translations, both because of the difficulty in communicating its deeper meanings and to avoid sounding redundant in Castilian. Thinking/feeling/dialoguing with the heart is a common metaphor that marks one's cognition and affectivity as inseparable, both in Nahua literature and everyday life. This view underlies the affective space of kinship and practices through reciprocity and community festivities, of seeing these practices as knowledge production as opposed to folkloric traditions. By emphasizing the heart, Nahuas do not reiterate the hackneyed depiction of Indigenous peoples as led by instincts. Instead, they foreground the ability to exercise this affective intelligence that recognizes the intimate weave of emotive and cognitive responses.

Perspectives encompassed by tlaixpan (that which is in front) link to ixtlamatilistli and yoltlajlamikilistli. Invoking the past as in front of the subject in a dynamic present and future, tlaixpan denotes altars made for festivities like the Day of the Dead. Deceased relatives' pictures rest on these altars, and the deceased, like the past, are at the fore. They constitute what is known and guide us into an unpredictable future. Nahuas use the strength from that past to project their own perspectives into a dynamic present and future. Contemporary literary references to weaving, farming, and other forms of expression tap into a long tradition of ancestors' creative production. This context is key, for example, in understanding Martín Tonalmeyotl's book of poetry *Ritual de los olvidados*, and its imagery of abandoned adobe homes (see chapter 2). With tlaixpan and the regeneration that it entails, I analyze how life and death metonymically parallel an agricultural regeneration.

A forward-looking view toward the past materializes, through Nahua literature, in other terms such as notsonyo (my genealogy or "the essence of my head, what is on top"), noneluayo (my ancestry or "roots"), nokuamekayo (my ancestors, or "head thread"), noixmatkauaj (relatives, or "those whom I know with my face"), and moikxipejpena (to retrace everywhere one has been during their life, or "gather one's feet"). Ancestors feature prominently at the base of genealogical trees, which are flipped from Western genealogies in which the deceased appear in branches and genealogy moves downward to descendants in the present. This view turns nationalist discourse—in its effort to confine Nahuas in the past—on its head. The past is not left behind in a teleological view of humanity. Similar to the Hawaiian conception of moʻokūʻauhau that Nālani Wilson-Hokowhitu and Manulani Aluli Meyer explore in the edited collection *The Past before Us*, tlaixpan is a "constellation of points in time" that marks genealogical relationships among human ancestors and the landscape (1–6).³⁵ It encapsulates a field of vision in which the land is sacred kin instead of real estate, and knowledge is relational as opposed to transactional (6). Native intellectual rights germinate in those interconnections, rather than in a transactional step in which one becomes an authority based on a university degree.

Ixtlamatilistli, yoltlajlamikilistli, and tlaixpan work in tandem. Yoltlajlamikilistli has tlajlamikilistli (knowledge/remembrance) at its core. That knowledge dialogues with ancestors' knowledges; rather than individualist, it is based on remembrance without the Western obsession of originality. The painting/textile by Eneida Hernández on this study's cover illustrates how these three perspectives combine. *Universo de las hilanderas* (Universe of Women Spinners; 2010) is inspired by a series of traditional images embroidered on blouses, but Hernández uses them innovatively to portray the connection between the sky and the earth. This textile canvas is oriented toward the east, effectively turning Western maps on their side. Reflecting these interconnections and movement, the altars prevalent throughout Nahua cultural production face the East to greet the morning sun. The arc over the altar represents solar passage across the sky.³⁶ Like the sun's movement, the care for ancestors' knowledges embodied upon the altar is far from static. In addition to their role in the articulation of Nahua identities, ixtlamatilistli, yoltlajlamikilistli, and tlaixpan function within literary analysis to better capture complex symbols, poetic and narrative arcs, and imagery within Nahua texts. The meaning of tlaixpan, the altar, signals that this perspective surfaces more in practice than abstract mulling. As research has attested, it is in ceremonies and everyday practices that Nahua views emerge.³⁷

Contemporary Nahua literature points to the past in front, in which wisdom is imparted by ancestors but then used in unexpected ways to tackle current challenges.³⁸ Eneida Hernández's art incorporates experiential knowledges; she learned textile symbols and how to create them through continual practice alongside ancestors. This communal effort not only weaves the cloth or canvas but weaves and reweaves kinship networks. The various threads can remind one of life events. Some blouses and garments are reserved for ceremonies.³⁹ Nahuas dress choice cornhusks in miniature versions of their apparel, highlighting a wider kinship that embraces the land and the harvest. Nahuas deploy their perspectives in defense of their Native heritage, within their texts if they are writers, and through their posts (both in the sense of *cargos* [community governance] and social media such as Facebook).

Carballo's image of the Serpent's Plumes comprises these Nahua perspectives and migrations. He privileges the insights of Indigenous migrants, who in their movement fly like the Serpent's Plumes and yet go unheard on mainstream media. These travelers develop a "heart knowledge" or affective intelligence in their struggles. Their intuition resembles Gloria Anzaldúa's concept of *la facultad* in which oppressed people obtain, through personal experience, a profound understanding of society that the advantaged are unable to comprehend (*Borderlands / La Frontera* 60). Carballo's innovation on Quetzalcoatl or the "Plumed Serpent" also reflects the view of the past in front, as his conceit of the Serpent's Plumes dynamically brings antiquity, Pre-Columbian symbols, to the forefront in unexpected ways. The Serpent's Plumes reminds him of his hometown Maguey Maguaquite, situating it front and center. Taken together, ixtlamatilistli, yoltlajlamikilistli, and tlaixpan undergird Nahua strategies and a Nahua aesthetic within contemporary literature.

Tied to Nahua knowledge production is an aesthetic in which maize operates as a central trope. Cultivation constitutes a metaphor for perspectives that can be described as maize-centric instead of logocentric.[40] To speak of *a* Nahua perspective poses serious pitfalls, since, like with any population, a multiplicity of viewpoints exists. There are Nahuas who self-identify as Protestant, Catholic, Mormon, and atheist, affiliated with political parties of the right, the alleged center, the left, and none at all;[41] Nahuas who do not speak Nahuatl and Nahuas in urban areas, rural municipalities, and places in-between, Gloria Anzaldúa's nepantla. Although not reflective of all, one sees within Nahua literature a general emphasis on maize and worldings linked to corn ceremonies.[42] Human growth, spiritual ceremonies, and writing itself are grounded in maize. The term used in Nahuatl for Native or Indigenous, macehualli or maseuali, carries with it the connotation of "peasant farmer."[43] The tending of the crop mirrors a Nahua view of who embodies an intellectual, because the harvester must carefully observe and possess experience with the terrain. An alternative time perception stems from the cyclical and dynamic nature of the corn crop itself. Respect for the landscape does not spring from a New Age romanticized notion but instead is rooted in recognition of the earth as the living source of one's sustenance. Situated within a nonanthropocentric worldview, Nahuas venerate ancestors and community.

Knowledges of elders and the past, not deemed temporally peripheral, can renew the present and future. Maize serves as the fundamental metaphor for all these perspectives—sacred landscapes, reciprocity, respect toward ancestors, cyclical temporality, and affective intelligence—as they play out in Nahua intellectual production in academics, politics, and the arts.

When I first began to analyze Nahua literature, I was unaware of these nuances and complexities that are, in many cases, codified within the Nahuatl language. As I studied Nahua cultural production, I found it imperative to place Nahua perspectives in dialogue with Native theorists from throughout Abiayala such as Aymara theorist Silvia Rivera Cusicanqui.[44] These perspectives emerge from Indigenous movements and descolonial strategies. "Decolonialization"—or "descolonialization" (*descolonización*) as Cusicanqui prefers to call it to distance the term away from English-based theorizations in the global North—searches for a new language that transcends coloniality and describes the complexities of gender, race, class, sexuality, knowledge, and spirituality.[45] It dialogues with non-Western forms of knowledge as an equal player on a heterarchical field of intellectual production. Cusicanqui calls for a descolonization of the theoretical debates over decoloniality. She argues that foreign theories should not overlay Indigenous writings with preconceived notions and models (*Ch'ixinakax utxiwa* 68–69). Superimposed frameworks tend to result in the divorce of Nahua knowledge production from its specificities and political movements.

Chickasaw anthropologist Shannon Speed similarly warns of the risk for research to recolonize if it fails to engage critically with the politics of knowledge production and ask what effect it will have on people's lives (*Incarcerated Stories* 8). As Speed asserts, to "decolonize our research or, at a minimum, not to recolonize ourselves in the research process" entails "not just taking Indigenous peoples' experience seriously but also taking *their understanding* of it seriously, while putting that in dialogue with the researchers' own critical analysis and directing them consciously toward some type of shared end that is of use in peoples' lives" (8–9). In this same vein, Eneida Hernández affirms in Tepeko meetings that the effects of research in the community take priority over the research project itself.[46] When Nahua concepts guide that understanding, the profound implications of their perspectives in defense of territory come into view and performatively center Nahua voices.

Azteca, Nahua(tl), Mexica, Mejikanoj, and Maseuali: Who Are Nahuas? What Are Their Literary Traditions?

At the most basic level, *Nahua* refers to people who speak the Nahuatl language or whose parents or grandparents spoke the language. Along with the term *Nahua*, popular (and academic) misconceptions abound. Part of a transnational network, the Nahuatl language belongs to the Uto-Nahua/Uto-Aztecan linguistic family. For the reasons mentioned previously, some researchers consider "Azteca" to be a misnomer and prefer to say Uto-Nahua. With its reference to Mexica origin stories telling of their migration from the north (Aztlan), "Aztec" is appropriate in this context. *Aztec* invokes a shared past among Nahuas, Mexicas, Utes, Shoshoni, Comanche, and additional Native Nations stretching from present-day Utah to Central America. Exactly where Aztlan was located has fueled debates, from claims that Aztlan was in Nayarit or Arizona to allegations that this mythic migration was perhaps wholly invented tradition. Regardless of its site or historical accuracy, what is clear both linguistically and culturally is that there are shared histories and exchanges across the Native Nations of Northern Abiayala.

Myths and equivocal etymologies persist concerning the Nahua toponyms that dot Mexican landscapes. Some claim that *Aztlan* means the "place of herons"; *Mexijko* is "the navel of the moon." Countless memes disseminate invented etymologies of Nahua words to express "how pretty" the language is.[47] With Eric Hobsbawm's concept of *invented tradition* in mind, this study does not seek to address which version is "accurate" or "inaccurate," as even invented etymologies take on a life of their own and become historical actors. Nahua authors at times avoid rehashing these much-vaunted toponyms and names to eschew paying homage to Mexican nationalist discourse's overemphasis on the "ancient Indian." If they do reference these terms, it is to play and innovate on them. Much like he plays on Quetzalcoatl, Carballo created a radio program called *Ombligo de tierra* (Navel of the Earth), as well as two television programs *De raíz luna* (From Moon Roots) and *La raíz doble* (Double Root). All these names allude to the attested etymology of Mexico as "the navel of the moon."

When Spaniards invaded Mesoamerica in the sixteenth century, Mexicas were the most prominent Nahuas within Mesoamerica (or notorious depending on the viewpoint). Their altepetl Mexihco-Tenochtitlan was one of the largest cities in the world; their fame owes itself to the widespread influence of the Triple Alliance. This Alliance or Ēxcān Tlahtōlōyan (Three Places Where You Dialogue), popularly known as the "Aztec Empire," consisted of the Central Valley altepemeh or "city-states" of Mexihco-Tenochtitlan, Texcoco, and Tlacopan. Alliance members would not have recognized the term *Aztec Empire*, which emerged in the nineteenth century from the works of English anthropologists and archaeologists.[48] The Triple Alliance dominated most of Mesoamerica from approximately 1428 until the Spanish invasion of Mexihco-Tenochtitlan in 1521. Spanish colonialism exploited and expanded on this system of domination, not only territorially but also linguistically. Nahuatl served as the lingua franca for Nahua and non-Nahua populations under Spanish rule from the sixteenth century into the early seventeenth century across the Viceroyalty of New Spain (present-day Mexico, Central America, and portions of the American Southwest). Colonial abuses decimated Native populations, which decreased by as much as 90 percent.[49]

An interregional solidarity based on speaking Nahuatl was highly unlikely, if not impossible, before Spanish colonialism. It was spoken throughout Central Mexico and surrounding areas by altepemeh often in conflict with one another. The sworn enemies of Mexicas in the fifteenth and sixteenth centuries, the Tlaxcaltecans, spoke Nahuatl. Nahuatl became the principal language of commerce and military incursions across Mesoamerica, although not imposed by decree as it later would be under the Spanish Empire. Tribute officials stationed across Mesoamerica assured that tribute was sent to Mexihco-Tenochtitlan. Within this context, multilingualism in local Native languages and Nahuatl was common.[50]

The term Nahua as a noun to denote people who speak Nahuatl derives from Castilian in the sixteenth century. In the introduction to his famed 1571 dictionary, Alonso de Molina pairs Nahuas with Mexicas in referring to "el lenguaje y frases de estos naturales [especialmente de los Nauas y Mexicanos]" (the language and phrases of these natives [especially the Nahuas and Mexicans]; *Vocabulario* n.p.). The term mexicanoh/mejikanoj to refer to Nahuatl is a colonial creation, combining Mexica with the Hispanicized ending "-ano" to indicate belonging (i.e., like castellano, belonging to Castile). Mexicanoh originally designated the prestigious Nahuatl used by Mexicas. Within Nahua communities it became increasingly common to refer to the many variants of Nahuatl as Mexicanoh rather than Nahuatl (even in Tlaxcala where Mexicas were despised), and to the present in numerous communities Mexicanoh is the preferred term.[51] *Nahuas* to identify people who speak Nahuatl, and subsequently the usage of this term to refer to an ethnicity, was born out of colonialism. *Nahuas* is Hispanicized to allow the pluralization with *s*, whereas *nahua* in the Nahuatl language can be integrated within another noun such *nauatlakatl* (a Nahua person). This historical and linguistic context is vital in understanding contemporary Nahua literary production and authors' adaptations of historical accounts.

There were myriad Nahua communities, altepemeh, in the sixteenth century. After conquest, Nahuas vied for privilege based on birth in certain communities or claims to Native nobility.[52] These specificities were acknowledged until the later part of the seventeenth century, when the blanket term *indio* gained prevalence and the Spanish crown's recognition of Nahua nobility waned.[53] In part this is what prompted well-known Nahua authors such as Tezozomoc and Chimalpahin to assert their nobility in the seventeenth century. Tens of thousands of "mundane documents" ("everyday" or administrative documents in Native languages from court proceedings, petitions, and so forth) in Nahuatl from this era uphold such claims, defend territory, and denounce injustices at the hands of Spanish authorities.[54] I trace this history because it is highly influential in the works of contemporary Nahua writers, either for writers to distance themselves from or to engage with it. In the late seventeenth century and afterward, one sees the emergence of a shared suffering among Native populations, referred to generally as macehualmeh or *indios*. Not until after nation-state independence did *Mexico* comprise areas beyond Mexico City. The use of the term *indio* (Indian) has a fraught and complex history. It was a legal term in the colonial era that afforded a limited level of autonomy and rights (Rappaport and Cummins, *Beyond the Lettered City* 46). In fact, after nation-state independence movements, some Native Nations opposed the adoption of the term *indígena* (indigenous), because this shift in language reflected states' design to strip away the special rights, albeit limited, afforded the Indian Republics. Nation-state governments erased their autonomy altogether and proclaimed that every individual was subsumed within a monolithic idea of the official, ideal citizen. *Indio* became a pejorative trope for the retrograde and unwanted under this nationalist discourse, and *indígena* a term with a nominal degree of celebratory discourse as a preliminary step toward the predestined foundation of the nation-state. It is in part due to this nation-state politique that the nineteenth century is less examined within Nahuatl studies. McDonough explains that this period is often portrayed as an empty interlude between Classical Nahuatl of prior centuries and present-day studies. Nonetheless, as she argues, that depiction is inaccurate.[55]

Although not the focus of this study, there is invaluable research on Nahua literary traditions stretching back from the sixteenth century onward. Two of the most influential texts in this regard are *The Florentine Codex* (ca. 1545–1590) and *Cantares mexicanos* (16th c.). Within the twelve books of *The Florentine Codex*, Fray Bernardino de Sahagún and a team of Nahua tlahcuiloh (scribes) document ornate discourse, ceremonial language, and sage council. *Cantares mexicanos* contains flower and song works that have inspired both nationalist narratives and contemporary Nahua authors. Miguel León Portilla's two-volume 2011 edition of *Cantares* is the most definitive to date.

Adding texts to these discussions, Arthur J. O. Anderson and Susan Schroeder translated and edited the extensive *Codex Chimalpahin* (ca. 1600–1630) into English. Seventeenth-century Nahua historian Don Domingo de San Antón Muñón Chimalpahin Quauhtlehuanitzin (1579–1660) relates approximately one thousand years of Mesoamerican history from AD 670 to AD 1631. Within an expansive scope of detailed genealogies and correlations between the Mexica and Gregorian calendars, he includes rulers' speeches and the lyrics of short song-poems. One of Chimalpahin's key sources was Fernando de Alvarado Tezozomoc's *Crónica Mexicayotl* (ca. 1598), which spans the history of Mexica Tenochca (1064–1579).[56] Within *Historia de la nación chichimeca* (ca. 1640), Fernando de Alva Cortés Ixtlilxochitl (ca. 1568–1648) offers the Texcoco version of this history up until the Spanish Conquest. There are hundreds of texts and studies authored and coauthored by colonial Nahua historians, Latinists, lexicographers, and students of Christianity.[57] These intellectuals share critical perspectives regarding myriad Nahua creative expressions over five centuries. Research on such works has increased exponentially in the last decades.[58]

In this study I have been careful to distance the analysis from reductive comparisons with more well-known *in xochitl in cuicatl* (flower and song). Flowered songs from *Cantares mexicanos* and *The Florentine Codex* are so prominent in the nationalist imaginary that they tend to overshadow contemporary Nahua literary production. Nevertheless, it would be remiss of me to ignore the profound impact of these works on present-day authors. Long-stretching Nahua literary traditions are by no means monolithic. It is impossible to speak of *a* Nahua literary tradition. Instead, multiple movements and scriptural practices weave and interweave. While scholars such as León Portilla point to specificities in their research, the nation-state has appropriated their studies to celebrate a monolithic past incognizant of those complexities. A case in point, the *Cantares mexicanos* is a collection of compositions from various regions, extending to songs translated from Ñhañhu ("Otomí") into Nahuatl. Nationalist citations of this text appearing on money, placards, and other media overlook these nuances in their celebration of "the Aztecs." Works such as *Cantares* particularly exert an impact on authors like Natalio Hernández who consult them. Whether or not they directly cite these texts, contemporary Nahua writers view themselves as part of a *longue durée* of literary production from manifold influences and communities. Official published sources omit the countless creative expressions—oral narratives, textiles, ceremony, and song—that went unrecorded on paper. Yet, these expressions passed down across generations are perhaps the most salient influence on contemporary works, an influence more appropriately cited with the names of entire communities rather than individuals.

A discourse of assimilation into Mexican nation-state citizenry proliferated throughout the nineteenth and twentieth centuries. Assimilationist discourse was so potent that prolific authors, among them Ignacio Manuel Altamirano, were not necessarily recognized as Nahua.[59] Faustino Galicia Chimalpopoca was a Nahua scholar who fell out of favor with the Mexican nation-state after his collaborations as an advisor for the Second Mexican Empire imposed after the French intervention in 1864. Recent scholarship brings back Chimalpopoca and recognizes his contributions.[60] Official histories laud the great caudillos of the Mexican War of Independence (1810–1821) and the Mexican Revolution (1910–). Nahuas' experiences within these struggles generally go unheard, although Nahuas joined Miguel Hidalgo's uprising and Emiliano Zapata's forces.[61] A far cry from the state-sponsored mythicized narratives of the Mexican Revolution, Nahuas' accounts of this conflict resemble the dystopic Revolution in Mariano Azuela's *Los de abajo* (1916). The unattained ideals of the Revolution premise stories after the conflict in the Huasteca. For example, as Natalio Hernández explores in his book of poetry *Patlani huitzitzilin* and unpublished novel *Ohtocani* (Sower of Paths), Nahua activist José Guadalupe Osorio Cruz (1892–1952) fought for community lands following the Revolution from the 1920s up until his assassination by large landowners.

The creation of the Secretaría de Educación Pública in the 1920s was perhaps more destructive against Nahua knowledge production than armed campaigns. Sent by the federal government with the task to "modernize" Native communities, teachers coerced children to cease speaking

Nahuatl. However, the twentieth century was no Dark Age for Nahua cultural production and activism. Nahua authors continued to publish.[62] For example, Jacobo Rojas (1842–1936) taught Nahuatl in the Museum of Archaeology in Mexico City. He published various works on the Nahuatl language and created a theatrical piece titled "Maquiztli" (1931). In this play the main protagonist Maquiztli drinks venom to escape a Spanish conquistador's attack.[63] Enrique Villamil (ca. 1890–1962) wrote lyrical compositions, among them "Quenin ka in yolli" (What Life Is Like) and "Kaxtiltecakah in Tenochtitlan ihuan Tlacoltica Yohualli" (Spaniards in Tenochtitlan and la Noche Triste) included in his *Descripción histórica de Tepoztlán* (1937). From the Huasteca Veracruzana, Pedro Barra Valenzuela (1984–1978) published an anthology of poems in Nahuatl titled *Nahuaxochimilli* (Nahua Garden; 1939). Various authors such as Miguel Barrios Espinosa published their works between 1943 and 1950 in the newspapers *Mexihcayotl* (Mexicanness) and *Mexihcatl itonalama* (The Mexican Times).

A watershed moment in Nahua literary traditions is Nahua author Luz Jiménez's participation with anthropologist Robert Barlow and later with anthropologist Fernando Horcasitas. Jiménez (1897–1965) was from the municipality of Milpa Alta, a delegation within Mexico City. She modeled for Mexican muralist Diego Rivera and later shared narratives with Barlow and Horcasitas in Nahuatl about her personal life and hometown. The posthumous publication of these narratives in *De Porfirio Díaz a Zapata: Memoria náhuatl de Milpa Alta* (1968) and *Cuentos en náhuatl de Doña Luz Jiménez* (1979) shifted an academic focus on colonial Nahua documents to contemporary Nahua production—although not without its problems, as Jiménez was often depicted more as a carrier of oral tradition and not recognized as the author of her narrations. The leading Nahuatl studies journal *Estudios de Cultura Náhuatl* published excerpts from her narrations alongside the works of other Nahua authors, particularly in the late seventies.[64]

Another pivotal publication is Miguel León Portilla's *Visión de los vencidos* (Vision of the Conquered; 1959). The book became a bestseller in Mexico and in the United States under the title *Broken Spears* (1962), especially among Chicanx activists. This text sparked interest in Nahuatl studies across Northern Abiayala. Since then, there have been numerous editions in Spanish and English. *Visión* compiles Nahua-authored accounts from the colonial period to give the "Other's" view of the Conquest. This compilation attributes voice and agency to Native peoples in the sixteenth century. Concomitantly, particularly since the 1980s, León Portilla sought to foreground Native agency in the present through collaborations with contemporary authors. He fought the misconception that Native Nations had fallen into disarray and vanished after Spanish colonialism.

In the twentieth century, language became the primary factor determining whether someone was Native, and groups delineated according to distinct languages.[65] It was most likely not until the mid-twentieth century that a cross-regional solidarity specifically among Nahuas began to emerge in response to Secretariat of Public Education (SEP) educational policies.[66] Principally in the 1960s Nahuas became teachers and fought assimilationist policies. In the 1970s a group of Nahua elementary and secondary school instructors created the Nechikolistli tlen Nauatlajtouaj Maseualtlamachtianej (Organization of Nahua Indigenous Professionals Civil Association, OPINAC), finding strength in numbers to battle the federal government's educational campaign to transition Nahuas to mainstream *mestizo* society.[67] Along with his brothers, Natalio Hernández moved away from his community to become a teacher. He later helped form OPINAC in 1973. In the late 1970s, Hernández championed the creation of the nationwide organization of Indigenous teachers Alianza Nacional de Profesionales Indígenas Bilingües (ANPIBAC).[68] They sought for the Native self-representation within the educational system. Members of these organizations later began to publish in *Estudios de Cultura Náhuatl*. As Indigenous activists and artists indicate, discourse from dominant sectors changed in the late 1960s and 1970s within academia and politics. With the active participation and self-representation of Nahuas and other First Nations, effective proposals questioning the status quo materialized.

While working for the SEP in the 1980s, Hernández published the first single-authored contemporary book of poetry in Nahuatl. Earlier in the 1960s, a vital movement had emerged with SEP-trained Nahua primary and secondary education teachers. The SEP instructed these teachers to assimilate their pupils into the national culture and transition them from speaking Nahuatl to using solely Castilian. Under the leadership of activists such as Natalio Hernández, they turned against the system and sought to reform it to respect Nahua cultural practices, knowledge production, and language. Nahua professors represent a school of thought that has received insufficient recognition for its educational proposals.[69] Nahua educators have obtained nowhere near the attention that teachers in Oaxaca and Chiapas have been given due to the latter's widely known role in the creation of the Coalition of Workers, Peasants, and Students of the Isthmus (COCEI) in Juchitán, Oaxaca, in 1973 and the Zapatista movement in Chiapas. Nearly all writers of what can be deemed a first generation of contemporary Nahua authors, generally born before 1967, served between the 1960s and 1980s as teachers for the SEP.

At the same time in the 1970s other Indigenous political movements began to command attention for Indigenous exigencies, notably radical responses in Guerrero, the Isthmus of Tehuantepec, and in Chiapas under the leadership of Catholic bishop Samuel Ruiz. Binnizá (Isthmus Zapotec) poet Irma Pineda's father, Víctor Pineda Henestrosa (Víctor Yodo), leader of the COCEI movement in Juchitán in the 1970s, was forcibly disappeared when Irma was a child.[70] In Guerrero, Lucio Cabañas Barrientos led the armed group Partido de los Pobres (Party of the Poor) in the 1970s. Nahuas took part in this uprising, and it encouraged the formation of later organizations. Such movements have influenced Indigenous literary production in many respects. They had a significant effect on Native authors and attracted the attention of literary critic Carlos Montemayor. Like León Portilla, Montemayor would become an outstanding promoter of Indigenous literatures from the 1980s onward. He acted as a mediator between the federal government and Indigenous-led armed uprisings, such as the Ejército Popular Revolucionario (EPR), in the 1990s.

Zapotecs played a key role in contemporary Native literary production alongside social and political protests. As Irma Pineda documents, Zapotec intellectuals exerted a profound impact with the creation of the Institute of Zapotec Language in 1935.[71] Zapotec writer and member of the Academia Mexicana de la Lengua Andrés Henestrosa (1906–2008) was an implacable proponent of the language. Renowned painter Francisco Toledo founded the Casa de la Cultura de Juchitán in 1972. This cultural center served as inspiration for Zapotec writers, among them Natalia Toledo and Irma Pineda. Víctor de la Cruz (1948–2015) explores specific Zapotec genres in his landmark book *Guie' sti' diidxazá / Flor de la palabra* (The Word's Flower; 1982), an anthology of Binnizá authors. De la Cruz traces the origins of this surge in contemporary Indigenous literatures to Zapotec song lyrics in nineteenth-century Tehuantepec. Poets began to publish in Zapotec in the Sociedad Nueva de Estudiantes Juchitecos's newspaper *Neza* (1935–1939) in Mexico City.[72] Founded by Víctor de la Cruz in 1975, the magazine *Guchachi' Reza* published compositions in Zapotec. Natalio Hernández cited the deep-reaching influence of de la Cruz in a speech given at his memorial in 2015.

Indigenous literary workshops, such as those led by Montemayor, began to form principally in the 1980s. Maya author Miguel Ángel May

May led the creation of the Taller de Literatura Maya (Maya Literature Workshop) in 1982 in Yucatán. With support from Dirección General de Culturas Populares and Carlos Montemayor, Maya Yucatec participants in this workshop developed the orthography for their language and created the newspaper *U yajal maya wiiniko'ob* (The Maya Awakening) in 1987. During this time, workshops developed in Chiapas for the promotion of Indigenous cultural production in other Maya languages as well as Zoque. The 1996 San Andrés Accords between Zapatistas and the Mexican government called for the formal creation of cultural centers promoting these languages and practices. This stipulation would materialize in the establishment of the Centro Estatal de Lenguas, Arte y Literatura (CELALI) in 1997, led by Tzotzil writer Enrique Pérez López. With support from Montemayor and the Rockefeller Foundation, initial efforts led to the two series Colección Letras Mayas Contemporáneas from 1994 to 1996. One series contains Maya texts from Yucatán and the other from Chiapas, with a total of forty titles published by the Instituto Nacional Indigenista.

In 1990, Native authors led a pivotal meeting to promote contemporary literatures in Native languages. Natalio Hernández and Carlos Montemayor coordinated the Primer Encuentro Nacional de Escritores en Lenguas Indígenas (First National Meeting of Writers in Indigenous Languages). They became two of the most active figures in organizing meetings and publications of Indigenous authors from throughout Mexico. Participants from the Primer Encuentro meeting contributed to an anthology of essays, *Situación actual y perspectivas de la literatura en lenguas indígenas* (1993). At this time, Hernández and Montemayor promoted scholarships for Indigenous artists through the Fondo Nacional para la Cultura y las Artes (FONCA), a program that continues to the present. Hernández's collaboration with many authors facilitated the creation of the anthology *Narrativa náhuatl contemporánea* (1992). This text contains short stories of Nahua authors from multiple regions. The same year Montemayor coordinated the publication of a two-volume anthology of Indigenous writers, *Los escritores indígenas actuales*. These various efforts led to the founding of the Association of Indigenous-Language Writers (ELIAC) in 1993.

A watershed moment during this surge in Nahua and Indigenous cultural production across Abiayala was the 1994 Ejército Zapatista de Liberación Nacional (EZLN) uprising in Chiapas. The EZLN denounced the North American Free Trade Agreement (NAFTA) as aspirations of an elite few who wanted to join the global North to the detriment of most of

Mexico's population.[73] The armed phase of the EZLN lasted twelve days, from 1 to 12 January 1994. This conflict quickly transferred to political mediations due to national and international pressure for a cease-fire. Two commissions were formed to facilitate these discussions, and the armed rebellion gave way to a series of social and political initiatives in the approximately thirty-eight municipalities that had declared themselves Zapatista autonomies. They rejected local leadership of the official government and established their own municipal councils to address issues such as education, health, agriculture, and judicial proceedings.[74] These widely broadcasted happenings brought worldwide attention to Zapatista demands and Native Nations writ large. Zapatistas formed alliances with a global network of Indigenous and non-Indigenous activists. The Mexican state subsequently attempted to combat the insurgency and critiques directed toward the federal government with an array of developmentalist projects during the nineties. One of these projects was increased funding for the publication of Indigenous literatures, which had already begun in part due to earlier demonstrations against the 1992 quincentennial celebrations of Christopher Columbus's invasion of the Caribbean.

In 2004 Montemayor directed the publication of another anthology that gained notoriety, *La voz profunda*. That year he led the creation of Festival de Poesía: Las Lenguas de América, a biennial recital hosted by the Programa Universitario México Nación Multicultural de la UNAM and that now carries Montemayor's name in memoriam. This recital gathers poets in the many languages spoken throughout Abiayala—without distinction of whether they are Romance or Native languages—to render vivid that Native languages are as valuable as hegemonic ones. This festival has garnered widespread attention for Indigenous literatures and since 2010 has filled one of the largest auditoriums, La Sala Nezahualcóyotl, on the campus of the National Autonomous University of Mexico (UNAM).

With literary critic Donald Frischmann, Montemayor directed a multilingual three-volume anthology, *Words of the True Peoples* (2004; 2005; 2007). These three volumes span theater, poetry, and narrative by authors from across Mexico. In 2008 ELIAC released its own two-volume anthology of contemporary Indigenous poetry and narrative, *México: Diversas lenguas, una sola nación*. In the 2010s, Mardonio Carballo promoted a series of publications by Native women authors.[75] Particularly in the last two decades, Abiayalan Native publications have multiplied in online magazines and newspapers, such as *World Literature Today*, *Nueva York Poetry*, *Círculo de poesía*, and the newspaper *La Jornada*'s special section *Ojarasca*. Martín Tonalmeyotl is a major promoter of Indigenous authors' publications in these venues. He has edited the poetic anthologies *Flor de siete pétalos* (2019), *Xochitlajtoli: Poesía contemporánea en lenguas originarias de México* (2019), and *24 poetas contemporáneas en lengua náhuatl* (2020).[76] The various publications described in this section give an overview of literary, cultural, and political traditions that weave in and out of contemporary Nahua authors' works.

Structure of This Study and Works Analyzed

In this project, I explore how Nahua writers Natalio Hernández (Tepeko, Veracruz; 1947–), Martín Tonalmeyotl (Atzacoaloya, Guerrero; 1983–), Ethel Xochitiotzin Pérez (Contla, Tlaxcala; 1973–), Judith Santopietro (Córdoba, Veracruz; 1983–), Mardonio Carballo (El Maguey Maguaquite, Veracruz; 1980–), and Ateri Miyawatl (Acatlán, Guerrero; 1988–) foreground an alternative aesthetic with its underlying Nahua epistemologies to assert the pressing relevance of their knowledges. Moreover, I consider the use of Nahua pedagogy and language to critique a flawed state-run educational system. These themes connect with the idea of territory, both physical and ideological. As mentioned earlier, Carballo's metaphor of the Serpent's Plumes is a subtle allusion to his own community of Maguey Maguaquite. Alongside Carballo, contemporary writers vie for mediatic territory filled with Nahua voices. They defend their hometowns—both their communities' knowledges and lands against incursions, be it from the federal government or transnational companies.

Natalio Hernández is reflective of what Nahuas generally term the elder (ueuej) generation of contemporary authors who opened spaces for contemporary Native literary production in the 1980s. In turn, Tonalmeyotl, Xochitiotzin, Santopietro, Miyawatl, and Carballo represent younger generations who acknowledge this previous generation's achievements, but also stress the need to denounce injustices and expand into venues like social media. Additionally, they highlight fluid Nahua identities, even using Spanahuatl or nahuañol (a mix of Spanish and Nahuatl) which is largely eschewed by older writers.[77]

In the first chapter, I compare Hernández's first book of poetry *Xochikoskatl* (The Flowered Necklace; 1985) with his book of poetry *Patlani huitzitzilin* (The Hummingbird Flies; 2016). I argue that both *Xochikoskatl* and *Patlani huitzitzilin* bring Nahua specificities to the forefront to disassemble the official Mexican nationalist discourse. These works are centered on and center Nahua perspectives. Hernández describes *Xochikoskatl* and *Patlani* as works thought out in Nahuatl.[78] They are situated in specificities from the Nahua region of Ixhuatlán de Madero, Veracruz, although *Patlani* mentions ceremonial elements and Nahua history more explicitly. Through these works, Hernández emphasizes the relevance of Nahua perspectives in his home community, Tepeko, and internationally. He has traveled across the world and currently resides in Mexico City, but Tepeko has always been his main node of enunciation.

This situatedness also holds true for Martín Tonalmeyotl. In the second chapter I analyze how Tonalmeyotl denounces social injustices committed against Nahuas in Guerrero, Mexico. In 2017, he opened a reading in Tlaxcala of his bilingual Nahuatl-Spanish book of poetry *Tlalkatsajtsilistle / Ritual de los olvidados* (2016) with the question, "How can you talk about 'father sun' and flowers when there are people dying in your community?" This question signals a critique toward an older generation of contemporary Nahua authors whom younger generations, which include Tonalmeyotl, perceive as too soft-spoken in the face of state and social violence against Indigenous communities. He declares that his "songs" seek to "tenakastlaposkej, / teixtlaposkej" (open people's ears, / open their eyes; *Tlalkatsajtsilistle* 94). Tonalmeyotl's poetry adds an invaluable feather to the Serpent's Plumage by disrupting the logic of settler colonialism and a multicriminal apparatus that usurps Nahuas' ancestral lands. In tandem with the perspectives of ixtlamatilistli, yoltlajlamikilistli, and tlaixpan, I deploy Chickasaw anthropologist Shannon Speed's concept of *neoliberal multicriminalism* and her application of the term *settler colonialism*—a theoretical framework usually reserved for Northern Abiayala. Tonalmeyotl casts performance of Nahua rituals and worldviews as deeply psychological experiences that oust the dominant discourse of *mestizaje* (i.e., assimilation) and the racial discrimination that this discourse inculcates.

Chapter 3 addresses how contemporary Nahua female authors transgress common metaphors within Nahua xochitlajtoli to position women as decision makers and intellectuals within and outside their communities. In doing so, they subvert instances of Nahua male authors' objectification of women and reiteration of patriarchy. I focus on the literary production of Tlaxcaltecan poet Ethel Xochitiotzin Pérez and her book of poetry *Tlaoxtika in tlajtol* (Shelling Words; unpublished manuscript, 2012; portion of the text published by the University of Warsaw in 2020). Writers like Xochitiotzin open spaces for dialogue among Nahua women and for the publication of their works. Many authors comment that doing so allows them to bypass male-dominated groups that have treated them condescendingly. Xochitiotzin reflects the three perspectives that serve as the methodology of this study while featuring inner struggles within her own community and literary circles to denounce sexism. In doing so, she displaces a patriarchal order rooted in a colonial system that portrays men as the *gente de razón* (people of reason) against a backdrop of Indigenous peoples and particularly women as objects devoid of reason and subjectivity.

Chapter 4 observes how poet Judith Santopietro contests the centrality of the Nahuatl language in identity constructions and expectations that one must speak Nahuatl to be Nahua. Her paternal grandparents were from the Nahua region of Ixhuatlán del Café and spoke Nahuatl, but later generations ceased to speak the language. Santopietro self-identifies as Nahua yet meets resistance to this assertion from within and outside Nahua communities. There is suspicion on both sides as to why one would assume a marginal identity unless one carries "inescapable" markers of Indigeneity, such as having grown up speaking a Native language. Her book of xochitlajtoli *Palabras de agua* (Words of Water; 2010) reclaims a Nahua identity. She has translated a selection of her poems into Nahuatl with the help of poet Sixto Cabrera González. As a theoretical framework, I apply the concept tlaixpan to examine how Santopietro's representation of her ancestors' ancient words, although broken up in her family line, return now with great force as a "storm of pebbles." Like the perspective of tlaixpan with the past in front, these ancient words form part of a dynamic present in which Santopietro uses them in unexpected ways. She proposes a fluid conception of who is Nahua that can work against the pervasive depiction of Indigenous peoples as "endangered." Such a move subverts the Mexican nationalist discourse of *mestizaje* and its implicit contention that increased distance from the markers of Indigenous identity signifies "progress" toward becoming a "modern" subject.

In chapter 5, I argue that, through his publication of xochitlajtoli-mixed lyrical essays in *Las Plumas de la Serpiente* (2012), Mardonio Carballo dismantles stereotypical portrayals of Nahuas by shifting trite metaphors that obscure Nahua innovation and cultural practices. Within *Las Plumas*, he immediately breaks with conventional approaches by the sheer act of writing the work almost entirely in Spanish rather than Nahuatl. For Carballo, Native language proficiency as a defining characteristic of Nahuas under government-imposed categorizations excludes the many Nahuas who do not speak the language. In the first essay of *Las Plumas*, Carballo invokes the symbol of an eagle devouring a serpent on the Mexican flag, based on the mythical foundations of the famed Mexica altepetl of Mexihco-Tenochtitlan. He repudiates official venerations of this site of memory and depicts the eagle as the oppressive Mexican nation-state and the deplumed feathered serpent as Native Nations. In subsequent essays, Carballo deconstructs victimized characterizations of Indigenous communities through the conceptual framework of ixtlamatilistli, yoltlajlamikilistli, and tlaixpan. He transgresses the fictitious demarcation between orality and written text to transmit his messages through numerous media such as his own nationally televised program, books of poetry, and radio programs.

In chapter 6, I analyze Nahua cultural promoter and writer Ateri Miyawatl's movements across diverse media through her trilingual Nahuatl-Catalan-English book of poetry, *Neijmantototsintle / La tristesa és un ocell / Sadness Is a Bird* (2018), and short theatrical piece *Tsintatak* (2020). Miyawatl represents flowered words as a cathartic outlet to articulate the sorrows in her region of Guerrero, Mexico, which the poetic voice describes as a quivering bird set upon her heart and a neijmankokolistle (sadness-sickness). She deploys the term xochiameya (water springs up like flowers) to render vivid this catharsis. The word xochiameya illustrates the tears pouring down one's face, and then the healing that comes by putting words on the page. Beyond the literal translations of "flower" or "flor," xochitl points toward Nahua spaces of ceremony, aesthetic, and affective intelligence as effective coping strategies to process trauma. Miyawatl's works are potent plumes in the Serpent's Quill to underscore how this healing intersects with a broad comprehension of territory that bridges language and the land.

Within each chapter, *The Serpent's Plumes* mostly discusses the sections of each work in the order they appear in the text. This mode of analysis seeks to respect the order intended by the writers. Moreover, since there are few studies of these texts and the works themselves can be difficult to obtain, it is especially important to be faithful to the original to give a better sense of their progression and serve a bibliographic function. In many cases, these publications are assembled cyclically and weave back and forth to previous themes. This cross-weave is apparent in the chapter analyses with a continual thematic reinforcement.

Despite its small readership (which decreases more when considering how many can read the texts in Nahuatl), literature is still one of Nahua artists' preferred methods for self-expression. Literature offers a compelling means of representation through which Nahuas revalue their culture and practices to uproot a colonial system of economic marginalization, epistemicide, and linguistic discrimination. This study is only an initial examination of Nahua artistic expression. Younger Nahua artists are gaining new spaces through digital media, and the works from these newer generations are tied to projects in film, music, painting, and social media. Across this diverse mediascape, they negotiate between their Nahua communities and urban spaces. Not wanting to be bound by preconceptions of authenticity nor by the supposed superiority of urban centers, they navigate a fluid politics of identity in which they question even Nahua cultural practices without ceasing to proudly self-identify as Nahuas.

With the emerging corpus of Nahua literature, authors create alternative genealogies that do not eclipse Native publications as behind the great literature of the West/North. While official discourse proclaims the importance of Indigenous languages, the notion pervades that Indigenous peoples are stuck in the past and any departure from a stereotyped pristineness constitutes an exit from Indigeneity itself.[79] All Nahua authors aver that the Mexican nation-state and general populace still fail to dialogue genuinely with Native Nations. Despite a wealth of contemporary literary production, their texts have received limited critical attention beyond an acknowledgment of their existence. I contend that an earnest exploration of contemporary Nahua literature raises pressing questions: Who is viewed as capable of offering ideas in the construction of the nation-state? Who wields the power of inclusion? Who defines "progress"? The Serpent-Plumed texts addressed in this project serve as forerunners in posing these questions and proposing answers, displacing colonial practices and giving flight to alternative knowledges in the (des)construction of the nation-state.

Chapter 1

More Mexican Because We Speak Mexican

Natalio Hernández Transgressing the
Borders of Nationalist Discourse

Natalio Hernández enjoys telling the story of a politician who visited a Nahua community. "Do you all feel Mexican?" this official asked the people due to the area's remoteness and their limited proficiency in Castilian. To his chagrin, they responded, "Yes, we are truly Mexican because we speak mejikanoj. *You* are the one who isn't Mexican because you don't speak Mexican."[1] A similar assertion appears within Hernández's famous poem "Na ni indio" (I Am Indian), from his first book *Xochikoskatl* (Flowered Necklace; 1985). He writes "uan namaj nij mati melauak ni mejikano / pampa ni tlajtoa mejikano" (and now I know I am truly Mexican / because I speak Mexican; 27). Centuries of historical trauma underlie the brief encounter between the politician and the community—and the effects of the federal government's linguistically oriented assimilationist programs can be particularly felt. Community elders, for example, still vividly recall the physical and psychological abuse to which they were subjected for speaking their Native languages in government reeducation programs in the 1940s and 1950s.[2] Clearly, however, the community's response does not stay mired in the past. By reminding the politician that Nahuatl holds the closest connection to the term *Mexican* (indeed, the endonym mejikanoj for Nahuatl is common in many Nahua regions), they not only provincialize the Castilian language but emphasize Nahuatl's centrality in the present. Simultaneously, they resist the politician's nationalist aspirations; they do not feel Mexican in the assimilationist sense the official has in mind.

In part due to federal reeducation programs in the Huasteca, ixtlamatilistli (face knowledge) has shifted meaning to denote someone who obtains book smarts in a university education (ix- referring to the pages or "[sur]faces" of a book). This shift underscores the importance of contemporary Nahua literature as a vehicle for processing generational trauma and proposing solutions that foreground experiential knowledges. Nahuas use the very instrument of alphabetic writing that marginalizes them to point toward a wider view of what constitutes script, text, and knowledge production. Authors return to the perspective of ixtlamatilistli and confront the colonial legacy imposed in federal curricula. For these reasons, I choose to keep the term ixtlamatilistli precisely because of the fraught history it encompasses. Ixtlamatilistli renders vivid how Western models have encroached on Nahua and Native frameworks in general, even linguistically, and how Nahuas reappropriate the concept and find healing. Similarly, in some Huastecan areas mejikanoj now signifies Castilian instead of Nahuatl since it is the hegemonic language of the nation-state called Mexico.[3] Within Hernández's anecdote, the people reject the out-of-touch peripheral depiction of their Nahua community intimated by the politician's question.

I argue in this chapter that Natalio Hernández's books of poetry *Xochikoskatl* and *Patlani huitzitzilin* (The Hummingbird Flies; 2016) bring specific, situated Nahua histories and knowledge production to the forefront to disassemble the official Mexican nationalist discourse that associates full citizenship with a Castilian-speaking, *mestizo* identity distanced from Native practices. *Patlani* and *Xochikoskatl* draw from and center Nahua perspectives and ceremonial spaces, the invaluable plumes portrayed in Carballo's potent metaphor. They are written mostly in the Nahuatl of Hernández's hometown Tepeko in the Huasteca Veracruzana. His choice of language reflects not only a Nahua target audience but also features the sheer act of writing in Nahuatl as resistance against colonial practices.

Hernández describes *Xochikoskatl* and *Patlani* as works thought out in Nahuatl and through Nahua spaces. Taken together, these two texts help trace Hernández's literary trajectory and his deployment of Nahua epistemes in fighting the Mexican nation-state's attempts to subsume Native Nations within its contours. This analysis sets the stage for the subsequent chapters in which later authors build on and respond to (and at times contest) Hernández's legacy. A key distinction in *Patlani* is its explicit appeal to the Nahua ceremonial elements and histories to which Hernández only alludes in *Xochikoskatl*. Hernández created—or as Arturo

Arias describes, "transcreated"—*Xochikoskatl* with a facing translation in Castilian.[4] In a departure from his previous publications and in defiance of a de facto linguistic hegemony, he wrote *Patlani* in Nahuatl and refused to translate the work into Castilian himself. This move highlights the language's vitality in conveying Nahua concepts. Hernández emphasizes the relevance of local Nahua perspectives projected out to Mesoamerica and the world. Although Hernández has traveled across the globe and currently resides in Mexico City, Tepeko has always served as his main locus and node of enunciation.

Hernández's foregrounding of the Huasteca—specifically knowledge production tied to ixtlamatilistli, yoltlajlamikilistli (heart knowledge), and tlaixpan (the past in front) in the Tepeko community—gains particular significance when considering the marginality usually afforded to this area in the nationalist imaginary. When Hernández wrote *Xochikoskatl*, Tepeko or Lomas del Dorado (the official name) did not appear on national maps. To borrow ethnic studies scholar Anne Mai Yee Jansen's observation about mapping in Pacific Islander literature, Hernández's writing locates Tepeko "at their [maps'] centers, not only physically but also culturally, historically, and socially" ("Writing *toward* Action" 9). Such a turn lends new meaning to "Contemporary Mexican Literature." Nation-state discourse ironically marginalizes the very people—*mexicanos* in its sense denoting Nahuas—who give name to the country itself.

The titles *Xochikoskatl* and *Patlani huitzitzilin* signal empowerment. Within *Xochikoskatl* Hernández articulates the Nahua perspectives ixtlamatilistli, yoltlajlamikilistli, and tlaixpan in Mexico City and the inner conflicts he feels. "Xochikoskatl" (the flowered necklace) is a ceremonial object for communal respect and kinship. "Patlani huitzitzilin" (the hummingbird flies) evinces the poetic voice's death and transformation into a hummingbird, a symbol of deceased warriors. *Xochikoskatl* consists of eighty lyric poems or "necklace beads" relating the poetic voice's—presumably Natalio Hernández's under the pseudonym José Antonio Xokoyotsin—varied experiences and responses to Mexico City. *Patlani* resembles an epic plotline in which the main figure, based on Hernández's father, Piltata, recounts his death and life.

When analyzed together, *Xochikoskatl* and *Patlani huitzitzilin* span a literary trajectory of over three decades. Especially since the 1990s, Hernández has stressed the need to focus on the positive and avoid dwelling on the sadness portrayed in *Xochikoskatl*. As shall be seen in later chapters, younger generations of contemporary authors question this peaceable attitude. For some of those authors, the threat of disruptive, property-damaging, or violent confrontation must exist for peaceful protests to exert a palpable effect. Younger generations' texts resemble Hernández's work during the 1980s when he wrote *Xochikoskatl*, ready to battle with an attitude of "arco y flechas" (bows and arrows) and openly denounce systemic discrimination.[5] While the approaches of *Xochikoskatl* and *Patlani* differ in some fundamental respects, both emerge from intense suffering and poverty, described as orphanhood, and then stake out a place in rural and urban territories. In *Xochikoskatl*, the poetic voice speaks from Mexico City. In *Patlani*, he speaks from Tepeko, the community alluded to in *Xochikoskatl*. In *Xochikoskatl*, the poetic voice describes being alive physically, but feeling dead emotionally inside Mexico City's urban milieu. In *Patlani*, the poetic voice is physically dead yet alive through his community's worldviews. Within this (re)vivification, the hummingbird serves as a metaphor for literary creation with its quill-like beak. The sight of a hummingbird in Tepeko also represents the return of a deceased relative. In this combination of literary creation and kinship, the hummingbird and flowered necklace—like the Serpent's Plumes—symbolize Nahua history and empowerment.

Flor y cuenta nueva: Truly Contemporary Mexican Literature

> Ma sampa mo echkauikaj ueuetlakamej
> ma sampa tijkakikaj ueuetlajtoli
> ma sampa tijyolitikaj
> xochikali uan kuikakali.
>
> (May the wise elders draw near again
> may we again listen to words of wisdom
> may we again revive
> the flowered house and song house.)
>
> —Natalio Hernández, *Xochikoskatl* (1985)

These lines from the poem "Iknotlajtoli" (Orphan Words) and similar ones throughout *Xochikoskatl* by Natalio Hernández have smacked, for some readers, of Pre-Columbian utopianism and an appeal to a Mexican state–sponsored nationalist narrative.[6] Because Hernández's poetics resemble Ángel María Garibay's and Miguel León Portilla's translations of the sixteenth-century manuscript *Cantares mexicanos* (Nahuatl Songs), several critics have depreciated his texts' evocation of this style as a Nezahualcoyotl imitator leveraging Aztec prominence. At a closer reading of *Xochikoskatl*, especially in Nahuatl, nothing could be further from the truth. Hernández skillfully displaces the nationalist narrative of the vanishing Indian. While ancient "flower and song" no doubt serve as inspiration for his texts, Hernández's deployment of contemporary Nahua aesthetics and perspectives have received much less attention. His emulation of flower and song has always been to center contemporary Nahua flowered words and practices.

Through maize-centered tropes in *Xochikoskatl* and *Patlani huitzitzilin*, particularly in Nahuatl, these texts offer insights into strategies against discriminatory practices. Hernández foregrounds corn aesthetic and its underlying epistemes to assert that Nahuas produce solutions for Indigenous and non-Indigenous peoples. He frames present-day oppression within a colonial space and time to denounce colonial practices or "coloniality"[7] (koyoyotl or "essence of the coyote" in Nahuatl, a concept resembling coloniality that I address in detail later). Hernández does so to imagine a space in which Native peoples actively participate in the (des)construction of the nation-state through worldings woven with the landscape, respect for elders, an alternative view of time, and affective intelligence.

In this section, I address Hernández's trajectory leading up to the publication of *Xochikoskatl* and subsequently *Patlani huitzitzilin*. Perhaps one of the principal reasons why close analyses of contemporary Nahua literature are so scant is due to a lack of familiarity among non-Native audiences with Nahuatl language and the contexts in which authors create their works. This unfamiliarity has led some critics to deem *Xochikoskatl* and Indigenous literatures insular and provincial. Much the same, though, could be said of well-known literary traditions if they too were relegated to obsolescence. I detail Hernández's biography to set the context for *Xochikoskatl* and *Patlani huitzitzilin* and debunk myths of insularity. The sections that follow give an overview of *Xochikoskatl*'s structure and the framework for the readings within the chapter—tracing "topographies" in both the sense of the physical landscape and the Nahua literary topos from which Hernández writes. I then outline the Nahua theoretical framework articulated within *Xochikoskatl*. This overview lays the groundwork to conduct readings of Hernández's poems.

Hernández is a poet, novelist, essayist, and activist who published his first work in the 1980s in Mexico City, at a time when there was a significant disparity between the progressive rhetoric of interculturality and bilingualism from the Secretariat of Public Education (SEP) and actual practices that posited Indigenous cultures as obstacles to national unity and industrialization.[8] With some notable exceptions, publishing houses supportive of modern Indigenous literatures would not emerge until the 1990s. Hernández released *Xochikoskatl* amid a milieu that pitted Nahuatl and other Native languages as antithetic to contemporaneity and even proper language as such.[9]

Born in the community of Naranjo Dulce in the municipality of Ixhuatlán de Madero, Hernández and his family moved to nearby Tepeko when he was about five years old. He considers Tepeko his true hometown. A majority of Huastecan Nahuas have as last names Hernández or de la Cruz (Natalio Hernández's maternal and paternal surnames are Hernández), due to the colonial evangelization in which priests imposed Christian surnames. Natalio Hernández published *Xochikoskatl* under the pseudonym José Antonio Xokoyotsin, "José Antonio Jr.," to combat this Spanish patronymic encroachment and honor his grandfather José Antonio. His grandfather is one of the poetic/narrative voices in *Patlani huitzitzilin*, giving counsel to Hernández's father Piltata and openly identifying elements that serve as inspiration for *Xochikoskatl*.

In interviews Hernández calls *Xochikoskatl* a product of "pure intuition."[10] He wrote this book while serving as SEP Deputy Director of Indigenous Education. By *intuition* he signals that *Xochikoskatl* exploded from feelings of outrage and frustration within a context that, as he describes, restricted his movement ("Afirma poeta"). Hernández also denotes with "intuition" that he was not readily aware of literary movements or styles at the time, aside from Garibay's and León Portilla's translations of flower and song; rather, *Xochikoskatl* was based on his foundational experiences in the Huasteca and subsequent service for twenty years as a bilingual teacher and deputy director (31). Hernández addresses poetry and literature as a visceral means to heal the scars of colonialism. This is something I have heard frequently in his home community—that xochitlajtoli "can heal," in Nahuatl, "timopajtisej." Hernández's decades of service in education from the 1960s and 1980s allowed him to observe a vicious cycle of discrimination that he seeks to end through his works.

When Hernández was an adolescent, he resided in Colatlán, then half a day's journey away from Tepeko, to complete part of his secondary education. Upon graduation, he returned to live in Tepeko for about a year. This return constituted a solidifying experience in which Hernández was initiated into the community as an adult and gained a deep respect for the knowledges there. He labored daily in the fields, came to appreciate the community elders, and participated in ceremonies throughout the year.

After this period in Tepeko, Hernández's father told him that he was not meant for work solely in the fields and should complete his studies at a *preparatoria* (three-year pre-university school similar to high school). Hernández moved to Hidalgo and labored as a domestic servant to pay for his studies. He recalls his vexation at having to fetch water (a target of jest from others, as it was viewed as "women's work") for an elderly *mestiza* who treated him with disdain as an *indito* (little Indian). Frustrated with this situation, he left the house and worked as an ice cream street vendor. The financial difficulties and discrimination faced during this time left an indelible impression on Hernández that has motivated him to fight the marginalization of First Nations.

In the mid-1960s, after completing his secondary school education, Hernández worked as a bilingual teacher in Puebla. In the early 1970s, he began his undergraduate studies at the Instituto Nacional de Antropología e Historia (INAH). While at INAH, Hernández led the creation of a pan-Nahua urban and rural association, Organization of Nahua Indigenous Professionals Civil Association (OPINAC). He served as the organization's first president beginning in 1973. OPINAC had three main goals: 1. Collaborate with Indigenous movements on a national and international level; 2. Foment political ideology for First Nations and by First Nations; and 3. Create a standardized grammar of contemporary Nahuatl that would stimulate its use and strengthen a Nahua consciousness (Nechikolistli, *Neluayotl tekiyotl* 3). The book *Xochikoskatl* has the OPINAC seal on its back cover. As Hernández notes, this political opening worried government officials—particularly the INAH director, who thought that Nahuas were bent on supplanting him.[11] This apprehension led to Hernández's transfer to Puebla to oversee bilingual education without having completed his studies at INAH (reflecting a common government strategy to neutralize threats by making them government officials in small offices).[12] Never having completed his *licenciatura* (undergraduate education), Hernández has confronted the pressure of teaching at the university level while not holding a bachelor's degree. He affirms that the knowledges gained from personal experience outweigh anything he could have learned within a classroom.[13]

As president of OPINAC and bilingual educator in various Nahua regions, Hernández became familiar with multiple variants of Nahuatl, a familiarity evidenced in his poetry. The SEP transferred him from Puebla to Hidalgo in the mid-1970s to direct Indigenous education for the entire state. Hernández recounts that he again came under suspicion from government officials due to his support of *campesino* (peasant farmer) uprisings in the Huasteca.[14] This stance led to his transfer to Mexico City as Deputy Director of Indigenous Education in 1978.

Hernández tells of walking around Mexico City in the early 1980s and feeling alienated.[15] He recounted his crisis to anthropologist Arlene Patricia Scanlon, who responded that he was not alone and recommended the novel *Brave New World* (1932).[16] Hernández identified with this novel, and his reading of it influenced poems in *Xochikoskatl*. Acknowledgment of this influence debunks any essentialism that depicts European work as incommensurable and anathema to "pure" Indigenous practices. Many lines in *Xochikoskatl* resemble statements in *Brave New World*. Like the character John, referred to as the Savage, Hernández voices his deep frustration toward the "brave new society" of Mexico City in an Indigenous language. Tempted to commit cultural suicide by disguising himself in Mexico City as a *mestizo* with his excellent Castilian, he chose instead to nurture his hometown's intellectual practices.

Garibay's and León Portilla's translations of *Cantares mexicanos* (Nahuatl/Mexican Songs) exerted a significant impact on the literary scene in which Natalio Hernández first published in 1985.[17] By the 1970s it was standard to include Garibay's and León Portilla's translations in anthologies of Mexican literature.[18] When Hernández wrote *Xochikoskatl*, he was reading their renditions of "flower and song" in Castilian. His personal copy of Garibay's *Poesía náhuatl* contains handwritten notes and even the beginnings of some poems from *Xochikoskatl*.[19] Although this text served as inspiration, Hernández does not copy its style. To the contrary, Hernández points to how this rich expression is alive and well in contemporary Nahuatl and present-day ceremonies. The title *Xochikoskatl* (Flowered Necklace) is a skillful allusion to "flower and song" and to modern-day ceremonies.

Hernández has succeeded in becoming a recognized literary figure in what Ángel Rama calls the *ciudad letrada* (lettered city).[20] He represents a compelling voice that deepens dialogues about Indigenous agency and questions the supposed Western monopoly over intellectual production. A point of reference for Indigenous letters in Mexico, Hernández is a founder of ELIAC and 1997 winner of the Premio Nezahualcoyotl. His extensive body of publications include the books of poetry *Así habló el ahuehuete*

(1989), *Canto nuevo de Anáhuac* (1994; 2007), *Papalocuicatl* (1996), *Semanca huitzilin* (2005), *Flores de primavera* (2012), *Patlani huitzitzilin* (2016), *Itoscac ahuehuetl* (2021), and *Tlilamatl* (2023). Hernández has gained international recognition as an intercultural education expert.[21] He was elected in 2013 as a member of the Academia Mexicana de la Lengua. Now perhaps the most prominent Nahua of the twentieth and twenty-first centuries, Hernández began to gain notoriety with *Xochikoskatl*. Considering this impact, it is puzzling that so few have examined the text. A return to *Xochikoskatl* offers crucial insights into Nahua perspectives and shifts discussions from Native victimization to dynamic agency.

Xochikoskatl helped launch Hernández's career and further opened a space for future Indigenous writers and the later creation of ELIAC in 1993. While a limited readership has seen *Xochikoskatl* in its entirety, a wider public has read selections in anthologies and partial republications such as its first part, "Sempoalxochitl" (Twenty Flower), printed by UNAM Press as a separate text in 1987.[22] Interest in Hernández's work soared after these publications along with Miguel León Portilla's adamant support, and Hernández leveraged his prestige to advocate for the creation of ELIAC. In 1994 he released through major publisher Editorial Diana an anthology of his poetry, *Yancuic Anahuac cuicatl* (New Song of Anahuac), with poems from *Xochikoskatl* and two subsequent texts. He went from being a little-known Nahua teacher working as deputy director in Indigenous education to being a leading figure in national and international debates over Indigenous rights and literatures less than a decade later. He attributes the origins of this success to the Editorial Kalpulli's willingness to publish *Xochikoskatl*.[23]

Due to Hernández's far-reaching influence, Native authors recognize him as a key protagonist alongside authors like Binnizá writer Víctor de la Cruz and Mazatec writer Juan Gregorio Regino in the promotion of contemporary literatures in Native languages from the 1980s onward. His first book of poetry and more recent work *Patlani huitzitzilin* are ideal points of departure for a consideration of Nahua literature as a whole and especially literature from the Huasteca, spanning portions of Veracruz, Hidalgo, San Luis Potosí, and Puebla. "Huasteca" (Huaxteca in Nahuatl) denotes a region in which the Huastecans, a Maya population, settled in the seventh century. It is a diverse space in which Totonacos, Ñhähñus, and Tepehuas coexist and share cultural practices.[24] Until approximately the 1990s, access to the Huasteca was difficult and, at the time Hernández wrote *Xochikoskatl*, government pamphlets advertised the area as a remote wilderness frontier ready for capitalists.²⁵ The region lies on the periphery of the Central Mexican Valley, such as Milpa Alta near Mexico City, studied more intently by Nahuatl scholars. In this sense Huastecan authors write within a marginality of the marginality of the marginality. Nahua authors from Central Mexico sometimes refer to Huastecan Nahuatl as "popular Nahuatl" (with negative connotations), "baby Nahuatl," and "vulgar Nahuatl" (*vulgar* with the dual meaning of both "common" and "full of vulgarities"). Hernández writes against these distortions propagated about the Huasteca. Alongside other Huastecan artists, he deploys Nahua images and symbols in his works to attest that contemporary literatures in the periphery deserve the same acclaim afforded Central Mexican Nahuatl and mainstream Mexican literary production.²⁶

The Textual Topographies of *Xochikoskatl* and *Patlani*

Xochikoskatl consists of four subdivisions or "necklaces": "Sempoalxochitl" (Twenty Flower), "Yankuik kuikatl" (New Song), "Yoloxochitl" (Heart Flower / Magnolia), and "Yankuik tonatij, yankuik tlanextli" (New Sun, New Sunrise). Each necklace bears twenty poems, referred to as "flower and song," for a total of eighty poems in the book's entirety. In the Huasteca Veracruzana such ceremonial necklaces symbolize dignity and authority for the wearer. Steeped in the rhythm and meter of Nahua ritual language, poems vary in length anywhere from a brief quatrain to three pages with stanzas ranging between two and eleven verses. Each composition is a *cuenta* (bead/count) on the subdivisions' strands of twenty; they progress from a cathartic expression of grief and protest to an assertion of power and knowledge.

The four parts coincide with cardinal points, beginning with the North (the place of wind and death). As *Xochikoskatl* develops, these four subdivisions circle the compass and culminate in the fundamental direction, East. The book advances like a Huastecan Nahua community guided by a tlamatini (ritual specialist, or literally "knower") through a xochikali (flowered house) ceremonial space.²⁷ Readers unfamiliar with such rituals would miss this significance because Hernández does not explicitly identify them in *Xochikoskatl* (by contrast, as we shall see, to his approach in *Patlani*). In xochikali ceremonies, the community adorns distinguished members and visitors with the flowered necklaces alluded to in the book's title, *Xochikoskatl*. A tlamatini first petitions harmful north winds to spare the corn crop and community members; within *Xochikoskatl* Hernández makes pleas like the tlamatini's invocations for dominant sectors of society to stop afflicting the landscape and Indigenous peoples. As a ritual develops, the community moves from the north into the xochikali, where members dance at an east-facing altar throughout the evening. At daybreak they then climb a mountain to greet the sun and the crop they hope will be successful. In *Xochikoskatl*, Hernández metaphorically traces these steps from colonial north winds to the welcoming of the "new sun" of an Indigenous empowerment that symbolically culminates in the collection's final part.

While it would be impossible to analyze all eighty poems within this study, I briefly describe the content to help give an idea of *Xochikoskatl*'s overall structure. Each part begins and ends with poems titled "Xochikoskatl," threading together the text's different themes. Poems are numbered with Mesoamerican bar-and-dot notation in the table of contents. The Mesoamerican structure of the book itself is circular, like crop cycles. Regeneration follows psychological storms and destruction.

In the first part, "Sempoalxochitl" (Twenty Flower), the poetic voice, José Antonio Xokoyotsin, feels isolated and orphaned in Mexico City. His suffering is reflected in titles like "Iknotlajtoli" (Orphan Words), "Maseualtlajtoli ipan koyomej inintlali" (Indigenous Words in the Land of the Coyotes), and "Kemantika nijmachilia nimiktoja uan nojua niyoltok" (Sometimes I Feel I Am Dead and Yet I Am Still Alive). He describes the need to defend against continual koyomej (*mestizo* and white, "coyote") encroachments. Many poems are apostrophic pleas to Indigenous brothers and sisters. Xokoyotsin acknowledges the continent as Native land. In Nahuatl the term *America* disappears and instead the continent is Maseualsemanauak (All the Indigenous Land among the Waters), similar to the Gunadule term Abiayala. A prominent aspect in this section is a trans-Indigenous framework (the term maseuali applies to Nahuas and all Native Nations) to reclaim the land and position Indigenous peoples as a locus of enunciation for its history.

Following "Sempoalxochitl," the second part "Yankuik kuikatl" (New Song) rallies a warrior defense of the territory, with *territory* understood to represent both land and the conceptual battlegrounds of history. The poetic persona declares that Nezahualcoyotl and Cuauhtemoc are alive and proclaims a new era of flower and song. The land encroached upon by the nation-state is named Anahuac (Among the Waters) instead of Mexico or the Americas (51, 71, 75, 89, 93, 97, 99, 103). *Mexico* specifically denotes Mexihco-Tenochtitlan, encompassed by present-day Mexico City. The third part "Yoloxochitl" (Heart Flower) focuses on an affectivity through metaphors of flowers and the heart, evinced by titles such as "Yolpakilistli" (Happiness with the Heart) and "Chokak noyolo" (My Heart Cried). Again the emphasis is on Nahuas' contemporaneity, and how they continue to plant the flowers of their artistic and epistemic creations. The fourth and final part, "Yankuik tonatij, yankuik tlanextli" (New Sun, New Sunrise), presages a new sun symbolizing an emergent period in which Native knowledges figure central to remedying environmental and social destruction.

Principally within the first part, "Sempoalxochitl" (Twenty Flower), Hernández confronts colonial perspectives and explores the culture shock he experienced in Mexico City. José Antonio Xokoyotsin articulates Indigenous empowerment amid a dismal context in which koyomej bury Nahuas under an oppressive discourse that obscures their very existence. Sempoalxochitl is the only flower used in ceremonies for both the dead and the living; it is rooted in the Nahuatl vigesimal base number and marks completeness or wholeness (indicative in its literal meaning of se pouali [one count of twenty]). Hernández repeats this number in the title of the first part, sempoalxochitl, and *Xochikoskatl*'s entire structure with twenty poems in each subdivision. With this reiteration, Hernández invokes the Mexica xiuhpohualli ("year count" / calendar) with its twenty-day signs, the twentieth being xochitl (flower). In *Xochikoskatl* the number twenty symbolizes the break with a period of discrimination and beginning of a new cycle, evident in the progress of the text. As the book advances, he resolves his own internal conflict over urban life in Mexico City and heralds the imminent arrival of an epoch of Indigenous leadership. Like Carballo's metaphor of the Serpent's Plumes, Hernández's text intervenes in the city to amplify Native voices and experiences.

The Nahua view of intellect is fundamental to understanding one of the main arguments of both *Xochikoskatl* and *Patlani huitzitzilin*—namely, that Nahuas and Indigenous peoples in general are modern knowledge producers. *Xochikoskatl* and *Patlani* shift fluidly between Pre-Columbian references and contemporary Nahua cultural production. As seen in the introduction, ueuejtlajtoli or huehuehtlahtolli, literally "old words," connotes words of wisdom. Ueuejtlajtoli in the Huasteca is acutely contemporary. Hernández highlights continuities between present-day philosophies and those found in colonial-period Nahuatl texts. In doing so, he locates Nahua thought within an unbroken millennia-old tradition to disassemble the pervasive notion that Indigenous subjects lack intellectual traditions from which they can draw for the present.

In relation to these perspectives, Native migrants, as Hernández himself was when he wrote *Xochikoskatl*, contest Western Modernity's disregard for Native intellectual traditions. Figuratively an "orphan" in the poem "Iknotlajtoli" (Orphan Words), this migrant negotiates between the worldviews of their communities and urban settings. Within this fluid context, the poetic persona José Antonio Xokoyotsin articulates Nahua views. They serve as a lens through which to interpret the experience of migration and position Nahuas as knowledge producers. *Xochikoskatl* constitutes a precursor to later self-representations of Indigenous migrant experiences. These movements shift discussions away from a fundamentalist rescue of a pre-Hispanic past and toward a dynamism in which Hernández mediates knowledges from his Huastecan community and urban landscapes.

Hernández places maize at the forefront in *Xochikoskatl*. He calls for a revival of the xochikali (flowered house) and kuikakali (song house). Kuikakali alludes to Pre-Columbian schools (cuicacalli), but xochikali refers to contemporary sanctuaries in which communities perform corn ceremonies. Hernández's appeal to "flower and song" carries deeper meanings associated with contemporary Nahua practices and is not strictly an invocation of the nationally celebrated flower and song. Huastecan Nahuas deem maize a flower. Indeed, the word often used for "flower and song," xochikuikatl, literally means "flowered song" or "maize song" and intimates xochitlatsotsontli (flowered music) played at modern ceremonies. Corn aesthetic transmits concepts codified within the Nahuatl language, specifically the approaches of ixtlamatilistli, yoltlajlamikilistli, and tlaixpan analyzed in the introduction. These perspectives are intrinsically tied to nemilistli (walk of life), in which philosophy is centered on close observation, affect, and a relational symbiosis of people with the landscape and their deceased ancestors.

Indigenous literary production like *Xochikoskatl* highlights how literature often anticipates future theoretical debates and performatively gives life to these perspectives. Storytelling and poetry are vital in communicating Indigenous theories.[28] *Xochikoskatl* blurs the demarcations among genres by mixing lyric poetry, narrative, epistolary, and ceremonial chant. Through the contact zones among these different forms of expression, Hernández's poetic persona articulates an account of Nahua agency and engages with the views that give Nahuas resilience to observe, create, and transform their surroundings.[29] This literature bridges abstract concepts with everyday personal experience—in keeping with the Nahua definition of intellectualism and the storied contributions of the Serpent's Plumes.

Sintli: Knowledge Production and Corn Aesthetic within Sacred Landscapes

The first of *Xochikoskatl*'s four parts, "Sempoalxochitl" (Twenty Flower / Mexican marigold), alludes with its title to preparations for the Day of the Dead (mijkailuitl or ueyi iluitl) in which paths of this flowers' petals lead ancestors home. My analysis of the third poem, "Iknotlajtoli" (Orphan Words), shows how a relational view with one's surroundings is interrupted by colonial practices within the urban context of Mexico City. The poetic voice, José Antonio Xokoyotsin, feels lost in a context where his philosophies are disregarded, affect is absent, and the connection with ancestors and the past is broken.

"Iknotlajtoli" serves as an ideal introduction to the vitality of maize and natural surroundings emphasized throughout *Xochikoskatl*. Iknotlajtoli means "orphan words" and connotes suffering. The landscape is an ancestor with whom one shares a reciprocity. As a migrant in Mexico City, Xokoyotsin is orphaned from both the members of his community and from proximity to natural surroundings. Rather than situate and articulate his being in dialogue with the landscape and fieldwork, Xokoyotsin's labor within Mexico City severs this connection and leaves him under the haughty gaze of koyomej (coyotes, within the postpositional *koyo*paj). He "walks and traverses," but seems to go nowhere:

> Ni iknochoka kemantika
> ni teikneltij ninentinemi
> tekuesoj ken nipanotinemi
> koyopaj ni tekipanoua. (25)

> (I sometimes cry like an orphan
> abandoned, walking around
> it's sad how I go about traversing
> working at the behest of koyomej.)

Ninentinemi literally means "I walk around walking" and nipanotinemi "I go around going around." Coupled with a Nahua view of an altepetl's (city's) natural surroundings is the indispensability of walking, which in turn correlates with the perception of an intellectual as one with personal experience; a person must know the earth face-to-face to properly comprehend it. The significance of this walk emerges in nemi, to live/walk, as the root word for nemilistli, which can be translated as *philosophy, feeling, thought*, and *way of life*. Nonetheless, as seen in "Iknotlajtoli," Xokoyotsin ambles around lost in synthetic cityscapes. The koyomej disrespect his views, and the land remains forgotten under pavement and buildings.

In the second stanza, Xokoyotsin expresses that, isolated from ceremonial fortification of a symbiosis with the landscape, he would want "xochitlatsotsontli nij kakiskia" (to hear maize ceremonial music; 25). Xochitlatsotsontli (flowered music) comprises an extensive sacred repertoire played solely at corn rituals ("flowered music" also denotes "corn music").[30] These religious practices are central in the articulation of the Nahua respect for place. Distinct xochitlatsotsontli compositions carry titles such as "Atl" (water), "Tlaskamatili" (gratitude), "Tlitl" (fire), "Tlaixpan" (altar), "Tepetl" (hill), "Ojtli" (path), "Tlanestiuala" (sunrise), and "Ejekatl" (wind), and maize is the epicenter of this music. The same natural elements of xochitlatsotsontli appear throughout *Xochikoskatl* (53, 61, 99, 183). Significantly, the poem "Iknotlajtoli" itself makes no explicit mention of these elements, since here the poetic voice laments how he is separated from them in Mexico City.

Walking guides maize ceremonies honoring Chikomexochitl (Seven Flower), to which the poem "Iknotlajtoli" alludes with the reference to flowered/maize music. Nahua communities climb sacred hills/mounts[31] to give offerings for an abundant crop. Chikomexochitl is a pair of sacred figures fashioned from cornhusks, who becomes a living entity when bound together and dressed in miniature traditional manta (men's white clothing) and kechtlajtsomitl (embroidered blouse).[32] This adornment contrasts with attempts to timokoyotlakentiaj (dress like koyomej) in the fourth stanza. The koyomej impose a singular system upon Nahuas and fail to respect a field of diverse aesthetics or sonorities.

The style of the poem "Iknotlajtoli," reflective of *Xochikoskatl* as a whole, resembles the diction and structure of Nahua ceremonial language. Tlamatinij (ritual specialists) often use the conditional mood during rituals to apprise divinities of their communities' desire for rainfall. Hernández adopts this ritual phraseology in "Iknotlajtoli." For example, in the second stanza he writes "nijnekiskia" / I would desire; "nij kakiskia" / I would listen; "nimijtotiskia" / I would dance; "ni pakiskia" / I would be happy (25).

Unlike in Castilian or English, the conditional mood in Nahuatl implies that what one requests should exist and that some aberrant state impedes its realization.[33] Initial repetitions of words and syntactical structures cross-stitch memories together (both figuratively and literally as a mnemonic device) and maintain an intimate connection with the land. Like a thread returning to the fabric to form a row, like the repeated sowing across furrowed fields, the lines in Hernández's poems and ceremonial songs reiterate similar diction and syntax. This ceremonial language echoes the Nahuatl aesthetic in the sixteenth-century text *Cantares mexicanos*.[34] The poetic voice marks continuity between classical language and present-day practices through parallel structures and repetitions.

One hears similar parallel structures from "Iknotlajtoli" in Nahua ceremonies, such as that of the New Year (Yankuik Xiuitl), in which a wise elder pleads for an auspicious future.[35] This language resembles the anaphora in the fifth stanza:[36]

> **Asijka tonatij ma**timoyolchikauakaj
> **Asijka tonatij ma**tiyolpakikaj,
> **ma sampa** tij kakikaj ueuetl uan teponastli
> **ma sampa** tijkakikaj akatlapitstli. (25; emphasis added)

(The sun/day **has already arrived** for us to be strong of heart
The sun/day **has already arrived** for us to be happy of heart,
Again may we listen to the drum and rattle
Again may we listen to the flute.)

These lines exemplify a Nahua aesthetic. For example, rhyming is not artistically appealing. Rather, sacred language and poems reiterate syntax, reincorporate internal structures, and tease out similarities among linguistic constructions. Repetition increases the intensity of the enunciation with each passing verse.[37] "Iknotlajtoli" features the rhythm and revisiting of syntactical forms fundamental to the literary aesthetic of Mesoamerican languages.

Within this context, referred to in the sixth stanza, kuikakali (song house) no longer constitutes solely a tribute to Pre-Columbian schools of music. Kuikakali correlates with the array of compositions taught in contemporary ceremonies. The poem's title, iknotlajtoli (orphan words), and the first line, iknochoka (cry like an orphan), contrast with the sonorities of the sixth stanza's xochikali (flowered/corn/ceremonial house) and kuikakali (song house). Iknotl (orphan) juxtaposes with xochitl (flower/

maize). Natural elements invoked in the "flowered song" titles accompany rituals within the xochikali, and they all contain life (yoltok) since without them Indigenous communities would fail to cultivate corn. Nahuas themselves have life within their hearts and minds because of the vital power supplied by maize and everything that goes into its production. Nonetheless, "Iknotlajtoli" limns a society that orphans and alienates Nahuas from the landscape and reduces everyone and everything to a cog in a commercial assemblage.

Hernández engages two disparate spaces within "Iknotlajtoli": Mexico City and his home community, for which he yearns. The conditional mood *iskia* in the second stanza marks this longing, as the poetic voice would listen to the xochitlatsotsontli (flowered music) and ayakachtli (rattle) if not confined within the city. In the first four stanzas the poetic voice describes how his surroundings lead him to wander around unable to situate himself, removed from his maseualikniuaj (Indigenous sisters and brothers). These lost steps then pivot toward the landscape in the final stanzas. Revival of the flowered house and song house corresponds with the resurgence of books and the amoxkali (library, or "book house") in the seventh stanza:

> Ma sampa nesikaj toltekamej
> ma sampa mo echkauikaj tlajkuiloanej
> ma tikin tlalanakaj to amoxuaj
> ma sampa tijketsakaj amoxkali. (25)

> (May the artists appear again
> may the writers draw close
> let us raise our books
> let us again erect the house of books.)

These verses link knowledge production with maize cultivation, drawing a parallel between the raising of texts and the growth of the crop. In this move, the act of raising books relates to the corn's centrality in helping elevate the spirit in ceremonial ascensions of sacred peaks. Hernández's words have the potential to return and lift his Indigenous brothers' spirits, linking them (like the maize crop and the ancestors) to past, present, and future. Maize itself in these readings is a text like the book raised in the seventh stanza. As Hernández explains in personal interviews, corn readings were on his mind when he wrote *Xochikoskatl*.[38] Presently, in some regions of the Huasteca, tlachianij (ritual specialists who foresee the future, or "seers") analyze corn kernels to predict future events and tell where a person needs healing.[39] Alluded to in the sixth and seventh stanzas of "Iknotlajtoli," maize functions literally/literarily as a text and foretells a resurgence of Indigenous knowledges and aesthetic. Corn receives its vitality from the new sun and then passes on that stored energy when people consume it.

The eighth and final stanza invokes this power with "yolchikaualistli" (heart strength), which serves as a metaphor of being "firm like a dried maize kernel":

> Ma tlami ni majmajtli
> ma tlami ni temiktli
> ma kotoni ni kuesiuistli
> ma sampa asi pakilistli uan yolchikaualistli. (25)

> (May this fear end
> may this nightmare end
> may this suffering burst
> may happiness and heart strength arrive.)

The incorporated noun yol-otl (heart) conveys "choice maize seed" and chikaua means "to harden." In Romance languages, "to be hard of heart" is a character flaw; in Nahuatl, due to the associations of yolotl with corn, it represents having a strength of character that resembles the durability of a dried, hardened maize kernel. "Iknotlajtoli" builds up in intensity with ritualistic diction to this final stanza in which Hernández's poetic persona pleads for a new era of Indigenous leadership. Like religious supplications for clouds to burst forth with rain, this petition seeks that the nightmare (temiktli) and suffering (kuesiuistli) cease, indeed burst (the ritual term kotoni for the "breaking" or "bursting" of an ailment). Xokoyotsin calls for happiness and strength of heart to return. Communal and individual health parallels with agricultural well-being in this link between Xokoyotsin's spiritual condition within Mexico City and the rainfall essential to plants. Flowered song invocations for a successful crop, mentioned in the second stanza, are intrinsic to his psychological health in an urban context of fear and oppression.

Nahua relationality communicates a view in which humans form part of a wide field of sonorities. Within this nonanthropocentric perspective, elements of the landscape like hills are animate and speak. Nahuas dialogue with these surroundings, as seen in "Iknotlajtoli" with its emphasis on listening: to the xochitlatsotsontli and Indigenous brothers in the second stanza; to musical instruments such as the ueuetl and ayakachtli in the fifth stanza; to words of the elders in the sixth stanza; to the burst of suffering in the final stanza (25). The reference to ueuetl in the fifth stanza cited earlier plays on three meanings of the word, as it signifies a pre-Hispanic ceremonial drum (made from a hollowed-out tree trunk), the wise elders (ueuejtlakatl), and the centenarian Mexican cypress tree (known as ahuehuetl or sabino) that symbolizes Nahua intellectual tradition. Ueuetl blends the individual with myriad sonorities. Elders' wisdom (ueuejtlajtoli / "wise words"), one's relationship with natural surroundings (xochikali / "flowered house"), and ritual music (xochitlatsotsontli / "flowered music") nurture this bond.

In a gesture that resonates with other Nahua authors' works, Hernández turns the gaze back on the colonizer in "Iknotlajtoli" and directs what can be described as an atypical inverse study toward the cities of conventional ethnographers and anthropologists. Traversing the city, he researches and reports on social penuries within urban settings. In the role of a critical observer, Hernández reverses the customary paradigm in which only non-Indigenous urbanites conduct such studies. Urban residents suffer in crisis because of their estrangement from the landscape. Xokoyotsin ambles around lost in the first stanza of "Iknotlajtoli" since he is unable to situate himself in a polluted concrete jungle. Within this representation urban inhabitants perpetuate regressive and unhealthy practices that inflict psychological and physiological harm. The poetic voice dismantles the supposed superiority of the koyotl's city and exposes it as inherently dis/placed due to its detachment from the land. Xokoyotsin recognizes the sacred sites of Mexico City and, as *Xochikoskatl* progresses, the text portrays his presence there more as a pilgrimage to Mexihco Tenochtitlan (the Nahua name for Mexico City) than a migration (40, 189, 207). In the first four stanzas of "Iknotlajtoli" (Orphan Words), Xokoyotsin traces a socially stratified topography dominated by koyomej, and in the final four stanzas he claims within the city a space of Nahua empowerment rooted in sacred lands. He situates himself in Mexico City by inviting the sonorities of flowered/maize music and the flowered/maize house within the sixth stanza to transform (or kotoni, to "break" or "burst") restrictive urban areas. He rearticulates and reappropriates this space that marginalizes him. Not only "more Mexican because he speaks Mexican," Xokoyotsin is more familiar with the Mexican territory and manifests

Native land rights through his deployment of Nahuatl toponyms venerating geographical features.

Although it has become commonplace to speak of a bond between Indigenous peoples and their ancestors, this intimate relationship should not be romanticized. Rather, kinship is better understood when framed within an ontological sense of what constitutes an individual. The profound implications of this view materialize in the Nahuatl word tlaixpan (that which is in front), the name for altars adorned with pictures of deceased relatives. The cogent past in front associated with tlaixpan constitutes what is known and helps guide us through the dynamism of the present. From this perspective, elders and their knowledge production are vital to decision making. "That which is in front" resembles what Abenaki historian Lisa Brooks, partially citing Vine Deloria, states regarding Indigenous perspectives on the landscape where "creation stories are actually much more concerned with geography, 'what happened here,' than with chronological origins and temporality, 'what happened then'" (xxiii). Landscapes serve as mnemonic devices in recalling and rereading ancestors' knowledges.

Anti-Coyotialismo/Colonialismo: Shifting Landscapes of Colonial Continuities

In this section I explore how Hernández unsettles a singular koyotl perspective propagated in colonial practices. Colonialism and koyoyotl (the essence of the coyote or coyotialism) are founded on the displacement of Native peoples' spiritual and physical territories. The agents of these discourses debase such territorial claims as superstitions or, at best, as tourist attractions that commodify the sacred. Koyomej invade Native territories in the name of progress and development. In *Xochikoskatl*, Hernández depicts the koyotl as one who in tragic irony steals land without ever truly inhabiting that land himself. The term koyotl is not limited to outsiders; it also applies to Nahuas who look condescendingly on their own communities. Rather than advancement, the koyotl brings destruction under a system devoted to overexploiting natural resources and dehumanizing First Peoples.

In "Na ni indio" (I Am Indian), one of his most famous poems from the first part of *Xochikoskatl*, Hernández firmly frames contemporary discrimination within colonialism. The poetic voice Xokoyotsin asserts in the first stanza:

Na ni indio:
pampa ijkinoj nech tokajtijkej koyomej
kemaj asikoj ipan ni yankuik tlaltipaktli. (27)

(I am Indian:
because that is how the koyomej named me
when they arrived here to this new land.)

Hernández translates koyomej as *blancos* (whites). From the context of the preceding poem "Iknotlajtoli" (Orphan Words) with the translation "blancos y mestizos" (whites and *mestizos*), he establishes a continuity between Spanish colonialism and twentieth-century *mestizaje* discourse. Colonial authorities claim the power to name and impose the exonym *indio* on Nahuas. As such, *indio* is purely a construct. The poem accentuates this artificiality to a greater extent by leaving it untranslated in Nahuatl: Na ni indio. This word is conspicuously awkward as a foreign construction because the phoneme *d* is absent in Nahuatl. In juxtaposition with a millennia-old Nahua intellectual tradition, Hernández exposes a colonial continuity through over four centuries of discriminatory practices.

To discuss coloniality in Nahuatl, it would be more appropriate to use koyotl instead. The former is deep-rooted in specific Huastecan contexts of abuse toward Native Nations and their lands. In fact, in contemporary Huastecan Nahuatl, koyotlakua (he eats like a koyotl) describes people who eat only the best cuts of the meat and wastefully leave the rest, mirroring how they lay waste to the land and fail to understand the people and surrounding landscapes. Upholding the opposite of a communal ethic, the koyotl only protects his self-interests and will cheat Indigenous peoples to fulfill his ambitions. As with the landscape, he labels Native Nations as merely another element to exploit. Echoing Aníbal Quijano's analysis of coloniality, those who embody koyotl associate Indigenous subjects with manual labor and an undeveloped magical landscape ("Coloniality of Power" 542–44, 554–56). Koyotl is a term that all Nahuas easily use, whereas *coloniality* in many respects lacks the emotional response that koyotl elicits. As seen in Hernández's poetry and generally within the Huasteca, koyotl is tied to specific agents of colonial discourse who distinguish themselves from Nahuas as "gente de razón" (people of reason). Rather than representing "reverse racism" in condemning "blancos y mestizos" (whites and *mestizos*), Hernández instead attacks the koyotl discourse of rationalist superiority and those who embody it.

As observed in "Na ni indio" and previously in "Iknotlajtoli," the koyotl imposes a singular vision of modernity. Aníbal Quijano refers to this stratification as a new "cognitive model" in which diverse peoples with their own histories, languages, discoveries, cultural products, memories, and identities were all "merged into a single identity: Indians" (15). He describes this "new identity" as "racial, colonial, and negative" (15). The power structure associated with this cognitive model held a "new perspective of knowledge within which non-Europe was the past, and because of that inferior, if not always primitive" (15). This paradigm not only persisted into "Modernity" but was constitutive of modernity itself. "Modernity" crafts an exclusive space and time.[40] Its cartography arises from the dichotomies of civilized/barbarian, cosmopolitan/provincial, and developed/underdeveloped.

Hernández denaturalizes this systemic discrimination. In the second stanza his poetic persona traces the genealogy of *indio* to Spaniards'/koyomej's self-deception when they first arrived to Abiayala. The poetic voice claims:

Na ni indio:
pampa mokajkayajkej koyomej
kemaj asikoj kampa tlanauatiayaj nokoluaj. (27)

(I am Indian:
because the coyotes deceived themselves
when they arrived here where my grandparents/ancestors
  ruled.)

The lines "pampa mo**k**ajkayaj**k**ej **k**oyomej / **k**emaj asi**k**oj **k**ampa tlanauatiayaj no**k**oluaj" exhibit a cacophony with the consonant *k* (27; emphasis added). Dissonance reflects the koyomej imposing sounds, language, and names such as *indio* with a foreign phonology. This cacophony repeats in the sixth stanza, "nij mati mo**k**uapoloj**k**ej **k**oyomej" (I know that the coyotes erred with their minds; 27). It is not the so-called *indios* who lack intelligence and power of observation. Koyomej are the ignorant and careless observers who disfigure Nahuatl words, concepts, and toponyms, like the conquistador Hernán Cortés who mistakenly used "Temixtitán" to refer to Tenochtitlan (*Cartas de relación* 92). Unlike the wise elders who know things with their faces, the koyomej lack perceptiveness and jump to erroneous conclusions.

The second stanza of "Na ni indio" amplifies the importance of language and speaking "kampa tlanauatiayaj nokoluaj" (where my grandparents/ancestors ruled; 27). Again, this statement does not hark back necessarily to the Pre-Columbian era, but to José Antonio Xokoyotsin's own grandparents (indicative in his pseudonym from his grandfather's namesake). On a linguistic level, a continuity with Pre-Columbian practices appears in Hernández's mixture of words from multiple variants of Modern Nahuatl and Classical Nahuatl. As mentioned earlier, he acquired this expanded vocabulary from his experience as a bilingual teacher and promoter of Nahuatl throughout Mexico. For example, while kuikatl for "song" is not used in the Huasteca (rather, the very similar uikatl is used in its place), it appears in other present-day variants and in Classical Nahuatl. Hernández highlights that no abysmal gap exists between Classical and Contemporary Nahuatl.

In contrast, Modernity's linear time was championed by the Enlightenment, in which history was seen as moving teleologically toward a bastion of ultimate progress. Westerners would naturally be the harbingers of this advancement, and others would either assimilate or be crushed in its wake. Tightly associated with this temporality is the supremacy of "rationality," which afflicts and "tramples" Nahuas. Natalio Hernández writes in the third stanza of "Na ni indio" that koyomej named him *indio* to "nopan nejnemisej" (walk on him) and "nechpinajtisej" (make him feel ashamed), which he translates into Castilian as *aplastar* (to crush) and *discriminar* (to discriminate):

Na ni indio:
pampa ijkinoj nech manextijkej koyomej
para uelis nopan nejnemisej uan nech pinajtisej (27).

(I am Indian:
because that is how the coyotes pointed at me
to be able to walk on me and make me feel ashamed.)

"Nopan nejnemisej" (they walk on me) carries a deeper meaning than physical violence. It implies epistemicide since, as previously mentioned, the root of the word nemi conveys a way of life or philosophy. Walking on Nahuas connotes the koyomej imposing their worldview. This degradation is emphasized with "nechpinajtisej" (they make me ashamed). Nahuas commonly use this phrase when they feel ashamed to speak Nahuatl, and this mortification is internalized and made to seem natural.[41] Such a naturalized stratification of society develops, as Michel Foucault theorizes, into a system of discrimination that governs itself without coercion ("Society Must Be Defended" 45–47). Abashment toward the language transmutes into a rejection of Nahua practices. As "natural" it goes unquestioned and is eventually obscured as the status quo.

The repetition of "na" (I) throughout the poem asserts José Antonio Xokoyotsin's subjectivity and debunks the myth that members of First Nations lack individuality. A pervasive stereotype maintains that *I* dissolves into an Indigenous collective identity. According to this falsehood, Indigenous peoples cannot think for themselves and are unfit to lead in politics, business, education, and so on. In the fourth stanza, a collective ethic appears in speaking of "timaseualmej tlen ni yankuik tlaltipaktli" (we Indigenous peoples of this new land; 27). Though an individual participates in a collective ethic, they are not subsumed within it. The knowledge production of this maseuali (Nahua/Native) collectivity does not hamstring a person but rather strengthens them when facing adversity. In the fifth stanza, Xokoyotsin underscores the importance of the individual in the line "uan namaj ika nimotlakaneki ni tlajtoli" (and now with this word I love myself as a person; 27). He transforms *indio* and maseuali to signify a strong, perspicacious subject, thus rebuking the connotation of tlapiyali (livestock) that koyomej foist upon them. Koyomej can no longer make Xokoyotsin feel ashamed. Writing in Nahuatl is itself a performative act against their attempts at silencing him.

Xokoyotsin in the eighth stanza reiterates that he has his own roots and his own worldview:

> Na ni indio:
> uan namaj nij mati nij pixtok
> no ixayak, no tlachialis uan no nemilis. (27)

> (I am Indian:
> and now I know I have
> my face, my observance, and my way of life.)

These verses return to the conception of intellectual as one who knows things with their face. Hernández imagines a nation-state in which the validity of one's own knowledge production is not dependent upon a purported superiority over nature nor the inadequacy of others' epistemes. To discuss decolonization, one can address *decoyotlization*, or when society ceases to embody the koyotl's perspective. Hernández foregrounds language in this decoyotlization with the declaration that he is truly Mexican because he speaks Mexican (27–28). As explained at the beginning of this chapter, many Nahuas call their language mejikanoj (Mexican) and perceive *nahuatl* as a word popularized by foreign studies. Hernández uses *nahuatl* only once in *Xochikoskatl*. He instead talks about Mexicans (Nahuas) and the Mexican language. It is through this language that Hernández articulates proposals for the nation-state. This move is significant on several counts. For one, it allows the poet to refer to the Mexican nation (i.e., Nahua Nation) without necessarily denoting the country Mexico (nation-state boundaries). Hernández implicitly argues for a plurinational state in which Nahuas, or any Native peoples, are not second-class citizens. He decenters the notion of a homogeneous state by claiming that the subalternized group is more Mexican—since Mexican means Nahua—than the prototypical citizen of nationalist discourse. Descolonial strategies would consist in people across the nation-state engaging with Nahuas and Native Nations and respecting their ways of life as equally valid alongside other worldviews.

The word *indio* turns into an anagram in the Castilian version of the ninth stanza:

Na ni indio:
uan namaj nij mati melauak ni mejikano
pampa ni tlajtoua mejikano, tlen inintlajtol nokoluaj. (27)

(I am Indian:
and now I know that I am truly Mexican
because I speak Mexican, the language of my grandparents/
    ancestors.)

Yo soy indio:
y ahora sé que soy verdaderamente mexicano
porque hablo el *idiona* mexicano, la lengua de mis abuelos.
    (*sic*, 28; emphasis added)

Hernández deconstructs and shifts *indio* with the word *idiona* (*idioma* or "language" written with an *n*) to represent Nahuatl as a language and not disdainfully as a "dialect" or, as popularly said, *indialecto* ([In]dia[n] lect). The cacophony of *k*s associated with the koyomej contrasts with the majority of *n*s and *m*s associated with Nahuas, phonetically reminding readers of *nahuatl*, *mejikanoj*, and *indio* (27). The apparent misspelling of *idioma* as *idiona* opposes the pejorative classification of Nahuatl as a subdialect or *india*lecto due to its similarity to the word *indio* (in fact, in some regions Indigenous peoples say *toindioma*, "our Indian language" or "our Indianguage," with the same empowering connotation).[42]

Idiona resembles the phrase "idioma *nacional*"[43] and displaces Castilian as the de facto language of the Mexican nation-state. Hernández asserts Nahuas and himself as subjects with valuable contributions and language. The Nahuatl language is intertwined with the land and surges forth from carefully observing social and physical landscapes. "Nation" in Nahuatl is ueyi altepetl (large city [water-hill]) or, in "Na ni indio," tonana tlaltipactli/totlalnantsij (our earth mother), both grounded in the landscape as opposed to the state-centered society that *nation-state* denotes. This sharp distinction appears in Hernández's 2010 translation of the Mexican Constitution, which I mention to underscore its importance in comprehending "Na ni indio." Where the original Castilian declares that the land pertains to the nation-state, in Nahuatl the text sustains that it belongs first and foremost to our earth mother.[44] With *Na ni indio* in Nahuatl and *Yo soy indio* (I Am Indian) in Castilian repeated facing one another in the poem, another anagram appears. The juxtaposed first person *na* in Nahuatl and *yo* in Spanish create a negation on the page: n(a)/(y)o, *no*, in other words, **No** soy indio. The written reiteration of "Yo soy indio" evokes the typical Western school punishment of "writing lines" on a chalkboard to drill into a student's mind that they must abandon problem behaviors. Here, though, José Antonio Xokoyotsin assumes control of how many times he repeats the phrase and transforms its meaning into one of empowerment. Instead of internalizing the pejorative connotations of *indio*, he purges himself of it and marks that he is different from the koyotl in positive ways regardless of the term deployed.

Like in the poem "Iknotlajtoli," in the twelfth stanza of "Na ni indio," Xokoyotsin proclaims, "namaj sampa yeyektsij nijkaki / ayakachtlatsotsontli uan xochitlatsotsontli" (now again I hear beautifully / the rattle music and the flowered music; 29). Once more the text welcomes corn ceremonies. Rather than only wishing for these ceremonies as stated in the previous verses, Xokoyotsin declares that he will hear them straightaway. He switches from voicing optatives to using the present tense with *now*. His words reflect how Nahuas view the past and ancestors in front, offering knowledges to guide dynamically through the present and future. Xokoyotsin undermines the implications of "new land" to signify Abiayala in the first stanza (29). "New land" popularly treats the hemisphere as if no peoples were present when Europeans arrived. Nonetheless, Xokoyotsin gives the term an alternative meaning. This new land alludes to images of a "new sun," "new day," and "new sunrise" in the tenth stanza. A new sun symbolizes a revival of Indigenous practices after colonialism. In this fresh cycle First Peoples no longer figure as objects of prehistory, but as agents in contemporary society. The repetition of the word namaj, "now," ten times, and various linguistic markers, stress this cogent presence in the present and future. A new sun highlights a cyclical time, as Nahuas spoke of patterns on earth passing with different suns. This poem treats the last five centuries of history not as "progress" toward some ultimate Enlightenment but rather as a cycle of suffering to be disrupted.

The sunrise sets in motion a new cycle. Seen earlier in the analysis of tlaixpan, this view of "that which is in front" permeates relationships, especially with elders. Ancestors provide insights that accompany people in making present-day decisions. Cusicanqui analyzes a similar perspective in the Aymara term Nayrapacha, a temporal framework shared among Indigenous movements across the continent: "the past, but not just any vision of the past; rather, 'past-as-future,' that is to say, as a renovation of space-time. A past capable of renewing the future, or turning over the lived situation" (Rivera Cusicanqui, *Violencias* 51).[45] Historical remembrance renews the present and future and is not abandoned on a linear, positivistic progression toward Modernity. Xokoyotsin states in the thirteenth stanza of "Na ni indio" (I Am Indian), "uan namaj sampa nikinita / uan nikintlakakilia ueuetlakamej" (and now again I see / and hear the wise-elderly people; 29). These ancestors serve as a locus for making decisions *now*.

Yolotl and Affective Intelligence: Thinking with the Heart

Within the Nahua empowerment portrayed in "Na ni indio," Hernández proposes an affective intelligence that does not separate emotions from rationality. He shares what he has seen and establishes firmly the first-person singular *na* throughout *Xochikoskatl*. This testimony enters a politics of memory that debunks the official state history of progress toward integration. In the apostrophic poem "Xijkakikaj koyomej" (Listen, Coyotes), the poetic voice shifts from the testimonial *na* to addressing an absent audience of "you all koyomej." Xokoyotsin leads with authority based on experiential knowledge and from this position now gives commands and recommendations to his oppressors. He speaks from a collective ethic that stresses the need to live "with the heart" and respect the environment.

The corporal metaphor of the heart appears throughout the poem. Xokoyotsin expresses in the third stanza:

> ijatsaj timatlantokej nojuaj ti**yol**tokej
> pampa **yol**tok to**yolo**, nojuaj ti**yol**chikauakej,
> nojuaj ueli tomo**yol**nojnotsaj;
> timo**yol**nejnemiliaj uan timokuanejnemiliaj
> kenijki sampa uelis timeuasej uan tinejnemisej
> kenijki sampa timo**yol**kuisej (59; emphasis added)

> (although we have suffered we **are** still here,
> because our **heart** is alive, we are still strong **in the heart**,
> we can still dialogue **with the heart**;
> we contemplate **with the heart** and we contemplate with the mind
> how we can again arise and walk
> how we can **recover from illness**)

The stanza is steeped in parallelisms where the noun *yol-otl* (heart) repeats with varying syntax. Timoyolnejnemiliaj (we contemplate with the heart) and timokuanejnemiliaj (we contemplate with the mind) represent a *difrasismo*[46] that conjugates affect and conscious decisions in subject formation as they parallel the roots *yol* (heart) and *kua* (mind/head). From the last line of the citation, yolkui refers to recovering from illness, but literally means "to take heart." Hernández translates this phrase twice in Castilian as "cómo podemos revivir, cómo volver a tener vida propia" (how we can live again, how we can again have our own life; 60). As stated earlier, timoyolchikauaj (we are strong of heart) centers on corn, as yolotl also signifies "seed" and chikauak (literally "hard") describes dried maize. Yolotl encompasses both physical and psychological well-being, and this wider purview is largely lost in translation. Unlike the Indigenous heart, the koyomej have a heart, mentioned in the second stanza, that has been slowly dying.

The distinction between Indigenous peoples and the koyomej should not be reduced to the romanticized vision in the "mythic-magic mentality" (Quijano 9). Rather than a simple following of instincts, affective intelligence constitutes the viewing of emotions as an integral part of one's reasoning. In this manner "Xijkakikaj koyomej" flips Western rationalism on its head and deems it unnatural and senseless in its disregard for affectivity. Hernández battles the reduction of cultural and religious practices such as corn ceremonies to unsound folklore divorced from the rational bounds of the sciences. The bodily metaphor of yolotl represents an (a/e)ffective resistance to epistemicide. This heart forms a lucid collective ethic in which capital is subordinate to carefully cultivated relationships with humans and other-than-humans.

Emphasis on feeling throughout *Xochikoskatl* (as well as *Patlani* and additional works by Hernández) argues for an affective intelligence as the basis of solutions to societal dilemmas. Such an approach, as philosopher Martha Nussbaum describes, "adopt[s] plausible rather than implausible pictures of ethical change, and we understand (in connection with our normative arguments) what it might mean for a political community to extend to its citizens the social bases of imaginative and emotional health" (15–16). With this affective intelligence, the visceral metaphor of yolotl combines with that of flowers and Mesoamerican deities to give an alternative genesis and framework to that of Modernity. Hernández hopes that these songs will find a place and "flower" in the heart of readers. A true intellectual not only understands things of the mind in relation to their personal experience but also recognizes emotions as a key part of cognition.

At odds with this affectivity, the pairing of "blancos y mestizos" (whites and *mestizos*) in *Xochikoskatl* unveils *mestizaje* as a cover for whiteness, in which Indigenous peoples must assimilate into Modernity's "progress." *White* and *mestizo* differ little in their result. Perceived *whiteness* "naturally" entails superior "rationality." The concentration of capital in the hands of those deemed "white" has perpetuated this racism.[47] *Xochikoskatl* contrasts koyomej's oppressive practices with the liberating Indigenous ones of the heart. *Mestizaje* discourse teaches First Peoples to integrate but marginalizes them even when they attempt to do so. Any marker of Indigenous identity in the present, whether in clothing, speech, or phenotype, is a certain path to discrimination. Those who benefit from the discourse of *mestizaje* are labeled white, speak Castilian with no "accent," and have assimilated into the "national" culture.

Out of this physical and epistemological violence surfaces Xokoyotsin's visceral resistance. In "Xokoyotsin moyolnojnotsa" (Xokoyotsin Has an Inner Dialogue with His Heart), from the first section "Sempoalxochitl," Hernández writes:

Asijka tonatij timo**yol**nojnotsas
miak tlamantli kiajokui mo**yolo**;
yeka tipatstlami, yeka ti**yol**kuitlamiki,
kemantika tiiknochoka,
kemaya timo**yol**pitsaua (23; emphasis added)

(The day has already arrived for you to dialogue with your
   heart
your **heart** holds many things;
that is why you get irritated, why you get furious of **heart**,
sometimes you cry as an orphan,
at other times you scatter yourself about with the **heart**)

Amid the hostile environment of colonialism emerges a feeling body with agency that transforms this situation. Yolotl is the symbol par excellence of survivance.[48] The heart confronts the assumed separation of mind and emotions basic to European Enlightenment and in turn the racial hierarchy that demeans the subaltern as too near nature, too emotional, and thus incapable of active participation in the "higher" forms of government, economy, and society.

Hernández uses the word *filosofía* (philosophy)[49] in the Castilian versions of poems to highlight that Nahuas offer valid knowledges that have been marginalized for centuries and that are essential to leaving the destructive time/space Quijano calls "colonial modernity" (4). This attention to philosophy is influenced by the work of Miguel León Portilla. He defines *philosophy* in his book *Filosofía náhuatl* as a "human inquietude, fruit of admiration and doubt, that impulses one to ask and inquire rationally regarding the origin, being, and the destiny of the world and man" (4). In the process of writing *Xochikoskatl*, Hernández read this text and the primary documents analyzed by León Portilla. Vital elements of philosophy from the heart are music, dance, song, the Nahuatl language, and an empathetic respect for and reciprocity with the landscape. This feeling is intrinsic to Nahuatl, and arguably yolotl is untranslatable without qualifying its meanings beyond mere "heart."

A person heart-strengthens themself (moyolchikaua) with Nahua cultural practices and accompanying philosophies. Song and dance unite in religious ceremony and actuate an ethic in which nature is respected, in which individuals laugh with the heart. This sensing body, as philosopher Erin Manning explains, disturbs the state apparatus, as the state seeks to retain citizens within static categories. Yet a politics of touch exceeds this restrictive organization. The sensing body is an "agrammatical invention" in that through "atypical expressions" it stretches and moves outside the strict confines of the state (xxi). It represents the "deterritorialization of language," or perhaps more accurately its *reterritorialization,* as it shifts elements beyond their "known forms and conventional functions" (xxiii). Speaking Nahuatl constitutes an agrammatical political statement. This affirmation unsettles a state discourse that, even in the guise of multiculturalism, disseminates a singular official history. Dance and music take on a powerful meaning, and, in that vein, Hernández invokes flowered/maize music throughout *Xochikoskatl* (25, 29, 37, 65, 223). These elements of dance and music are explicitly manifest in Hernández's book of poetry *Patlani huitzitzilin.*

The Hummingbird's Plumes: Defense of Nahua Territories within *Patlani huitzitzilin*

In this final section I examine Hernández's *Patlani huitzitzilin* (2016) to follow his trajectory since the publication of *Xochikoskatl* and address the significance of Nahua ceremonies present in both works. Since Hernández wrote *Xochikoskatl* while working for the Secretariat of Public Education (SEP), he felt limited in what he could say and concealed his identity with a pseudonym. Hernández experienced intense frustration, a sentiment reflected in the title of another poem from *Xochikoskatl,* "Toseltika matinejnemikajya" / "Caminemos solos" (Let Us Walk Alone [i.e., not depend on koyotl saviors or state recognition]). Hernández now avoids reading his earlier poems. He comments that he wants to write a poem instead titled "Caminemos juntos" (Let Us Walk Together).[50] *Patlani* exemplifies this shift as the poetic voice invites readers to trace Hernández's father's steps through the Huasteca. The text centers local knowledges from Tepeko and foregrounds the perspectives that undergird them: ixtlamatilistli, yoltlajlamikilistli, and tlaixpan.

Within Nahuatl, *Xochikoskatl* and *Patlani* deconstruct the false binary of city/town. While the distinction between altepetl (large settlement) and chinanko (small settlement) can have reductive connotations like *city* versus *village,*[51] in *Xochikoskatl* and *Patlani* the chinanko is a locus of intellectual contributions. Across many areas of the Huasteca, ueyi altepetl (large altepetl) denotes a large city like Mexico City and pilaltepetsij (small altepetl) refers to a smaller city or community. The difference is not qualitative but rather quantitative and eludes the reductive undertones of *community* or *town*.[52]

Readers will notice immediately in *Patlani huitzitzilin* a shift in orthography from *Xochikoskatl*. Hernández considers his current writing system more aesthetically appealing. It resembles what the public is accustomed to seeing throughout Mexican landscapes, street names, and proper names (i.e., Nezahualcoyotl rather than Nesaualkoyotl). This change echoes Hernández's reconciliatory approach by building on terms with which non-Indigenous readers are familiar. However, while Hernández's orthography resembles "classical orthography," he has developed his own idiosyncratic adaptation of it (for example, only using *z* when it follows a *t*, and otherwise opting for an *s*). With this seemingly minor change, Hernández signals to readers Nahuas' contemporary vitality and that what they are reading possesses continuities with Classical Nahuatl, but it also innovates in the present.

Patlani contains a series of thirty-one numbered lyric "prose poems" in free verse, varying in length from eleven verses to multiple pages to tell the history of Tepeko territory. This prose-poetry style allows Hernández to relate the community's history with a xochitlajtoli mix of ceremonial language, textiles, music, narrative, and verse. Hernández views this region through the eyes of his father, Piltata (left untranslated, meaning "royal/little/dear father"). Like Pacific Island authors in ethnic studies scholar Anne Mai Yee Jansen's article "Writing *toward* Action," Nahuas feel the obligation to take on the "dual work of educating and critiquing" (6). This protreptic thrust in part contributes to Hernández's poetry often reading more like prose. Piltata retraces from burial Tepeko's trajectory and his place in it.

While Hernández transcreated his earlier works with facing translations in Castilian, he wrote *Patlani* in Nahuatl and refused to self-translate. He did, however, assert control over the process and rejected the first translator's rendition as too free with the original. He subsequently chose a different translator, his brother, Nahua professor Severo Hernández, whose version was ultimately published alongside the Nahuatl text. Natalio Hernández's refusal demands a space for contemporary Nahuatl literature within mainstream literary circles where professional translation is readily available. Equally important, he foregrounds the original Nahuatl language to express Nahua conceptions of the land. In the interstices between Nahuatl and Castilian, distinct perspectives emerge, among them ixtlamatilistli, yoltlajlamikilistli, and tlaixpan. Hernández's defense of Nahua knowledges intersects with defense of territory in the wide sense, encompassing linguistic, epistemic, social, and topographic spaces. Unlike the open denouncements against koyomej in *Xochikoskatl*, the nation-state and koyomej are nearly absent in *Patlani*. They figure as peripheral elements in a Nahua narrative. The nation-state and koyomej appear briefly in negotiations for land claims and subsequently their complicity in the assassination of a Nahua leader. The poetic space is almost entirely centered on Tepeko. The poetic voice, Piltata, focuses on the solutions Nahuas offer.

Tellingly enough, Piltata's poetic journey begins not at the start, but at the end of his life. The first person, indeed, opens in medias res, with Piltata relating his own burial: "Nihuetztoc / nitlacactoc / nicactica tlatzotzontli / tlen ica nechmacahuah; / notlacayo sesec, / huipictic, / ayocmo nimohmolinia, / san notonal tlachixtoc / ica inon nohua hueli niquita / tlen quichiticateh nochanehuah" (I have died / I listen / I'm listening to the sacred music / with which they send me on my way; / my body is cold, / rigid, / I no longer move, / only my tonal is awake / and that is why I can still see / what my kin are doing; 14). However, the fact that Piltata's body is dead and that we hear only from his first-person experiences does not signal a separation from his community. The first six poems detail burial rituals. Musicians came straightaway and all evening performed the xochitlatsotsontli, the same music to which the poetic voice alludes in *Xochikoskatl*. Although his body is cold and rigid, Piltata's tonal lives. In Castilian, Severo Hernández translates tonal as *espíritu* (spirit). Yet, in later poems he leaves this term untranslated; *espíritu* does not quite capture its meaning. Tonal derives its energy from the sun (tonatij) and can also signify "shadow" and a person's *don* or life calling.[53] In some Nahuatl variants, tonal can refer to one's animal companion at birth. As described in Tepeko, the tonal emanates from the individual and encompasses them. This energy connects with surroundings (maize possesses tonal) and provides the power to live and observe.

In this relationality between the landscape and the crop, Piltata explains in Poem II that he has requested his grave be filled with earth rather than cement. Cement would represent an estrangement from the land. Instead, his kin plant flowers over the tomb with the numerous implications of flowers analyzed in relation to *Xochikoskatl*. Flowers serve as a nexus between both life and death. These flowers, according to Piltata, "quinescayotia totlachialis / ihuan tonemilis / ipan tlaltipactli" (mark our worldview [observation] / and our way of life / upon the earth; 16). They signal Piltata's connection with his ancestors, specifically his adoptive father José Antonio Tepetolo (Hernández's maternal grandfather, the inspiration for the pseudonym in *Xochikoskatl*) and future descendants (such as Natalio Hernández), as petals strewn on the ground guide them to one another within ceremonial spaces. This flower conceit is rooted both literally and figuratively in land, territory, language, and the body. As mentioned previously, rather than apply the term *revitalizar* (revitalize), Nahuas commonly use yolchikaua (strengthen, or "become firm like a maize/flower seed"), xochiyoua (flourish), chamani (sprout), or kueponi (bud). All these metaphors relate to horticulture. The human body itself is made of flowers, as the primordial bloom, maize, is the main food staple. Moreover, Piltata's burial is described like planting. The same word for *to sow*, toka,¹ is used for burials, nechtlaltohqueh (they buried/planted me in the ground; 19).

The knowledges that Piltata has left with his community will endure and resurge each year. As with yolotl (heart / seed) in many poems, xochitl could seem redundant without awareness of its deeper meanings. Piltata invokes flowers nine times in the first two brief poems alone. He deploys the first-person plural to speak about the views they hold: "titlachixtoqueh" (we observe/live), "totlachialis" (our observance), and "tonemilis" (our way of life / philosophy). One will rarely hear the words tlachialistli and nemilistli used without a possessor—*our* observance and *our* philosophy. This grammatical structure reflects that the spaces created by this observance and heartfelt intelligence hinge on communal praxis.

Piltata passed through intense trials in his life, growing up "niicnotzih" (an orphan; 26). In Poem IX, he tells of meeting a noble man, José Antonio Tepetolo, who possessed a "great heart" and took him in (32). José Antonio Tepetolo was the equivalent of a distinguished doctor in multiple practices within the community. He presided as ueuejtlakatl (officiator at marriages and special events), tlachiani (seer), tlamatini (officiator at xochikali ceremonies), and tepajtiani (healer). In the xochitlajtoli that follow, Piltata shares Tepetolo's huehuetlahtoli (wise/old words) to show "huehuetlahtoli yoltoc / amo polihtoc / amo cotontoc" (the wise words are alive / they have not died / they have not been broken; 90). As in *Xochikoskatl*, huehuetlahtoli refers to Pre-Columbian knowledge production and present-day philosophies. Piltata wants Tepeko to protect these words, "tlen monextia ipan toltecayotl, / ipan xochimecatl / itechpan xochitlahtoli" (which appear in toltecayotl [culture/philosophy], / in the flowered string /

in flowered words; 92). The xochimecatl (flowered string) hanging from the altar to the entrance leads the reader into a ceremonial space. The words enunciated in this space are malhuili or "sacred."

One of those "words" or histories that Piltata features in Poem XXIII is the work of Nahua land rights activist Guadalupe Osorio. A leader in the Huasteca shortly after the Mexican Revolution, Osorio guided Nahua communities with wise words in defense of their territory. Piltata refers to the Revolution as "hueyi mahmahtli" (the great scare), a description far removed from official idealizations of that conflict (104). Most likely with the complicity of the nation-state, large landowners assassinated Osorio to repossess land that Native people had recovered from the caciques. Despite the much-vaunted land redistribution to oppressed communities within nationalist narratives, Nahuas struggled to defend their territories from *mestizo* squatters and large landowners during and after the Revolution.[54]

Osorio grew up as a Nahua masehuali speaking Nahuatl and wearing traditional clothing. Like Piltata, he "icnotzin moscalti[h]" (grew up an orphan), a recurring metaphor throughout *Patlani* and *Xochikoskatl* (104). Piltata employs the term ixtlamatilistli to describe Osorio's knowledge, suggesting its experiential implications: "quinyecanqui masehualmeh / ihuan quinpalehuihqui / ica ixtlamatilistli" (he guided the Indigenous people / and helped them / with ixtlamatilistli; 104). Piltata expresses that he carries Guadalupe Osorio's wisdom in his heart; he marks an affective connection with this knowledge. He accentuates Osorio's skills at negotiation with koyomej and prominent leaders. With this Nahua history, Hernández fulfills Chadwick Allen's and José Antonio Lucero's calls to reformulate histories outside the "settler survey" and "the limited repertoire of their sanctioned performances" to explore historical events from Native perspectives in which Euro-Americans are peripheral to the varied and creative ways Native peoples engage with colonial and nation-state administrations (Allen, *Trans-Indigenous* xvi; see also Lucero, "To Articulate Ourselves" 3). Piltata highlights the respect demanded by Osorio's transformation of the political landscape.[55] While Osorio is little known outside of the Huasteca, he is well remembered among Huastecan elders as a defender of territorial rights. Osorio's engagement with the nation-state emphasizes Nahua agency, and the various ways in which Nahuas have negotiated with state entities.

Piltata shifts focus, in Poem XXVI, from Nahua political agency to the ceremonial space of the Xochikali (Flowered House), where Chikomexochitl (Seven Flower / Maize) resides. This extensive ten-page poem identifies Chikomexochitl as maize's multigendered tonal and body. The *seven* in Chikomexochitl refers to the seven food staples that accompany maize, namely chili pepper, beans, squash, cotton, amaranth, sesame seeds, and tomato. These plants form humans: "tlen sentica mocuepah / intlacualis tlacameh / toeso ihuan tonacayo / mocuepah" (who together transform / into people's food / into our blood and our bodies / they transform; 122). Cultivated as a polycrop, maize is an epicenter in a relationality with other foods, the surroundings, and people. Piltata tells how many years ago Chikomexochitl abandoned Native communities because humans ceased to give flower offerings on the altars. Amid the ensuing drought and famine brought on by Chikomexochitl's departure, the Ñhähñu Nation pleads for the deity's return. Ñhähñus "lay themselves down like orphans" (moicnotecah) before Chikomexochitl and give offerings of flowered necklaces, sacred flowered music, libations, and animal sacrifices (126). In this manner Ñhähñus pay the spiritual debt for all Native Nations, and Chikomexochitl returns (128). Ñhähñus continue to officiate ceremonies in many Nahua communities. For Hernández, these trans-Indigenous dialogues and mutual aid embody the interculturality needed for contemporary coexistence across society.

Poem XXX addresses another vital flower, the sempoalxochitl (Mexican marigold), arrayed in Chikomexochitl ceremonies and other special occasions. According to Piltata, sempoalxochitl is truly "our flower" because it shows "mexicayotl" (*mexicanidad* or Mexicanness; 154). Related to the anecdote shared at the beginning of this chapter and the analysis of "Na ni indio," these references to Mexicanness affirm "Mexico" as a region and yet signal the cracks within nationalist discourse. In Native communities effaced by that discourse, the sempoalxochitl adorns the Day of the Dead, or Mijkailuitl (Festival of the Dead) and constitutes the sole flower displayed within all festivities as a nexus of the living and the dead (156). Piltata describes how sempoalxochitl appear when sowing corn, tending the crop, and gathering corncobs. Sempoalxochitl lace flowered necklaces on the altars and within marriages, funerals, and postpartum rites. This flower unites all ceremonial elements introduced in previous poems. This depiction in *Patlani* evidences the notable shift in Hernández's writing from *Xochikoskatl*. In *Xochikoskatl*, Hernández openly condemns discrimination, particularly within the first part titled "Sempoalxochitl"; in *Patlani*, when speaking of sempoalxochitl, he foregrounds communal practices and the perspectives transmitted through that praxis. Implicit in Piltata's descriptions is a denunciation of discrimination, but with greater emphasis on what Nahuas propose in the face of oppression.

In the final xochitlajtoli, Poem XXXI, Piltata can now rest after recounting his community's history. Far being from a victim of his surroundings, Piltata expresses that his fearless warrior-tonal will transform into a hummingbird. He did his work "ica miac paquilistli / ica yolchicahualistli" (with great joy / and with heart-firmness; 160). This statement encapsulates Hernández's emphasis on positivity and strength. The title, *The Hummingbird Flies*, situates a powerful connection with ancestors who *fly* in the present, as underscored with the present-tense patlani. Piltata feels that again "totlamatilis" (our knowledge) will become a Xochimili (Flower Field), where hummingbirds visit and observe "Anahuac ihuan Semanahuac" (Land among the Waters and the Universe; 162). As in *Xochikoskatl*, he uses the term Anahuac (near or among the waters) to name Mexico and position it in relation to the landscape. The deceased will return to watch "nochinanco / notlalpan / nochantzinco / Mexihco totlalnantzin" (my community / my land [my *tlalpan*] / the place of my precious home / Mexico our earth mother; 162). Significantly, Tlalpan is the Mexico City delegation in which Hernández has lived for decades. Here he shifts the meaning of tlalpan to Tepeko territory. Moreover, Mexihco or Mexko usually refers to Mexico City / Mexko Altepetl. Piltata adds totlalnantzin (our earth mother) to mark the affective connection to the land and move the focal point effectively away from the capital. The xochitlajtoli in *Patlani* decenters the nation-state to focus on Tepeko's region.

Piltata concludes, remembering "ixochitlahtol / tocoltzin Nezahualcoyotzin / queman quiihtoh: // Namah melahuac, / quicuamachilia noyolo, / nihcaqui cuicatl / niquita yeyectzi xochitl / melahuac nihnequisqua / amo queman maixpilinican" (the flowered words / of our noble grandfather Nezahualcoyotzin / when he said: // "Now truly, / my heart understands, / I hear a song / I see beautiful flowers, / truly I wish / they would never wither"; 162–64). Hernández adapts into contemporary Huastecan Nahuatl the words in Classical Nahuatl attributed to Nezahualcoyotl. Above all, this reference ties into the knowledges passed down from his grandparents and parents, as Nezahual*coyotl* resembles Xokoyotsin or "junior" of the family, the pseudonym Hernández deployed in *Xochikoskatl*. Hernández's defense of contemporary Nahua practices within *Xochikoskatl* and *Patlani huitzitzilin* link with his grassroots efforts to renovate the Tepeko ceremonial flowered house and establish a Nahua-run university and cultural center there. Tepeko continues to serve as the main locus of enunciation for his writing and projects.

The Same Questions Persist: Present-Day Relevance of *Xochikoskatl* and *Patlani huitzitzilin*

This exploration of *Xochikoskatl* and *Patlani huitzitzilin* traces Natalio Hernández's decades-long trajectory of publications and activism. These two works invite readers to contest monolithic nationalist discourse and contemplate the plurinational nature of the regions denominated Mexico (or Anahuac). The connective material between language and territory is salient; the locus of enunciation is Tepeko in both books. A parallel analysis of these two texts highlights the continuities and shifts across Hernández's literary production.

More broadly, this overview of Hernández's career has laid the groundwork to understand the context of younger authors who write in dialogue and debate with him. They innovate on a contemporary literary tradition that he has helped move. He saw in literature a backdoor to meaningful discussions about Nahua worldviews, land, territory, and language. Hernández has placed his bets on interculturality, focusing on the positivity evinced in his speech of flowers and hummingbirds. Younger authors use similar metaphors but deploy them as part of denunciations. They alter, innovate, and transform their communities' practices while simultaneously respecting them.

"More Mexican" because he speaks Mexican, Hernández dismantles any monolithic notion of what is considered Mexican by centering Nahua knowledge production. The assertion that he is more Mexican implies a greater understanding of this region's diversity. It entails a familiarity with the complexities within Anahuac, the Native languages spoken, and worldings through ixtlamatilistli, yoltlajlamikilistli, and tlaixpan. Nahua heartfelt lexicon carefully observes the situations people face. This language recognizes the past in front and Native Nations—at the forefront—acting upon the present and future.

Since the 1990s, Hernández has stressed dialogue over confrontation. For Hernández, his reconciliatory approach constitutes a means to persuade people to listen, rather than react defensively. When a state governor asked Hernández at an event in Chiapas, "Pardon me, Professor

Hernández, do Indigenous people feel Mexican?," Hernández replied with the same anecdote shared at the beginning of this chapter where a Nahua community considered that they were true Mexicans (*De la exclusión* 59). The governor was so impressed with Hernández's answer that he invited him to talk to local officials on Native Nations' rights (60). His encounter with this politician manifests the power that stories can exert on peoples' perspectives. If Hernández had responded by aggressively critiquing the governor's ignorance, opportunities for further reflection would have vanished. In fact, Hernández considers that many younger authors have an attitude resembling his infuriated mindset when he wrote *Xochikoskatl*; he affirms that he has since learned that more can be achieved through dialogue and an emphasis on Native agency in a myriad of contexts.

Salient in Hernández's acceptance and celebration of different cultural traditions is language's role as a bridge among distinct practices. One of his most well-known pieces is a speech he gave in Castilian and Nahuatl to the Eleventh Congress of the Royal Academy of the Spanish Language in the city of Puebla in November 1998. It was published the following year in *Estudios de Cultura Náhuatl*. Titled "Noihqui toaxca caxtilan tlahtoli" (Spanish Is Also Ours) and representative of the shift in Hernández's writing, this speech claims Castilian as a Native language, since Nahuas and other First Peoples have appropriated it. Such a viewpoint confronts the Mexican political system's use of maternal tongue as a determining factor in deciding who is Indigenous. Along with underscoring Nahua influence in the Castilian language, Hernández advocates a harmonious relationship among different ethnicities. From the mid-1990s to the present, he has written tirelessly on the imperative for this harmony—particularly in his book of poetry *Semanca huitzilin* (Hummingbird of Harmony; 2005) and essay collections—and he has championed educational projects to this end.

Xochikoskatl and *Patlani* raise urgent questions: Who is capable of offering ideas in nation-state (des)construction? Who wields the power of inclusion? Who defines "progress"? Hernández's *Xochikoskatl* serves as a forerunner in posing these questions, condemning discriminatory practices as products of a colonial era, and proposing alternative knowledges in the construction of a plurinational state. This begets the question of the implications of the legacy of the first Nahua writer to publish a single-author book of poetry in Nahuatl. In addition to demystifying prevalent stereotypes toward Native Nations, Hernández offers alternative views of what constitutes representation, progress, and intellectualism that are pertinent to our present. Tracing earlier explorations of the topics addressed in discussions of postcoloniality and de(s)colonialization, as Cusicanqui notes, reveals a series of intellectuals south of the US-Mexican border who tackled these issues in innovative and effective ways well before Global North academics gave them adequate attention (Rivera Cusicanqui, *Ch'ixinakax* 63–69). While primary documents of the SEP and the National Indigenista Institute (INI) paint an image of progressive rhetoric, Hernández writes in counterpoint to them and through poetry depicts how official discourse contrasts with actual practices, giving a window to a richer comprehension of this history. To use a visceral metaphor, this text puts affect and flesh—the Serpent's Plumes—on the skeleton of a historical period in Mexican bilingual education insufficiently researched.

Especially since the early 2000s, *interculturalidad* has become a byword in government-run Indigenous education, and no mention is made of this term's origin with SEP and Gonzalo Aguirre Beltrán's pedagogy for Indigenous education in the early 1970s. The question of who sets the framework and the terms of this interculturality is mostly approached rhetorically or not raised at all. "Interculturality" runs the risk of becoming a one-way process in which nation-state administrations "allow" Indigenous people to keep their practices but require that they learn "superior" ones to integrate into the Mexican state. A case in point is the creation, beginning in 2004, of the Intercultural University system targeted toward Native students, rather than more appropriately toward all students.[56] If anyone is in less need of a formal intercultural education, it is Native students whose families passed through a traumatic, coercive intercultural experience over five centuries. Hernández calls for a genuine, wide-reaching interculturality, in which Indigenous epistemologies are on a level playing field of knowledge production, like the bilingual lines of *Xochikoskatl* and *Patlani* performatively produce. Interculturality was far from Hernández's mind when he wrote *Xochikoskatl* in 1985, but this text is key to understanding his espousal of this concept from the 1990s onward.

The perspectives of ixtlamatilistli, yoltlajlamikilistli, and tlaixpan combine and take Serpent's flight in Hernández's works to move beyond misrepresentations of Native Nations. These perspectives serve as a lens to delve into Nahua texts and descolonizing strategies. While younger authors deploy them in arguably a more combative way than Hernández and an older generation of contemporary authors, they all use them with the goal of achieving systemic changes. Alongside Hernández, there is a broad corpus of Nahua writers who reject victimization. There are numerous paths of research suggested in this chapter, such as the need to explore Nahua literature in relation to Native literatures throughout Mesoamerica and Abiayala as a whole. Synergies exist among these Native Nations, and trans-Indigenous studies prove promising. The influences from other languages and Indigenous Nations in Nahua literary production are compelling. In the Huasteca, Tepehuas, Totonacos, and Ñhähñus live together and collaborate across Nations. Hernández's works also encourage trans-Nahua dialogues among the thirty Nahuatl variants. He does so by including words from multiple variants of present-day and older Nahuatl. Trans-Indigenous exchanges are even more apparent in urban contexts, where Hernández wrote *Xochikoskatl* and *Patlani*. There Nahuas network with the many Serpent-Plumed Native Nations of Mesoamerica and with Native Nations from throughout the world.

Chapter 2

Ritual Shouts of the Forgotten

Anti-colonial Protest in Martín Tonalmeyotl's *Tlalkatsajtsilistle*

Kema noyolika nikake nokualis
niman tlaka nokuikaluan
kinekej tenakastlaposkej,
teixtlaposkej
niman kinekej kinpajtiskej noche tlakamej
uan melauak kintlauelmiktsia kalmaseualtin.

(When with my heart I listen to my song
I realize that my songs
want to open people's ears
to open their eyes
and cure all people
who truly murder Nahua communities.)

—Martín Tonalmeyotl, "Kuak nikneke ninokuikatis"
(When I Want to Sing)

"How can you talk about 'father sun' and flowers when there are people dying in your community?" Nahua poet Martín Tonalmeyotl asked at the beginning of a 2017 public reading of his book of poetry *Tlalkatsajtsilistle / Ritual de los olvidados* (Shout of the Forgotten / Ritual of the Forgotten; 2016) in Tlaxcala, Mexico.[1] Tonalmeyotl's rhetorical question intimates a critique toward an older generation of contemporary Nahua authors whom a younger generation, which includes Tonalmeyotl, deeply respects and yet also perceives as soft on state and social violence against Native communities. In the poem "When I Want to Sing" from *Tlalkatsajtsilistle*, he declares that his "songs" seek to "tenakastlaposkej, / teixtlaposkej" (open people's ears, / open their eyes; 94). In contrast to Natalio Hernández, who, as we have seen from the previous chapter, emphasizes interculturality and harmony, Tonalmeyotl deploys an aesthetic of violence to unsettle colonial logics of belonging and denounce territorial encroachments in Guerrero, Mexico. Binnizá writer Irma Pineda describes this Guerrerense literary production as "la poesía de la ausencia, el dolor, el desplazamiento de las tradiciones, el secuestro, la trata de personas, la migración por pobreza, la militarización, los asesinatos" (poetry about absence, pain, lost traditions, kidnappings, human trafficking, desperate migrations, the military state, and assassinations; Pineda, "Xtámbaa").[2] Rather than a *poesía resurrecta* (resurgent/resurrected poetry) with connotations of revitalizing moribund Native cultural practices, this is a *poesía insurrecta* (insurgent poetry) of denunciation that moves readers to feel the violence inflicted on Native Nations.[3] Both Hernández and Tonalmeyotl defend Nahua territories in the broader sense, albeit with divergent styles and strategies toward achieving that end. This tension is generative of ideas and underscores the complexities within contemporary Nahua literary production.

In Tonalmeyotl's *Tlalkatsajtsilistle*, narcotraffickers and state officials are indistinguishable from one another in a massive-scale illegal economy that nullifies even the thin promises of validation made under what anthropologist Charles Hale terms *neoliberal multiculturalism*.[4] Tonalmeyotl exposes the cracks of those thin promises, akin to a "gilded flowered neoliberalism" that celebrates diversity while simultaneously oppressing those populations with structural inequities and transnational megaprojects.[5] Generally, younger authors like Tonalmeyotl view the older generation of contemporary writers who began writing in the 1980s and 1990s as overly invested in state-sponsored celebrative discourse. This chapter explores how Tonalmeyotl writes with the Serpent-Plumed perspectives of ixtlamatilistli, yoltlajlamikilistli, and tlaixpan against what Chickasaw anthropologist Shannon Speed terms *neoliberal multicriminalism*.[6] I argue that Tonalmeyotl's poetry disrupts the settler colonial logics of a multicriminal apparatus that operates with impunity while usurping Nahuas' ancestral lands as well as acoustic, visual, and political territories.

Many scholars within Latin American studies may oppose the application of the term *settler colonialism* to Mexico, or, for that matter, to Latin America in general.[7] As Speed explains, one of the principal objections to this framework in Mexico is the claim that the Spanish Empire relied upon forced manual labor and labor extraction rather than land theft and the establishment of colonies (*Incarcerated Stories* 14–16). Although colonial practices permutated over different regimes and time periods within Abiayala, all administrations insidiously represented Native Nations as being prime for cheap manual labor, full of superstitions, and racially inferior. While resource and labor extraction no doubt took place under that guise, land theft was an integral part.[8] The Spanish Empire did not merely extract resources but also settled the land and dispossessed Native Nations. After the proclaimed independence of Latin American nation-states in the nineteenth century, colonial practices of violence and dispossession in many ways intensified and became more entrenched as newly independent governments like the Mexican nation-state eroded special legal protections for Native Nations within Pueblos and Repúblicas de los Indios.[9] All citizens (and the land itself) were expected to assimilate into the general citizenry (and territory) for the country's welfare. Native Nations effectively would cease to exist under this paradigm. *Mestizaje* discourse in Mexico in the twentieth century allegedly forged a mixed racialized melting pot in which "we the people" (i.e., settlers) could no longer be distinguished from "them" (Native Nations). Precisely because of this misperception, settler colonialism is an effective and much-needed framework for understanding Mexican contexts. This lens aids particularly in analyzing the deep implications of Tonalmeyotl's *Tlalkatsajtsilistle*. While within academic circles it is common to speak of displacement and land dispossession in US and Canadian contexts, this is not so within Mexico or Latin America writ large. *Mestizaje* discourse has so naturalized land theft that the underlying assumption is that *mestizos*—part Indigenous themselves—inherited it.[10]

Along with Hernández's *Xochikoskatl*, Tonalmeyotl's work highlights that, within Nahua communities, *mestizo* is equated with *blanco* to expose an opaque white-supremacist discourse employed to justify Native dispossession. In the study *Por mi raza hablará la desigualdad*, sociologist Patricio Solís calls this narrative a "racist discourse that denies racism" ("Discriminación México").[11] Thus concealed, this "racist antiracism" becomes even more difficult to question. Tonalmeyotl seeks to break with that context and openly denounce Native dispossession through his xochitlajtoli.[12] His work invites readers to view economic inequities and racism as intrinsically interconnected. Both are grounded in territorial dispossession—in the literal sense of land and in the wider meanings touching on knowledge production explored in the previous chapter—and in spurious justifications of that theft. Speed's concept of "neoliberal multicriminalism" points to a growing amalgam of actors—state entities, organized crime, transnational companies, and foreign nation-state governments such as the United States—complicit in this dispossession and in the perpetuation of colonial practices.

Denunciation of this neoliberal multicriminalist system is at the heart of Tonalmeyotl's poetry, as is echoed in his question regarding the type of literature needed to face an oppressive milieu that renders Native people vulnerable. This vulnerability is imposed by unjust structural conditions and does not constitute some sort of innate Native frailty. As Speed avers, Native Nations are *rendered vulnerable* "by the structures of the settler-capitalist state," in Castilian *vulneradas* (made vulnerable) as opposed to *vulnerables* (vulnerable; *Incarcerated Stories* 3). Tonalmeyotl signals that these forms of colonial violence follow Nahuas when they migrate from their hometowns to other areas within Mexico, the United States, and Canada. Neoliberal multicriminalism melds with settler structures of Indigenous dispossession and elimination across the continent (Speed 5). In light of real and tangible threats, Speed calls for a reduced focus on postmodernist debates over truth within fields such as anthropology to examine the "much-needed critical engagement with the politics of knowledge production (the understanding that all knowledge produced has political effects on its subjects)" (8). With his question regarding what type of literature is requisite amid violent conflict, Tonalmeyotl calls for a similar engagement within literary circles. He questions what good poetry does if, in his view, it remains merely an authors' self-interested quest for "art for art's sake" with no benefit to one's Nation or community.

Tonalmeyotl accentuates the potentially descolonizing effects of literary production to process what Ned Blackhawk describes as the pain inflicted by "violence over the land" and confront the "imperial visions that assumed a priori the dispossession of Native communities" (121). Through literature, writers like Tonalmeyotl assert control over the historical narrative regarding Nahua territory and imagine systemic change. Inversely, Tonalmeyotl addresses the potential colonizing force of literature, and he warns that Native writing may play into the formation of an intellectual elite incognizant of or unwilling to engage with contemporary injustices. Tonalmeyotl's remark about "father sun" and flowers signals that risk. This reference alludes to a romanticized discourse surrounding Native practices promoted by multiculturalism at the expense of genuine engagement with contemporary Native issues.

Tonalmeyotl's criticism of a "flowery view" is especially intriguing when one considers that the term for "poetry" in Nahuatl, xochitlajtoli, is itself a reference to flowered words. In his critique, Tonalmeyotl refers to "flowers" in a Western sense—a flowery, abstract poetic conceit or dead metaphor associated with a "rose-colored" toxic positivity. In moving away from that sense, he invites readers to explore the wide articulations of xochitlajtoli that do not necessarily entail beauty or unfettered sanguinity. Xochitlajtoli itself nestles close to the land in its literal meaning and its associations with telluric ceremonies, which partly explains why territory is a frequent theme. In this sense, xochitlajtoli resembles descriptions of other Native languages, such as the meaning of Mapudungun as "language of the land."[13] It also resembles Abiayala, "land in fruition," as opposed to an empty landscape available for the taking. Xochitlajtoli asserts Nahua agency in the face of attempts to destroy and appropriate their territories. As reflected in Mardonio Carballo's statement regarding the multivocality of the Nahuatl language that I shared at the beginning of the study, xochitlajtoli can be just as harsh or beautiful as texts in any "mainstream" language. Times of linguicide call for a "ruthlessly committed poetry" through which the public observes and feels the pain inflicted on the Serpent's Plumes.[14] Tonalmeyotl himself explicitly invokes the combative potential of xochitlajtoli when, in the introduction to his eponymous anthology, *Xochitlajtoli: Poesía contemporánea en lenguas originarias de México* (Xochitlajtoli: Contemporaneous Poetry in Native Languages of Mexico), he explains that xochitl does not equate to the Western conceit of *flower* or *flor*. Within Pre-Columbian and early colonial-era sources, "flowered" operates as a metaphor for war (3). The Serpent's Flowered Plumes are poised to fight.

The same multivocality appears in present-day usage of xochitl. With its ceremonial connotations, xochitlajtoli emerges in times of intense suffering. This is especially true during droughts, to which the title *Tlalkatsajtsilistle* alludes.[15] As often occurs with self-translations, or transcreations, *Ritual de los olvidados* is not a literal translation. *Tlalkatsajtsilistle* denotes "the shout/yell of the forgotten." Tonalmeyotl's xochitlajtoli speaks out—lays blows—against injustices and labors against a politics of forgetting. The word *ritual* in the Castilian translation highlights how this protest pulls from the *longue durée* of opposition against centuries of colonial practices. These (emp/fl)owered words constitute a space of catharsis to cope with intergenerational trauma from colonial oppression. Tsajtsilistle can denote "ritual," specifically the ceremony petitioning or "shouting" for water. In this ceremony with abundant flower arrangements, people dressed as tekuanij (tigers) box one another to produce the rain.[16] Out of conflict emerges healing. Nahua ritual seeks remembrance of ancestors, underscores the value of the community's knowledges, and foregrounds an affective intelligence—of *feeling* Native Nations' losses and pain.

Although he alludes to ceremonial practices, Tonalmeyotl's work is not meant to be an ethnography of "the Nahua perspective." Along with Yásnaya Elena Aguilar Gil, he contests the category of "Indigenous literature" itself in part because of the tendency to read Indigenous literature as peripheral ethnography.[17] On social media and in interviews, Tonalmeyotl cites various influences on his work such as Edgar Allan Poe, Elsa Cross, Charles Simic, Mikeas Sánchez, Vicente Huidobro, Humberto Ak'abal, María Auxiliadora Balladares, Juan Rulfo, Franz Kafka, and César Vallejo.[18] Like Natalio Hernández's work, the focus in Tonalmeyotl's work is on Nahuas observing through dynamic and unexpected contexts rather than being observed. The importance of this shift in the locus of enunciation cannot be overstated. If there is an ethnography here, it is of Nahuas themselves conducting a study of contemporary society and the persistent ills of colonialism. The locus for Tonalmeyotl's observations is his home region of Chilapa Álvarez, Guerrero; rather than creating a sense of narrowness, this situatedness acts like a prism, as a moving angle that allows for the observation of myriad situations.

Native displacement in mainstream media obscures this complexity and mirrors acts of land dispossession. According to Tonalmeyotl, in addition to its excessive focus on ethnography, *literatura indígena* is treated as a subcategory and promoted by the state to typecast Native Nations. This second-class relegation in the media is clearly evidenced in the federal government's attempt to limit Native Nations to radio stations designated as *indígena* (more on this in chapter 5). In this sense, the current official use of *indígena* resonates with the problematic nineteenth-century origins of the term. The word *indígena* never appears in Tonalmeyotl's *Tlalkatsajtsilistle* or, for that matter, in any of his works, unless in the context of criticism. He rejects the category "Indigenous literature" because for the public it insinuates that Native authors are incapable of competing with mainstream writers. Moreover, conglomerating all Native languages under one term elides the unique genres, styles, and literary traditions within each of the over sixty Native languages in Mexico. According to Tonalmeyotl, if a general term is employed, it should be "Mexican literature"—a broader category including all languages (both Native and colonial) on an equal footing. The *mestizo* readership concentrated in Mexico City is accustomed to "flowery celebrations" of Native practices and the country's Pre-Columbian roots; they do not expect Tonalmeyotl's violent aesthetic of protest against contemporary problems. He wants the public to engage seriously with his poems, which will be unattainable if people consider them an inferior form of writing or ethnic tributary.

Tonalmeyotl and younger generations of contemporary Nahua authors (he describes two younger generations) relate that they in many respects have had to self-constitute themselves with limited support.[19] Perhaps more than their age, however, what most marks their works is the fact that they began to write and publish in the 2000s. Two key events that formed their views are armed Native movements in Southern Mexico—among them the 1994 EZLN uprising—and the misbegotten "War on Drug Trafficking" officially declared in 2006 under President Felipe Calderón's regime.[20] The divide between generations is especially salient in the limited collaborations between authors of the older generation with the younger.[21] More recent authors tend to take greater advantage of different media such as Facebook, especially given their limited access to traditional publishing houses. Social media constitutes a way to publish freely online and bypass the perceived elite who head these publishers.[22]

Tonalmeyotl and many younger authors attest that, while recognition of Nahua cultural practices and knowledge production can shift public perceptions of Indigenous peoples, no major changes in structural inequities will come to fruition without massive protest and even armed defense against nation-state colonial practices.[23] In contrast, according to earlier writers such as Natalio Hernández, recognition of Nahuas as knowledge producers will reduce discrimination and injustices against Indigenous peoples. Tonalmeyotl's *Tlalkatsajtsilistle / Ritual de los olvidados* (Shout of the Forgotten / Ritual of the Forgotten) is representative of the friction between different generations of Nahua authors. Tellingly, this tension is already evident in the title, which—through its invocation of a "shout" of rage from and for the "forgotten" who have suffered under state-sponsored oppression and neglect—breaks with Hernández's less confrontational celebration of intercultural harmony. In this chapter, to explore the visceral protests within *Tlalkatsajtsilistle* more at length, I expand on the Nahua perspective of ixtlamatilistli (knowledge with the face) and how it constitutes a view "with both eyes," an optic aware of class oppression coupled with ethnic and colonial oppression.[24] It is a perspective in which "emotions" are not viewed as separate from "reason," nor is one's subject position objectively independent of knowledge production. This depth-perceiving perspective resists the monocular "eye of reason" of Modernity/colonialism that constructs Indigenous peoples as victims of social retardation and irrational traditions.

A view of the past in front relates to ixtlamatilistli in that they both point to Indigenous founding experiences that collide with Western Modernity. With these alternative imaginaries, Nahuas see reality differently and in conflict with developmentalist discourses that paint the past as just that—having passed behind the modern subject. Much like yoltlajlamikilistli (knowledge with the heart) denotes a conjugation of rationality with emotions, tlaixpan conjugates the past with a present and future. It is an approach in which the past constitutes a resource for the present. The concepts of ixtlamatilistli and tlaixpan aid me in identifying how Tonalmeyotl employs visceral metaphors to imagine a plurinational space in which Nahuas actively construct historical remembrance and defend their social rights.

Tonalmeyotl employs these approaches in open condemnation of colonial practices. As various Nahua authors recount, Nahuas who are told to "preserve" their language often respond, "Mi lengua no me da de comer" (My language does not put food on the table).[25] According to Tonalmeyotl and many others of the younger generation, government institutions readily support programs that seek to preserve the language and protect traditional practices because this does not alter—and in many instances it distracts from—the fundamental social and economic inequities in the country. Like many authors of a younger generation, Tonalmeyotl seeks to publish and at the same time avoid being co-opted by the state as an *indio permitido*.[26] Ultimately, taken together, Natalio Hernández's and Tonalmeyotl's approaches reflect the diversity among Nahua literary production and complement (or counterpoint) one another toward achieving similar aims.

Tonalmeyotl and the Maize Fields of Guerrero

Martín Tonalmeyotl (Martín Jacinto Meza, 1983–) first and foremost identifies as a Nahua *campesino*, and this positionality encompasses his approach to additional *cargos* as poet, storyteller, radio host, columnist, language promoter, professor, translator, photographer, and father. Relationality with the environment is intimated in his artistic pseudonym's reference to the sunrise (tonal [sun/day] + meyoa [shine]). The land and agricultural ceremonies play a key role in his literary production. He is from Atzacoaloya, in the municipality of Chilapa de Álvarez, Guerrero, a community in which more than half the population of 3,500 dedicates itself to farming.[27]

Tonalmeyotl obtained his undergraduate degree in Hispanic American literature from the Universidad Autónoma de Guerrero and subsequently completed an MA in Indigenous linguistics at the Center for Research and Higher Studies in Social Anthropology (CIESAS). His MA thesis, directed by well-known Nahua scholar José Antonio Flores Farfán, was one of the first studies to document the Nahuatl of his home region. After having attended literary workshops promoted by Nahua authors in Guerrero, Tonalmeyotl began to give readings in 2012. His initial collection of poems would later become *Nosentlalilxochitlajtol / Antología personal* (2017). He has worked as a Nahuatl professor at the Universidad Intercultural del Estado de Puebla while completing a PhD in Hispanic American literature at the Universidad Autónoma de Puebla. Tonalmeyotl has authored three books of poetry and edited three anthologies of Nahua and Native writers throughout Mesoamerica. His work and promotions of other authors who write in Native languages appear in numerous magazines and newspapers.[28]

Tonalmeyotl views the promotion of other authors' texts as one of his primary responsibilities. His collaboration within the Suplemento Ojarasca in the newspaper *La Jornada* has been groundbreaking; he has helped to include many authors' texts in Native languages. His work with the series Xochitlájtoli (Flowered Words) in the online magazine *Círculo de poesía* has been fundamental in circulating the texts of Native authors.[29] Tonalmeyotl has edited three anthologies of literature in Native languages. One anthology focuses on authors in Native languages writ large, another specifically on women authors, and the third is a collection solely of Nahua writers. As part of this promotion of other authors' projects, he hosts the radio interview program *Ombligo de tierra* (Navel of Earth). Through *Ombligo de tierra*, Tonalmeyotl interviews many Native activists, academics, and authors. Situated in Mexico City on the radio station CDMX, this program features Native authors occupying one of the largest urban areas in the world.

As an avid Facebook user, Tonalmeyotl champions contemporary Nahua literary production and underscores its political implications. In his social media posts, he is a tireless defender of the Nahuatl language. As part of that language activism, he attended the 2017 Nahuatl revitalization conference in Tlaxcala mentioned at the beginning of this chapter, where he commented on the tone deafness of speaking about flowers and father sun in times of state-sponsored violence. Many Nahua authors (including Natalio Hernández and Ethel Xochitiotzin) were present at this meeting. During the COVID-19 pandemic, Tonalmeyotl participated in numerous online meetings to promote the Nahuatl language and Nahua knowledge production.

His book of poetry *Tlalkatsajtsilistle* was published in 2016 through Jaguar Ediciones, a local publisher in the state of Colima that specializes in regional poetry, with support from the Universidad Intercultural del Estado de Puebla. *Tlalkatsajtsilistle* has not been widely distributed.[30] Despite its limited circulation in print form, this book is significant in its attention to protest. Additionally, poems from *Tlalkatsajtsilistle* have a wider reach through other publications and formats. They appear in online magazines, anthologies, and social media.

Hubert Matiúwàa has written a synopsis of *Tlalkatsajtsilistle* in which he describes Tonalmeyotl's social commitment to "caminar con la palabra, para que a través de ella, miremos como ha cambiado su pueblo, por eso escogió ser poeta en el lugar más violento de México" (to walk with the word, so that through it, we can watch how his community has changed, this is why he chose to be a poet in the most violent place in Mexico; "Los hombres zanate" 15). Along with Tonalmeyotl, Matiúwàa is one of the most prominent denunciatory poets in Guerrero; they both view words themselves as a daily ritual that can reinforce unjust practices or remediate that context. In discussing Tonalmeyotl's work, Matiúwàa goes on to reject the moniker "la nueva generación de poetas indígenas" (the new generation of Indigenous poets; 15). Like Tonalmeyotl and Yásnaya Elena Aguilar Gil, he criticizes the term *indígena*, given its links to the mythologized idea of an "indigenous literature." He also discards the term *new generation* because these writers come from a long line of creators. It is important to note that, although tension exists between older and younger generations of contemporary authors and they may disagree in their approaches, they deeply respect one another. Respect toward elders—and an invective against the pernicious absence of that veneration—is a prevalent theme throughout Tonalmeyotl's *Tlalkatsajtsilistle*.

Tlalkatsajtsilistle consists of thirty-four bilingual Nahuatl-Spanish poems. The poems seek to represent the knowledge production of the forgotten, reflected in the title in Castilian, *Ritual de los olvidados*. In the first seven, the poetic voice decries violence directed at people in his community. To foreground the Nahuatl language, the Nahuatl version of each poem appears in its entirety before the Castilian version to persuade readers to look more at the Nahuatl. This contrasts with the practice of providing facing translations that is commonly used in collections of poetry written in Native languages.

The text begins with references to silence and absence in an epigraph from K'iche' poet Humberto Ak'abal: "*Hablo / para taparle / la boca // al silencio*" (*I speak / to cover / the mouth // of silence*; 5). A key theme of the book is the valorization and amplification of oppressed voices. Unexpectedly, as shall be analyzed more in detail, at the book's end the poetic voice tells the reader/listener precisely *not* to speak. While sounding those silences, Tonalmeyotl leaves key absences in *Tlalkatsajtsilistle*. The text never refers to the nation-state explicitly, and state-sponsored nationalist discourse is excised. In part, this move signals a rejection of the multi-mythic/culturalist celebrations of "The Aztec." There are no direct references to the *flor y canto* (flower and song) lauded by the state. Instead, the Serpent-Plumed personal experiences and people's fears in Tonalmeyotl's region of Guerrero take precedence. Xochitl (flowers) do appear in his poetry in Nahuatl, but often these references go untranslated into Castilian to eschew any misinterpretation of them as flowery celebrations rooted in (sh/f)allow Western conceits. For example, Tonalmeyotl self-translates "xochikouatsin" (flowered serpent) as "serpiente de sonaja delicada" (serpent of delicate rattle; 29–30). When flowers do appear, they do not hark back to the pre-Hispanic era. In the introduction to the anthology *Xochitlajtoli*, of which he was editor, Tonalmeyotl explains, "La palabra *Xochitlajtoli* está compuesta por dos raíces morfológicas de la lengua náhuatl: *xochitl* 'flor' y *tlajtoli* 'palabra,' término **contemporáneo** usado por los hacedores de la bella palabra" (The word *Xochitlajtoli* is composed of two morphological roots from the Nahuatl language: *xochitl* "flower" and *tlajtoli* "word," a **contemporary** term used by the creators of the beautiful word; 9; emphasis added). Here *bello* departs from "beautiful" in the romanticized sense criticized by Mardonio Carballo to invoke carefully curated and respectful language. Tonalmeyotl goes on to state that xochitlajtoli comprises poetry as a literary genre and "al pensamiento nahua en toda su extensión" (Nahua thought in its entirety; 9).

Nahua metaphors and metonymy centered on flowers and the heart, and the affective intelligence communicated through them, can be seen as examples of what Javier Sanjinés calls catachresis. According to Sanjinés, subaltern subjects deploy words that describe what the dominant society cannot grasp and for which the hegemonic language lacks a term.[31] Yolotl and xochitl lose deeper meanings when simply translated as "heart" and "flower." Through these metaphors Indigenous migrants such as Tonalmeyotl articulate the tension between Modernity and Indigenous knowledges, which have cultivated a healthier psyche with their close conjugation of cognition with affect. Within *Tlalkatsajtsilistle*, metaphors rooted in the heart and flowers elucidate this tension. When the flower does appear, principally in reference to Tonalmeyotl's poetry or xochitlajtoli, it foregrounds protest and empowerment through a visceral struggle against colonialism.

Both in interviews and within *Tlalkatsajtsilistle*, Tonalmeyotl reflects upon the efficacy of poetry. Why write? This medium can serve as a tool to confront the daily violence he sees. Literary production can confront systemic inequities by denaturalizing the ideas that intersect and undergird them. Concomitantly, poetry is perhaps perceived as more innocuous than an explicit news report. If Tonalmeyotl wrote news articles that included the names of those involved in illicit activities, he would likely receive death threats. Many of his poems, meanwhile, have come out in a newspaper, *La Jornada*'s special section *Ojarasca* dedicated to Native perspectives. While explicit in their activism, his poems have not led to nearly as dangerous consequences. This does not diminish the power of poetry, however; on the contrary, poetry can carry the voices of those previously minoritized and unheard. A key theme of Tonalmeyotl's writing is the lack of affect in a society accustomed to violence and desensitized to hearing, touch, sight, and taste. More specifically, frequent references to an inability to see clearly allude to mass media, which support a complicit elite while failing to report on the many environmental, social, and economic challenges directly affecting the lives of Indigenous people living in Guerrero.

Visceral Shouts: Intelligent Affectivity within *Tlalkatsajtsilistle* amid a Context of Violence in the Land of Dogs

I now turn to the initial seven poems of *Tlalkatsajtsilistle* to analyze how the poetic voice calls for the reader to feel a tragic context to which many have become numb. These poems denounce how people involved in illicit activities are more vicious than canines and bloodier than a butcher. The continual threat of violence forces youth to leave the community. A sense of surveillance and a risk that one may be targeted by or recruited into criminal entities are ever present. To underscore a double complicity, the text is ambiguous regarding whether the government or criminal organizations pose this menace.

In the first poem, "Chichetlaltipak" / "Tierra de perros" (Dog Land),[32] Tonalmeyotl criticizes the generalized violence that people now treat as quotidian. This poem consists of five stanzas that progress (or *deteriorate*) from shorter octosyllabic verses to eighteen syllables in the third and fourth stanzas, mirroring the increasing presence of threats against the people and the ongoing theft of the land. The final stanza contains shorter verses to emphasize the despondency and territorial reductions that arise out of these encroachments. The first stanza states, "Notlaltipak tlachijchijtle / ika tlakamej uan xtlachaj, / tlakamej uan xtlakakej / niman tlakamej uan nontsitsintin" / "Mi mundo está hecho / de hombres ciegos, / hombres sordos / y hombres mudos" (My land is made / of men who do not see, / men who do not listen / and men who do not speak; 13, 15). From the initial verses, the context described stands in stark contrast with Natalio Hernández's poetry analyzed in the previous chapter. As in many other poems within *Tlalkatsajtsilistle*, these verses carry dual meaning. People are oppressed to the point that they can no longer see, hear, or speak, but also oppressors fail to observe, listen, and dialogue.

"Notlaltipak" is translated into Castilian as "mi mundo" (my world) but signifies more specifically "my land." This word appears as part of the anaphora "Nichante ipan se tlaltipaktle" (I make my home in a land), repeated three times in the following stanzas to firmly situate the poetic voice's locus of enunciation in Tonalmeyotl's region and underscore violence inflicted against the land. Each stanza begins with a reference to land and home: nichante (I live / make my home) from nochaj (my home). The anaphora with nichante serves as the unifying thread bringing together the verses. Focus lays on the land with notlaltipak (my land), nichante (the place I make my home), and kampa (where). It is important to keep in mind that the book's title points to a ritual petition for the earth. Language centered on anaphora and syntactical repetition resembles ceremonial syntax. Besought through supplication, earth possesses the ability to cleanse. Nonetheless, here the people are divorced from the milpa. Society has dismembered itself to such an extent that the parts no longer serve the whole. This land has been overrun and transformed into a "land of dogs," where people viciously compete, relationships break, and many fail to hear and see one another. Missing body parts and missing senses are a recurrent trope to metonymize this disintegration of the community. The oppressed, blinded by systemic oppression, are made vulnerable (in the sense of *vulneradas* described by Speed). These references can also denote that oppressors (those who *vulneran*) do not observe or listen.

The poem "Chichetlaltipak" shifts from the more personal "my land" to the anonymized "a land," as competing forces attempt to steal and appropriate the Native territories of Guerrero. Land has been stripped of reciprocity and converted into "un lugar" (a place), as translated into Castilian (15). A Western conception of the land is extractive—objectifying, commercializing, and privatizing it. In this context, even the people are treated as property or "food" for a ferocious neoliberal multicriminalist economy. "Nichante" and "notlaltipak" are invaded by "high race/breed dogs" who thrive off that system. Far from a hagiography of Nahuas, people from inside the Nahua community also participate in this unjust system. The land has become a place of "dogs" where the people compete at a level of viciousness that surpasses the ferocity of literal dogs. Competition for wealth fractures all relationships. Women speak, but as the poetic voice goes on to show, no one listens. The women dream, but violence and deaf ears drown their voices. In a hypermasculinized environment, their wings are clipped and their arms figuratively severed. The translation of "notlaltipak" as "mundo" (world) marks the wider context of criminality in which the area is ensconced.

The speaker describes the inequities of this system by calling attention to the starkly contrasting opportunities of the community's children in which some grow up in privilege due to no merit of their own: "Nichante ipan se tlaltipaktle / kampa kokonej tojtomajkej niman tejteuakej, / kampa siuakokoneh ikxitsotsoltikej niman kakyejkej" / "Vivo en un lugar / de niños gordos y flacos, / de niñas descalzas y de zapatos" (I live in a land / of skinny and fat children, / girls barefoot and with shoes; 13, 15). References to clothing signal a level of poverty that prevents some from fulfilling basic necessities. The lines call attention to a system of discrimination fixated on outward appearance and dominance.

This is a land where men have outdone dogs ("han sido rebasados"), and canines fear the people (15). A distinction that emerges in the version in Nahuatl is the use of the word "chichi." In Guerrero, chichi refers specifically to street dogs. In contrast, itzcuintli or "notzcuin" is one's pet dog (the xoloitzcuintle [Mexican hairless dog] or any other cherished dog). So "Land of Dogs" is really "Land of Street Dogs." This marks a separation from the family and home repeated throughout *Tlalkatsajtsilistle* and relates, again, to poverty, homelessness, and government mismanagement. Such disintegration signals a separation from the past and the land of the dead. Connected with one's ancestors, a commonly known belief (whether still believed today or not in specific communities) is that the itzcuintli or xoloitzcuintle will lead a person through the land of the dead back to their deceased relatives. Nonetheless, here the poetic voice describes a land of dead for the living where the enablers of a multicriminalist apparatus, the "dogs," tear apart society. Unlike the Mesoamerican xoloitzcuintle, chichi are a symbol of Spanish conquest. Most infamously, Hernán Cortés was accompanied by them.

"Dog Land" offers no hopeful resolution. Instead, it ends by emphasizing the deeply entrenched inequality at the root of the community's persistent problems: "Uan ache uejueixtokej, / uan sa yejyektin tlakamej, / kikuaj nakatsintle uan amo / yajuamej okinotekitilijkej" / "Los más finos, / los de raza alta, / comen la carne / que no han ganado" (the big ["finer" in Castilian] ones, / the pretty [highbred] ones, / eat the meat that they have not / worked for ["earned"]; 14, 16). Those "de raza alta" (high race/breed), in Nahuatl "the pretty ones," eat what they have not "ganado" (won/earned). In streets marred by normalized inequities, people fail to see, listen, and speak out. Tonalmeyotl turns racialized discourse on its head by likening it to a brute competition among animals with no basis in any actual system of superiority. As Tonalmeyotl describes in interviews and in the article "¿Qué ganamos los pueblos originarios?" (What Do We the Native Nations Win?), there is no translation of *ganar* from Castilian into Nahuatl that does not carry connotations of unjustly taking what you have failed to earn with the necessary work and suffering. Tonalmeyotl explains, "En la cultura náhuatl el término 'ganar' es violento y negativo. *Tetlane* (ganar) sólo se usa en una pelea de perros, gatos, gallos y otros animales. El que domine y lastime más es el ganador" (In Nahuatl culture the term "ganar" is violent and negative. *Tetlane* [to win] is only used in a fight among dogs, cats, cocks, or other animals. He who dominates and injures most is the winner; 4). He goes on to state, "En nuestra cultura, la palabra más cercana a 'ganar' es el *timoyolkokoltis* ('hacer doler el corazón a uno mismo' o 'hacer doler el corazón para llegar a algo') traducido al español como esfuerzo" (In our culture, the word closest to "ganar" is *timoyolkokoltis* ["to inflict pain on one's own heart" or "to inflict pain on one's heart to obtain a goal"] which is translated into Castilian as *esfuerzo* [effort]; 4). As seen in the previous chapter, many Nahua writers and authors of other Indigenous Nations deploy this strategy of marking words or concepts absent in Indigenous languages or Castilian. A person who truly triumphs has suffered with their heart. Nahua communities offer solutions from a wisdom forged in that travail, as repeatedly stated in *Tlalkatsajtsilistle*, but they find themselves in a context that renders them vulnerable with few opportunities. Tonalmeyotl foregrounds the Serpent-Plumed experiences of those Nahuas. In response, the "uejueixtokej" (the big people) and "yejyektsin tlakamej" (pretty men) disrespect Nahua communities to depict themselves as superior/greater in size and polished in appearance.

By way of contrast with the dog land, Tonalmeyotl emphasizes the need to cultivate spaces of affectivity. Yoltlajlamikilistli constitutes a viscerality that can be understood as intimately related to affective intelligence, in which emotions are treated as an integral part of a person's thought processes. The concept of "affective intelligence" has its roots in debates surrounding the term *emotional intelligence* used by Daniel Goleman in his best-selling book *Emotional Intelligence* (1995). This emotional intelligence is, as Gerald Matthews describes, the "competence to identify and express emotions, understand emotions, assimilate emotions in thought, and regulate both positive and negative emotions in oneself and others" (xv). Affective intelligence differs from emotional intelligence in that the latter focuses on self-awareness and the management of emotions as a means to meet company objectives, maximize profits, and score personal gains—in other words, emotional intelligence is understood as a tool to score "wins."[33] As anthropologist George E. Marcus posits, affective intelligence "conceptualize[s] affect and reason not as oppositional but as complementary, as two functional mental faculties in a delicate, interactive, highly functional dynamic balance" (2). Solutions to political, economic, and social challenges must be created with the "active engagement and interaction of both mental faculties" (2). Also evident in Natalio Hernández's texts, affective intelligence constitutes a focal point of resistance in numerous Indigenous movements against state assimilationist projects.

Along with Hubert Matiúwàa in Mè'phàà, Tonalmeyotl has cultivated an aesthetics of violence within Nahuatl expressive forms to denounce oppression in their region. The sounds and images that burst from these unjust conditions are a mix of metonymy (individual pieces representing divisions and conflicts, that, taken together, in a sense constitute a "whole of pieces"), violent metaphors, and continual antithesis between oppressor and oppressed. Both Matiúwàa and Tonalmeyotl mention how their language is highly influenced by Native ceremonies that attempt to alleviate the ethically arid context in which they find themselves. Dismembering to remember is a constant theme throughout their literary production. To process and recover from this systemized violence, one must first recognize its dire reality. Under the sign of neoliberalism of this reality, social and political plights depicted in news cycles serve as reminders of the need to find "free market" solutions to problems and confirmation that privatization functions best. In this context, identity politics represent new venues of consumption rather than any potential systemic transformation. Structural inequities go unaddressed, and the focus falls on individual circumstances and occurrences. The way these plights are presented in *Tlalkatsajtsilistle*, in many cases without specific names, is to underscore systemic problems that represent many Nahuas' experiences. Media is a key theme in the text regarding what gets reported and how. *Tlalkatsajtsilistle* could mistakenly be seen as imitating the tendency in news outlets not to name specific Indigenous people who have died. Tonalmeyotl's text differs, however, in exploring the people's experiences in the community—people who, like the butcher in the poem that I will discuss next, struggle to survive in oppressive and disheartening circumstances.

In "Tlamiktijketl" / "Carnicero" (Butcher),[34] a butcher worries about his grandchildren's possible career paths and the dearth of opportunities available to them. This poem consists of three stanzas in free verse ranging from four to fifteen syllables in Nahuatl and three to twelve in Castilian—a quintet, a sextet, and a septet—increasing in magnitude and desperation. The experiences of the community are told from the perspectives of numerous poetic voices throughout *Tlalkatsajtsilistle*, sometimes with an ambiguity that allows for multiple readings. "Tlamiktijketl" is told from the perspective of the butcher's son. His father is "melauak yotekikualan" / "cruelmente molesto" (truly/cruelly angry/troubled; 17–18). The poetic voice denounces how killing has become an "oficio" (career) like the butcher's work. The father worries that his children will become killers instead of butchers. In conjunction with the previous poem, the Nahuatl version plays on the words tlatemikej (they dream) and its resemblance to tlamiktijketl (killer/butcher). "To dream" and "to die" share the same root, miki. Women in the previous poem dream ("tlatemikej"), but those aspirations are lost in the face of killers ("tlamiktijkej"). Instead of dreaming, society has developed habits rooted in oppression.

In Nahuatl, the poem "Tlamiktijketl" focuses on the eyes: tlauelchoka (cries excessively), ixtenchachapaka ika choka (pours out tears crying), kinkixtis ixtololohuan (pulls out his eyes). The father wants to bury his eyes in the earth. This description, however, should not be misread as a surrender. Instead, this is a common trope in Nahuatl literature; burying has the potential to spawn a rebirth like that of a newly planted corn crop. The text emphasizes an affective capacity that can sense the impact of this violence so difficult to observe, in contrast with the killers who threaten and "xteiknelianej" (do not love the people; 17). They kill "inminiktsitsiuan" (their dear sisters and brothers; 17). The butcher's heart grows sick, as he feels the pain of those around him. The father worries that his grandchildren (perhaps the speaker's children) will "ixpoliuikan" (disappear or literally "lose their face or their eyes"; 17). This facial reference connects with the first stanza in which the father wants to tear out his eyes and bury them so that he no longer is forced to witness this pain. In the final stanza, he fears that his descendants will end their lives in criminal activities. They may also begin to disrespect their elders (the speaker and the grandfather who is the butcher) and destroy their own community.

Read more figuratively, the poem "Tlamiktijketl" connects with the previous criticism of capitalism, in which people are described as biting like dogs. In Nahuatl there is ambiguity, as tlamiktijketl literally means "one who kills" (either a butcher or assassin), while in Castilian *carnicero* specifically denotes a butcher. In Castilian the poem speaks of competitors, the theoretical heart of a market economy, while in Nahuatl it simply states that "killers are all around" who disregard others' welfare (17). The land is a key locus of enunciation, somewhat indirectly as the speaker denounces its exploitation. Treated as an object for material production, earth is no longer respected for its potential to cleanse. Contrasting such profit-driven attitudes, Nahua traditions value the land as a place of continual renewal—as is highlighted, again, by the image of the butcher who seeks to bury his eyes in the ground to counter the violence around him. The land remains a potential space for renewal.

In the face of these hostilities, the poem "Itlan tlayouisyotl" / "Bajo la noche" (Under the Night) describes the desire to speak while being unable to do so. Its verses echo the silences spoken by Humberto Ak'abal in the epigraph to *Tlalkatsajtsilistle*. "Under the Night" highlights strategies against generalized violence. Each stanza begins with the anaphora "Najua" (I) in Nahuatl and "Soy" (I am) in Castilian. This "Najua"/"I" forms part of a communal ethic through participation in ceremonies. In the first stanza, the poetic voice wants to yell but is unable to speak. In the second, he invokes ceremonies in which he participates to petition water.

In the final stanza the poetic voice cites a legacy left by "Nesaualkoyotl" (Nezahualcoyotl): "Najua te ixochiponaltsin Nesaualkoyotl, / tlajtoltsintle uan xkaman poliuis" / "Soy el fruto de Nesaualkoyotl, / la palabra que nunca se acaba" (I am the fruit of Nesaualkoyotl, / the word that never disappears; 29, 30). This is one of few pre-Hispanic references in Tonalmeyotl's *Tlalkatsajtsilistle*. The poem recognizes the significance of that legacy, of the past as part of the present and future. The spelling as Nesaualkoyotl (as opposed to Nezahualcoyotl) adapts it to contemporary orthography. This minor change underscores that one respects the past but at the same time innovates upon it. Altered spellings like Nesaualkoyotl "unsettle" colonial logics, disrupting official claims to Nezahualcoyotl made by the Mexican nation-state through commemorations on money, historical sites, and school curricula. Tlajtoltsintle in Nahuatl, with the reverential -tsin, can mean "word" and "language," referring to the Nahuatl language. This is emphasized more in the Nahuatl, with "tlajtoltsintle uan xkaman poliuis" (word/language that will never be lost; 29). The Castilian version could make one think that it refers specifically to the words of Nezahualcoyotl. The last line in Nahuatl, however, suggests that the language will never be (nor ever has been) lost, as antiquating discourse surrounding Nezahualcoyotl often intimates.[35]

The fruit of Nesaualkoyotl (the coyote who fasts) contrasts with the insatiable consumerism and the virulent dogs described in the first poems. As Shannon Speed notes, debates surrounding "coloniality" or "internal colonialism" fail to address a settler politics of supposed belonging (an entitlement that embraces figures like Nezahualcoyotl) and naturalize the purported contours of the nation-state (the entity in which colonial practices take place internally). Idealization of an Indigenous past is a settler logic of belonging mirrored in organized criminal organizations.[36] From the colonial period on, *criollos* (children born in Latin America of Spanish parents) lay claim to the land by appealing to an Indigenous past they allegedly inherited and subsequently surpassed. Tonalmeyotl seemingly appeals to Nezahualcoyotl and the "flower and song" (underscored even more by the literal meaning of "fruit," xochiponaltsin, "flowered bloom"), but he does so, importantly, to emphasize contemporary Nahua literary production. Here, amid a multipronged attack on Native Nations, this "flower and song" is invoked in protest. The meaning of the book's title, *Tlalkatsajtsilistle* (Shout/Yell of the Forgotten), alludes to a coyote's "yell" or howl to denounce injustices.

Shannon Speed's analysis aids greatly in understanding the settler colonial logics and "the invaders" depicted in *Tlalkatsajtsilistle*. By not distinguishing among federal and state soldiers and police, government officials, and narcotraffickers, Tonalmeyotl's work ruptures the discourse of "la Guerra contra el narco" (the War against Drug Trafficking). Speed explains that a neoliberal colonialism or neoliberal multicriminalism acts "with its brutal extractivist logics—that continues the work of forcing indigenous peoples to slave on their own expropriated lands for others' benefit while deploying interlocking race and gender tropes against them in ways that further suppress their inherent sovereignty as peoples and render their dispossession acceptable" ("Structures of Settler Capitalism in Abya Yala" 788). Tonalmeyotl seeks a fundamental structural change that challenges these undergirding colonial logics by asserting Nahua sovereignty over land and knowledge production.

The three perspectives of ixtlamatilistli, yoltlajlamikilistli, and tlaixpan form part of a strategy among Nahua authors to recuperate their territories. Highlighting the contributions of their ancestors as present, underscoring an affective intelligence, and emphasizing the value of knowledges gained from personal experience undergird an effective strategy against discriminatory practices brandished to justify territorial theft. The Nahua community is left to defend itself against state and criminal organizations requiring a tax for "protection." Tonalmeyotl's text calls for the community to rise and fight. As evidenced in Tonalmeyotl's work, Nahua frameworks break with settler colonial logics and neoliberal multiculturalism. They promote an affectivity that recognizes Nahuas and other Native Nations as key knowledge producers with millennial rights to the land.

Violence over the Land

The poems that follow focus on the violence exerted against the land, and how those incursions intersect with aggression against the people and the Nahuatl language. "Nipeua nixtentlapoue" / "Primeros párpados" (I Begin to Blink) represents a space of dismemberment and destruction. Body parts and clothing strewn about parallel the land's anguish. Neoliberal multicriminalism converts both people and their surroundings into mere objects to render profits. The first stanza describes six different items, each with double meanings. "Chikuasen xijtin sakayojkej" / "Seis años de pasto" (Six years of pasture) can refer to six years of goats grazing on the land, but also to *pasto* in the sense of fuel for a fire (33, 34). There are six "chivos de largos cuernos," which can signify literally the long horns of six goats tended to by the speaker, or else AK-47s (this weapon's magazines are called "cuerno de chivo" because of their resemblance to a goat's horn). A pastoral space is interrupted by "seis relámpagos golpeando a las casas de carrizo" (six lightning bolts hitting the reed homes).

The second stanza describes mutilated body parts of dehumanized people. In the third stanza, strewn across the ground are worn pants and shirts in "se ojtsintle kampa xaka nejneme / niman se tlamachilistle / uan xe yaka kitlakuijkuilia" / "un camino no transitado / y un pensamiento aun, / no explorado" (a road untraveled / and a thought still, / unexplored; 34). The initial verses count sets of six in the first stanza, then descend to two, and then to one to represent this dismemberment. They depict the difficulty living in a Guerrero overwhelmed with AK-47s, hungry eyes, mutilated arms, and bare feet, and perhaps beyond this region in possible allusions to unsuccessful migration across the desert to escape hardship.

In the fourth stanza, the poetic voice emerges using the first person: "Kinaman peua nixtlapoue / niman chachapaka nixayo se uaktik. / Kinaman peua ninehnemej / niman melauak tekokojkej tlaltetsitsintin" / "Practico los primeros párpados / y de mis ojos caen lágrimas secas. / Hago los primero[s] pasos / y duele caminar sobre piedras filosas" (I practice the first blinks / and from my eyes fall dry tears. / I take the first steps / and it hurts to walk on sharp rocks; 34). The speaker has witnessed this destruction and attempts to make sense of the dismemberments described within previous stanzas. In the final stanza, he observes and contemplates with affect: "Nitlatlacha niman niknemilia, / kana kechmej tokniuan nanka yopanokej / niman kana kechmej nanka onokajtikiskej, / konistokej on ikxiojtsintle uan xkaman tlame" / "Observo y pienso, / cuántos hombres han transitado estos caminos / y cuántos de ellos han quedado solos, / mirando una vereda que nunca acaba" (I observe and think, / how many men have transited these paths / and how many of them have ended up alone, / looking at a path that never ends; 34). "Niknemilia" (to think/feel) has "walking" at its root; the poetic voice feels these losses and intimates a close connection to them as he walks in thought and remembrance of those who have perished. To signal this affectivity, in Nahuatl the text states "toikniuan," "our brothers and sisters," rather than simply "hombres" (men), as translated in the Castilian version. The poetic voice speaks of people's body parts and clothing as if they were a part of him to mark this empathy and journey with those who suffer: "*my* two hungry eyes," "*my* cut arms," and "*my* bare feet."

The poem "Tokatsitsintin" / "Las arañas" (The Spiders) is key in highlighting the perspective of tlaixpan in these dire circumstances.[37] The first verse states that "algunas veces, es necesario caminar solos" (sometimes, it is necessary to walk alone; 38); finding new paths sometimes entails leaving unaccompanied and participating in other forms of life. Nonetheless, a person needs to return to their homeland. The third stanza states, "Tla san tajuamej tinejnemej, uelis uejka tasiskej. / Onixpoliue in ojtsintle kuak se sanka seka yo / kampa tokatsitsintin tla kitaj xok yaka chante, / kinkajteuaj sanka seka innakatekatsaualuan ijtik on / kaltsitsintin" / "Solo, se puede ir hasta lo infinito. / Se pierde esa eternidad cuando no hay regreso / porque las arañas, al no notar movimiento alguno, / abandonan las casas y huyen de su propia telaraña" (Alone, it is possible reach the infinite. / That eternity is lost when there is no return / because the spiders, upon realizing there is no movement, / abandon their homes and flee their own web; 37, 38). The spiders' string ties back to poems speaking of the "tejidos" (textiles) and the following of a path. Meeting people in other places can be satisfactory for one's memory and to construct one's identity in contrast with those people. In the final stanza, the poetic voice states, "Uelis tsiaskej uejka maske kineke oksejpa matiuajlakan. / Maka matikinkauilikan san yajuamej mamikikan tokniuan / kampa yajuamej inka inchikaualis, / nookintlapojkej yankuikej ikxiojtin, / ojtin kanka aman, tojuitsiaj" / "Es necesario oír y regresar. / No dejar morir a los demás también es de humanos / pues con sus vidas, algunos de ellos / abren nuevas veredas, / atajos por donde hoy, transitamos" (It is necessary to listen and return. / To not let others die is also human / for with their lives, some of them / open new paths, / shortcuts through which we now, travel; 38). The poetic voice emphasizes that, even when walking by oneself, a Nahua is never alone. Nahuas follow in the trajectories left by a long history of pathfinders and a return to one's land.

To highlight that idea of walking in the company of ancestors, the Nahuatl version emphasizes a *comunalidad*: "Kemaniantika, nokineke ma**ti**nejnemi**kan** san **tajuamej**" (may only *we* walk; 37; emphasis added).[38] The first-person plural in Nahuatl, tajuamej, becomes exclusive through its absence in Castilian in "Tokatsitsintin" and throughout *Tlalkatsajtsilistle*. This gesture resembles Yásnaya Elena Aguilar Gil's analysis of an exclusive *we* in the Ayuujk language. She describes an ambiguity in Castilian where *nosotros* may or may not include a listener. Her language eliminates that ambiguity. Ayuujk contains an inclusive and exclusive *we*, and the speaker must decide whether the recipient of their message forms part. By extension, Aguilar Gil argues that identity formation depends on these moments of distinction, where "[e]s necesario el contraste para crear categorías distintas, reconocerse no sólo distintos sino también contrastantes. La identidad, al igual que los fonemas, necesita del contraste para configurarse" (juxtaposition is necessary for creating separate categories, for seeing ourselves as not only different but also contrasting. Identity, much like phonemes, relies on contrast to shape itself; "Ëëts, atom" 19).[39] Tonalmeyotl's exclusive first-person plural in Nahuatl (trans)created through its elision in Castilian marks this contrast and constitution of a Nahua community in solidarity. Without realizing it, the reader who only accesses this text through the Castilian is not included in this community. The poetic voice calls on Nahuas to defend themselves, to act, and to break with a patronizing state that depicts them as victims and targets. The poetic voice states that we can travel far away, but "kineke oksejpa matiuajlakan" (we need to return; 37). We should not let *our brothers* die. They give strength, "inchikaualis," and open new foot paths, "ikxiojtin," in which *we* traverse.

These paths and the "earth's back" are damaged, as described in the poem "Notlaltsin" / "Mi tierra" (My Land). The reverential -tsin is added to notlal to address the land with respect. The first stanza begins, "Itla kokoua ipeyoyotsin notlaltsin. / Kimate kampa yekase totonke" / "Algo le duele a la piel de mi tierra. / Se siente invadida por la fiebre" (Something pains my earth's skin. / It feels invaded with a fever; 39, 40). The land has turned dry in response to climate change, and it wants to submerge itself in water like an axolotl (a Pre-Columbian animal in danger of extinction). In the second stanza, the ahuehuetes (Mexican cypress) have gone silent: "xok tlajtlajtouaj" (they no longer speak; 39). The land grieves because it is no longer caressed by ocelots and other animals. The wind blows harder now since there are no trees to tame it: "El viento solo la observa y no se detiene / todo por tener lastimada la espalda" (The wind only observes her [the earth] and does not stop / all because the earth's back is hurt; 40). In the final lines the poetic voice states that the land cries because men have lost respect for it, "xok kinojnotsaj ken tokojkoltsitsiuan kinojnotsayaj" / "ya no dialogan con ella como lo hacían nuestros abuelos" (they no longer dialogue with her like our grandparents did; 39, 40). They have forgotten to "vestirla de palabras, / perfumarla con humo de copal" (dress her with words, / to scent her with copal smoke;

40). Ceremony and sacred words call out that neglect in a hope to spark remembrance. The book's title, *Tlalkatsajtsilistle*, refers to the rituals of forgotten people, but also to the rituals themselves being forgotten. The land agonizes where humans no longer view the earth as a person (39). Memory can confront extractivist logics.

These poems highlight a relationality with the landscape in which human suffering parallels the suffering of other-than-human beings. This move insists upon a relationality that disrupts the isolating and objectifying effects of neoliberal multicriminalism, which extols individual gain and (w/h)ealth over collective well-being. As *Tlalkatsajtsilistle* contends, the land cannot be treated as a resource for extraction; rather, people must live in dialogue with it. Tonalmeyotl marks the importance of viewing the land as central to our own *existence*, rather than as a separate entity. He defends an ecology of being and speaks through his xochitlajtoli to fight a continual destruction of the earth reverberating through all society.

The Forgotten, Assassinated, and Disappeared

The five poems that follow consider specific individuals targeted by state-sponsored violence and neoliberal multicriminalism. Introducing these individuals, the sixteenth poem comprises a brief tercet titled "Uan xaka techita" / "Invisibles" (And No One Sees Us; 49, 50). Nahuas occupy public spaces but still go unseen:

> Tajuamej tej titlakatsitsintin uan yotechelkajkej.
> Tlakatsitsintin uan tinejnemej niman xaka techita,
> uan titlajtouaj ika totlajtol niman xaka techkake. (49)

> Nosotros somos los olvidados.
> Aquellos invisibles que caminamos sin que nos vean,
> aquellos que hablamos en nuestro idioma sin ser escucha-
>   dos. (50)

> (We dear people have already been forgotten.
> We dear people walk and no one sees us,
> and we speak in our language and no one hears us.)

The poetic voice addresses "those of us who speak in our language and no one hears us"; in print, the blankness on the rest of the page surrounding this brief poem mirrors this invisibility. It is not necessarily that people do not understand what Nahuas say, but they will not even hear the language. Totlajtol (our word/speech) can be interpreted to mean both a specific language (Nahuatl) and in general the perspectives Nahuas offer (speech/ideas). Nahuas speak and *act*, emphasized in the reference to walking. Parallelism marks the final words of each verse: yotechelkajkej (already been forgotten), xaka techita (no one sees us), xaka techkake (no one hears us; 49). Forgetfulness echoes not being heard and ties back to the title of the book—the rituals of the forgotten or a ritual/habit of ignoring the cries and yells of those forgotten. Colonial practices attempt to interrupt both Nahua remembrance of deceased and living relatives and Nahua contemporary knowledge production / speech writ large. This acoustic colonial-scape drowns out the names of Nahuas, a fact that is especially ruinous in this context. As accentuated in Day of the Dead ceremonies, a person whose name is forgotten wanders aimlessly and puts at risk a community's integrity. Affect and experiential knowledge deteriorate in this oblivion.

To battle that stupor, subsequent poems remember jailed or murdered activists. The eighteenth poem speaks out against the 2014 forced disappearances of students from Ayotzinapa, Guerrero—suggesting a larger collective and shared suffering (more on Ayotzinapa in chapter 6). With the title "Intajtsitsiuan ayotsitsintin no uelej patlanej" / "Los padres de las tortugas también saben volar" (The Parents of the Dear Turtles Can Also Fly / The Parents of the Turtles Also Know How to Fly; 55, 57), Tonalmeyotl alludes to the forty-three disappeared students from Ayotzinapa (place of revered turtles upon the water).[40] This allusion is more evident in the title in Nahuatl since one can readily identify Ayotzinapa with "ayotsitsintin" (dear turtles). The poem begins with anaphora focused on the ability of the parents to patlanej / volar (fly): "Uelej patlanej inkuatipan sokitlalkontin / inkuatipan miktlalkontin / Uelej patlanej inkuatipan tepossayolimej / Ipan ojtin techichikuitoltikej niman xalyojkej" / "Volar sobre pantanos / y fosas clandestinas / Volar más allá del ruido de las moscas de fierro / Volar sobre carreteras curvuosas y arenosas" (To fly over swamps / and clandestine graves / To fly further than the noise of the flies of iron / To fly over curving and sandy highways; 55, 57). Many of the missing students are Indigenous. The parents forcefully protest their children's disappearances and enter with strength where no one speaks up. They are "strong of heart" (translated as *sobrevivir*, to survive), despite their thorn-pierced hearts. In the Castilian, the references to this deep affection are sometimes absent. For example, in the Nahuatl text, Nahuas "kintlasojtlaj" (deeply care for) their relatives.

In an act that demonstrates their survivance and affection, the parents in "Intajtsitsiuan ayotsitsintin no uelej patlanej" direct thousands of turtles to scoff at silence and break the fences of the "tekapotschichetsopilomej" / "perros-zopilotes hambrientos" (hungry dog-vultures; 55, 57). In Castilian there is no punctuation, and numerous verbs highlight a communal agency: *tienen alas* (they possess wings), *volar* (to fly), *sobrevivir* (to survive), *dirigir* (to lead), *burlarse* (to scorn), *luchar* (to fight), *defender* (to defend), *gritar* (to yell), and *romper* (to break). Their agency prevails in "Gritar con ellos para crear ecos" (Yelling with them [the disappeared students from Ayotzinapa] to create echoes) to force those who will not listen to pay attention (58). The "turtles" struggle against "pingüinos gordos" (fat penguins), in Nahuatl referred to as tsopilomej (vultures). The poem describes how the fathers of these students ". . . atlanelouaj ipan inayeualuan on tetojtomaktikej / tsopilokotsmatiltin / uan xtla kimatej, uan amo itla kinkokoua" / ". . . nadan y nadan / sobre mares arremolinados / sobre lagos de pingüinos gordos / e inhumanos" (. . . swim and swim / over seas of whirlpools / over lakes of penguins who are fat / and inhumane; 56, 58). These descriptions allude to economic inequities, as the vulture is a common symbol of capitalist abuses—especially given its association with economic opportunism through the means of vulture funds (*fondos buitre* in Castilian). The speaker connects the Ayotzinapa case with widespread corruption based on economic exploitation. The poem constitutes a clear indictment against the neoliberal multicriminalist zeitgeist of putting profits above people's lives and erasing marginalized groups. Having the Nahuatl version invites the reader to recognize that many of those disappeared were Nahua or from other Native Nations, a fact little reported in coverage of Ayotzinapa.

The eponymous poem "Nestora Salgado" further denounces these general surroundings of neoliberal multicriminalism. Specifically, it does so through the figure of Nestora Salgado García, one of the most prominent Nahua women in Guerrero to have led *policías comunitarias* (community police forces unauthorized by state and federal government). Salgado's community-centered activism led to persecution and imprisonment at the hands of the Mexican state. Tonalmeyotl dedicates the longest poem, four pages, to underscoring her strength and importance.

The first stanza identifies Salgado's powerful animal companion (tonal) as a jaguar, dressed with "alas de lepidópteros" (butterfly wings).

She plants flowers for the butterflies as a symbol of local efforts aimed at preventing tragedies like Ayotzinapa. The third stanza, the longest of *Tlalkatsajtsilistle*, describes how with her roots—her founding experience as a Nahua—Salgado defends the community Olinalá. She forms part of a larger fellowship that exercises its agency and a communal conscience in which "san achijtsin ouajnoskalte ouel okitiak tlinon / nochijtok ichan" / "[b]astó con crecer un poco / para poder mirar desde cientos de ojos" (she only needed to grow a little / to be able to observe from the perspective of hundreds of eyes what has occurred in her hometown; 59, 63). Olinalá is famous for fashioning elaborate boxes with dynamic designs that simulate movement. The name for these boxes, olincuahuitl (movement-wood), alludes to the social movements Salgado leads, as well as to the migrations that many from her community have made. She had left her hometown and resided in the United States. When she returned to Olinalá, she found the region overrun by "perros y coyotes hambrientos / quienes regían al pueblo a punta de amenazas y colmillos" (hungry dogs and coyotes / who ruled the community with threats and fangs; 63). This insatiability contrasts with the reference to Nesaualkoyotl, the coyote who fasts, in the poem "Under the Night." Opposed to these ravenous animals, Salgado defends the community with her "jaguar nahual" (itonalnahual on tekuane), her animal companion symbolizing fortitude.

In the poem "Jueves kuak nokua posojle" / "Jueves de pozole" (Thursday When Pozole Is Eaten), a bowl of pozole (stew made with hominy and meat) is a metonym of the unmitigated, routine violence against which activists from previous poems struggle. A family is eating out at a restaurant when suddenly two armed men forcibly abduct the father. The first stanza begins, "Melauak tej amo kualtsin kuak se tlakatl uan kana kipiya 35 / niman yeuatok ipan se silla istak mixpan kixteke / ome tlakamej, se kana de 18 niman okse kana de 23 / kampa ipan on naue inmauan kuikaj ome miktepostle" / "No es lúcido ver que un hombre de 35 / sea levantado de una silla blanca / por otros de 18 y 23 siendo la gran diferencia / cuatro manos jóvenes y dos fierros de muerte" (It's not good to see a man who is 35 / kidnapped from his white chair / by two men, one 18 and another 23 / with four young hands and two iron tools of death; 66, 68). The young ages underscore disrespect toward an older member of the community. The interrupted bowl of pozole symbolizes the disintegration of a family, and the incursion of criminality into everyday experiences. It is "abnormal" to, as stated in the second stanza, "mamitskuiteuakan kana 11:30 ika okualkan / kuak kinaman otikonsele moposol"

/ "privar a alguien a las 11:30 am / de un pozole que apenas se prepara" (take you away at 11:30 a.m. / right when you're about to receive your pozole; 66, 68). The various numbers suggest the reduction of society to statistics like the ever-increasing number of homicides reported in the news. "Jueves kuak nokua posojle" breaks with the quotidian nature of this context in which similar events are casually (un)reported.

The poetic voice bears witness to this abduction in the fourth stanza: "Xkualtsin tej kuak timotlalia itlajkotsian motonan / niman mochpotsin uan sa yektle niman sa kualtelotsin / niman kema mamitsuikakan sankaseka / niman xok kaman uelis tikimitas" / "Es injusto sentarse en medio de la esposa / y una hija de alegre y tierna sonrisa / para después abandonarlas involuntariamente / hasta un tiempo de jamás regreso" (It's unjust to sit between your wife and your daughter who smiles so happily and sweetly / to later abandon them involuntarily / until a time of no return; 66, 68). The family is separated, and the reason for the kidnapping goes unstated. The Nahuatl version switches to the second person, "timotlalia" (you sit down), "mochpotsin" (your daughter), "mamitsuikakaj" (they seize you), "tikimitas" (you will see them; 66), and "*you* will never see them again" (66). As in previous poems, the use of anaphora with *you* invites the reader to *feel* the tragic loss portrayed.

Military presence does nothing to protect the streets, suggested in the sixth stanza: "Xkualtsin tej kampa ika tonajle niman ika yeuajle / mikipijpiyakan ajakatsintle ipan ojtin / niman san kana omponka kalkuitlapan yokonkajkayajkej / on tlapijpixketl / niman sa chokatok se siuatsintle uan kana kipiya 30 niman / okse kana de 7" / "Es anormal mantener vigilado día y noche / al viento traicionero de las calles / mientras que a dos cuadras del vigilante / se revientan unas lágrimas femeninas de / 30 y 7 años" (It's abnormal to maintain a watch night and day / on the treacherous wind of the streets / while two blocks away from the watchman / cries a precious woman who is 30 and / another who is 7; 67, 69). The mention of ages and no names again suggests a reduction to numbers. Moreover, the word *anormal* alludes to the forced disappearances of students from the Escuela Normal (Normal School) of Ayotzinapa.

The poetic voice laments the unpleasantness of seeing another person murdered Friday morning: "Xkualtsin tej kampa ipan se viernes okualkan / ipan se periódico oksejpa tikitas on tepostlauilanajle istak / on telpochxayakatl, on tsontsintle uan kine okonxinkej / niman on ixtololojtsitsintin yejyeualtikej sa tlaltsintle, sa / tlikonextle" / "No es agradable que un viernes por la mañana / en un periódico local, uno vuelva a mirar al mismo / coche blanco / el mismo rostro joven, los mismos cabellos recién / cortados / y los mismos ojos redondos hechos polvo y ceniza" (It's not pleasant that on a Friday morning / in a local paper, you again see the same / white car / the same young face, the same hair recently / cut / and the same round eyes turned to dust and ash; 67, 69). It should not be normal, but the word "mismo" (the same), alongside daily references to *viernes* and *periódico*, suggests that such events have become quotidian. The fact that the poetic voice deliberately trivializes the experience by understating that "it's not pleasant" speaks volumes to this systemic problem.

It is unjust to have to abandon one's land, as addressed in the final stanza. The poetic voice itself has been witness to these crimes and may need to flee. People leave the community because of threats for reporting what they have witnessed (which the speaker does through this xochitlajtoli) or must leave to avoid being recruited into organized crime. "Jueves kuak nokua posojle" is based on one of Tonalmeyotl's personal experiences.[41] He witnessed a father being forcibly taken away from a restaurant in broad daylight and in front of his wife and daughter. Rather than frame this as an individual experience, however, Tonalmeyotl sets up the poem as a means of expressing collective suffering.

Language with Face and Head

The final poems focus on language. "Nonauatlajtol" / "Mi lengua náhuatl" (My Nahuatl Language/Tongue) speaks of the violence exerted against the Nahuatl language. I cite the poem in its entirety:

> Kijtouaj kampa notlajtol nauatl
> yokechtejkej,
> yokikxisalojkej
> niman yokixtlapachojkej.
> Najua uan niualeua Atsakualoyan,
> niteititis kampa xmelauak.
> Yajua kipiya itsontekontsin,
> ikxiuan makajtokej
> niman melauak tlacha uejka.
>
> Najua nikmastika
> kampa notlajtol nejneme,

kampa xtsasalijtokej imauan niman iyoltsin,
sa tsikuintok ken se aokokapostsintle. (86)

Cuentan que a mi lengua náhuatl
le han cortado la cabeza,
amarrado los pies
y vendado los ojos.
Yo, un hombre de Atzacoaloya,
mostraré lo contrario,
ella tiene cabeza,
goza de pies ligeros
y una vista inalcanzable.

Estoy seguro
que camina,
que posee brazos libres y que su alma
palpita como el corazón de un encinal. (87)

(They say that my language, Nahuatl,
has already been beheaded,
that they have bound its feet
and covered its eyes.
I who come from Atsakualoyan,
will show people that is not true.
It has a precious head,
its feet are light
and it truly sees far.

I know
that my language walks,
that its arms are free and that its soul
beats like the heart of an encinal.)

"They" have severed the Nahuatl language's head, tied its feet, and prevented it from walking. The speaker declares that, despite these attacks, the language is still very much alive. Weakening of the Nahuatl language parallels the loss of land and key perspectives, as the decapitation symbolizes a separation from ancestors, the covering of the eyes implies a lack of observation, and the general mutilation of the language through a slit throat signifies an inability to defend Nahua territory and concepts. It would seem strange to blindfold a decapitated head, yet this symbolism carries profound meaning. In Nahuatl "yokechtejkej" literally translates as "they have already cut the throat" (86). This act emphasizes the direct attack against speech. "Kijtouaj" (they say) signals that this moribund state "they" allege is a falsity circulating like gossip. Without the head, the language is no longer able to observe and offer ideas. "[Y]okikxisalojkej" / "amarrado los pies" suggests that it can no longer walk. This description has wider meanings in Nahuatl due to its associations with personal experience and thought explored earlier. A surprising description added, "niman yokixtlapachojkej" (they already covered its eyes), in Nahuatl carries the additional connotation of not only covering the eyes but pressing against and smashing them. Even though the language has been beheaded, the oppressors obstruct—crush—the eyes to accentuate this epistemic violence.

Ruthlessness against the language converges with violence exerted against the people and earth in previous poems. The importance of the land is underscored in the poetic voice's declaration at the beginning of the first stanza "Najua uan niualeua Atsakualoyan" (I who come from Atsakualoyan; 86). Atsakualoyan is a little-known community, but here the poetic voice suggests that being from there gives him authority to speak. In contrast with what "they say," the poetic voice stresses that the language "has a precious head, / its feet are light / and truly sees far" (86). Optical and kinetic depth emphasizes the perspectives gained from personal experience. This is reiterated in the second stanza, with the statement that the language still walks, "notlajtol nejneme" (86). The language has hands and a heart (translated into Castilian as "su alma" or "its soul"; 87).

In the penultimate poem, "Kuak nikneke ninokuikatis" / "Intento de melodía" (When I Want to Sing / An Attempt at Melody), the speaker reflects on how he cannot sing a melodious song while his community suffers. The poetic voice has a sense for detecting injustices and an urge to report events so they will be remembered. As quoted in the epigraph to this chapter, Tonalmeyotl's poetic persona reflects on his previous poems with the heart. He realizes that these songs seek to "tenakastlaposkej," to open ears, and "teixtlaposkej," open eyes (94). They want to cure all people "uan melauak kintlauelmiktsia kalmaseualtin" (who kill the Nahua/Indigenous homes/communities), in Castilian rendered as "hombres impacientes ante la sociedad" (impatient men before society; 94, 95). *Impatient* marks the rush of neoliberal multiculturalism, a time that precludes kinship and quickly decimates Native communities to convert them into commercial products.

The last stanza expresses a longing for a melodious song, but unbridled sanguinity would be unethical in the face so many injustices. The speaker's surroundings, described as "tepantlakamej" (wall-humans) in Nahuatl, "xkauiliaj maueiya nokuikaltsin, / xkuauiliaj manokuepa se xijtlapajtiketl / kampa kijtoua tla kauiliaj, / melauak miyak ualixuas ken ixua xijtle / niman kuajkon miyak tokniuan kinmakixtis" / "no permiten que mi canto / sea una hierba curativa, / porque, si se le permite, / se multiplicará como maleza sobre la tierra / y dañará a una gran parte de la sociedad inhumana" (don't let my song grow, / don't let it become a healing herb / for, if you allow it to, / it will spread like weeds [in Nahuatl: plants] over the earth / and harm a large part of inhuman society [in Nahuatl: then it will save a lot of our sisters and brothers]; 94, 95). If given space to grow, these songs would "melauak miyak ualixuas ken ixua xijtle" (truly spread like a plant; 94). "Xijtle" can be read two ways in Nahuatl, as a weed (as suggested in Castilian, *maleza*), but also as a medicinal plant. From the oppressors' perspective, these verses are a weed, whereas for Nahuas they can be redemptive and healing. The speaker's words need to sting to change this context. Then these words could sprout like plants and save "our sisters and brothers." The rejection of "pretty songs" constitutes an invective against neoliberal multiculturalism and its failed promises of democracy and social rights. The poem concludes with the verses: "kuajkon tej, oksejpa san ompa ninokaua, / kan niknektok ninokuikatis / niman xaka nechakake" / "Por ello, vuelvo a quedar / solo en el intento / de ser escuchado" (Because of that, I again remain alone, / when I attempt to sing / and no one listens to me [in Castilian, "in the attempt / to be heard"]; 94, 95). The word *kauitl* (time) plays on *kaua* (to let happen) and *nokaua* (to remain), from which *kauitl* is derived. Those who will not let (*kauilia*) the song grow fail to recognize the ephemerality and preciousness of life (signaled in their impatience that murders Native communities), and the value of this xochitlajtoli, which endures from one generation to another.

The final poem, "Amo xchiua" / "Recomendación" (Don't Do It / Recommendation), can be read as contradicting all the previous poems. The initial stanza begins, "Amo xkisa, / amo xmotlalo, / amo xtlanemile" / "No salgas, / no hables, / no pienses" (Don't go out, / don't run, / don't think; 96, 97). "Don't speak," which appears in the Castilian version, is exchanged for "don't run" in Nahuatl. This linguistic mix suggests the parallel between walking/running and speaking. The poetic voice recommends that "Amo xkisa" / "No salgas" (Don't go out) because "In ikxiojtin kimpiyaj intlapijpixkauan" / "Las veredas que pisas tienen sus espías" (The footpaths have their spies; 96, 97). With the word *espía* (spy), the speaker possibly refers to people who report on others to the government and criminal organizations, and that could be anyone, even people no one may suspect—described as "wind-men," "grandmothers," or "flower children" (96, 97). The second stanza goes on to recommend, "amo xchoka, / amo xuetska, amo xmijyote" ("don't cry, / don't laugh, / don't breathe"; 96). If you breathe, ". . . poliuis tlaltipaktle, / tlaltipaktle kan chantej toniuan uan tlachistokej, / tlaltipaktle uan ijkatok ipan se mitlaltipak" / ". . . se perderá el mundo / que parece de los vivos, / cimentado sobre una tierra de muertos" (the land will be lost, / land where our brothers who observe live, / land established on a land of the dead; 96, 97). The land turns into a haunted space, like Comala in Juan Rulfo's famous novel *Pedro Páramo* (1955) alluded to by poetic voice. The speaker again recommends that the audience do nothing. This is not a world that one would want to live in, but in irony the poem addresses it as one to maintain.

The concluding stanza declares, "Amo xtlanemile, / amo xisteuetska, / yamok xtlajkuilo / xkinkauile san noyajuamej matlajtokan tonaltsitsintin" / "no pienses, / no sonrías, / deja de escribir, / que el presente hable por sí solo" (Don't think, / don't smile, / stop writing, / let the present speak for itself; 96, 97). This apparent invitation to remain silent and "let the present speak for itself" ties into prior admonitions, in particular a poem in which a parent tells their child, "Don't go . . . but no, you'd better" (20, 22). If the present only speaks for itself, then past oppression is ignored. This acquiescence could afford a person protection from retaliation, but they would also be allowing society to linger in dire circumstances. The connection with ancestors would be lost, and instead this present world would become a land of dead unfit for the living.

Tlalkatsajtsilistle is a book of protest, underscoring the irony of the final poem in which the poetic voice invites readers to stay silent. The speaker in "Amo xchiua" / "Recomendación" echoes the common recommendation not to get involved because only those who interfere get hurt. In Nahuatl, the title "Don't Do It" (rather than "Recommendation" in Castilian) contradicts Humberto Ak'abal's call to cover silence's mouth in the epigraph to *Tlalkatsajtsilistle*. The poem consists of three stanzas, going down from seven, six, four verses, suggesting a decline in speech. In one possible reading, "Amo xchiua" / "Recomendación" is a stinging criticism of the indifference and detachment for which many people opt. In this sense, the poetic voice is distinct from previous poems in telling the listener/reader to cease speaking and doing.

On the other hand, a possible reading of this poem is as a warning against the elitism that writing can create. In this sense, one should let the present speak for itself and not let literary production distract from the horrors of that present and people's experiences on the ground. What is the point of writing poetry about hyper-ethnographed rituals and melodious speech if that is an inauthentic reflection of people's knowledge production and lived experiences? This second reading is enforced in the Nahuatl version. Intlapijpixkauan, translated as *espía* (spy), means "protector" or "watchman" and is the same word used in the poem, "Thursday When Pozole Is Eaten," to refer to the patrols, possibly federal or state police, who do nothing when they hear the cries of a girl being raped a few blocks from them. This meaning coincides with the previous reading of "Amo xchiua" / "Recomendación" in which the poetic voice calls on people to remain quiet and avoid becoming targets by calling attention to themselves. Nonetheless, intlapijpixkauan can also refer to true protectors who defend the community. One may stand aside to allow those protectors to confront injustices.

This ambiguity and multiplicity of meanings reflect Tonalmeyotl's own internal debates as to the value of his writing. He questions whether one can dismantle the master's house with the master's literary tools.[42] The act of writing tends to focus on the individual, yet Tonalmeyotl stresses the need to listen to the community and recognize their actual situation. Poetry for poetry's sake, or language revitalization for revitalization's sake, fails to effectuate the systemic changes needed. Essentially, Tonalmeyotl asks where the line exists between xochitlajtoli, in the proper sense, and becoming engulfed in a *letrado* world disconnected from Nahua communities.

Displacing Homogeneous Nationalist Narratives

Tonalmeyotl questions Western Modernity's horizon of expectations and imagines a space in which Native knowledges and practices are validated for our present-day world. To this end, he advocates open protest, even physical force (such as community police) for defense if necessary. In Tonalmeyotl's texts the metaphors of the heart and flowers play a key role in the visceral resistance to the discourse of Modernity. He envisions a world in which affective intelligence thrives. As Ned Blackhawk argues in his influential work *Violence over the Land*, change cannot be achieved until people comprehend the pain inflicted against both the people and the land (5). Through his poetry, Tonalmeyotl invites readers to feel that pain. As Speed argues in relation to Indigenous migrant women sharing their stories, there is power in taking control of the narrative to contest a system that renders one vulnerable.

Descolonization can only take place when those on the supposed margins dismantle colonialism. Hernández and Tonalmeyotl conceive a space in which Indigenous subjects participate actively in the (des)construction of the nation-state. They underscore the importance of local knowledges transmitted through the Nahuatl language and attempt to transform a political and social structure that, from its inception, was configured to dispossess them. I read Tonalmeyotl's *Tlalkatsajtsilistle* more closely with the Nahua perspectives ixtlamatilistli, yoltlajlamikilistli, and tlaixpan. Ixtlamatilistli aids in understanding the many metaphors centered on the face and the insistence on careful observance—specifically, an observance capable of recognizing the persistence of colonialism within a neoliberal multiculturalist milieu and its coupling of ethnic discrimination with economic inequities. Yoltlajlamikilistli validates the affective responses to five centuries of oppression, and tlaixpan highlights the potential of Nahua knowledge production from that past to guide toward contemporary strategies in overturning colonial practices.

This chapter and the previous one point to insights gleaned from a South-South dialogue between two Nahua intellectuals of different generations. Such dialogues are needed to propose valid solutions untethered to hegemonic knowledge production centered in "the North"/West. Natalio Hernández and Martín Tonalmeyotl widen our understanding of Native Nations' movements and the place of literature within these efforts. Both Tonalmeyotl and Hernández are committed to promoting genuine exchanges with Native knowledge production and demands for land rights. Although they have distinct approaches to achieve this, they view literature as a means to help rectify inequities. In the following two chapters, I address the works of contemporary Nahua female writers who critique many male authors for their problematic depictions of women as well as for excluding them from literary circles. These writers take up the same Nahua perspectives as their male counterparts but then articulate them to underscore Nahua women's agency against representations of women as merely carriers of tradition.

Chapter 3

Grinding Words

Ethel Xochitiotzin Pérez's Subversion of Nahua and Nation-State Patriarchy in *Tlaoxtika in tlajtoli*

Sé semilla
sé manantial
al pie de la Malintzi.
Tetepetla lugar donde nace tu rostro.
Hace siglos nuestros ancestros construyeron tu historia,
diseñaron ollas,
cada una lleva el color, el sabor y el aroma de esta tierra.
Cuando llegaron los españoles, fueron quebradas,
quedaron esparcidas en tu cuerpo.

—Ethel Xochitiotzin Pérez, "Donde nace el arcoíris,"
Tlaoxtika in tlajtol / Desgranando la palabra (2012)

El símbolo de la entrega es la Malinche, la amante de Cortés.
Es verdad que ella se da voluntariamente al conquistador, pero éste, apenas deja de serle útil, la olvida. . . . Y del mismo modo que el niño no perdona a su madre que lo abandone para ir en busca de su padre, el pueblo mexicano no perdona su traición a la Malinche.

—Octavio Paz, "Los hijos de la Malinche,"
El laberinto de la soledad (1950)

"Why are there no publications of Nahua women authors?" I asked a Nahua male author in Mexico City. The year was 2009, and this glaring absence contrasted with other Indigenous languages at that time.[1] This writer thought about it for a moment and replied, "Es que ellas no quieren escribir" (The thing is that they [Nahua women] don't want to write). This "explanation" surprised me. Uninterested in writing? In my earlier studies of Nahuatl, I had seen academic and literary circles dominated almost exclusively by men. It appeared to be more a question of systemic elision than a dearth of interest. I suspected that what this author said about the categorical absence of women writers was wrong—especially considering that there are more than three million Nahuas, and Nahuatl is the most widely spoken Indigenous language in Mexico, as well as all Northern Abiayala.

Certainly, this male writer *was* mistaken in assuming there were no Nahua women writers. Female authors from numerous regions write, demand to be heard, and have published in increasing numbers since 2009.[2] Tlaxcaltecan poet Ethel Xochitiotzin Pérez is one of those authors who speak out against the marginalization of women's voices. In "Donde nace el arcoíris" (Where the Rainbow Is Born), her poetic persona exclaims the need to "be seed" and "be a spring of water" at the foot of the Malintzin. The volcano Malintzin is the most prominent feature of the Tlaxcaltecan landscape and is named after Doña Marina, popularly known as the "Malinche." Mexican nationalist discourse depicts both the state of Tlaxcala and Doña Marina as traitors due to their alliance with the Spanish conquistadors.[3] Mexican poet and essayist Octavio Paz puts forth his (in)famous misogynist interpretation of these events in "Los hijos de la Malinche" (Sons of the Malinche), in which he describes the Malinche as delivering herself sexually over to Cortés. Nahuatl scholar Frances Karttunen counters, "Today in Mexican popular imagination [Malinche's] reputation has fallen victim to the blame-the-(sexual)-survivor syndrome. Like many a woman who has so suffered, her own character has come into question, her survival become distasteful, her collusion with rapists reprehensible" ("Rethinking Malinche" 311). Through her poetry, Xochitiotzin uproots this entangled representation transferred to Nahua women in general—particularly Tlaxcaltecan women—and offers a remapping in which she highlights their agency within a Nahua landscape (emphasized through the deployment of Nahua toponyms such as Tetepetla).[4] These women created ceramic pots, but the Spaniards broke them and the shards were scattered throughout the women's bodies—symbolic of rape rather than the supposed voluntary surrender to conquistadors' advances. The call to "be seed" and "be spring" at the foot of the Malintzin challenges nationalist depictions of Nahua women as traitors and invokes their ability to observe—in other words, to possess ixtlamatilistli or "knowledge with the face"—and their creative potential to transform their communities beset by a colonial heritage of male chauvinism.

Despite Nahua women's important literary production, academic and editorial spaces have historically been closed off to them or else only open to a certain degree—provided their participation does not question traditional male patriarchy within literary and intellectual production. Karttunen notes that the Nahuatl studies program at UNAM was apparently a space that mostly elided Nahua women ("Indigenous Writing" 441). Beginning in the 1970s and up to 1992, UNAM's journal *Estudios de Cultura Náhuatl* (Studies of Nahuatl Culture) published selections from the literary production of sixteen writers, all men. Karttunen comments on this hostile environment: "It is disconcerting that the twentieth century, which opened with a publication by Isabel Ramírez Castañeda and into which Doña Luz brought forth her work, is concluding with Nahuatl literature practiced, as in the colonial period, largely by men" ("Indigenous Writing" 441). Ramírez Castañeda and Julia Jiménez González (Doña Luz Jiménez) published decades before the surge in contemporary Nahuatl texts post-1985.[5] Yet, as Karttunen argues, academia has not recognized their participation as creators and intellectuals. In response, this chapter acknowledges a distinct history and literary trajectory centered on contemporary women authors who debunk their presupposed absence and the fallacy that "they don't want to write."[6]

The following questions guide my analysis: How do depictions of Nahua women shift when they represent themselves? How do Nahua women differ from the traditional depictions of them by men? What strategies can be gleaned from Nahua women's experiences that would be of value to struggles for feminist rights across the globe? And what do they teach us about gender discrimination and how it intersects with the persecution of minority languages and cultural practices?

If one considers the negative experiences Nahua women have had in attempting to publish their works, it is true in part that they do not want to write—they do not want to labor under the norms of a male-dominated intelligentsia. Instead, Nahua women rewrite and transform this environment. These ixtlamatinij (intellectuals / close observers)[7] do so by incorporating innovative metaphors into their works that position women as agents of change instead of muses for male authors' poetry. As do their male counterparts in the texts analyzed in the previous chapters, women writers offer theoretical perspectives rooted in the Nahuatl language. Nonetheless, they differ significantly in locating women as the source of articulation for such perspectives. In this chapter, I address the work of Ethel Xochitiotzin Pérez, one author among many who seek to undermine male-dominated spaces. I argue that Xochitiotzin's book *Tlaoxtika in tlajtol / Desgranando la palabra* (Shelling Words) reshapes common metaphors within Nahua poetry to position women as decision makers and ixtlamatinij within and outside their communities. In doing so, she inserts a neglected narrative into the Serpent's Plumage to subvert both the Nahua male authors' objectification of women and their reinforcement of male dominance.

This chapter goes against the traditional framework that is not only applied to Xochitiotzin but to Nahua women authors in general—an attitude of "Qué bonito que escriban" (It's so nice [literally "pretty"] that they write), which I heard repeatedly when telling male authors about women's works.[8] Reflective of the depreciation of earlier women writers' texts and a doubly marginalized echo of the comment "Qué bonito es el náhuatl" criticized at the beginning of this study, such a condescending attitude contributes to the dismissal of female writers as incapable of producing literature as innovative as that of their male counterparts. I draw attention to the pioneering ways in which Nahua women authors challenge the male-dominated status quo. While it is true that Nahua authors' writing is generally skimmed for content, it is even truer for women authors who receive insufficient support for publication. In the present chapter I focus on Xochitiotzin because her work addresses the resistance to women's writing within her community and beyond.

In the sections that follow I revisit the Nahua perspectives employed in Xochitiotzin's poetry and frame the context in which Nahua women writers subvert chauvinist metaphors. I explore selections of these writers' texts and give a brief introduction before beginning the analysis of a selection of poems from Xochitiotzin's *Tlaoxtika in tlajtol*. I describe Xochitiotzin's background and her struggles to write. Familiarity with this context helps significantly in more fully understanding and appreciating *Tlaoxtika in tlajtol*. This book offers a distinct view of Xochitiotzin's ancestors, foregrounds maize-centered metaphors, and articulates her identity as a Nahua woman. She writes against the "traditional" male-centered depictions of ancestors, maize, and women to cultivate an alternative space that embraces Nahua women's Serpent-Plumed knowledge production and active participation in society.

Theoretical Framework for Analysis of *Tlaoxtika in tlajtol*

As in previous chapters, the theoretical framework of this chapter centers on perspectives tied to ixtlamatilistli, yoltlajlamikilistli, and tlaixpan in Xochitiotzin's work. Connected to ixtlamatilistli, the term tlachialistli (observation) appears repeatedly in *Tlaoxtika in tlajtol*. Tlachialistli constitutes the need to carefully observe one's surroundings and personal lived knowledges. In addition to framing my own approach to detailed analysis of texts in this study, tlachialistli and ixtlamatilistli are key in understanding Xochitiotzin's poetry. Opposed to a depiction of women as mere recipients of a tradition articulated by men, she situates women as knowledge producers. They possess the ability to carefully observe surroundings and propose solutions to societal challenges.[9]

Within Xochitiotzin's text, perspectives tied to tlaixpan and ueuetl (literally "old") are correlatives to tlachialistli and ixtlamatilistli. As already seen, the "old" or the past is not situated "behind" the subject. Rather, the past constitutes what is known and lies in front of the subject as a guide. Lessons from earlier years serve as more than anchors to tradition; they play a role in a dynamic present and future. Xochitiotzin observes and looks to deceased female relatives for guidance (these relatives' pictures lie on the tlaixpan or altar). She then uses the strength from that heritage to project her own perspectives into the present and future. Her references to weaving and other forms of expression tap into a long tradition of creative production by women ancestors and break with a privileging of the written word.

Furthermore, as analyzed previously, yoltlajlamikilistli represents a fundamental metaphor linked to affective space in which emotions are conjugated with rational thought. This is particularly important when addressing Nahua women's texts, as women are traditionally depicted as excessively "emotional" and "weak." Xochitiotzin instead weaves a space of strength in which Nahua women possess and shape the word through their texts. Every poem in *Tlaoxtika in tlajtol* explicitly mentions yolotl (heart) or else alludes to it. Such repetition may seem unnecessary if one ignores the wider implications of this metaphor. By emphasizing the heart, Xochitiotzin is not reiterating the hackneyed depiction of Nahua women as overloaded with affect but rather foregrounding the ability to exercise an affective intelligence that recognizes emotive and cognitive responses as intimately interwoven.

In this chapter I explore the way in which Xochitiotzin leads the reader to look at tlajtol or tlajtoli (literally "word[s]"). She points to tlajtol's wider meanings of "sentence(s)," "discourse(s)," "literature(s)," and "language(s)." Xochitiotzin teases out this polysemy in her poetry. The different possibilities for tlajtol are especially significant when considering that she works within the gaps between Nahuatl and Spanish as she writes. In interviews, she tells of shifting back and forth between the two languages.[10] "Tlaoxtika" or "desgranando" (separating the kernels of) language(s) can mean multiple languages, as inanimate objects in Nahuatl do not carry any plural marker.[11] In these linguistic shifts, Xochitiotzin disrupts essentialist representations of Native authors as limited to authentic displays of their "original" tongue. This is more exceptional when one recalls the depiction of the Malinche in the Mexican nationalist narrative as "the violated" who possessed the word by interpreting for Cortés. Instead of depicting women as vehicles of conquest, Xochitiotzin establishes women as descolonizing knowledge producers battling the Mexican nation-state's inheritance of colonial practices.

As noted in the introduction, maize itself constitutes a vital element tied to ixtlamatilistli, yoltlajlamikilistli, tlaixpan, and language. Corn, tlayol in Tlaxcala, figuratively represents "the word" and literary creation. Maize is the main staple that strengthens the heart and points toward close observance of the landscape with the necessary care for the crop. Agricultural death and regeneration guide a perspective in which the past continually surfaces in the present. Although traditionally a task associated more with men, maize cultivation in Xochitiotzin's text is one in which she takes part metaphorically through writing. She positions herself as a farmer with command over literary production through maize-centered metaphors in which women direct every step of the cultivation.

I place these perspectives from Xochitiotzin's *Tlaoxtika in tlajtol* in dialogue with the approach of Joyce Green, within what she terms Indigenous feminism (*Making Space for Indigenous Feminism* 4–17). Xochitiotzin would not self-identify as *feminista* (or *intelectual* for that matter), for many of the same reasons Green identifies regarding the term *feminist* throughout Abiayala. This opposition is even more salient in Southern Abiayala, as shown in the works of such intellectuals as Aura Cumes and Yásnaya Elena Aguilar Gil.[12] Green notes that many Native peoples consider *feminism* anathema to Native scholarship, as a term limited to white settler colonialist women's privilege (Green, "Taking More Account of Indigenous Feminism" 1-8). In contrast with mainstream feminism's focus on individual privilege, Green defines Indigenous feminism as both a framework and strategy that "draws on core elements of Indigenous cultures—in particular, the nearly universal connection to land, to territory, through relationships framed as a sacred responsibility predicated on reciprocity and definitive of culture and identity" (4). In Green's sense of the term, Xochitiotzin is without doubt feminist.

The disavowal of feminist scholarship and its far-reaching implications within Indigenous studies and descolonizing strategies risks a perpetual postponement of Native women's rights. Michi Saagiig Nishnaabeg scholar Leanne Betasamosake Simpson indicates that, when topics like domestic violence arise, male Indigenous leaders often sidestep the matter, with "a hierarchy of issues" according to which "[l]and claims, treaty violations, blockades, and political negotiations are positioned as righteous work, while issues regarding children, families, sexual and gender violence, and bodies are positioned as less important—issues that can wait until we have the land back" (*As We Have Always Done* 53). In the name of solidarity within struggles for land rights and national sovereignty, these leaders stall critical perspectives within the community that question the status and treatment of women.[13] Xochitiotzin has also come up against similar opposition, and criticism of male chauvinism within Nahua communities is met with accusations of betrayal. Nonetheless, like Simpson, Xochitiotzin considers it important to bring about this dialogue now.

A conspicuous absence in Xochitiotzin's text is any reference to the Mexican nation-state. Her omission of nationalist discourse resembles what IllumiNative leader Crystal Echo Hawk (Pawnee) describes as a sovereignty that is a "living process within this knot of human and spiritual relationships bound together by mutual responsibilities and obligations" (21). Menominee activist Ingrid Washinawatok echoes this perspective: "Our spirituality and our responsibilities define our duties. We understand the concept of sovereignty as woven through a fabric that encompasses our spirituality and responsibility. This is a cyclical view of sovereignty, incorporating it into our traditional philosophy and view of our responsibilities" ("Sovereignty as a Birthright" 12). The views that Xochitiotzin articulates in her text are reflective of this spirituality and responsibility. These perspectives offer alternatives to the male-dominated nation-state model, which inherently reifies a patriarchal order.[14]

Patriarchal and patronizing perspectives toward women surface in many male Nahuas' texts. This observation in no way is meant to target specific authors or show dismissiveness toward their works. Quite the opposite, this is to seriously engage with representations in their works and note a critique that could be leveled toward numerous literary publications today across the world. Mazatec poet Juan Gregorio Regino warns against complacency and superficial readings.[15] Mirroring Aguilar Gil and Tonalmeyotl's opposition to the (sub)category "Indigenous literatures," Regino criticizes a tendency to have low expectations for literary quality or to treat this literature like an achievement by virtue of its existence. Nahua women writers offer a critical approach that questions the problematic representations of women and literary production in Native languages.

Xochitiotzin's empowerment contrasts with depictions of Nahua women as passive receptacles of tradition. Butterflies, flowers, the sun, and rainbows are recurrent tropes in many male authors' works and in Xochitiotzin's poetry, but she uses them as metaphors to empower women. Common depictions place women in a position of reproduction as carriers of oral tradition without originality. According to this framework, they are receptacles, locales where dreams or poetry may be born but not through their own agency. Portrayed as informants, Nahua women go unrecognized as authors with their own ideas. They are an inspiration for male writers to produce their works, muses for those who create poetry. They pass on memories and preserve tradition. In that same sense, they teach the language to children and give birth to new generations. It is through men, however, that language becomes literature. This criticism of the representation of women within Nahua literature distances itself from any attempt to discard male authors as chauvinists severed from "modern" gender equity in "developed" countries. Such an erroneous conclusion perpetuates the Euro-American characterization of Native communities as backward. Machismo is by no means a phenomenon limited to Indigenous communities nor supposed "Third World" or "Fourth World" countries. The colonial tendency to relegate Indigenous peoples to a false binary of saint or devil has contributed to a paucity of discussion over women's rights. Held to an iniquitous higher standard, Native Nations that acknowledge internal discrimination are perceived as proof of their communities' inferiority and need for outside aid. State-sponsored programs and incursions into Indigenous communities such as the Mexican nation-state's Oportunidades welfare program and ethnographic studies played an influential role in the perpetuation of this presupposed

Indigenous dependency.¹⁶ Nahua women authors remedy this problem through their works and debunk the notion that they lack the agency to do so themselves without outside intervention.

Introduction to Contemporary Nahua Women Authors

While research of present-day Nahuatl literature is scant, attention to contemporary Nahua women authors is even more limited and constitutes a field in need of serious consideration. As mentioned previously, this inattention is not due to a shortage of Nahua women writers. There are numerous authors, among them Yolanda Matías García (Guerrero), Yankuik Metztli Nopaltecatl (Sierra de Zongolica), Ethel Xochitiotzin Pérez (Tlaxcala), Fabiola Tieco Carrillo (Tlaxcala), Calixta Muños Corona (Tlaxcala), Zabina Cruz (Puebla/Tlaxcala), Eugenia Ixmatlahua Tlaxcala (Sierra de Zongolica), Salustia Lara de la Cruz (Morelos), Delia Ramírez Castellanos (Morelos), Eustacia Saavedra Barranco (Morelos), Olivia Tequiliquihua Colohua (Sierra de Zongolica, Veracruz), Ángeles Tzanahua (Sierra de Zongolica, Veracruz), Delia Ramírez Castellanos (Morelos), Judith Santopietro (Córdoba, Veracruz), Araceli Patlani (Zitlala, Guerrero), and Ateri Miyawatl (Acatlán, Guerrero).

Publications by the Colectiva Editorial de Mujeres en Prisión Hermanas en la Sombra (Sisters in the Shadows Editorial Collective of Women in Prison) are of great significance. These texts are by incarcerated women in the writing workshop Taller de Historias de Vida (Life Histories Workshop) at the Atlacholoaya, Morelos Correctional Facility (Centro Estatal de Readaptación Social / State Center for Social Readaptation [CERESO]). Many of the women who participate in and direct this workshop are Nahua and from other Native Nations such as Mè'phàà. In their narratives and poetry, they address gender and racial discrimination faced in their own communities and in their interactions with the state government.¹⁷ Their life stories constitute an indictment of the harsh conditions throughout the Mexican nation-state. They describe the absence of court translators for Nahuatl and other Native languages as a compounding factor in their imprisonment. Among the Nahua women in the Sisters in the Shadow Editorial Collective are Perla Negra (Alejandra Reynoso), Flor de Noche Buena (Santa María Soyatla), and Morelitos (Honoria Morelos). Echoing the sentiments of fellow participants in Hermanas en la Sombra, Alejandra Reynoso describes how she "ha encontrado en él [el mundo de la escritura] una salida para sus emociones, una puerta para sacar al exterior la historia de violencia que ha marcado su vida y la manera en que fue construyendo el camino sinuoso que finalmente la trajo a este lugar" (has found in the world of writing an outlet for her emotions, a door to let out the history of violence that has marked her life and the way in which she went on constructing the sinuous path that brought her to this place [the correctional facility]; Aída Hernández Castillo, *Bajo la sombra del guamúchil* 95). Many Nahua women authors comment on how literature opens an outlet for processing traumas and imagining spaces in which healing can emerge (see chapter 6).

In this brief survey, I describe works from a selection of authors whom I had the opportunity to interview, specifically Yolanda Matías García, Isabel Martínez Nopaltécatl (Yankuik Metztli), and Fabiola Carrillo Tieco. With notable exceptions, Nahua male authors and publishing houses have treated these writers as marginal voices and have not given them space to share their writing. An understanding of this position shared among Nahua women authors will help frame the context in which Ethel Xochitiotzin Pérez writes.

Yolanda Matías García is the most experienced author and the only woman whose poems appear within an Indigenous literary anthology from the 1990s.[18] Support for her work at that time did not go beyond the two poems in *México: Diversas lenguas, una sola nación*, and her texts have often been dismissed as "overly emotional." Matías García has a compelling story behind what led her to start writing in Nahuatl. She is from the municipality of Tixtla, Guerrero, an area of conflict not far from Tonalmeyotl's home municipality of Chilapa. Her husband was assassinated in social movements during the nineties in Guerrero.[19] After her husband's death, Matías García saw the surge in Indigenous publications in the 1990s and decided to participate with her own literary production. In our meeting she recited much of her poetry from memory, as she has lost her sight. Her lyrical poetry seeks to elicit a strong affective response from the audience. She has released a CD, *Xochitlahtol ika moyollot / Palabra florida para tu corazón* (Flowered Words for Your Heart; 2005), with many of the compositions accompanied by guitar; published a book of poetry, *Tonalxochimeh / Flores del sol* (Sunflowers; 2013); and coordinated the publication of a Nahuatl anthology, *Semanauakuikatl / Canto al Universo* (Song for the Universe; 2018).

Similar to Ethel Xochitiotzin Pérez in her opposition to metaphors that privilege men, Isabel Martínez Nopaltécatl does not view the sun as masculine and claims both solar and lunar space. She comes from the municipality of Zongolica, Veracruz, and uses the pen name Yankuik Metztli (New Moon). Unlike most contemporary Nahua authors, Metztli refuses to translate her poetry into Castilian. Her pen name Yankuik Metztli combines with the figure a New Sun and claims a metaphorical space that symbolizes an opening for women's voices. She calls for a landscape in which Nahua women represent their own voices.

Significantly, the Nahuatl from her region has a unique pronunciation and vocabulary.[20] In part due to these distinctive aspects of their linguistic variant and geographical remoteness, Nahua authors in Zongolica voice concern over the difficulty in finding venues in which to publish—a barrier that is even greater for women. Authors have resorted to creating their own collectives and publishing houses to distribute their works. Confronted with this situation, Metztli posts her poetry on Facebook. The following is one of Metztli's poems, perhaps indicative of this absence of an audience:

amika nechkaki,
nokxipa ninehnenti,
nikakti:
in kuikalmeh tekolomeh;
tlen nechyolosewia.

okuitzo, owetzke wan otlanke. (Metztli, "amika nechkaki")

(No one listens to me,
I am always walking,
I am listening:
to songs of the owls;
that extinguish my heart.

It choked, they fell and ended.)

Yankuik Metztli is the songwriter for a Nahua heavy metal band in Zongolica. "Songs of the owls" alludes to this musical genre, as tekolotl, the ominous owl, is a symbol of its harsh sonorities. Yolosewia (extinguish my heart), meanwhile, can signify both to extinguish and to calm. Heavy metal, because of its unvarnished approach, serves as a cathartic mode that can give better expression to the daily effects of inequality than the flowery lyrical modes encouraged by nationalist discourse. Giving voice to these plights, which are often obscured in public discourse, the genres of rap, hard rock, and heavy metal have attracted several Nahua artists.[21]

They more closely resemble the perspective of ixtlamatlistli, focused on actual, lived experiences on the ground. This visceral space relates to yoltlajlamikilistli, knowledge with the heart, and to the importance of affectivity in cognition. Heavy metal compositions subvert stereotypes tied to Nahuatl, among them the misconception that it is not a modern language. Audiences are often surprised to hear, within a contemporary music genre, lyrics composed by a Nahua woman in what the public deems an extinct dialect.

Metztli takes great pride and comfort in her language, as seen in the following poem:

> No tlahtol;
> ich atl motlelowa.
> No tlaltzin
> nowan wetzkatok
> yeh tlen nochipa nech tlamaka.
>
> (My language;
> blown upon the water.
> My precious land
> rejoices with me
> it always gives me sustenance.)

Much like Ethel Xochitiotzin, Metztli parallels her language and literary production with the landscape. This language to her is as important as the physical sustenance provided by the land. The choice words within ceremonial spaces, "blown upon the water," are essential to petitioning for the necessary rain that brings forth sustenance. Metztli finds that poetry provides a medium through which to express her own words, discourse, and language.

Fabiola Carrillo Tieco is from San Pablo del Monte, Tlaxcala, and she is completing her PhD in history at the Universidad Autónoma de México. Carrillo Tieco's opposition to marginalization of women is evident in her short story "In tlazinque" (The Lazy One).[22] In this narrative, Aurelia, the "lazy one," refuses to care adequately for her elderly mother, Doña Margarita. Aurelia spends most of the day asleep. When she marries the sacristan's son, the townspeople hope that this will cure her stupor, described as a mysterious disease. Nonetheless, these efforts are to no avail; Aurelia becomes even lazier and neglects her family. Her husband leaves, Doña Margarita passes away from neglect, and Aurelia ends up on the street selling chamomile branches door-to-door to survive. While it might be tempting to read this story as a lesson for women to comply with domestic responsibilities, this narrative instead serves as a warning not to lose the affective attachment with one's mother. The one thing for which the townspeople cannot forgive Aurelia is the abandonment of her mother. The act of writing this narrative itself in Nahuatl invokes that connection with ancestors and a respect for their knowledges—something that in many instances younger generations forsake or even openly reject.

This brief overview highlights just a few of a diverse group of female authors who share a common desire to transform literary circles dominated by men. While these women have encountered obstacles, this context is rapidly changing. Particularly since 2010, there has been a growing surge in publications of Nahua women's works. Judith Santopietro (the focus of chapter 4) released her book of poetry *Palabras de agua* (Words of Water) in 2010. That same year the Mexican government's Institute of Indigenous Languages (INALI) printed the anthology *Pensamiento y voz de mujeres indígenas* (Thoughts and Voice of Indigenous Women). This collection contains essays, short narratives, and poetry from eight Nahua writers (including one poem from Ethel Xochitiotzin Pérez). Near the end of 2013, Yolanda Matías published her first book of poetry. In 2014 Fabiola Carrillo Tieco released her first book of short stories, *In xinachtli in tlahtolli: Amoxtli Zazanilli* (Seedbed of Words: Book of Short Stories). Ateri Miyawatl (chapter 6), Martín Tonalmeyotl, and Mardonio Carballo (chapter 5) have been key promoters of Nahua women's publications. Miyawatl leads the publishing house Originaria, dedicated to Native women authors, which will print poems by Araceli Patlani (Araceli Tecolapa Alejo / Astronauta de Tlaltipaktli) in 2024. Tonalmeyotl directs the series *Xochitlájtoli* in the online magazine *Círculo de la palabra* and in 2019 released the literary anthology *Flor de siete pétalos: Espina florida de siete poetas mexicanas* with poetry by Araceli Patlani. Ethel Xochitiotzin's book of poetry *Tlaoxtika in tlajtol*, completed in 2012, was published by the University of Warsaw as a monolingual Nahuatl edition in 2020.[23] Although Mardonio Carballo has not been directly involved in publishing Nahua women authors' works, he has invited them to participate in his television and radio programs to promote their literary production.

On 6 December 2020 *La Jornada Semanal* circulated an ill-informed article that elided this contemporary literary production. Titled "La literatura indígena de México: Desigualdad de género y olvido" (Indigenous Literature from Mexico: Gender Inequality and Oblivion), the piece claims,

"Beyond the precariousness, marginalization, exclusion, and poverty that they suffer, the scarce support for their culture, above all made by women, continues to perpetrate a machista preference" (Albarrán Solleiro). In addition to containing factual errors, the article ignores Native women authors' numerous efforts and publications in the last decades. Native authors slammed this article after Tonalmeyotl shared and criticized it on Facebook (Tonalmeyotl, post from 6 December 2020). I cite this dispute because it signals the importance of avoiding the extreme of victimization and the fallacy that women have not responded creatively to this context. While Nahua female authors comment on battles with male chauvinism, this situation has improved markedly because of their resilience and proposals. The sensationalism evident in the *Jornada Semanal* article exaggerates gender discrimination and victimization at the expense of recognizing Native women's successes. Literary publications are only one area in a multifaceted movement to open spaces for Native women's voices. The following section analyzes more in depth one of those works, Ethel Xochitiotzin Pérez's *Tlaoxtika in tlajtol*.

Worded Flowers: A Brief Biography of Ethel Xochitiotzin

Ethel Xochitiotzin Pérez is from Santa María Tlacatecpac, municipality of Contla de Juan Cuamatzi in the state of Tlaxcala. She has written poetry and narrative in Nahuatl for more than two decades, despite an unfavorable context within and outside her community. She tells of pressure from her own community to confine herself to domestic responsibilities.[24] Xochitiotzin has continually gone against this pigeonholing, obtaining a *licenciatura* (bachelor's) in Hispanic literature from the University of Tlaxcala, working as a professor of Nahuatl, and participating in organizations such as the Jóvenes Creadores en Lenguas Originarias (Young Creators in Indigenous Languages) and the Nechicoliztli Zohuatlahtolxochitl (Women's Worded Flower Collective), the latter of which she had helped form.

In 2013, Xochitiotzin, along with Fabiola Carrillo Tieco, Calixta Muñoz Corona, and Zabina Cruz, formed a writers' collective in Tlaxcala, named Nechicoliztli Zohuatlahtolxochitl (Women's Worded Flower Collective).[25] She and cofounders have opened new spaces for dialogue among Nahua women and for the publication of their works. They comment that doing so allows them to bypass male-dominated literary circles that have tended to treat them condescendingly. The name of the organization itself reflects this desire, as it would be more common to say xochitlahtol (flowered word) instead of tlahtolxochitl (worded flower). The latter is innovative and places emphasis on the flower, a common Nahua metaphor for women in addition to its many valences discussed in previous chapters.

In interviews Xochitiotzin describes how Nahua male authors take on a patronizing attitude when she shares her work. After looking at her poetry, one male author put her out completely by commenting: "Tienes mucha madera, pero aún te falta mucho" (You have a lot of potential [literally "you have a lot of wood" as in "raw material"], but you still have a ways to go).[26] She would need the discipline and refinement taught by male writers to achieve publishable quality. Another male author mentioned that she had ueyi iyolo (a big heart), referring to her bravery to continue writing in such an adverse context. These comments, rather than recognize her work, only acknowledge that Xochitiotzin has an uncanny determination to keep writing; they fail to treat her as an equal or encourage the publication of her literature. A male author even went as far as to suggest that Xochitiotzin would need to obtain an MA or PhD to improve her writing, even though the author himself holds no degree.[27] In fact, few male authors have completed a bachelor's, while Xochitiotzin has. The underlying logic to this author's comment suggests that women need to have an extra amount of formal education to offer valuable contributions outside the domestic space. That is, they are incapable, in and of themselves, of offering ixtlamatilistli, since their personal experiences are confined to narrower contexts.

At the time Xochitiotzin was born in Contla in 1973, there was a swift decline in the number of Nahuatl speakers. According to anthropologist Jacqueline Messing in her study "Multiple Ideologies and Competing Discourses: Language Shift in Tlaxcala, Mexico" (2007), the 1970s marked a dramatic downturn in the population of speakers forty years old and younger (557–58). Xochitiotzin grew up a heritage speaker of the language in this context. Her parents avoided speaking Nahuatl with her due to discrimination, but she did hear the language from her grandparents and on the street. Not having grown up using Nahuatl actively, Xochitiotzin decided to study it upon seeing the surge in Indigenous literary production in the 1990s, as she was completing her degree. The fact that she is a heritage speaker and did not turn to Nahua literature until adulthood has led other authors, particularly male authors, to dismiss her as incapable of producing high-quality literature. In fact, one writer observed that the title of *Tlaoxtika in tlajtol* (Shelling Words) is grammatically "incorrect" and should instead be *Koxtikaj in tlajtol*, since *tlaoxtikaj* is intransitive and thus cannot specify an object.[28] Such structures evidence, according to this writer and others, that Xochitiotzin thinks in and translates from Castilian.[29] Nonetheless, as Xochitiotzin describes in interviews, she thinks in both languages and the poems are a product of going back and forth. For this reason, I include both the Nahuatl and Castilian versions of her poetry either side by side or with the Castilian version in endnotes. My translations are based on a comparison of these two versions, as sometimes the Nahuatl carries additional meanings not evident in the Spanish and vice versa. Rather than being "inauthentic" or "grammatically wrong," her literature evidences a fluid dynamic between the two languages that makes a bilingual (or translingual) reading all the more intriguing and relevant.[30]

It was not only in her turn to Nahuatl that Xochitiotzin faced criticism but also in her study of Hispanic literature. She began to write while completing her degree in Hispanic literature at the University of Tlaxcala in 1999. In interviews she speaks of resistance to this specialization within her community. They warned, "[V]as a morir de hambre" (You're going to die of hunger). In reply, she would say that there were other kinds of wealth than money.[31] Poetry represented a means to make her voice heard. In the following section I begin my analysis of her first book of poetry written under these conditions.

"Soatsin" (Revered Woman): Analysis of First Poems of *Tlaoxtika*

Xochitiotzin's book of poetry *Tlaoxtika in tlajtol / Desgranando la palabra* (Shelling Words) consists of fifteen lyric poems, varying in length from a quatrain to two pages. *Tlaoxtika* progresses from remembrances of the past to the center of the book, which focuses on maize. The final poems explore how the poetic voice will speak despite discrimination. It is difficult to translate the title *Tlaoxtika in tlajtol* into English, as *tlaoxtika* refers to drying corncobs and brushing off the kernels. Xochitiotzin translates the title into Spanish as "Desgranando la palabra," literally "shelling" or "dekerneling the word."[32] I choose to translate it also as "grinding maize" because the kernels are brushed off to grind them and make *masa* (ground-up corn for making tortillas). This action becomes a metaphor for writing, as writers bring words together, each grapheme like a kernel, to create something new. Such imagery embodies Xochitiotzin's work and Nahua female authors in general, as they "mix and grind Nahuatl words" to transform them into a space where women are centered as agents.

Throughout her poems, as the title of the book suggests, Xochitiotzin imagines rewordings and societal transformation. In the introduction, written in Castilian, Xochitiotzin explains that the verses address love, denounce discrimination, vindicate Nahuatl, and play with that language: "Cada verso desgrana soledad, discriminación, amor, sabor y color del idioma de esta comunidad [Municipio de Contla de Juan Cuamatzi]" (Each verse removes and collects kernels of solitude, discrimination, love, flavor, and color from the language of this community [Municipality of Contla de Juan Cuamatzi]; i). This description can apply to each poem, since Xochitiotzin's poems are open to multiple interpretations. Thus, a love poem can be analyzed as a reflection about a lover or as a meditation about an intimate connection with ancestors and the Nahuatl language.

The first poems "Soatsin" (Revered Woman), "In tonal tomiketsitsi" (Day of Our Dead), and "Kanik tlakati in kosemalotl" (Where the Rainbow Is Born) begin not with a "look back" but instead a "forward look" to the past and remembrance. As opposed to being an anchor that draws the subject "back," ancestral remembrance projects toward a dynamic present and future. At the book's center, Xochitiotzin focuses more explicitly on maize as a metaphor for writing. My reading examines the poems "Niknekiskia" (I Wish), "Ixtololotsin tlen kitsakuilia ixayak tonantsi intlali" (Eyes That Detain the Face of Our Mother Earth), "Xochitlaoltsin" (Flowered Maize), and "Achtlitonaltsin" (Sun's Seed). Xochitiotzin's maize metaphor challenges traditional depictions of Nahua symbols and the marginalization of women. In the final poems, her poetic persona turns inward and dialogues with herself and her Nahua identity through the poems "Malinalli" (Entanglement) and "Teskatl" (Mirror). She refuses to let her voice be relegated. These three parts of *Tlaoxtika* combine to illustrate how Xochitiotzin asserts an alternative poetic framework in which women make history rather than just carry it, actively produce knowledge rather than passively receive, and articulate their own identities instead of accepting an imposed one.

The first poem, "Soatsin" (Revered Woman), is centered on women's voices. Much can be gleaned from the title itself. The words soatl and soatsin with the reverential suffix -tsin conspicuously represent the Nahuatl variant of Tlaxcala. Soatl contrasts with cihuatl (also "woman") of the prestigious Nahuatl from Mexico City.[33] That is, cihuatl is more common within the male-dominated academic and literary circles described at the beginning of this chapter. Xochitiotzin's use of soatl reflects her transgression of Nahua literary and linguistic hegemony as she knew well that this "dialectical" word could be frowned upon.

In her introduction, Xochitiotzin identifies the poems as being written in free verse (i). Her descriptions of writing reflect her own desire to break free from prior convention both in Castilian and in Nahuatl. According to Xochitiotzin, "Soatzin" was meant to be set to music with her own melody:

Soatsin	**Mujer**
Popokatsi kosemalotl	Niña arco iris
Monauaktsi tlajtol yes in metsintli	Junto a ti la palabra es luna
Timauiltia ika in tonaltsi	Juegas con el sol
Kuikatia in yolotl	Arrullas el corazón.
Oajsiko se papalotsi	Llegó una mariposa,
Uan omotlakenti ika motlajtol	Y se vistió con tus palabras
Poliui	Se pierde
kajtok ajuiak ipan tlen tlali	Dejando el aroma de la tierra
Ichpopokatsi kosemalotl	Niña arco iris
Tlajtol tonaltsi. (1)	Palabra de sol (2)

(Revered Woman

Rainbow girl

Beside you the word is moon

You play with the sun

You lull the heart

A butterfly has arrived

And dressed in your words

It vanishes

leaving a scent of earth

Rainbow girl

Word of sun)

Xochitiotzin employs the metaphor of a "rainbow girl" (literally a "young woman rainbow") to represent women, the soatl (woman) of the title. The rainbow depicts women as exercising agency and self-representation. Sun and water interact to form its colors.[34] The mix of light and water symbolizes literary creation. These colors also allude to the weaving of clothing and the wide spectrum of hues that go into its design. Traditionally made by women in Contla, textiles here serve as an apt metaphor for Nahua women's literature (alluded to in the sixth line, "dressed in your words").

An element that appears in the following verse and continually throughout the book is the moon; in "Soatsin," specifically, Xochitiotzin writes that next to the rainbow "the word is moon." Like Yankuik Metztli, Xochitiotzin rejects portrayals of the moon as exclusively feminine and the sun as masculine. Instead, here the sun is associated with women and underscores their power to observe and create texts—from weaving tapestries to expressing themselves through other visual, auditory, and written media gathered under the umbrella of textuality. Xochitiotzin's poetic persona is the butterfly who, to strengthen the heart, arrives and dresses with the words that are both sun and moon. Throughout the whole collection one senses a constant threat of loss of words. In "Soatsin" this motif is suggested by the sole Nahuatl word in the seventh line: Poliui (It vanishes / It is lost; 1, 2).

The final verse speaks of "Palabra de sol" (Word of sun; 2). Distanced from male authors' self-depictions as "men of sun," Xochitiotzin's words are of astral strength. The poetic voice addresses another woman, perhaps Xochitiotzin herself, telling of this potency. These apostrophic verses encompass all the senses, of sight (the rainbow), hearing (song), smell (aroma of the earth, which in Nahuatl can also refer to taste), and touch (dressing with words). It is a synesthetic experience in which the poetic voice sees, hears, and dresses with the word. "The word" denotes significant power, especially in Nahuatl, as tlahtoani (literally "the one who speaks") can mean "ruler" or "governor."[35] This term is usually associated with men, but Xochitiotzin asserts power over speech. These words are at risk of being lost because of the pressure for women to be silent.

The second poem of *Tlaoxtika*, "In tonal Tomiketsitsi" / "Día de Muertos" (Day of Our Dead), shifts from living women to invite a deceased female relative to return home during the Day of the Dead:

Miketsitsi in miktla tiuitse	Ánimas, del Mictlan vienen
¿Omiteyoj kan tonnemi?	Huesuda, ¿Dónde andas?
¡xonuiki!	¡Ven!
¡Xonkalaki!	¡Entra!
¡kuali yo ton ajsiko itech mo yeyantsi!	¡Bienvenida a tu casa!
¡xonnenemi ipan ojtli xochitl!	¡Camina hacia el camino de flor!
Ye mitson chia in atsintli	Ya te espera el agua,
In ajuialis kopal,	el aroma del copal,
In sempoalxochitl	la flor de muerto,
In panchichiual	el pan,
In tlemol	el mole,
In tamal	el tamal
In ayojtsopelik	el dulce de calabaza,
In xokotl....	la fruta....
¡Xkonana in tlanex uan istatl!	¡Toma la luz y la sal!
Mitsonpaleuis ijkuak tonmokuepas	Te ayudará a tu regreso
¡Xkoni moneuktsi!	¡Toma el pulque!,
Mouintia moyolotsi	Embriaga tu alma.
Axa nimitsontlaokolia nin tlauili tlen yes noxochitlajtol. (3)	Hoy te regalo esta luz que es mi poesía. (4)

(Spirits come from the land of the dead
Bony lady, Where do you go?
Come!
Enter!
Welcome to your home!
Walk toward the pathway of flowers!
Water awaits you,

the aroma of copal,
sempoalxochitl, flower of the dead,
bread,
black *mole*,
tamales,
pumpkin sweets,
fruit....
Take the light and the salt!
It will help upon your return
Drink the pulque!
Intoxicate your soul.
Today I give to you this light, my poetry.)

The poem's structure resembles ceremonial language by listing ritualistic elements, constituting a blend of colors that invoke the rainbow of "Soatsin": sempoalxochitl (cempasuchil/marigold flowers), panchichiual (bread), tamal (tamales), ayojtsopelik (sweet squash), xokotl (fruit), and tlemol ("mole prieto" or "black *mole*," a labor-intensive, sacred dish of pork with black *mole* sauce that is cooked in the ground; this dish is unique to Xochitiotzin's region). "In tonal Tomiketsitsi" sets the stage in the first verse by announcing that the deceased souls are approaching. The poetic voice calls out to one relative, omiteyoj, and, in Castilian, *huesuda* (bony one) to come home.[36] This deceased relative follows the path of cempasuchil flowers scattered on the ground leading to the front door. She consumes the light and food at the altar ("toma la luz y la sal"); this sustenance will give strength and direction for her eventual return to the land of the dead. Xochitiotzin's poetic persona ends by speaking of her own words as a light to guide the ancestor on her way.

"In tonal Tomiketsitsi" highlights the nexus with ancestors, here specifically a female ancestor. The path both directs predecessors back to their homes and points the attention of the living toward deceased relatives. Although most often men direct ceremonies, Xochitiotzin interjects her voice like a religious leader officiating a ceremony in honor of the dead.[37] It is significant that this poem follows "Soatsin," as Xochitiotzin speaks of the power of women's voices and then directs her attention in the following poem to a deceased female ancestor. She connects with a tradition of strength and avers that she is not alone in the power of her voice. Kinships cross over into death and help cultivate the "relationships framed as a sacred responsibility predicated on reciprocity" that Joyce Green and numerous Native feminists propose outside the confines of nation-state teleological and territorial frameworks ("Taking More Account of Indigenous Feminism" 4).[38] Against government depictions of the need to "move forward" toward a future of modernization, the poetic voice of "In tonal tomiketsitsi" looks instead to the past—again, casting a look forward to communal relationships based on reciprocity. She shares food and light from the altar to nourish the relative.

In the fourth poem, "Kanik tlakati in kosemalotl" / "Donde nace el arcoíris" (Where the Rainbow Is Born), Xochitiotzin continues to foreground women's voices. Named in the first line, her poetic persona represents a rainbow with its powerful colors and words:

> Ethel Xochitiotzin Pérez
> Maseual tlale.
> Itech moikpa tlakati Kosemalotl
> Ikpame tlen kitlajkiti nouipil uan nech tlauilia nonakayo.
> ¡xinechiuili se ilpilkatl,
> Ma ki paleui no ijte!
> Ti achtli,
> ti ameyal
> tlani in Malintzi.
> Tetepetla
> Altepetsi kanik tlakati moxayak
> Ye uejkaui tlen tokojkoluan okitlajkitijke motlapoal,
> okichijchijkej komimej,
> tlen kiuika in tlapal, in ajuialis uan in uelika nin tlali.
> ijkuak oajsiko in kastilla tlatlaka seki kiposteki,
> omokajkej oxexelo mo nacayo.
> kineluayotia Contla
> axan motlakayo ikpame omotlalo,
> ikpatl tlen kuika moneluayo.

acuic
axolhuaca
xochayatla
xicotenco
cuatzincola
aztatla
Tlacomulco
xelhua
Juárez
ikpatl tlen kitlajkiti in ayatl, in tilma, in ilpilkatl.
ikpatl tlen kixtilia ajuiak tlilmol
ikpatl tlen moneneloa ika in xochipitsauak uan ueuexayakatl
ikpatl tlen kitlajkiti iyolotsin in Conteco. (7–8)

(Ethel Xochitiotzin Pérez
Indigenous land.
The rainbow is born upon your weaving
Threads that weave my huipil and fill my body with light.
Make me a sash,
give strength to my womb!
You are a seed
you are a spring
at the foot of Malintzin.
Tetepetla
Place where your face is born
A long time ago our ancestors constructed your story,
they made pottery,
which carries the color, flavor, and smell of this earth.
When the Spaniards arrived, they broke some,
shards remained scattered in your body.
Contla is founded
now threads run through your body,

threads that carry your roots.

Juárez,

Aztatla,

Tlacomulco,

Xelhua,

Xicotenco,

Xochayatla,

Cuatzincola,

Acuic,

Axolhuaca.

Threads that weave blankets, *saltillo*, *ceñidores*,

threads that release the aroma of black *mole*,

threads that move to the music of *Xochipitzauatl* and of the *Catrines*,

threads that weave the heart of the *conteco* and the *conteca*.)[39]

The poetic voice equates Xochitiotzin with *tierra morena* (brown land) in Castilian and maseual tlale (Indigenous/campesino land) in Nahuatl. Although it describes her as a landscape, this imagery does not seek to objectify women by fusing their bodies with the scenery. The combination of *moreno* (in the context of Xochitiotzin's poetry used to denote darker phenotypes that *mestizos* conceal) and maseual (Indigenous) mark a racialized subject. Implicit in this description of Xochitiotzin's pride in her territory and skin color is a criticism of those who attempt to "whiten" themselves.[40] This topic surfaces repeatedly in *Tlaoxtika* with descriptions of her body as "tierra morena."

The rainbow—Xochitiotzin's poetry—is born within the land's weaving. This imagery ties together ancestors' artistic production with Xochitiotzin's literature. *Urdimbre* in Castilian can refer to weaving as well as to an intriguing turn in a work of literature, which Xochitiotzin seeks to create through her poetry. These ancestors' threads form her huipil (loose-fitting embroidered blouse or dress). The poetic voice asks to be made a *ceñidor* (a "tightener" or "sash") and for her womb to birth new ideas. She wants her words to "be seed" and "be a spring" at the foot of the Malintzin. In the following line she invokes Tetepetla, now a small archaeological zone near Contla. As mentioned earlier in this chapter, Xochitiotzin's references to the Malintzin challenge the traditional depiction of the Nahua woman as a traitor. From this Indigenous geography Xochitiotzin's "face is born." This area has a long history, and Contla (the name itself derives from komitl or "pot") were known for earthenware. Remembrance of this artisan work is a sensorial experience in which each pot carried the color and aroma of the land. Paralleling the description of Xochitiotzin's body as the earth's hue, the pots are a metaphor for Nahua women.

The poem's center disrupts the creation of pottery, as Spanish colonialism invades and shatters earthenware. Their pieces, representing the history of her people, are scattered throughout Xochitiotzin's body. They are now in shards due to pervasive colonial practices. The name of the volcano Malintzin is significant. Rather than blame Doña Marina for the conquest, Xochitiotzin displaces such depictions and blames the conquest discourse that still prevails in men's treatment of women.

Xochitiotzin's poetic persona relates the founding of the municipality of Contla and its formation from nine smaller communities, described as different threads that carry its roots. In doing so she features an Indigenous descolonial geography: Juárez, Aztatla, Tlacomulco, Xelhua, Xicotenco, Xochayatla, Cuatzincola, Acuic, Axolhuaca (9).[41] This list resembles the series of ceremonial elements in Day of the Dead observations. All the senses converge in the literal and metaphorical weaving together of these communities, threads that unite the unique sights, smells, and sounds of the region: weavers, black *mole*, and the traditional sounds of xochipitzahuatl.[42] This portrayal goes against common depictions of Contla as an area in decline.[43] The poetic voice speaks of a region rich in history and knowledge production for the present. As emphasized in this section, Xochitiotzin looks to the history of her municipality and to her ancestors' traditions as an inspiration for unexpected and untraditional turns in her own literary production. Such a turn emerges in the maize-centered metaphors that she decenters in the poems that follow.

Grinding Words:
Maize Metaphors at the Center of *Tlaoxtika in tlajtol*

"Niknekiskia" marks a shift to emphasize maize.[44] This fifth poem of *Tlaoxtika* can be understood to embody both an address to a lover and an intimate relationship with the word, figuratively represented as maize:

Niknekiskia

Nik nekiskia nies ni amatl,
uan ijkon notech
tej titlakuilos.
Nik nekiskia nies ni metsintli
ijkon tinechmauisos.
Nik nekiskia nies ni tonaltsin,
ijkon ni mitsontlanextilis mo tlajtol.
Nik nekiskia nies ni atsintli,
ijkon ni mitsonkixtilis moamik
Nik nekiskia nies ni neuktli,
ijkon nimitsonuintia.
Niknekiskia nies kuali tlali
Ijkon in achtli uelis nikanaskia.
Niknekiskia nies nisemikak
   xopanistli,
Ijkon nimakaskia semijkak
   xochitlajtolistli. (11)

Quisiera

Quisiera ser papel,
Para que sobre mí
tú escribas.
Quisiera ser luna,
para que me contemples.
Quisiera ser solecito,
para alumbrar tus palabras.
Quisiera ser agua,
para poder saciar tu sed.
Quisiera ser pulque,
para poder embriagarte.
Quisiera ser tierra fértil,
para poder tomar tu semilla.
Quisiera ser eterna
   primavera,
Para darte siempre poesías.
(12)

(I Wish

I wish I were paper
so you could write
on me.
I wish I were the moon,
so that you could contemplate me.
I wish I were a little sun,
to shine on your words.
I wish I were water,
to quench your thirst.
I wish I were pulque,
to make you drunk.

I wish I were fertile soil,

to take in your seed.

I wish I were eternal spring,

To give you poems always.)

The poetic voice begins by stating that she *wishes* or *would like* to be paper, so that the person or thing to which she directs the verses could write on her. Especially in Nahuatl, the conditional mood indicates that some obstacle impedes this relationship. Pervasive discrimination makes literary production more difficult. The symbols of sun, moon, and water appear in the following verses. All these are key elements in corn harvesting as well as calendric indicators of when to harvest. The poetic voice would like to be a fertile land to receive "your seed." Especially in light of the whole collection, "Niknekiskia" can be read as an intimate relationship with the maize crop, and the poetic voice positions herself as a subject with valuable contributions toward a successful harvest. Corn gives Xochitiotzin the capacity to live, think, and produce her literature—the paper to be written on—and in turn she wishes to offer all the elements necessary to achieve an abundant maize crop. The repetition of ni (I) at the beginning and center of every other verse emphasizes Xochitiotzin's own agency and desire to participate in this agricultural production equated with literary production. The erotic nature of the poem relates to how Xochitiotzin and other female writers defy gender norms and expectations. Here she is not a passive recipient of lover's seed (i.e., passive vessel for reproduction) but rather an active agent.

The sixth poem, "Ixtololotsin tlen kitsakuilia ixayak tonantsi intlali" (Eyes That Detain the Face of Our Mother Earth) foregrounds "close observation"[45] that develops in this agricultural and literary creation, the tlachialistli analyzed previously:

Ixtolotsin tlen kitsakuilia ixayak tonantsi intlali

Se tonal oajsik motlachilis,

Onejne ipan nonakayo.

Tlachilis tlen kitsakuilia in kauitl

Ixtololotsin tlen kitlapoa in yolotsin tlen maseual tlalli.

Tlachilis tlen tlajtoa uan mouetska ika in tlanesi.

ika in Malintzi, uan in Cuatlapanga

ika in maime tlan tlajkiti in kosamalotl,
ika in iljuitsintli altepetl.
Tlachilis tlen kixexeloa in ajuyalis in kuauime,
in tiopantsintle,
in mixtle,
in tlajtlakaj,
in tlaxkal.
Tlachilis tlen patlani nochi in altepetsin.
Nejnemi, amo tikauas mikis in kauitl.
Tlachilis tlen patlani nochi in altepetsin.
Tinejnemi, amo tikauas mikis in kauitl. (13)

**Ojos que detienen el rostro
de nuestra madre tierra**
Un día llegó tu mirada,
Caminó por mi cuerpo.
Mirada que detienen el tiempo,
ojos que abren el corazón de la tierra morena.
Mirada que habla y ríe con el crepúsculo,
con la Malintzin, la Cuatlapanga
con las manos que tejen el arco iris,
con la fiesta del pueblo.
Mirada que desprende el aroma de los árboles,
De la iglesia,
De la nube,
De la gente,
De la tortilla.
Mirada que vuela por todos los rumbos.
Camina, no dejes morir el tiempo. (14)

(Eyes That Detain the Face of Our Mother Earth
One day your observation arrived,
It walked over my body.

Observation that detains time

Eyes that open the heart of the dark earth.

Observation that talks and laughs with sunrise,

with Malintzin, and Cuatlapanga

with hands that weave a rainbow,

with village celebrations.

Observation that parses the aromas of the trees,

of the church,

of the cloud,

of the people,

of the tortilla.

Observation that flies over all communities.

Walk on, you will not let time die.

Observation that flies over all communities.

You walk on, you will not let time die.)

This poem was inspired by an art exhibition Xochitiotzin attended in Tlaxcala.[46] The paintings depicted Tlaxcalan landscapes such as the Malintzin. Ekphrastic verses describe the act of viewing this landscape art as "detaining time" and leading the speaker to find her own body. Tellingly, as the "observation" or "look" is said to "walk over" her body, it is as if the artwork gazes back at the speaker—making her, the viewer, the exhibit.[47] This reciprocal observation emphasizes an affective connection between the speaker and her surroundings, which calls to mind the paralleling of the speaker's body with the *tierra morena* (dark-skinned land), maseual tlalli (Indigenous land), in "Donde nace el arcoíris." Cuatlapanga from the sixth verse is the name of a small volcano near the Malintzin. In Tlaxcala, this volcano is also called "el cerro del rostro" (mountain of the face) because it resembles a yelling face. As with the Malintzin, there are multiple narratives associated with Cuatlapanga, among them a story of golden church bells having been hidden within the volcano's crater during the Mexican Revolution. Xochitiotzin's poem imagines the landscape with a face—not only in the literal image suggested by the silhouette of Cuatlapanga but also in the sense of being able to communicate narratives. The story regarding the golden bells reminds community members of the destruction and theft brought on by the Revolution, providing a counternarrative to laudatory remembrances of official government discourse.

Within the body-landscape symbiosis of Xochitiotzin's poetry, humans are not superior to their physical surroundings. Both Xochitiotzin, with her ability to observe, and the landscape, which communicates histories through its own face, enact a "look" that produces poetry (the rainbow) and constitutes a sensorial experience that goes beyond physical eyesight or solely cognition. In its associations with literally walking as well as careful thought, tinejnemi (you walk) in the final verse highlights an affective intelligence. This observation leads the poetic voice to explore her own physicality and relationality. Rather than an "out of body" experience or fixed gaze, the "look" described is one that helps her to know her body. This close attention—nurtured by the maize in the tortillas referenced in the third to last verse—keeps time from dying because it can then be transmuted into artistic production that will survive the artist's death.

"Xochitlaoltsin" / "Flor de maíz" (Flowered Maize) is at the center of the fifteen total poems and is key to understanding *Tlaoxtika in tlajtol*. This poem focuses on corn as a metaphor for writing and the Nahuatl language:

Xochitlaoltsin

Titlaoya motlajtol itech in ilkaualis
    Yalua,
    Oniktlati no tlajtol
    Ijkon amo nikaki motlajtolmej.
    onia uan onikilka,
    nikmati ke nikatki.
    In mayanalis in papalotl nechyolchikajti.
    kuentla kichiaj notekitl,
    in tonaltsin,
    metsintli,
    atsintli,
    kitlamaka no yolo.

    ¡X' kitta!
    Mo nakayo motema imaseualtlajtol,

tlapoualis kitlakijti mo tlajtol.
Neluame kitemoa mo xayak,
uan kitlatia in kauitl. (15)

Flor de maíz
Desgranas tu voz en el olvido.
Ayer,
escondí mi voz,
para no escuchar tus palabras.
Emigré del olvido,
sé que existo.
El hambre es la mariposa que me acompaña
afuera esperan mi trabajo.
sol
luna,
Agua,
Alimentan mi corazón.

¡Mira!
Tu cuerpo se baña de voces morenas,
la historia teje tu voz.
Raíces que buscan tu rostro,
y ocultan el tiempo. (16)

(**Maize Flower**
You unkernel your voice in oblivion
> yesterday,
> I hid my voice [language],
> so as not to hear your words.
> I have left behind oblivion,
> I know I exist.
> Hunger is a butterfly that strengthens me of heart.
> Outside, they await my work,

sun,

moon,

water,

nourish my heart.

Look!
Your body fills up with Nahuatl,
history will weave your voice.
Roots search out your face,
and conceal time.)

This poem begins by once more using the metaphor, common throughout Nahuatl variants, that associates maize cultivation with writing. Humans are also composed of corn, and the writer is made of her poetry. They are inseparable. The removal and (re)collection of corn kernels represent speech and script, in lines like rows on the cob—but in the poem these words are lost in oblivion or forgetting (in Nahuatl the word kiilkaua, in the fifth verse, denotes "leaving behind memories"). Knowledge that not a single kernel should go to waste makes this loss especially tragic,[48] and with this metaphor Xochitiotzin suggests that not a word of what she states in her poetry should be squandered. The displacement of tlajtol (language) alludes to the marginalization of the Nahuatl language in general, but also more specifically to Xochitiotzin's marginalization as both a Nahua woman and writer. She feels that she has important messages to communicate through her literature, but these messages are not heard; they are memories left behind. Outside pressures and criticism have led the poem's speaker at certain points in her life to give up writing, or at least not to share it openly—as is reflected in the third verse, when she states, "Oniktlati notlajtol" (I hid my language).[49] As mentioned earlier, tlajtoli in Nahuatl means language, individual words, and discourse in general.[50] With these different significations of tlajtol, Xochitiotzin refers to both the systemic marginalization of Nahuas and their language, and also to a personal experience connected to her individual words and discourse.

A poignant reflection on the effects of this marginalization occurs in the third and fourth verses, when the speaker confesses to having hidden her voice in order not to hear "tus palabras" (your words). This could refer to not wanting to hear the words of those who discriminate against Nahuas as well as to Xochitiotzin's own prior internalization of this discrimination and avoidance of the Nahuatl language. The poetic voice fears that people might mock her for speaking Nahuatl. The enjambment "yesterday" is set apart to emphasize that the temptation to abandon her tongue has passed. She emigrates out of "oblivion/forgetting." This image relates to Xochitiotzin's own migration from her hometown in Contla to the capital of Tlaxcala. Xochitiotzin was tempted to conceal her background when she moved to the city to study at the University of Tlaxcala.[51] She now resists this temptation and accepts her language as an ancestral gift, and, from the perspective of tlaixpan, Xochitiotzin uses it to question sexism within and outside her community.

In the ninth verse Xochitiotzin's poetic persona speaks of hunger as a butterfly, which could represent a desire for her xochitlajtoli to take flight and be known. She then states that "kuentla kichiaj notekitl" (outside they await my work). Kuentla (outside) plays on a resemblance to the name of Xochitiotzin's home municipality of Contla. The poem's speaker alternates between addressing an "outside" public and directing her voice toward her own community. She describes the hunger she feels as stronger than physical famine. This poetic persona regains strength from the sun, moon, and water, listed in the final verses of the first stanza. As mentioned previously, these are the key elements in maize production, and as such they serve as a metaphor for literary production and spiritual sustenance.

In the second stanza the poetic persona once more accentuates observation with the single line "¡X' kitta!" (Look!). She speaks of "your body" being bathed in synesthetic voices that evoke brown. In the poem "Donde nace el arcoíris," these "brown voices" represent a racialized body with an intimate connection to surroundings. "Xochitlaoltsin" critiques those who attempt to hide their phenotype and Native cultural practices by using cosmetics and changing their clothes. Regardless of what they do, the poetic voice asserts that Native heritage survives.[52] Nahua characteristics embody a history that weaves "your voice." The roots "hide time" because they carry a history that needs to be known. With the mixing perspectives between nej/*yo* (I) and tej/*tú* (you), the poetic voice could be speaking to herself and to her own words. "Your voice" and "your face" are the voice and face of Xochitiotzin's poetic persona and can also refer to the voice and face of community members.

"Achtlitonaltsin" / "Semilla de sol" (Seed of the Sun), the eighth poem, expands on this communal voice:

Kajkoki in achtle tonaltsi,	Levanta la semilla de sol,
Kitlapoua ueyatl in ilkauilis.	abre el mar del olvido
¿kox moteskatl petlani?	¿Es tu espejo que brilla?
¡kema!	¡sí!
xnexti in ajuyalis in nakayotl	Descubre el aroma del cuerpo
xkixmati in metsintli.	Conoce la luna.
Ye kiuintia in xochitlakatsin,	Ella embriaga al poeta,
Tlajtol kualtsitsi	Seduce las palabras.
Tlanesi ijtek in mixtle in nektle	Amanece entre las nubes del pulque
yejua kiteki in neljuatl in nakayotl.	ellos cortan la raíz del cuerpo.
Poliui in kauitl	Se pierde el tiempo
¿tlika?	¿Por qué?
¿Tlika tlatia motlajtol?	¿Por qué ocultar tu voz?
tla motoka moyekoa tlaol.	Si tu nombre sabe a maíz.
¿tlike mopatla moneljuayo?	¿Por qué cambiar tu raíz
tla in tlaltsintli tlajtoa in te	Si la tierra habla de ti?
¿tlika tikixtilia mokuikatil?	¿Por qué desplazar tu canto
tla in kauitl nejnemi ika ye.	Si el tiempo camina con él?
¿Tlika amo tiktoka motlajtol?	¿Por qué no sembrar tu voz?
tla mostla niknechikos mo xokotl.	Si mañana recogeré tu fruto.
¿tlika amo timouintia?	¿Por qué no embriagarnos?
Uan timopoliuiste ika in sitlallimej (17)	Y perdernos con las estrellas. (18)

(She raises the seed of the sun,
she opens the sea of forget.

Is it your mirror that shines?
>Yes!
Discover the smell of the body
acquaint yourself with the moon.
It intoxicates poets,
Seducing words.
The sun rises among clouds of pulque
they cut the root from the body.
>Time is lost.
Why?
Why hide your voice?
If your name tastes of maize.
Why alter your root
If the precious earth speaks of you?
Why displace your song
If time walks with it?
Why not sow your voice?
If tomorrow I'll gather your fruit.
Why not get drunk?
And lose ourselves among the stars.)

As in "Niknekiskia," the poetic voice overturns the metaphor of the male farmer by positioning herself as the sower, and by extension the writer. In the initial stanza, Xochitiotzin focuses on the pressure to forget her roots. The temptation to *salir adelante* (to get ahead) in Tlaxcala, as anthropologist Jacqueline Messing argues, propels attempts to discard signs of indigeneity (559–60). Public lexicon features "verbs of motion, action, and change" to indicate leaving behind the traditional in order to become modern (560). In the second stanza, Xochitiotzin rejects this discrimination, asking a rhetorical question of why one would stop speaking. Eschewing the shades of backwardness with which Nahuas are typically portrayed, she cultivates knowledge production from her community as part of a dynamic process.

The poem's title, "Achtlitonaltsin" / "Semilla de sol," foregrounds corn. The Nahuatl language commonly associates maize with the sun, and here maize is described as the sun's seed. Notably, achtli or xinachtli, the choice corn seed, is another word for semen. In turn, women are traditionally associated with the moon and its weaker light. Nonetheless, Xochitiotzin claims the space of the sun and seed for women, metaphorically representing the connection of corn with literary production and demanding a forum for Nahua women's potent voices and writings. The word for "choice corn seed" in Nahuatl can mean "heart," and with it Xochitiotzin constructs an affective space of cognition interwoven with emotions and rituals petitioning a plentiful crop.

The one-word lines of ¡kema! / ¡sí! (yes!) and ¿tlika? / ¿Por qué? (why?) underscore that markers of Nahua identity still surface despite attempts to suppress them. The *sí* and *por qué* rise in opposition to those who would cut the root of Nahua cultural practices. As the corn harvest reemerges from death in its agricultural cycle, constant since the Spanish invasion, Nahua knowledge production will also continue to thrive. The mirror similarly evinces acceptance of Nahua identity, against a "sea of forget" that disassociates the poetic voice from her Indigenous perspectives and practices. This sea shines like a mirror reflecting the deep history from which she comes. This look again discovers the aroma of the body and closely observes its surroundings. It is an observation that transcends the everyday, symbolized in the waking amid clouds of pulque. Nonetheless, "ellos" (they, colonizers) interpose and cut "the root from the body." Time, in other words historical remembrance, is lost in this violence. As in the previous poem, "Flor de maíz," this severance symbolizes the epistemic and physical violence exercised against Nahua populations. Like the koyomej depicted within Huastecan literature, "they" are those who wield a colonial discourse.

Like the corn crop, this history can be recuperated. This is the focus of the second stanza. The poetic voice repeats the question tlica / ¿por qué? directed toward those who would deny their Native history. The question implies that it would be senseless to hide her voice and not speak Nahuatl. The poetic voice asserts the power of her words that grow with the strength of maize. Throughout Nahua regions the lines on a page are described as furrows in the fields. The poetic voice argues that Nahua women sow valuable words on the page. Each "why?" confronts the desire to conceal Indigeneity: Why hide "your voice"? Why try to change roots? Why displace the community songs? Why not plant "your voice"? These words bring one to a heightened experience, symbolized by being inebriated and losing oneself "among the stars." The tlika of each line calls the reader to question discrimination and to value Indigenous knowledge production, an idea that is more fully explored in the concluding poems.

Entanglements: Articulation of Nahua Identity in the Concluding Poems of *Tlaoxtika*

The final poems explore an inward-glancing dialogue between the speaker and her surroundings. In "Malinalli" / "Enredadera" (Entanglement), the poetic voice addresses the word "entangling" her heart. She speaks to "the word" in the second person informal *tú*:

Tlajtol tlen tikmalina noyolotsin	Palabra que enredas mi corazón
tiktemoa itech in mesintli	¿Qué buscas en la luna?
¡Xijsa!	¡Despierta!
timahuilti itech nonauak,	Juega conmigo,
amo ximopolo,	no te pierdas,
amo ximopolo,	no te pierdas,
amo. (21)	no. (22)

(Word entangling my heart
What do you seek in the moon?
Awake!
play with me,
don't get lost,
don't get lost,
don't.)

The poetic voice asks "the word" what it seeks in the moon and at the poem's center exclaims that it must "awake!" This petition stresses the imperative not to leave the word or the Nahuatl language dormant. The poetic voice tells this word to play with her and not to be lost, as is emphasized via the repetition in the final three verses. As analyzed in the previous chapters, poliui commonly refers to linguicide: polijtikaj tlajtoli (the word is being lost). Xochitiotzin counters this loss with tlaoxtika in tlajtol (shelling words).

The book title's use of the present progressive emphasizes that this shelling and grinding of words is happening now. A categorical no in the final monosyllabic line of "Malinalli" defies those who eradicate the language. The poem's title is especially significant since Malinalli (entanglement) is popularly considered to be Doña Marina's original name before baptism, and Marina (from María) was chosen because of its phonetic similarity.[53] The poetic voice in "Malinalli" breaks with depictions of Doña Marina as a traitor, or one engaged in sexual "entanglements," and instead calls for a reawakening of Nahua women's words/writing.

Xochitiotzin continues reflecting on Nahua identities in "Teskatl" / "Espejo" (Mirror):

Mo ixtololotsin okitak notesca,	Tus ojos vieron mi espejo,
teskatl temiki,	espejo lleno de sueños,
temiktli amo kipia xayak.	sueños sin rostro.
Xayakatsin.	Rostro,
tlajtol tlapokjtok. (25)	palabra abierta. (26)

(Your eyes saw my mirror,
mirror full of dreams,
dreams without a face.
Precious face,
word that is open.)

Ojos and ixtololotsin visually resemble what they signify with their double *o* and triple *o o o* vowels: the eyes. This visual on the page imitates a looking glass, as though the eyes of the speaker were gazing into the mirror and being reflected back to the reader by its surface. Mirror imagery is tied to the poem's play on point of reference. Keeping in mind the dynamics of a reflection, the line "your eyes saw my mirror" could be interpreted as an internal dialogue of Xochitiotzin's poetic persona with herself. She wishes to see this mirror full of dreams fulfilled. These dreams lack a face, symbolic of them not yet having been realized. The poetic voice sets "Xayakatsin" (precious or revered face) apart in its own verse for emphasis with a reverential suffix. This "face" is then described as "tlajtol tlapokjtok" (open words). These words are "open" because the poetic persona aims to open up, realize, and put a face on her aspirations. She has the power to shape these words and desires. While *Tlaoxtika* emphasizes the importance of language and ancestors, these connections to the past do not restrict her. Xochitiotzin stressed this in a personal interview, where she spoke of how she seeks to break with "lo trillado" (hackneyed representations) in previous Nahua poetry and to provide her own unique contributions in Nahuatl and Castilian.[54]

Near the end of *Tlaoxtika*, in "Xolko temiktl" / "Surco de sueños" (Furrows of Dreams), Xochitiotzin's poetic persona alludes to the physical and emotional abuse she has suffered within and outside her community:

Ipa in yeyantsi oajsik in chokalis
Oteten in tepetl
Non ichpopokatsi okipolo ni ajauil
Okikajteua se xolko temiktl
Nikan amo yen tej
Mostla tikalakis ipan tlanex
¡Xnejnemi! Xkaua ipan nin amatl moyolkokolis. (27)

Sobre esta hacienda llegó un mar de llanto
inundó la montaña.
Esa niña perdió sus juegos,
dejó un surco de sueños.
Aquí no eres tú
Mañana entrarás al crepúsculo,
¡Camina! Deja en el papel las cicatrices de tu llanto. (28)

(A sea of tears swept over this *hacienda*
flooding the mountain.
That little girl lost her games,
leaving behind a furrow of dreams.
Here you are not yourself
Tomorrow you will enter dusk,
Walk on! Leave the scars of your weeping ["heart-illness"] on paper.)

The poetic voice tells of anguish on the *hacienda*, or large estate on which Nahuas are commonly employed for low wages. The suffering of these workers inundates the community: "Oteten in tepetl" (It flooded the mountain). Water and hill/mountain constitute a town or city (the meaning of altepetl, as mentioned in previous chapters), but here water, linked symbolically with tears, is a destructive force. The *haciendas* seized large tracts of land, thus displacing (or "flooding") community members and in turn hiring them under unjust conditions.

The oppression undergone by Xochitiotzin's poetic persona parallels the author's own experiences with trauma. As a young girl, Xochitiotzin was abused by a man in her community.[55] The recovery from that occurrence has in part fed her desire to uproot the discourses of male domination that fuel such incidents. She represents the effects of this through the poetic voice of "Xolko temiktl." As a child this poetic persona "lost her games" and "left furrows of dreams." Her innocence and youthful optimism were stolen and she is no longer herself: "Nikan amo yen tej" (Here you are not yourself). The poetic voice does not remain in a victimized state of mind but rather exclaims in the final line: "¡Xnejnemi! Xkaua ipan nin amatl moyolkokolis" (Walk on! Leave the scars of your weeping on paper). "Leaving the scars of your weeping" on paper symbolizes the cathartic transference of past trauma onto the page; this affective response is accentuated in the word moyolkokolis (your heart-illness). In this turn, the verses themselves visually suggest the image of both the furrows in a field and scar lines across the paper. With the imagery of furrows and the water that originates from tears, the poem hints at a possible renewal through the expression of this anguish—as embodied by both Xochitiotzin's personal traumas and the generalized suffering of those in her community under dire economic circumstances—and at a strength cultivated to allow them to walk, xnejnemi. This walk is symbolic of the active Nahua participation in confronting economic and social inequities, as well as of the knowledge production that the root nemi suggests in Nahuatl. As I have analyzed in this section, Xochitiotzin in the final poems accentuates her own articulation of a Nahua identity in which women have a potent voice and denounce discrimination.

Beyond "Receptacles of Tradition"

In this chapter, I introduced contemporary Nahua female authors and offered a close observation of Xochitiotzin's *Tlaoxtika in tlajtol*. I analyzed the three main themes of the past and remembrance within the first poems, maize metaphors at the center of the text, and the articulation of a Nahua identity within the final poems. I further demonstrated how key Nahua perspectives—principally ixtlamatilistli (knowledge with the face) and its companion concepts tlachialistli (observance), yoltlajlamikilistli (knowledge with the heart), and tlaixpan (that which is in front)—operate with Xochitiotzin's poems. Xochitiotzin transforms recurrent metaphors within Nahua poetry to position women as decision makers within and outside their communities; they offer wise solutions that foreground close observance and ancestral knowledge production. In effect, *Tlaoxtika in tlajtol* points toward new directions in Nahua literary production that debunk the erroneous presupposed absence of Nahua female writers described in the introduction to this chapter.

Despite having more publications, women of other Native Nations have met with similar challenges in distributing their works. A case in point, of the seventeen writers who have received the Premio Nezahualcoyotl, Maya novelist Marisol Ceh Moo and Zapotec poet Natalia Toledo are the only women among the awardees. Ceh Moo was the first woman to receive the Premio de Literaturas Indígenas de América (PLIA), now the most prestigious prize for Indigenous literary production across Abiayala, at the Guadalajara Book Fair in 2019. Not one to mince words, she brought to everyone's attention in her acceptance speech that, even though she had already chosen her chair, she was moved to the end of the table. In interviews Ceh Moo tells of similar micro- and macroaggressions throughout her career. As she herself suggested, the organizer perhaps had no intention of placing her on the periphery, but that does not matter. There is systemic discrimination against Native women of which the public must be made aware. While Native female writers have gained extensive access to publication venues, Nahua women are considerably less known in these circles. This chapter identifies some of the reasons why, among them a resistance both inside and outside their communities to their participation. A propitious setting would entail more Nahua women entering positions of leadership in which they themselves are the editors, like Ateri Miyawatl at the head of Originaria, deciding what gets published and assisting new authors—a structure that elides approval of the "male editors of the sun."

There exists fear that critique of male chauvinism within Native Nations could hinder struggles for autonomy and reparations. Mirroring accounts by Leanne Betasamosake Simpson's and numerous Native feminists' experiences shared at the beginning of this chapter, one male author told me that first Nahua authors must win the fight for recognition before turning inward to critique community practices. According to him, it is a conversation that needs to occur, but now is not the time. The postponement becomes a perpetual excuse that prevents it from being addressed. This is obviously not an issue restricted to Indigenous Nations but one that encompasses the globe. Rather than reinforcing stereotypes, addressing the problem instead defies the persistent idea that Nahuas themselves cannot analyze and question their own communities. It also shows the diversity of voices within societies popularly believed to be homogeneous and monolithic. Nahua female writers do not add to a discourse of victimization but rather act as agents of change. Since they are firsthand observers, who better than they to offer solutions?

Through the texts explored in this chapter, we see strategies of self-representation common to women's literary movements in many parts of the globe, such as the overturning of metaphors that attempt to objectify women and the deployment of perspectives that break with male-dominated approaches. They help us question the artificial borders that nation-states attempt to impose and upend the nationalist discourses that most often favor male subjects and ignore the great diversity of languages and communities—Nations in the proper meaning of the word—within state borders. This cultural production elucidates topics such as linguistic diversity, migration, and gender across the globe. The present study points to the importance of seriously engaging with this literature, which underscores the multiplicity of voices and perspectives within Abiayala, as well as among Nahuas themselves.

A promising area of research that this analysis suggests is future studies not only of contemporary Nahua women authors from the last two decades but also of the artists' works from the 1980s and earlier. A different narrative could be told about the beginnings of the Nahua literary movement than the one painted by the selection of a near majority of male authors in *Estudios de Cultura Náhuatl* and other publications. For example, Frances Karttunen points to Isabel Ramírez Castañeda, Julia Jiménez González, and Luz Jiménez as key figures in the beginnings of contemporary Nahuatl literature. Likely there are more authors whose works should be studied as well as numerous authors like Xochitiotzin who write without receiving a serious reading.

Giving space to the dissenting views of Nahua female writers enriches Nahua and Indigenous studies at large. They join publications that similarly condemn gender discrimination, such as those by LGBTQ+ authors from

Nahua communities, like Mardonio Carballo in Mexico City, and from other Native Nations, such as Víctor Cata in Juchitán, or Manuel Tzoc and Adela Delgado Pop in Iximulew (Guatemala). Nahua women today expand the horizons of contemporary Native literatures and Abiayala cultural production. Representative of these writers, Xochitiotzin seeks to correct sexist male lineages of Nahua literature and create a space for women's voices. Nahua women are not passive "receptacles" of tradition, as stereotypically portrayed, but rather they are Serpent-Plumed knowledge producers who shell, grind, question, transform, and innovatively rewrite the knowledges both within and beyond their communities.

Chapter 4

Words of Water

Fluid Nahua Identities in Judith Santopietro's *Palabras de agua*

Nahua poet Judith Santopietro grew up in Córdoba, Veracruz. There she often heard her aunt tell the story of a family friend who visited his *compadre* (kin / close friend) to seek his daughter's hand in marriage. When the young man arrived, the family offered him a bed to stay the night. They said tamales would be served in the morning. During the evening, awakened by sounds outside the wood-thatched home, he saw through slits in the wall that the *compadre*'s family had transformed into mapachimej, raccoons. They were nahuales, people with the ability to turn into animals. He watched in horror through the night as the family raced back and forth from the cornfields. They regurgitated maize and used this peculiar masa to make the tamales promised for the morning meal. At the break of dawn, Santopietro's family friend, now frightened and dismayed, invented an excuse to leave. He hurriedly left—abandoning his plans to wed the raccoon-nahual daughter.

    I begin with this story because it was influential in Santopietro's life and work—particularly in her book of poetry *Palabras de agua* (2010), where it serves as inspiration for a bilingual Castilian-Nahuatl poem titled "Izcaltitla." Her aunt shared it in Castilian, but Santopietro discovered later that this history was likely told originally in Nahuatl.[1] Around 2005, after they had moved to Mexico City, her aunt mentioned in passing that Santopietro's paternal grandmother spoke the language. This knowledge had been hidden away, while the family celebrated their Italian surname. In interviews, Santopietro quips that, beyond her last name, there was little presence of Italian heritage in the family.[2] Throughout her youth, Santopietro believed her aunt's Nahua/nahual narrative. Today she still believes in it—not necessarily for its literal sense but rather for the narrative's deeper significance. Like the nahuales with the power to transform, she found in these words, in Nahua knowledge production and history, the determination to confront racism in her own family and society writ large. Santopietro's aunt related this story as a quaint superstition long abandoned. This deracination is symbolized in the young man's flight from the home upon discovering nahuales, as though hurrying along the path of *mestizaje* in which white and Indigenous races fuse until the markers of Indigeneity (i.e., language, dress, diet, beliefs, and so forth) are subsumed or mythologized.

When Santopietro's aunt told her that her grandmother spoke Nahuatl, Santopietro replied that the family was Nahua. Her aunt, offended, rebutted the assertion that Santopietro's grandmother was Indigenous or Nahua, as if unwilling to herself be associated with this heritage. Unlike her aunt, Santopietro recounts this narrative to underscore the living knowledge production of contemporary Nahuas, epitomized in the nahuales' capacity to turn into animals and closely observe their surroundings. Instead of being scared away by such empowerment, as the young man is frightened by the shapeshifting nahuales and her aunt is driven to distance herself from her own heritage, she embraces her family history and her Nahua identity. Santopietro evidences this shift in the Nahuatlization of her artistic name and Facebook profile as Juditzin Santopietro or Juditzin Santopietritzin (the reverential/diminutive -tzin resembles -*ita* in Castilian, roughly the equivalent of "Juditita" and "Santopietrita"). For Santopietro, -tzin connotes endearment and humility in the sense of being in contact with people and facilitating workshops.

In this chapter, I examine how in *Palabras de agua* Santopietro contests the prevalent view in Mexico that one must speak Nahuatl to be Nahua. Her family is from the Nahua region las Altas Montañas de Veracruz. They moved to the industrial city of Córdoba, where Santopietro was born. She did not grow up with the Nahuatl language. Because of her background, she meets resistance to her self-identification as Nahua from within and outside Nahua communities. There is suspicion on both sides as to why someone would assume a marginal identity unless that person carries the "inescapable" markers of Indigeneity such as having grown up speaking a Native language.[3] In response to these critiques, I argue that Santopietro's *Palabras de agua* proposes a fluid conception of who is Nahua. She combats the pervasive depiction of Indigenous peoples as "endangered" and opens a Serpent-Plumed path for Nahuas who do not speak the language due to centuries of state-sponsored discriminatory practices.

As a theoretical framework, I continue to deploy tlaixpan, and the perspective this term communicates of the past in front. Santopietro brings to the forefront her grandparents' knowledges, which are rooted in the experience and intelligent affectivity analyzed in previous chapters. She does so to break with a Western "Modernity" that disrupts that connection with her past. *Palabras de agua* represents a nearly decade-long search of her origins with poems written from 2001 to 2010. This book retraces her Nahua heritage and questions government-promoted categories for deciding whether one is Indigenous (enough).

Santopietro's work contests the primacy given the Nahuatl language, which can benefit Indigenous and non-Indigenous elites with access to academia-approved writing. Prioritizing the language risks divorcing academic and literary circles from territorial struggles. On this point María de Jesús (Marichuy) Patricio Martínez—prominent Nahua activist, former presidential candidate, and spokesperson for the National Indigenous Congress (CNI)—avers that federal and state administrations divide potential trans-Indigenous alliances by turning Native peoples against one another.[4] Government entities cause rifts through state-sponsored programs, such as literary awards that laud a select few at the expense of their communities.

This issue becomes increasingly complex when one considers that there are writers who grew up speaking Nahuatl but who are not Nahua. They lived on their families' large estates or in Colonia Roma–like homes in which they learned the language from their *hacienda* or domestic workers.[5] In these contexts, the children of wealthy families learned Nahuatl or other Native languages to "better manage" their future workforce. (This was not the case with Santopietro's great grandparents who were maseualmej and dedicated their lives to working the land). As the estate arrangement demonstrates, Indigenous languages can be used to exercise political and economic control—a tradition that stretches back to the sixteenth century.[6] Continuing to place primacy on the Nahuatl language at once provincializes it as something only "true Indigenous" people of remote communities speak, but it also obscures the historical complexities by which Nahuatl was politicized for the benefit of non-Indigenous communities. Thus, for example, state-sponsored programs and institutions, like the Instituto Nacional de Lenguas Indígenas (INALI), tend to move away from wider territorial struggles toward limited cultural and linguistic revindications.

As explored at length in previous chapters, discrimination persists against Nahuas, particularly against those proficient in Nahuatl.[7] Such oppression arguably far exceeds the marginalization one may face for claiming Nahua heritage without having grown up speaking the language. Nonetheless, Yásnaya Elena Aguilar Gil and María de Jesús Patricio Martínez warn that excessive focus on language—although still vitally important—weakens alliances among Native Nations and with non-Native communities. The divisions along linguistic and dialectical differences obscure Indigenous alliances stretching back centuries. Nahuas, Totonacos, Ñhähñus, and Tepehuas in the Huasteca Veracruzana share more in common, given their physical proximity, than do Nahuas in the Huasteca with Nahuas in Guerrero (for more on this, see chapter 1). Santopietro touches upon broader synergies in her poetry by foregrounding solidarity with Zapotecs, Mixes, Polish, and Valencians in *Palabras de agua*, even translating one of the poems into Catalan with the help of poet Pere Bessó i González. Through her work Santopietro establishes a reciprocal relationship with her family's past as a living entity that guides through a dynamic interplay of trans-Indigenous and non-Indigenous dialogues. Santopietro is learning the Nahuatl language to give back through remembrance rather than to extract exotic metaphors or overidealize that past.

Her work, however, reflects more than a critical reexamination of language. Much like Xochitiotzin's *Tlaoxtika in tlajtol* (see chapter 3), Santopietro's poetry dismantles the patronizing attitude directed toward female Nahua writers, who are dismissed with the comment, "Qué bonito que escriban" (It's so nice [literally "pretty"] that they write). Even when Nahua women grow up speaking Nahuatl, their proficiency is deemed a "kitchen Nahuatl" fit for domestic spaces, but not for "universal" literature. This dismissal goes further with Santopietro, as some authors refuse to acknowledge she is Nahua.

Santopietro began to openly identify as Nahua in 2010, after an international conference in New Delhi, India.[8] At the conference she met people from Native Nations in Australia. They were Indigenous without speaking a Native language and recognized Santopietro as Indigenous. In Northern Abiayala and Australia, in part because fewer people speak Native languages, greater prominence is given to narratives that trace one's origins, land claims, theoretical lenses, and ethical orientations.[9] These histories dismantle nation-state totalizing discourses and assert autonomy. In Northern Abiayala (Turtle Island), such narratives confront the colonial legacy of American Indian boarding schools (the rough equivalent to *albergues* or *internados* in Mexico) in which children were forcibly stripped of their languages and anything deemed Indigenous, a process more far-reaching and "successful" in Northern Abiayala than Mexico to the extent that the number of speakers of Native languages was decimated.[10] Proficiency in Native languages is not inherently liberating, and, as Yásnaya Elena Aguilar Gil warns, can become a tool to weaken Indigenous movements.[11] Due to the traumatic history and experiences associated with them, speaking these languages in unsafe spaces can in fact harm personal health if promoted separate from communal support and isolated from wider demands for justice and reparations.[12]

The nahual narrative retold by Santopietro's aunt represents a Nahua ancestral connection for Santopietro. As Sandra Gonzales posits in "Colonial Borders, Native Fences," such narratives serve to transgress nation-state borders and foreground Native networks among different lands, peoples, and practices that colonial and nationalist myths divide and dole out. These narratives show that "what is now called 'the Americas' were once vibrantly interconnected" (309–10). Santopietro's own life represents this bridging across multiple borders. She has guided projects to amplify the histories of Nahuas in New York, formed the magazine *Iguanazul* to share Native publications from across Abiayala, completed an MA in Iberian and Latin American languages and cultures at the University of Texas at Austin, studied creative writing at the University of Houston, lived in Bolivia to study Indigenous movements there, resided for years in Oaxaca, and completed a residency in the International Writing Program at the University of Iowa in 2022.[13] She has worked with New York City Nahuas in a vital South-South by Northeast dialogue. The two Castilian-Nahuatl poems analyzed in depth in this chapter were published in *The Brooklyn Rail* in New York with only the Nahuatl and English translations.[14] Santopietro's work questions the arbitrary borders imposed by essentialist nation-state policies.

Words of Water: A Decade-Long Search of Origins

Before examining the two Castilian-Nahuatl poems in depth, I give an overview of *Palabras de agua* to situate these poems within the work as a whole. The book begins with a dedication to Santopietro's family that, in recalling the past in a specific geographical setting, calls attention to the poet's concern with heritage: "A mis padres, a mi familia nacida el siglo

XIX en Boca del Monte e Ixhuatlán, Veracruz" (To my parents, to my family born in the nineteenth century in Boca del Monte and Ixhuatlán, Veracruz; 9). The idea of a "return" or "revisiting" of her Nahua heritage grows as the text progresses, or, more accurately, as the poetic voice recognizes the influence of that past on the present and future. Santopietro introduces this exploration of origins with epigraphs quoting Eduardo Galeano and *I Ching*. Galeano refers to the impossibility of utopias but stresses that they still give something to strive toward. His words allude to the EZLN and their seeking of a "world where many worlds fit," a moment of realization for many authors, including Santopietro, that Native Nations are not a distant memory. Similarly, the second epigraph from *I Ching* states, "El retorno sirve para el conocimiento de sí mismo" (The return allows the knowledge of oneself; 11). The journey itself produces knowledge and brings the past to the present. In effect, this search of origins is a recurrent trope in *Palabras* that positions the past continually in front.

The text is divided into five sections, each one showing an increasing recognition of Santopietro's Nahua heritage. After an overview of the book, I focus my analysis principally on two poems she translated, with the help of Nahua poet Sixto Cabrera González, into the contemporary Nahuatl of Soledad Atzompa, Veracruz. The first, "Estela de voces" / "Neskayo tlajtoltij" (Stella of Voices), is only five verses in length; the second, "Izcaltitla," is eleven verses. Both are in the fourth section, "Se incendia la palabra, 2008–2010" (The Word Is Ignited, 2008–2010). Together they reflect a generative exchange that serves as a model for trans-Indigenous dialogues. The conversations between Santopietro and Cabrera González constitute a South-South descolonial dialogue, as Silvia Rivera Cusicanqui would describe it, among two Native poets in Mexico.

The five sections of *Palabras de agua* stretch nearly a decade from 2001 to 2010. The first section, "Raíz de vuelo, 2001–2009" (Root of Flight, 2001–2009), consists of fourteen poems that vary in length from nine verses to longer poems extending to three pages. The trope of flight mixes with a search for one's roots—a continual motion upward and simultaneously downward—to describe the poetic voice's identity. Those roots serve as strength to move forward and metaphorically fly. From this first section, the eponymous poem "Raíz de vuelo" (Root of Flight) is dedicated to people who share with Santopietro "el viaje de cuentos y leyendas" (the journey of stories and legends; 19). These stories are not exotic relics but instead narratives that aid in knowing oneself. The poetic voice speaks of a "sonrisa de carbón que emerge de las manos" (carbon smile that emerges from the hands) to describe the writing on the page like the black soot left by fire (19). This metaphor of fire and its residual soot represent literary production throughout the text. The poetic voice stands before a fire of memory that can reignite. Rekindling occurs in "esta tierra parida de los ojos" (this land born of eyes; 19) that alludes to key images of the land and eyes within the Castilian-Nahuatl poem "Izcaltitla," analyzed at length later in this chapter. The poetic voice continues, "el colibrí asido a las ramas / bebe por su túnel de garganta estrecha / para despertarnos en el umbral de la carcajada del cuervo" (the hummingbird clung to the branches / drinks through its tunnel of narrow throat / to wake us in the threshold of crow guffaws; 20). As seen in Natalio Hernández's *Patlani*, the hummingbird, with its extended beak like a quill, suggests the writing of ancestral narratives. The alliteration of the *c* (such as in *chi*sporroteo [the crackle of the fire], *crepúsculo* [twilight], and pór*ti*co *co*nstante de *chi*cha*r*ras [constant portico of cicadas]) is reminiscent of the crackling sound of the fire symbolic and metonymic of community wisdom, creativity, and histories shared around the family hearth. From death and fire spring life and literary creation.

Some of Santopietro's earlier poems within *Palabras de agua* reference regions of Italy, such as Florence. She discovers later that her family had deeper connections to Nahua communities. In interviews, Santopietro describes how she herself had internalized her family's celebration of their Italian surname.[15] The poems in this first section trace the realization that this celebration was rooted in racism. Later poems portray her shift toward embracing Nahua histories.

A commitment to social justice is voiced explicitly in another poem from the first section, "Ciudades de arrecife" (Cities of the Reef), which is dedicated to the EZLN with the words "20 y 10: el fuego y la palabra: EZLN" (20 and 10: fire and word: EZLN; 31). This dedicatory commemorates EZLN preparations twenty years prior in the 1980s, and subsequently the famous uprising in 1994. Santopietro credits the Zapatista movement with paving a path for the revindication of Native rights. The EZLN's words were training for the "fire" or the battle. The poetic voice speaks apostrophically to the "*Madre de los caracoles*, / cavamos ciclos en el mar / para buscar el trozo enardecido / de la historia amarga" (*Mother of the shells*, / we dig cycles in the sea / to search for the inflamed piece / of the bitter history; 31). Santopietro's poems reflect a growing recognition of Native knowledge production. In her search for origins, water serves as a trope for fluid identity construction. Within the second section of *Palabras de agua*, "Tendal de yerba, 2004" (A Canopy of Plants, 2004), Santopietro revisits her youth and the region of Veracruz with a series of thirteen poems. Like Xochitiotzin's gathering of pieces in *Tlaoxtika*, Santopietro's poetic persona gathers the pieces of her identity in her self-searching.

In response to a violent context that disrupts this pursuit, the poetic voice denounces Ciudad Juárez femicides in a series of eight poems in the third section, "Ciudad de polvo, 2003–2009" (City of Dust, 2003–2009). Like Tonalmeyotl and Xochitiotzin, Santopietro joins a younger generation of contemporary Nahua authors who expressly condemn injustices. The poetic voice recounts the experiences of murdered women to keep their memory alive. In this same section appears an untitled poem translated into Catalan. It underscores a history of suffering that crosses borders to dialogue with voices that oppose the status quo and the nation-state supremacy.[16] Translating the poem into Catalan suggests this sought-out autonomy from nationalist campaigns and recognizes other languages to declare "la palabra negada" (the denied word; 60). Moreover, this translation communicates that femicide is a global problem prevalent not only in Ciudad Juárez but also in Spain. At a deeper level, this transatlantic dialogue signals the effects of colonial discourse in both the Iberian Peninsula and Abiayala to suggest that present-day epistemic and physical violence against women is rooted in Spanish colonialism.

Focusing on the role of language in the face of colonial discourse, Santopietro includes the two poems translated into Nahuatl and traces her revalorization of her Nahua heritage in the fourth section, "Se incendia la palabra, 2008–2010" (The Word Is Ignited, 2008–2010). This section is the most extensive with a total of twenty-three poems reedited from a previous publication in 2008 under the same title.[17] The poetic voice addresses Nahua history on the stone walls as the history "escrita sobre el lomo de la roca" (written on the stone's back; 69). At the same time, these walls are ever fluid like water, thus eschewing essentialist relegation to the past. Putting forth these metaphors, the Castilian-Nahuatl poems "Stela of Voices" and "Izcaltitla" constitute one of the principal changes from the 2008 publication of "Se incendia palabra," with Sixto Cabrera González's Nahuatl translations added. In the remaining poems of this section, the poetic voice touches upon the trope of a return of origins to center Nahua narratives.

The fifth and final section, "2006–2009," covers a wide range of themes. Santopietro's poetic persona has undergone a socially committed resurgence, particularly in the poem "Proética" (P[r]oet[h]ic, a play on "poetic" and "pro-ethic") which begins "Algunos poetas se masturban con palabras" (Some poets masturbate with words; 100). The depiction of some writers masturbating with words critiques the attitude of artists who create literature only for literature's sake. Moreover, this description constitutes a strong criticism of men, suggested by the masculine algun*os*, dominating the poetic panorama. A probe into literature's effectiveness echoes Martín Tonalmeyotl's pondering the social responsibility of good poetry. Santopietro's poetic persona imagines a text that "me hace los mandados, / me carga las maletas, me acerca las pantuflas" (runs errands for me, / carries my luggage, brings me my slippers; 100). Such poetry embodies movement, materiality, and relationality *in reality*. In contrast, mainstream poets "construyen palíndromos hasta el cielo" (construct palindromes reaching the sky; 100). Noncommitted poets fail to question the status quo and instead reiterate the same systems—be they lexical or social—like a palindrome. These verses allude to the Tower of Babel, and the implicit monolingualism (and ensuing portrayal of multilingualism as something negative) in this biblical reference as its creators spoke only one language and sought in their unfettered pride to breach the heavens. The poetic voice of "Proética," conversely, points toward a myriad of voices that dismantle monolingual schemes. As Santopietro retraces her family's origins, she does so in dialogue with Native and non-Native international movements. An understanding of this context in which she wrote *Palabras de agua* and its general structure elucidates the two Castilian-Nahuatl poems.

Stela of Voices and Storms of Pebbles: Reclaiming Nahua Identity

I now turn to an in-depth analysis of the Castilian-Nahuatl poems "Estela de voces" / "Neskayo tlajtoltij" (Stela of Voices) and "Izcaltitla," in which the poetic voice reclaims a Nahua identity. "Estela de voces" begins with a quatrain and ends with a single verse:

Monumento de la palabra,	Tetlamanal tlajtol,
la génesis en las paredes	peualistli itech tepamimej,
tan antigua	satekitl yauejkika
como la vírgula de roca,	kemi i machioyo texkali,
tormenta de guijarros que caen de la montaña. (82)	ejekatemej tlen uetsij itech tepetl. (83)

(Monument of the word,
genesis on the walls
as ancient
as the stony diacritic,

storm of pebbles that fall from the mountain.)

Santopietro plays on the word *vírgula* (diacritic) and the imagery associated with the diacritic on the *i* of the word itself. The accent on the *i* of *vírgula de roca* (diacritic of stone) alludes to the volute or shell-like symbols that represent speech in Mesoamerican pictographic codices.[18] These ancient words, although broken up in Santopietro's family line, resurge with great force as a "storm of pebbles." Like the perspective of tlaixpan, this past and ancient wisdom are in front as a guide; they influence a dynamic present in which Santopietro adapts them in new and unexpected ways. Fluid movement is reinforced with the etymology of *vírgula* from *virga*, lines or branches of condensation that fall from clouds. Besides its sense as stela or inscribed stone slab, *estela* puts fluid imagery in motion with its meaning as a "trail" or "wake" left by someone and combines with the image of a trail emanating from the clouds. *Estela* also threads a resemblance with *es tela* (it is cloth/canvas) to evoke the medium of inscription on embroidered cloth. In Nahuatl *neskayo* from the poem's title signifies "where it appears," or the "essence of its appearance," and renders vivid the word. Etchings on stone suggest alternative writing systems, akin to the Maya concept *tzib'* studied by Palacios and Worley. Durable stone material intimates that this writing endures.

More broadly, various forms of writing are interwoven/etched, such as on stone, on cloth, on the air as "speech-writing," and on the landscape itself as a text to be read. Within an expanded repertoire, watery stone and weaving mark dynamic languaging and wordsmithing. Notably, enjambment and the absence of a verb in the first stanza of "Estela de voces" create the sensation of the words falling to the final line. The use of the present tense indicative *caen* (they fall) highlights that this movement occurs in the present moment. Connected to this imagery, word *volutas* that descend like rain are reiterated by the paratextual first and last pages of *Palabras de agua*, with "palabras de agua" and "Judith Santopietro" forming spiraling *volutas* that fill the pages. Furthermore, the speech scroll's significance is underscored with references in earlier poems to the *caracoles* (conch shells), autonomous regions of the EZLN. Images of their shells mirror the spiral form of a voluta; this symbol asserts Indigenous autonomy, dynamism, deployment of a wide array of media, and above all an inconspicuous presence in the present.

Within this remediated empowerment, the "tormenta de guijarros" (storm of pebbles) in the poem "Estela de voces" is a flow of letters and diacritics.[19] Consequently, a semantic relationship pairs the *palabra* (word) and the *pared* (wall) in the repetition of *pa*; this association carries over into pamitl in Nahuatl. Tepamimej signifies "stone furrows," tying into allusions to the crop. As explored previously, pamitl is also the word for lines on the page. Tepamitl (wall) is composed of te(tl) (rock) + pamitl (furrow or line on a page), reinforcing allusions to writing. With that in mind, it is important to consider that the stela is inscribed on the mountainside, linking with the second Castilian-Nahuatl poem in which the raccoon-nahuales are at the top of a *loma* / hill (as mentioned earlier, "mountain" and "hill" are tepetl in Nahuatl). *Loma* is an elongated hill or elevation, and the word derives from *lomo*, the back of a person or animal, as well as the rise between each furrow in the fields evoked by the term pamitl. Throughout *Palabras de agua*, elevation is a recurrent trope that signals Native knowledge production raining down with force from above and surfacing from below with the subsequent resurgence of the crop.[20]

Santopietro proposes a fluid conception of who is Nahua that breaks with the continual depiction of Nahuas and other Indigenous peoples as "endangered." Government policy creates a framework in which Indigenous populations inevitably decline. According to the Mexican nation-state paradigm, once a generation ceases to speak the language, there is apparently no return to Indigeneity as future generations who choose to learn it cannot be considered Nahua. Santopietro's position subverts the nationalist discourse of *mestizaje* and its portrayal of distance from markers of Indigenous identity as "progress" toward becoming a "modern" subject. If language ceased to be a determining factor, the official number of Indigenous peoples in Mexico would increase to much more than 6.1 percent of the population.[21] That said, the goal is not to achieve a statistical increase unless it evidences a fracture within the nationalist *mestizaje* narrative, revindicates contemporary Native knowledge production, and calls for public officials who reflect the country's population. Santopietro seeks not only to create a space for Nahua women's artistic production but also to help expand our notion of who is Nahua. A key choice was translating *Palabras de agua* into contemporary Nahuatl with Sixto Cabrera González, as opposed to Classical Nahuatl as many non-Indigenous authors do.[22] The book highlights that Nahuatl is a living language.

Santopietro explains she collaborated with Cabrera González, who is from a region near where her grandmother was born, on the Nahuatl translations because she wanted to "give [the work] a Nahua voice"—not just in the two poems they translated but throughout the book (personal interview, 9 December 2013).[23] Fluid pebbles falling like rain (underscored in Nahuatl with tlaauetsi; *water*, a[tl], incorporated into the verb meaning "to fall") are an apt metaphor for the perception of the past as in front and integral to a dynamic present. The storm of volutas battles clichéd nationalist depictions of speech scrolls carved into a far-removed antiquity. A fluid and transformative past in "Estela de voces" comes to the forefront with vigor. The volutas are the "words of water" to which the title, *Palabras de agua*, refers.

The mention of diacritics, the *vírgula*, elicits debates over orthographies, and the artificial binary of orality and writing. Regarding orthographies and grammars, Santopietro expresses that they are not a pressing issue for her.[24] She focuses on the power of words rather than how to write them (or not) with Latin graphemes. This is significant in the context of diacritics referenced in the poem. Santopietro relates that she met with Nahuas who defended competing alphabets for the Nahuatl language. She was surprised at how heated discussions could get over graphemes.[25] Cabrera González uses an idiosyncratic orthography and does not necessarily agree with the alphabets employed by other writers. Regardless of the writing system or medium used, Nahua knowledge and literary production come to the forefront with strength in Santopietro's work.

Cabrera González's translation of *vírgula* in "Estela de palabras" as imachioyo is notable: "kemi i machioyo texkali," literally means "like the stone's model." Machiyotl can signify model (the loanword in Spanish *machote* for miniature architectural models comes from it), example, template, draft, and more importantly *metaphor*—machiyotlajtoli (model word) are lexicon and images that help someone understand another contexts. The dialogues between Cabrera González and Santopietro, and the metaphors that emerge from them, are themselves a model for dialogues between Nahuas and youth who seek to recover their Nahua heritage. Linked to the narratives Santopietro grew up hearing, among them histories of genesis or creation, the poem plays with the incidental diacritic or accent mark in the word *génesis*. The accent surges from the grapheme *e* like the pebbles described in the poem. *Genesis* suggests the creation story imposed by Christian missionaries to the detriment of local narratives. With "genesis" and the fluid stone, "Estela de voces" alludes to the prophet Moses striking a stone and water gushing from it. In Santopietro's poem, the stone breaks into a flood of little pebbles. This image hints at Santopietro's surname, "Santo Pietro" or "San Pedro" / "Saint Peter/Stone." Mesoamerican creation narratives are alluded to in earlier poems, particularly the syncretic narrative of a rabbit who reached the moon during the great flood (explicitly referred to in Huastecan Nahuatl as "Noah's flood").[26] Santopietro's poetic voice values Nahua wor(l)ds/narratives, in this case how the world has been birthed and subsequently destroyed on multiple occasions to return like the crop. Rather than acting as a rigid stone centered on an invented Eurocentric past, fluid pebbles break with a Western framework that had once seemed enticing to Santopietro as she grew up idealizing an Italian ancestry. She now shares narratives as part of a Nahua identity in flux. "Estela de voces" sets up the following Castilian-Nahuatl poem, "Izcaltitla," in which she shares one of those histories composed by a storm of wor(l)ds.

Consequently, "Izcaltitla" is dedicated to Enedina Piña Cogco, the aunt who related the Nahua narrative from her family's hometown. The title refers to a community near the Nahua hometown of Santopietro's father and grandparents in Ixhuatlán del Café, Veracruz, where the narrative may have taken place:

> *In memoriam Enedina Piña Cogco, por*
> *contarme las historias del pueblo de mi padre*

Los hombres de la loma taciturna
se desvisten ante una fogata de sabiduría;
    sueltan en la oscuridad las formas
        de un ojo lleno de costumbre.

Cada uno en la danza pega el cuerpo al corazón de la tierra,
pide al ave sus alas desplegadas,
    desea los negros ojos del mapache.

Alguna vez seremos la mirada del nahual
que sobrevuela la barranca
    y pariremos maíz por la boca
para arroparlo en el chisporroteo del brasero. (84)

Tlakamej inon katej itech tleokoyal tepetl
moxijxipetsouaj ixpan tlikuil tlamatilistli
      kikajkauaj ijtik tlapoyaual, tlachiualtij
          nekaj se ixtololotl tentok ika ajsikamachilistli.

Sejsenmej, itech ijtotilistli kiuiteki inakayo itech yolotlal,
kitlajtlanilia tototl i ajasuan tlapotiuij,
      kineki i ixtololouan tlilikej mapachin.

Kemantis tietoskej itlachialistli nahual
tlen majkoktinemi ik uarrankaj
      iuan tikpiluaskej tleoli ijtik tokamak
pampa sektlakentis itech tliko tlikuisalotl. (85)

            (*In memory of Enedina Piña Cogco, for*
         telling me the stories of my father's village

Men from the taciturn hill
undress before a wisdom fire;
      they let loose in the dark their shapes
          of an eye full of custom.

Each in the dance brings their body close to the heart of the earth,
asking the bird for their unfolded wings,
      desiring the dark eyes of the raccoon.

Some day we will be the vision of the nahual
who overflies the ravine
      we will give birth to maize through our mouths
to dress it in the crackle of the brazier.)

In the first lines the men undress before a fire. The family removes their clothes to transform into raccoons. Beyond that literal meaning, the poetic voice values the stories told from the Nahua region in which Izcaltitla lies, symbolized in a "fogata de sabiduría" (fire of wisdom) around which they come together with "un ojo lleno de costumbre" (an eye full of custom). This fire is likely on a *tenamastle*, a cooking surface made of three hearthstones and used specially to prepare tamales. In this process, the *tenamastle* or hearth is the principal symbol of the home space where maize enters its final stage to become food. Yet, the raccoon-people gather in the dark, on a taciturn hill, suggesting that their ceremony must be performed in secrecy. They must conceal their full powers. With the translation of "costumbre" as "ajsikamachilistli" (with *feeling* at the root of the word), the poetic voice manifests the affectivity tied to these practices. Furthermore, *costumbre* carries a meaning beyond "custom," since in Mexico "usos y costumbres" is a legal term defending the rights of Indigenous communities to their own systems of governance.[27] On this point, as analyzed in depth by Nahua anthropologist Abelardo de la Cruz, Huastecan Nahuas deploy *el costumbre* with a masculine article as opposed to the standard *la* to signal its distinct meaning within Nahua ceremonies ("The Value of *El Costumbre*" 267–70).

In the second stanza, the raccoon-people dance around the fire, with their bodies hitting/attached to the "corazón de la tierra" (heart of the earth; 84). In Castilian, the verse plays on the verb *pegar*, which can signify both "to attach" and "to hit." In Nahuatl, kiuiteki means specifically "to hit." The wordplay in Castilian describes the rhythmic dancing on the ground, like the beating of the heart (in Nahuatl, uitoni, approximate to kiuiteki, to hit), and this rhythm connects the dancing raccoon nahuales with the earth and marks their affective nexus with the territory.

The black and white of the raccoon, as well as the *masa* (corn dough) they produce, reinforces an interpretation of the poem as a symbol of literary creation, with the image of black ink on white pages to reclaim a Nahua heritage and territory. The nahual dancers petition birds for their unfolded wings and they desire the raccoon's black eyes. As in other poems, the artificial binary between orality and writing collapses into myriad forms of expression. Dancing itself is a form of writing on the ground.[28] This reference to dance in the second stanza implies there is music; perhaps the raccoon-people are even moving to the rhythm of the poem itself. The nahuales in "Izcaltitla" hide and dance at night, and with good reason. People accused of being nahuales, or even believing in their existence, have suffered centuries of persecution.[29] Now in many communities "nahual" is synonymous with the pejorative "brujo/a" (sorcerer or witch); they are linked to the devil, and discussing them is taboo. Beyond invoking older associations, these masked raccoons suggest a more contemporary group who has needed to take cover: the Zapatistas. As mentioned previously, an earlier poem cites "20 y 10," the tenth anniversary of the EZLN 1994 uprising and the ten years of preparation that preceded that. In "Dancing with the Zapatistas," Diana Taylor describes a twenty-year anniversary of the uprising with a party. A similar celebration was held ten years earlier, and her observations can be applied to the time Santopietro wrote. Reflecting on the power of dance, Taylor describes a "practice-based approach" that entails "embodied experience and practice—*being there*—as an entry point for learning and theorizing, and not just the other way around. In other words, our presence, acts, and interactions could produce new ways of knowing and theorizing that would be different than, say, learning from the findings of others through lectures or articles" ("Dancing with the Zapatistas"). The relationality communicated through this performance not only extends to the people but also to one's general surroundings.

Like the EZLN, the nahuales in "Izcaltitla" must mask themselves, when in fact, politicians are the ones who wear disguises, echoing Philip Abrams's observation: "The state is not the reality which stands behind the mask of political practice. It is itself the mask which prevents our seeing political practice for what it is" (qtd. in "Dancing with the Zapatistas"). As Yásnaya Elena Aguilar Gil argues, state-sponsored *mestizaje* discourse fashions a discriminatory mask that smothers people's identities and precludes their knowing who they are.[30] In contrast, the *mapache* nahuales conceal themselves and yet become even more visible for it when the poem brings attention to their presence and strength. Like the Zapatistas who redefined the ski mask—commonly associated with anonymity in committing criminal practices—the poem "Izcaltitla" reconfigures depictions of Nahuas and Zapatistas to underscore their capacity to create. The dance brings the reader into the fray with the first-person plural, suggesting alliances across numerous movements: "Alguna vez *seremos* la mirada del nahual" (Some day *we* will be the vision of the nahual; 84; emphasis added). This could be an exclusive "nosotrxs" that does not include the reader or an invitation to join them in developing this observation.[31] Such an invitation and *compadrazgo* relationship/alliance were rejected by the suitor who fled from the raccoon-nahual family.

In the final stanza, the poetic voice addresses learning to see our surroundings with a deep perception that "sobrevuela la barranca" (overflies the ravine) like the bird in the previous tercet. Reminiscent of ixtlamatilistli in earlier chapters, this ability to observe permeates each stanza: "ojo lleno de costumbre" (eye full of custom/practices), "negros ojos del mapache" (dark eyes of the raccoon), and "mirada del nahual" (vision of the nahual). These descriptions value the Nahua(le)s' personal experiences and thus overwrite the popular narratives that depict them as vestiges of the past. Indeed, Nahua knowledges serve as the basis for the entire poem. In this regard, traits associated with raccoons are telling, as they are characterized as an animal that loafs, steals, destroys, and scavenges—some of the stereotypical portrayals of Nahuas and Indigenous

Nations at large within the media.[32] "Izcaltitla" turns that representation on its head to position Nahuas as knowledge producers.

Santopietro charts a new mapping that centers Nahua intellectual production. Cartographic reorientations are hinted at in a semantic play on mapachin (raccoon) and *mapache*, a loanword from Nahuatl, with their resemblance to *mapa* (map) in Castilian. Furthermore, this redrawn imagery is reinforced with "alas desplegadas" (unfolded wings), *desplegar* constituting a verb used to describe the unfolding of a map. Gestures toward a new cartography increase in complexity when one realizes that *mapa* in Nahuatl carries connotations of territorial defense.[33] Tracing back to the sixteenth century, colonial administrators authored maps to steal Native lands. Nahuas fought these encroachments with histories that defended their millenary land claims.[34] In "Izcaltitla," Nahuas take cartographic control to fortify territory in its wide sense and to feature the region of Ixhuatlán del Café, specifically mentioning Izcaltitla, a community that did not appear on most maps. In this process, tamales over the fire are like literary creation, with the different pages bound and wrapped in a cover. Productively underscoring allusions to mapmaking and bookmaking, "se desvisten" (they undress) from the first stanza parallels "desplegados" (unfolded) from the second stanza. These bodies are exposed in self-expression shared with the reader to then be "wrapped" in the leaves/pages of the final stanza. Raccoon-nahuals' mouths do the work of the metate in grinding the corn, a metaphor for literary production present in Ethel Xochitiotzin's poetry (see chapter 3).

In association with the procreant fire of this creation, the final verses of "Izcaltitla" alliterate with the plosive sounds "p" and "b," simulating the noise of the "chisporroteo del brasero" (the crackle of the brazier) and alluding back to the *fogata de sabiduría* around which the nahuales gather. Along this logic, repetition of *ma* in *loma, formas, mapache*, and *maíz* wrap these words and what they symbolize semantically together in literary creation around a fire of wisdom. "We will give birth to maize through our mouths / to dress it in the crackle of the brazier" in a literal sense refers to the raccoon nahuales vomiting corn and wrapping it with cornhusks or leaves to make tamales. Notably, giving birth to corn links with cycles of death and rebirth associated with the crop. Perhaps one might think that corn is in fact dead at this stage, which raises the question as to how they give birth to it. Yet, maize grants life when people consume it. In this way, cycles of life and death are an integral part of tlaixpan. Like the maize crop that continually dies and renews, ancestors pass away and return every year—in a literal sense during the days of the dead, and, as represented in Santopietro's poetry, continually throughout the year. Relatedly, "arroparlo" (to dress it) parallels with the men who undress in the first quartet and pairs semantically with "*pariremos*" (we will give birth). In this process, a sensorial shift emerges among sight, taste, feeling, the sounds of the crackling fire, and the smells of the cooked maize. This synesthetic mix brings together the dance, the cooking of the tamales, and the *sabiduría* / wisdom (from saber, which means both "to taste" and "to know"). To put it another way, viscerality renders vivid an affective intelligence that does not dismiss Nahua narratives as irrational.

Within these descriptions, the artificial binary between orality and writing collapses, a message underscored in the previous Castilian-Nahuatl poem. Maize renews the nahuales, and after undressing and transforming they are, in a sense, dressed (*arropados*) like the tamales at the end. Food cooked on the "fire of wisdom" provides them life and strength, like the knowledge production of which the narrative related here is an example. To be sure, "Izcaltitla" casts light on a perspective where reciprocity—a key concept of tlaixpan, as the living remember their ancestors and in turn receive their ancestors' blessing—moves beyond human relationships into other-than-human surroundings and interconnections with animals, such as the birds and raccoons in this poem. Accordingly, tamal preparation is a communal event that forges kinship (evinced in the nahual wedding that was not to be) and effectuates ceremonies to commune with the dead. Alongside forging kinship, implications of "Izcaltitla" in relation to language are underscored with the similarity between "nahual" and "nahuatl" (in some variants Nahuatl is pronounced "Nahual"), and the power derived from language. Nahuas' look/vision/sight (*mirada*) sees far into the distance—extending out wide like the unfolded wings. "Izcaltitla" lends close observation to Nahua surroundings and traditions, with the possibility of transformation as deemed necessary, especially as Nahua women decide.

Mapache Mapping across Anahuac and Abiayala

This chapter has examined how Santopietro reclaims her Nahua heritage through *Palabras de agua*. The raccoon-nahual narrative is indicative of a revaluation of her Nahua ancestry. More broadly, her approach to identity has a potential to increase dramatically the number of Indigenous peoples in the census calculations of Mexico. With this change, Santopietro proposes a fluid conception of who is Nahua that combats depictions of Nahuas and other Indigenous peoples as "endangered"—depictions tied to language loss with the insinuation that Nahuas will cease to exist if Nahuatl ceases to be spoken. She disrupts Mexican nationalist assimilation of Afrodescendant and Indigenous peoples within a homogeneous notion of the ideal *mestizo* citizen.

This approach carries significant implications. Authors such as Hubert Matiúwàa ask why Native languages continue to decrease despite mounting rhetoric about their rescue ("El día bajo la sombra"). Has any Native language in Mesoamerica truly been revitalized by government-sponsored revitalization programs? A pitfall seems to lie in the tendency to prioritize language and to see it as isolated from the wider ramifications of community and territory. Santopietro gestures toward a view of language as a starting point in a battle against discrimination more broadly.

Distance from Indigenous markers of identity remains a sign of supposed progress. In that disjuncture, many choose to stop speaking Nahuatl. Santopietro describes her travels to other countries as an exile forced upon her due to death threats against her family in Córdoba, Veracruz. Her poetry processes historical and present-day traumas. In the so-called "War on Drugs" and during the COVID-19 pandemic, Native communities have been the most severely affected. As seen particularly in the previous chapter on Tonalmeyotl's work, Nahuas see historical traumas and present-day struggles as related. Current violence is an extension of colonial practices.

Santopietro's work seeks to reverse that process—to value Nahua knowledge production and the narratives she heard in her youth. She is learning, or relearning in the sense of tlaixpan, the Nahuatl language. Nonetheless, she is not studying the language to become Nahua, but rather because it merges with an expansive revaluation of her already being Nahua. Much as English is the lingua franca of many Native Nations in the US and Canada, Castilian is the lingua franca among most Nahuas. They have appropriated the colonizers' tongues, and, as Santopietro's work suggests, they are no less Nahua for speaking them.

Palabras de agua points toward the Serpent-Plumed complexities and myriad experiences of Native peoples. By bringing attention to these nuances, Santopietro fights Native erasure. As Natasha Varner states, "The idea that only those Indians who dressed and performed a certain way were 'real' Indians laid the foundation for narratives of Native extinction, since relatively few actually conformed to those specific standards" (149). *Palabras de agua* invites reflections on heated debates throughout Native Nations, especially bearing in mind "Pretendians" who have "played Indian" to receive recognition, access to publication venues, and scholarships. A similar apprehension is expressed by Native authors in Mexico who have stated that it is acceptable for Santopietro to claim she is Nahua provided she does not siphon off resources meant for Indigenous people fluent in their mother tongues. Native authors warn against a "Playing Indian 2.0" in which Mexican nationalist discourse shifts from "We Are *Mestizo*" to "We Are All Indigenous."[35] This extended version of settler colonialism creates a sense of settler belonging that dilutes and weakens Native territorial claims.

While one must guard against disingenuous claims, it is also imperative to appreciate the complexities among Native Nations. Santopietro's work features those nuanced histories and transcends stock characterizations complicit with Native erasure. She foregrounds genuine engagement with Native narratives. Her texts are an authentic search not for authenticity, but a deeper understanding of contexts, land claims, and Native knowledge production. Not all claims are equal. To be Native growing up in a rural community and/or speaking the language is not the same as growing up in Mexico City speaking Castilian. But the latter experience is no less Native. To not embrace one's Native history is to reproduce colonial violence. Like Santopietro, who did not discover her Nahua heritage until her teens, many people have been denied access to their family narratives. Nonetheless, as Cherokee literary scholar Joseph Pierce posits, this is also a Native experience ("In Search of an Authentic Indian"). Pierce raises this issue in addressing his own experience as the biological son of a Cherokee father who was adopted out of his community and did not know he was Cherokee. In Santopietro's case, it was her family's acquiescence to discriminatory discourses that kept her from knowing her own history. Pierce's separation from his Nation was caused by the social and economic exclusion, forced monolingualism, forced acculturation, and stigma that his grandmother experienced. Failing to acknowledge that history and that Native heritage, "however distant and bureaucratic it has been, is to participate in the erasure of the Indian populations of the Americas. It is to continue to silence that history. It is inauthentic" ("In Search"). Pierce argues that one must be honest with these complicated stories, and that differs starkly from the deception of Pretendians who pass as Native. In a gesture resembling Santopietro's, he recognizes, "I do not have the ability to belong to the Cherokee Nation in the same way as someone who grew up on the reservation. I do, however, have the ability to tell this story. In fact, this story is the most authentic thing I have to honor the trajectory of my own racial history. And it is in this spirit, in this unlikely sense of self, that I continue to imagine a more historically grounded sense of belonging to a community that was never meant to be mine, but which I approach slowly, openly. Authentically" ("In Search"). Santopietro tells her family's stories in a similarly painstaking and sincere search of her family's origins, histories, and language. She argues that to deny that history is to reproduce the erasure of Native histories.[36] Like Pierce, she has participated in trans-Indigenous dialogues to get to here.

This analysis of Santopietro's *Palabras de agua* signals the need for future studies of more Nahua women authors' works, regardless of whether they are in Nahuatl. Numerous writers in the United States identify as Nahua or Mexica and do not speak the language. Nahuas reside throughout the United States with all the complexities, diversity, and differences that entails. Dialogues among Nahuas in the US and Mexico fight the tendency to speak of Nahuas and other Native Nations as vanishing and dwindling—with language loss cited as proof of this supposed extinction. In fact, overturning the vanishing Indian myth would probably draw more people, in particular youth, toward speaking a Native language and exploring their Native heritage than would the usual nagging and coercive appeals to learn a "dying culture." The Nahuatl language constitutes one component within a wide network of territorial practices that encompass Serpent-Plumed family histories, land, and, most importantly, accountability and kinship.

Chapter 5

Redressing the Eagle and Feathered Serpent

Mardonio Carballo's Trans-Indigenous Dialogues
and Descolonizing *Contrapunteo*

Tengo mi mamá...
        mi mamá no está conmigo
        iajki Estados Onidos
        lava coches
                (como mi abuelita nixtamal)

(I have my mom...
        my mom is not with me
        she went to the United States
        and washes cars
                [like my grandma washes nixtamal])

Nahua artist Mardonio Carballo's verse "iajki Estados Onidos" (she went to the United States) in his first book of xochitlajtoli *Ueuejtlajtoli* (2006), copublished with Binnizá poet Irma Pineda, transits like the migration it describes between nations and languages—Spanish (Estados Onidos [sic]) and Nahuatl (iajki), a sort of *nahuañol* or Spanahuatl (13).[1] Carballo's code-switching in this wing-shaped stanza breaks with the popular depiction of the language itself as static and temporally frozen. This epigraph is a fitting window into a principal trope within the translingual poetics of Carballo's multimedia text *Las Plumas de la Serpiente* (The Serpent's Plumes) and contemporary Nahua literary production in general—that of movement, transit, and migration. In addition to the plays on language described in the introduction to this study, the title *Las Plumas de la Serpiente* alludes to how Carballo's radio broadcasts fly through the airwaves.

In shifting and sifting across regional, nation-state, linguistic, and epistemic borderlands, Carballo offers valuable perspectives on crucial issues such as decolonizing methodologies, linguistic diversity, land rights, criminalization of migrants, and gender constructions. The conception of the past as in front constitutes a key part of these movements (reflected in the title *Ueuejtlajtoli*, "old/wise words"). These movements are both spatial and temporal migrations among philosophical practices across millennia. Although it is not explicitly cited in *Las Plumas*, Carballo was working on the book *Ueuejtlajtoli* while initiating his radio program, which first aired in 2004. The epigraph from *Ueuejtlajtoli* serves as a subtext to this program in centering the knowledge production from his family's hometown of Maguey Maguaquite as well as from Native Nations writ large. Carballo's works contribute to an expansive network of artivism aimed at flooding mass media with Native voices to, in his own words, "investigar, intentar hacer medios de comunicación y meter el tema indígena en los que son masivos" (to research, attempt to make media, and insert [or sneak] Indigenous themes within mass media"; *Las Plumas* 16). *Las Plumas* forms part of a wide gamut of tools—encompassing poetry like *Ueuejtlajtoli*, short stories, television, radio, social media activism, documentaries, and progressive rock—that Carballo deploys against what Mapuche literary critic Luis Cárcamo Huechante terms acoustic and visual colonialism.[2] Movement, exchange, and circulation are constitutive metaphors in this effort.

The fact that the mother in the poem washes cars instead of nixtamal (maize soaked in limewater in preparation for making dough for tortillas and other corn-based dishes) suggests a displacement of Nahua practices that Carballo and the artists explored in this study overturn through their work. The reference to nixtamal symbolizes the contributions Nahuas offer and a context in which their knowledge production is recognized for its importance—not sequestered for poorly remunerated manual labor such as cleaning cars. As seen throughout this study, maize constitutes a metaphor for artistic production. Moreover, Carballo describes in *Las Plumas* how Nahua histories are exchanged in practice and praxis within spaces where people perform tasks like washing nixtamal, working the fields, and preparing life-sustaining maize-based food staples. This knowledge production revolves around reciprocity, which is symbolized and embodied in maize cultivation, as people and the crop live in mutual dependence. By contrast, washing cars represents a transactional economy that distributes resources inequitably, alienates the workforce, and offers poor compensation, barring workers from affording the very cars they clean.

Extending this metaphor further, both the maize seed and the car are durable. Washing maize seeds in limewater softens them for tortilla dough. In these final stages, maize dies to give life to humans, who in turn work the fields to resurrect maize in a reciprocal cycle. Cars on the other hand are unsoftened by washing, and symbolically, as well as quite literally, any system of reciprocity is broken under an economy designed to maximize profits and conceal the identities of the workers who made the vehicles. Although racial capitalism prides itself on circulation through exchange rates, free trade, and currency, it blocks reciprocal flows from a broader conception of territory and of what possesses value in contemporary Nahua literary production.

Of great significance, "iajki Estados Onidos" can refer to leaving for Mexico City (where Carballo's sister, the mother described, lives now), as the official name for Mexico is the Estados Unidos Mexicanos. Such a move reveals the cracks within nationalist discourse's attempts to paint a unified Mexican nation-state. The states are not united, which Carballo ironizes by changing the *u* of unidos to onidos. *U* and *o* are interchangeable in Nahuatl. This Nahuatlized version of the word accentuates the divisions within Mexico. The internal word *nido* (nest) suggests the irony that the nation-state is not a welcoming space, a "nest," for Indigenous peoples. Carballo highlights this foreignizing of First Peoples within Mexico by using *migración* even when Indigenous peoples move to different Mexican states in search of work (*Las Plumas de la Serpiente* 56–58).

In this chapter, I focus on Mardonio Carballo's book *Las Plumas de la Serpiente* (2012), a transcribed selection of radio shorts spanning the first seven years of his radio program beginning in December 2004. I argue that *Las Plumas*, both in its thematic content and performatively through filling mediascapes with marginalized voices, promotes what Cárcamo Huechante calls "acoustic ecology" against a ubiquitous backdrop of media colonialism that dominates the circulation of sounds and images ("Indigenous Interference" 50–51). Acoustic ecology constitutes a space "where animal, human, physical, and spiritual planes of sonic activity intersect and engage with one another" ("No + *Wingka* Word" 109). Comparable to the relationship between land/territory and voice/language in Mapudungun, Nahuatl is described by Carballo in a relational epistemology with humans, animals, the landscape, and maize. In contrast, mediatic colonial practices obscure the intersection of language, territory, and economy. To speak of acoustic and visual colonialism is especially useful in underscoring that this oppressive sound/sightscape is intimately linked with territorial dispossession. We must acknowledge not only Native land but also Native mediascapes appropriated by colonial project(ion)s.

This mono-mediatic staging does not exist "naturally"; nation-states and corporations maintain it explicitly or implicitly. What else can explain the introduction in 2014 of Article 130 of Mexico's Federal Telecommunications Law, which prohibited Native languages on national media? In response, Carballo has fought media colonialism through his xochitlajtoli and in federal court.[3] While Mexico differs from Chile in aspects such as *mestizaje* discourse and a long-standing state-sponsored strategy of co-optation, the end result of Mexican nationalist discourse resembles what Cárcamo Huechante describes as a "linguistic, graphic, and acoustic regime of language within the Chilean nation-state [that] entails a prevailing monolingual practice in the realms of poetry, literature, and print culture in Chile, a sociolinguistic regime that is part of a broader deployment of acoustic colonialism in society" ("No + *Wingka* Word" 104). Like Mapuche poets, Carballo "registers in figurative and performative modes the acoustic ecology of the linguistic, cultural, and territorial" Native imaginary against "the dissonant omnipresence of a colonial history" (104). He publishes and performs his works in an array of formats, and these works emerge from an expansive understanding of text encompassing textiles, ceremony, dance, music, and maize cultivation. Content from *Las Plumas* has served as a weekly radio short, magazine articles, lyrics for his prog rock group, documentaries, and a node for artivist campaigns.

Land dispossession transects with denied access to print and acoustic media fora. Mainstream publishing houses claim that the "niche" of "contemporary Indigenous literature" is economically unviable. The antiquating encasement of Native languages within nationalist discourse (discussed in the introduction) compounds this situation, which in turn increases publishing houses' reticence to take up these works and stunts the growth of a readership. Tied to these obstacles, land dispossession severs Native activists' access to a critical mass of support, resources, and spaces to make their voices heard. A telling example are *radios comunitarias* (unlicensed Indigenous community radio stations) persecuted by the state, such as the Zapotec stations in Oaxaca referenced by Carballo in *Las Plumas* (107).

Literary scholar Matt Cohen signals that this intersectional coloniality assumes Native peoples lack sophisticated forms of communication and are thus an empty space fated for colonization (cited in Dowling, *Translingual Poetics* 45). Carballo promotes Native deployment of numerous technologies in a takeover of these colonized mediascapes. He avoids positioning Native communication technologies, as Sarah Dowling warns, as "artifacts" that run "the risk of erasing contemporary Indigenous peoples and furthering the project of colonization by reducing Indigenous cultural materials to symbols of difference to be activated within non-Indigenous artistic and philosophical contexts" (54). Carballo rejects Mexican nation-state discourse's "artifacting" mythologization of Indigenous cultural materials such as the state-sponsored appropriation of figures like Quetzalcoatl.

Carballo does not seek solely to fill mass media with Native voices. He promotes spaces where Native authors are the directors and sponsors of that communication. Otherwise, this work could reproduce structural inequities and, as Rita M. Palacios and Paul M. Worley caution, leave art networks in the hands of "regulators who grant entry under their regulations, thereby perpetuating the relations of power that legitimize their authority" (*Unwriting Maya Literature* 164). Carballo situates Nahuas as reporters, researchers, media hosts, and producers. This epistemic turn circumvents a simplistic nativist binary of Indigenous and non-Indigenous.

Although he strategically employs binaries to distinguish descolonizing actors from colonial agents, these binaries repeatedly segue into complex contrapuntal analyses where no one is spared from criticism. Carballo underscores how everyone is potentially complicit in colonial practices. This movement back and forth, or *contrapunteo*, constitutes a recurrent trope throughout *Las Plumas*. This *contrapunteo* resembles Cuban anthropologist Fernando Ortiz's well-known use of the same term in his analysis of transculturation within *Contrapunteo del tabaco y el azúcar* (1940). He proposes a contrapuntal transculturation to reflect "the extremely complex transmutations of culture that have taken place here [in Cuba] . . . and without a knowledge of which it is impossible to understand the evolution of Cuban folk, either in the economic or in the institutional, legal, ethical, religious, artistic, linguistic, psychological, sexual, or other aspects of its life" (*Cuban Counterpoint* 98).[4] In reference to Carballo's work, I understand *contrapunteo* to be, as sociologist Agustín Laó-Montes describes by drawing on Édouard Glissant's work, a "historical totality" conceptualized as "*archipelagos, assemblies, constellations, or montages*, heterogeneous and discontinuous formations of subjects, classes, genders/genres, communities, peoples, countries, regions, diasporas, et cetera, that configure historical processes and translocal spaces, whose relations we interpret and represent as counterpoints" (my trans.; 29). This open and contradictory process catches sight of a complex dance of descolonial praxes and persistent imperial powers. Contrapuntal method allows us to articulate diverse historical spaces and see movement in both a totality and its parts. Fittingly, Carballo transposes across local, national, and global spaces, past and present, identity and flux, and an arpeggiated articulation of an ever-moving totality at play with exteriority.

With counterpoint in mind, Carballo invites Indigenous musicians on set to play and speak about their compositions on his radio programs. *Las Plumas* radio shorts have background music, frequently traditional *sones* from the Huasteca sampled with styles ranging from jazz to Mozart to "La llorona" in Nahuatl. The fact that the genre of *sones* is traditionally associated with Afro-Caribbean cultures is not lost on Carballo. Through *Plumas* and his documentary series *La raíz doble*, he highlights Afro-Mexican contributions. Like the polyphony and tension that reverberate in the interstices of such encounters, the program articulates alternative perspectives within what Sarah Dowling calls a "'colonial cacophony' of linguistic collision" (169). Immersed in this transposition among multitudinous artistic and epistemic influences, Carballo centers the contributions of people excluded from the figurative dance of knowledge production.

In this contrapuntal strategy where different modes of interacting with the world are juxtaposed and transposed, Carballo adapts the perspectives of ixtlamatilistli, yoltlajlamikilistli, and tlaixpan. He features the experiential knowledge of subalternized subjects, an affective intelligence gained through their struggles, and their knowledges from a long line— more accurately circle or spiral—of ancestors. Ixtlamatilistli interrupts colonial discourse, with Nahua voices moving through the soundscape in the same way that Nahua people transit space and time. In contrast, agents of colonial practices, who can be Indigenous or non-Indigenous, dismiss Native communities' knowledges to embrace a state-sponsored, Euro-American-centric positivism.[5]

The introduction to *Las Plumas* refers to the eagle devouring a serpent found on the Mexican flag. This state-appropriated Pre-Columbian symbol represents the mythical foundation of famed Mexica altepetl Mexihco-Tenochtitlan. Carballo breaks with official venerations of this site of memory within Mexican nationalist discourse by describing the eagle as the oppressive nation-state (or nation-states, including the US, whose official national bird is also an eagle) and the serpent in the eagle's depluming grasp as Indigenous populations.[6] That serpent, Native Nations, lives and can strike back. Throughout *Las Plumas*, Carballo deconstructs bromidic portrayals of Indigenous communities as victimized populations through approaches rooted in ixtlamatilistli, tlaixpan, and yoltlajlamikilistli. As seen in previous chapters, this framework insists upon a space of affectivity that views Indigenous subjects as modern producers of knowledge and not as vestiges of a premodern era.

Carballo capitalizes Las Plumas de la Serpiente as a name like Quetzalcoatl (in Castilian only the first letter of titles is upper case). Aside from mirroring its play on Quetzalcoatl, capitalization underscores the proper naming within the radio program of people, the plural *Plumas*, who go unnoticed. Carballo cites family members, such as his mother, father, and brother-in-law, throughout *Las Plumas*. All contributions on this program are based on his personal experiences in dialogue with Native and non-Native activists, artists, and academics to strengthen a collectivity emphasized in the introduction to *Las Plumas*: "Por eso preferí—preferimos—hablar de los pueblos indígenas vivos, de *Las Plumas de la Serpiente*" (7). The serpent's feathers are a fitting metaphor for Carballo's work and for contemporary Nahua literature in general. He describes the weaving in and out through *Las Plumas* episodes like a textile composed of interlacing threads, serpents, and feathers. What is at stake in this mediatic warp and weft? What happens when Native authors and artists disseminate their own materials in mass media, representing themselves instead of being represented by others? Carballo's work responds to these questions. Discriminatory images against Native Nations abound within mass media. Through *Las Plumas*, Carballo foregrounds trans-Indigenous perspectives to dismantle those visual and sonic distortions.

Dreaming in Another Language: Mardonio Carballo's Trajectory

Mardonio Carballo has a grueling schedule. In the summer of 2013 alone, he was responsible for presenting a nationally televised documentary series in Mexico, conducting another program of interviews on Internet television, giving his weekly *Las Plumas de la Serpiente* radio spots on Carmen Aristegui's news program and a weekly one-hour radio program on the

National University's radio station, being the lead singer and composer for a progressive rock group, and doing a book tour for the recently published *Las Plumas de la Serpiente*. That same summer, he gave a rock concert in an economically disadvantaged area of Mexico City, wrote a weekly news column, published a book/CD of xochitlajtoli and experimental music, went on tour to present the volume, participated in protests denouncing the killing of reporters, and created a bilingual Nahuatl-Spanish children's book. Faced with questions about his itineraries, he responds, "I sit a lot of the time and talk, and talk, but out in the cornfields my family does intense physical work. When I think of that, I can't complain."[7] The comparison of his projects to a higher standard of laboring in the cornfields is an apt metaphor for Carballo's own work, and one that explicitly appears within *Las Plumas*. He cultivates fields of music, literature, and mass media with Nahua and Indigenous voices, perspectives, and experiences—voices largely inaudible in mass media that among other things demand land rights to work the cornfields he describes.

His influence on social media constitutes a potent example of Indigenous strategies of transiting among these fields through recent technology. He is intensely active on Facebook, or ixamoxtli—literally ix, face, and amoxtli, book.[8] Indeed, most Nahuas in urban areas are active on Facebook to stay in touch with rural communities and build kinship within places like Mexico City. *Las Plumas* reflects Carballo's own conceptualization of what a book should be—a multimedia work that reaches beyond the pages, networks with its readers, and challenges the conventional view of Nahua amoxtli as archaic and restricted to Pre-Columbian or early colonial periods.

Carballo is from the Huasteca Veracruzana, home to the largest Nahua population in Mexico. He has nonetheless spent most of his life outside of this region. In his teens, he moved to Mexico City to complete his high school studies, and he has lived there since, joining a large pan-Indigenous urban population. Among the most eclectic artists of contemporary Indigenous cultural production, Carballo works with many types of media and *géneros* (the Castilian word *género* referring to both *genre* and *gender*). To really read *Las Plumas*, one must see it connected to a wider project uprooting stereotypical, patriarchal, and heteronormative representations of First Peoples. This is evident in *Las Plumas* and on Facebook with Carballo's participation in LGBTQ+ movements. Acceptance of a gender spectrum encapsulates Carballo's aim to defend linguistic diversity and convene large groups in protests against social injustices. He has promoted the campaign "Salgamos todxs del clóset. ¿Qué lengua hablas tú?" (Let's all come out of the closet. What language do you speak?).

Carballo's xochitlajtoli joins a larger project of introducing Indigenous perspectives and aesthetics into every medium possible, particularly mass media such as film and social networks. In explaining how he learned to enter this foray, Carballo describes himself as self-taught. From 2018 to 2022, he served as Director of Culturas Populares, Indígenas y Urbanas with the administration of President Andrés Manuel López Obrador. As director, he continually corrected people when they added the title *licenciado* (college graduate) to his name. In his biography for *Las Plumas*, Carballo states, "Soy un hombre que tuvo la fortuna de desarrollar dos partes de su cerebro. Desde pequeño hablo castellano y náhuatl. Soy autodidacta, soy escritor porque no queda de otra" (I'm a man who had the fortune of developing both parts of his brain. I have spoken Castilian and Nahuatl since childhood. I'm self-taught, I'm a writer because I have no other option; inside cover). He describes the publication of *Las Plumas* as follows: "[C]uando las editoriales lo permiten, les infrinjo un diminuto gol en forma de libro que después grito en silencio, en papel, en páginas, en tinta y en el escenario si se me permite. De ahí soy" (When publishing houses allow it, I score a minute goal past them in the form of a book and later shout in silence, on paper, on pages, in ink, and on the stage if I'm allowed. That's where I'm from; inside cover). He recognizes mainstream publishing houses' reticence to print a work like *Las Plumas*. Faced with this politics of funding, it is telling that the book was a self-funded project through Carballo's one-time press/collective Amoch Libros. Carballo first presented *Las Plumas* at the Guadalajara International Bookfair (FIL) in November 2012. He was concerned the book would go unsold, especially considering the high costs of presenting at FIL, but recounts that his fears quickly dissipated when he saw the room filled to capacity and all copies on hand sold out.[9] This success shows the appeal of *Las Plumas* to a wide audience, and Carballo's outstanding ability to bring Native perspectives into myriad expressions.

The Warp and Weft of *Las Plumas*: Textual Tapestry and Overview

The essays of *Las Plumas* are framed by a prologue and epilogue from two eminent Mexican reporters, Carmen Aristegui and Ignacio Rodríguez Reyna. These bookends highlight the relevance of Carballo's words to conversations regarding the role of news outlets. They confront the misperception that Indigenous peoples' words are more fit as ethnographic objects than as journalistic research. As stated in the introduction to this study, Carballo created *Las Plumas* after he contacted Aristegui's news program to protest references to Native language as *dialectos*. In the prologue, Aristegui recounts how she invited him to educate a non-Indigenous public about Indigenous Nations. In the epilogue, Rodríguez Reyna describes Carballo as an "escritor, periodista, poeta y buscador de metáforas" (writer, journalist, poet, and seeker of metaphors) who does not pursue "una nostalgia ni una idealización del mundo indígena, tan lleno de virtudes y sabiduría como lastres e injusticias" (a nostalgia or an idealization of the Indigenous world, a world as full of virtues and wisdom as it is of burdens and injustices; 134). He situates Carballo's work as journalism in search of dignity, respect, and justice for Native Nations without "commiseration" or "pobretología" (poortology). In his move away from the victimization of Native peoples within mass media, Carballo bears testament to the danger reporters face, especially if they are Indigenous. Several journalists he mentions in the *Las Plumas* book and radio program were assassinated. The back cover of *Las Plumas* includes a blurb from renowned Nahuatl studies historian Alfredo López Austin. By choosing a quote from López Austin to promote his book, Carballo appeals to an audience of Classical Nahuatl enthusiasts and then breaks with their expectations regarding Nahua texts. With this format, Carballo moves from the field of Nahuatl studies, associated with ethnography and Pre-Columbian history, to journalism in order to position Native intellectuals as reporters and commentators on current events.

In its expansive scope, *Las Plumas* consists of fifty radio shorts. Identifying an arc to the arrangement of episodes can be challenging, and topics addressed near the beginning of the print version reappear at the end. The internal structure of most essays[10] shares a similar cyclical or spiral structure with initial sentences reappearing near the end. There is no table of contents, some pieces go untitled, and episodes appear out of chronological order. Despite this seeming fragmentariness, Carballo and his editorial team carefully curated the text to underscore its circular conceit. The small outline of a coiled snake appears by nearly every page number and at the beginning of untitled pieces. This image represents how, through time, worldings spiral and continually transform. *Las Plumas* relates how discriminatory practices incessantly permutate and return to haunt society. In the face of these practices, the knowledges produced by Indigenous communities endure and adapt to offer solutions to present-day societal problems. The contrapuntal poly/cacophony among Native knowledge production and colonial oppression can be both replete in creativity and potentially destructive in clashes among incommensurabilities. *Las Plumas* examines those cycles of creation and destruction. Carballo describes the Serpent's Plumes, Native Nations, as repeatedly shedding their skin in a continual becoming. He pulls at the threads of readers' assumptions regarding Native Nations in a style of writing that dances back and forth, contests and responds.

Consequently, the essays are roughly divided according to fifteen Mexican marigold (sempoalxochitl)–colored pages introducing general themes. The pieces that follow the respective orange pages have a white background and begin with sempoalxochitl-colored text in the title and initial two lines. These graphemes appear like sempoalxochitl petals guiding ancestors and their families to one another. In effect, remembering the deceased is a recurrent theme throughout the book. In this sense *Las Plumas* is more an intergenerational network than a linear narrative. The fifteen sempoalxochitl-colored pages dispersed through the text remember the dead and their knowledges, such as Carballo's mother in the first piece. Furthermore, the color of the pages resembles an orange-tinged variety of Huastecan maize, and in this sense each letter is arranged in a line like maize kernels. The subsequent black font on white pages also alludes to corn (in Nahuatl "blue corn" is black, yatsij). Throughout *Las Plumas*, Carballo explores, as the "roots" of his xochitlajtoli, an intersection of maize cultivation and flowered invitations to ancestors to return home (13; 26; 47; 102; 106).

The book concludes with a glossary of Nahuatl words and one Tzotzil term, followed by a final sempoalxochitl-colored page with Carballo's farewell aired at the end of every broadcast. The terms in the glossary point to creation, communal practices, and strength: chuj (Maya Tzotzil black wool cloth used in textiles), kuetlaxotl (leather, skin), maguaquite (bothrops asper or "four-nosed" snake), omitl (bone), pique (bean tamal), tziktli (gum), and zacahuil (large tamal with ground maize). In the book launch of *Las Plumas*, Carballo describes these Native words as "incrustadas" (inlayed) in his Castilian like precious stones.[11] In this sense, Nahua concepts refract through these words into the Castilian to insert a prismatic expansiveness of Native voices.

Carballo's words on the final page appear untranslated in an enlarged font: "Tlaskamati miak. / Xij kaua ma / kueponi mo / tlajtol" ("Thank you very much. / Let / your words [or language] / blossom"; 133). This phrase with its flowered reference alludes to xochitlajtoli. Most radio/internet listeners are in Mexico City; Aristegui in her prologue states that the main audience of *Las Plumas* is non-Indigenous. Nevertheless, these episodes are meant for a Native audience also, as the untranslated state of the final words suggests.[12] He speaks directly to Nahuas in urban and rural spaces. Additionally, the orthography of this last phrase reflects how Carballo reaches out to Native and non-Native audiences. He uses an idiosyncratic Nahuatl orthography that he argues is accessible and easier to read for all audiences.[13] Carballo's underlying argument with his personal orthography is that academic debates over writing systems are ancillary. Instead, the focus should rest on the message communicated and the affect it elicits.

In this process, the rhythm of the pieces throughout *Las Plumas* is a rapid stream of images, words, and sounds, reflecting a dynamic counterpoint that highlights the framework of personal experience (Native knowledges and contemporary relevance in dialogues and debates), the past in front (evinced by the overall structure, continual shifts and spirals), and an affective intelligence (cultivated and amplified by the music). This staccato pace is even more evident on the spoken program as Carballo often speaks quickly. Perhaps this is partly due to time restrictions on the radio (episodes last approximately six minutes at most), but more importantly that speed gives the sensation of Native voices overtaking mass media. This swiftness confronts the mediatic tropes of Native figures painstakingly speaking broken Castilian or of the slow-speaking, contemplative Native spokesperson who seems to reach out from a physical and temporal distance. *Las Plumas* points to a multiplicity of texts with an interplay of metaphors based on textiles, text on the page, and furrows (lines) in the field. The program shifts among numerous formats with the text on the page, spoken word on Aristegui's radio program, online articles in the weekly magazine *Emeequis*, YouTube video recordings with added visuals, and content for Carballo's televised programs. This multimodality displays how Carballo uses text as a counterpoint to the spurious way in which Native peoples are misrepresented in the lettered city, to in turn reimagine this scholarly commonplace in a way that shows the potential anticolonial stakes of nonliterary reading.

Confronting Origins: Facing Native Histories

Carballo begins and concludes the introduction to *Las Plumas* by describing how time runs like ants (6). This image possibly alludes to the destruction of Macondo by a horde of ants in the circular structure of Gabriel García Márquez's *One Hundred Years of Solitude*, representing a labyrinth of violence in which Latin America appears trapped. The image also recalls Mesoamerican narratives about how ants brought maize to humans, allowing them to thrive and establish altepemej (cities). These two interpretations reflect how life cycles entail destruction or creation. Carballo states that in the face of challenges "estamos poniendo de puente nuestra mano; este es nuestro grano de arena, nuestra mano vuelta, nuestro puñado de tierra, por los otros" (we're extending our hand as a bridge; this is our grain of sand, our *mano vuelta* [collective work, literally "returned hand"], our fistful of earth, for others; 6). Carballo then repeats "Las Plumas de la Serpiente somos todos" (We are all the Serpent's Plumes; 6). Additionally, he intimates that most of Mexico's population is Native.[14] When Carballo speaks of Nahua heritage, he does not address this topic in the distance as nationalist discourse or popular mediatic tropes do. He poses a rhetorical question repeated in two episodes within the book and additional radio shorts not included in the print text, "¿Qué es la flor sino la raíz?" (What is the flower but the root?; 6) instead of "¿Qué es la flor sin la raíz?" (What is the flower without the root?) to feature an inseparable relationality with one's ancestors and the land. Xochitlajtoli is etymologically tied to those relationships with ancestors as flowers and words/languages serve as the vehicle to link generations.

The xochitl, flower, is the root of kinships metaphorically and quite literally in the sense that they are strewn on the ground to prepare paths for deceased relatives during the Day of the Dead. As explained in the introduction, Nahua genealogical trees position ancestors at the bottom as the roots. This theme reappears throughout *Las Plumas* and reflects the past-in-front temporality of tlaixpan. Carballo refers to the deceased in a sort of past-present tense by combining preterit and present conjugations within Castilian, a grammatical calque from Nahuatl in which preterit and present tenses commonly mix (*Las Plumas* 13, 16, 51, 92, 126, 130–31). He posits that there is much to glean from personal knowledges, the ixtlamatilistli inspired by ancestors. Carballo speaks of "nuestra palabra de papel" (our paper word), suggesting that these words on paper are only one tool among many (6). This word in book form connects with myriad modes of communication that foreground performance and personal experience.

After addressing this collective work, the introduction shifts to recount a Native protest in Chiapas. Demonstrators carry the Mexican flag, "[e]l símbolo máximo de un país que los ha despreciado" (the supreme symbol of a country that has despised them; 6–7). The flag serves simultaneously as a standard of Native struggles and symbol of the very nation-state against which they protest. This image inspired the name of the program *Las Plumas de la Serpiente*. Carballo states, "La serpiente somos los pueblos indígenas de México. Pero igual que en el escudo de México, el águila no se ha devorado a la serpiente. No aún. . . . La bandera y el escudo son parte del suspenso. También nuestra oportunidad" (We, the Native Nations of Mexico, are the serpent. But just as in the coat of arms on the Mexican flag, the eagle has not devoured the serpent. Not yet. . . . The flag and the coat of arms are part of the suspense. And our opportunity; 7). Carballo's reinterpretation of this image reflects an iconoclastic gesture throughout his work to turn mythologized nationalist symbols on their heads. He does so to accentuate that Nahuas are alive and thriving; the serpent symbolizes the defense and power of Native Nations. Nonetheless, these Nations are in the clutches of a nation-state that has stolen their lands and appropriated their iconography. As mentioned earlier in this study, within official nationalist discourse the supposed "fall of the eagle," intimated in the false etymology of the last Mexica tlahtoani's name Cuauhtemoc, reincarnates into the modern nation-state.

Along with his emphasis on the contemporaneity of Native experiences through a subverted analysis of national symbols, Carballo combats the relegation of Nahuas to the past. He declares in a passage partially cited in the epigraph to this study's introduction:

> Cuando uno escucha Quetzalcoatl piensa de inmediato en "La Serpiente Emplumada"; en el pasado glorioso de México, pasado que, de tan glorioso, nos estorba. Por eso preferí,—preferimos—hablar de los pueblos indígenas vivos, de *Las Plumas de la Serpiente* que siguen dotando a nuestro país de rostros y posibilidades múltiples. De los olvidados. De seres humanos con piel y huesos y caminando y que han sido ignorados en aras de seguir perpetuando la memoria de la pirámide. (7)

> (When someone hears Quetzalcoatl, they think immediately of "The Plumed Serpent"; of the glorious past of Mexico, a past

so glorious that it gets in our way. That is why I preferred,—we preferred—to speak about the living Indigenous nations, of *The Serpent's Plumes* who continue to endow our country with multiple faces and possibilities. Of the forgotten. Of human beings of flesh and bone and walking and who have been ignored in the name of continuing to perpetuate the memory of the pyramid.)

"En aras de seguir perpetuando la memoria de la pirámide" alludes to massive state investment in perpetuating this myth. "En aras de" (literally "at the altar or sanctuary of") carries religious overtones that suggest sacrificing an Indigenous past for the present "Progress" of the nation-state. This temporality of ancientness and novelty contrasts with the tlaixpan view of that past at the forefront. The state has invested immense wealth in museums of Pre-Columbian artifacts, such as the Templo Mayor and the National Museum of Anthropology in Mexico City. Meanwhile, comparatively little has been done to engage genuinely with living Native people.

Within the circular structure of *Las Plumas*, this juxtaposition is underscored in the penultimate essay, "¿Cuánto cuesta México?" The episode appears between two pieces that address the tens of thousands killed in the "War on Drugs." As shall be explored more in detail, "¿Cuánto cuesta México?" imagines an auction of Pre-Columbian and nationalist emblems. *Las Plumas* criticizes the transactional reduction of Mexican symbols to commercialism and people to statistics in the exponential tally of those killed in the so-called War on Drug Trafficking. To break with this mode of statistics, the first sempoalxochitl-orange page initiates a thematic focus on origins with a dedicatory to Carballo's mother: "Estas Plumas de la Serpiente alzan su vuelo / por Anatolia Manuel, mi madre" (These Serpent's Plumes take flight / for [or because of] Anatolia Manuel, my mother; 9). Carballo signals that his mother is at the head of his work he does. A subtext to this dedicatory is that his mother was the person who exclusively spoke Nahuatl with him growing up.

Despite foregrounding the value of living tradition, Carballo eschews nativism and observes his Nahua community with a critical eye. Anatolia pressured him to marry and have children.[15] Instead, he chose to challenge the gender norms of his community. Carballo alludes to this tension in the poem that follows this dedicatory and later essays. He scrutinizes his hometown. Below the dedicatory to his mother, he includes a right-aligned xochitlajtoli that invokes the practice of burying the umbilical cord to mark one's homeland: "¿De dónde es uno? / ¿Del lugar donde ha dejado enterrado su ombligo / o de donde se entierra todo lo demás? / ¿De dónde es uno? / ¿Del lugar donde ha sido plantado su árbol / o de donde muere el animal que le corresponde?" (Where is one from? / From where one has left their navel [umbilical cord] buried / or from where one has buried all the rest? / Where is one from? / From the place where one's tree has been planted / or from where one's animal companion dies?; 9). The reference to a person's animal companion spirit evinces an intimate relationality with surroundings. Carballo suggests that one is from all these places and the spaces in between. He invites an inexorable negotiation among multiple origins, practices, and experiences. The questions posed in this xochitlajtoli reappear through *Las Plumas*.

The text transitions from these questions regarding origins to the radio short, "Nahuatlaco en Europa" (Nahua in Europe), to contest Europe's supposed superiority. Carballo battles the depiction of Indigenous peoples as stuck in place and flips the traditional narrative of Euro-American researchers traveling to investigate Nahua communities. Here a Nahua reporter critiques Europe. In "Nahuatlaco en Europa" and throughout *Las Plumas*, Carballo spotlights himself and other Indigenous peoples in what Dakota historian Philip J. Deloria calls "unexpected places" where they exercise agency to reveal and overturn pernicious ideologies (*Indians in Unexpected Places* 9). The title, "Nahua in Europe," resembling the title of Federico García Lorca's book of poetry *Poeta en Nueva York*, conveys the presence of someone in an unexpected or estranging location.

Carballo begins "Nahuatlaco en Europa" by contemplating life and death. There are oppressive situations in Mexico, but similarly repressive situations exist in Europe. Octavio Paz's famous writings within *El laberinto de la soledad* on Mexican views regarding mortality are a subtext. Nonetheless, Carballo explores Europe rather than the "Mexican psyche." He describes people and their cities as belonging to a symbiotic relationship in which they resemble one another. Carballo ponders the mounting death toll in Mexico reported in European news outlets. He visits the Holocaust Museum in Germany and the Reina Sofía Museum in Madrid, where he sees Pablo Picasso's *Guernica*. For Carballo, these images call into question the Eurocentrism that has traditionally overshadowed Native worldviews. The name of the museum, the Reina Sofía, and the comment in the final lines that "[n]i los Reyes nos podrán Salvar" (not even the Kings will be able to save us; 12) accentuates the irony of representing Europe as "modern" when some European countries defend an antiquated system of kings and queens.

In the following essay, "El regreso" (The Return), Carballo travels from Europe to the Huasteca, and then back to Mexico City. The tlaixpan or altar is prominent in his trip to the Huasteca for the Day of the Dead. He visits those who have long since died. Carballo features the affective connection to those ancestors and links it with maize cultivation. He has ambivalent feelings when he returns to his hometown Maguey Maguaquite. While he looks forward to reconnecting with kin, he is saddened by conflicts and corruption within the community. He repeats, "No es fácil el regreso" (Returning is not easy) five times to underscore his feeling of not belonging completely in either Maguey Maguaquite or Mexico City (14). In the first and final line of the piece, Carballo observes internal divisions and impoverishment upon his return to Maguey Maguaquite as "[l]a raíz irrumpe como pico de colibrí en el pecho" (roots irrupt like the stabs of a hummingbird's beak in one's chest; 13, 15). This image contrasts starkly with Natalio Hernández's celebratory use of the hummingbird in *Patlani huitzitzilin* (The Hummingbird Flies).

One might expect "The Return" to suggest Carballo's arrival to his Nahua community in Veracruz or his home in Mexico City. Nonetheless, it refers simultaneously to both and neither. There is ambiguity regarding exactly from/to where he is returning, especially given the trip to Europe in the previous piece, "Nahuatlaco en Europa." He goes to the Huasteca Veracruzana to visit his father and remember deceased relatives, but this is difficult because of injustices and poverty in the region. Carballo then describes returning to Mexico City as entering "la selva que elegí como vivienda" (the jungle I chose as a dwelling; 13). Mexico City is a "jungle of asphalt that fills every pore with caresses and pollution" (13). He calls into question the city's supposed superiority. As mentioned in the first chapter, the Huasteca is commonly portrayed as a wilderness or jungle similar to how Carballo represents Mexico City. With his ambivalent descriptions of the Huasteca and Mexico City, Carballo is far from any static positioning. He moves and observes through the interstices of rural, urban, and international contexts. In its insistence on this dynamic close observation of surroundings, ixtlamatilistli affects (and adds affect to) research and journalistic methodologies.

Inseparable from ixtlamatilistli is respect, an indispensable ingredient in the subsequent essay, "Padres de maíz" (Mothers and Fathers of Maize). The title plays on the common phrase "hombres de maíz" (men of maize) used in Guatemalan writer Miguel Ángel Asturias's eponymous novel. *Padres* emphasizes a relational kindred connection, as opposed to simply "men." Carballo tells his father about the goal to inundate mass media with Nahua voices. His father responds that it is a "llamarada de petate" (a pipe dream or literally "a petate ablaze"), an ephemeral effort that will fail as quickly as it takes flames to consume a petate reed mat (16). Carballo then relates to his father the federal government's recent acceptance of GMO corn into the country. Carballo explains that "los científicos van a buscar la manera de mejorarlo, semillas que sirvan mejor para los distintos climas de México, cuál es mejor para hacer palomitas, para el pozole y los tamales" (the scientists are going to look for ways to improve it, seeds that work better for the different climates of Mexico, which variety is better to make popcorn, for pozole and tamales; 16). His father exclaims, "¡Ah que los científicos, siempre queriendo apropiarse de lo que ya está conocido! Si quieren saber cuál maíz es bueno *pal* tamal que le pregunten a tu mamá . . ." (Ah those scientists, always wanting to appropriate what's already known! If they want to know which maize is good for tamales they should ask your mom . . . ; 16). His father says they should ask his mother, even though she has died. They speak about her in the present tense. For Carballo and his father, transgenic corn constitutes scientists' attempts to appropriate maize and separate it from the deep affective attachment reinforced through Nahua ceremonies and ancestors'—his mother's—knowledge production.

Carballo comments that maize resembles people, with a wide range of hues/phenotypes totaling more than fifty. Nonetheless, in society certain phenotypes and elites, like the scientists cited, are favored over others. Moreover, this disparity applies to language. A subtext not mentioned in the piece is that Carballo's father only speaks Castilian with him. Perhaps due to the discrimination he himself experienced, his father insists on speaking that language unless the listener is monolingual in Nahuatl. He felt that his children needed to use Castilian so as to achieve success in life.

Despite his reservations about the Nahuatl language, Carballo's father still holds a profound affective attachment to maize and the Nahua perspectives linked to the crop. Carballo states that "hay que saber cantarle [al maíz]" (one must know how to sing [to the maize]; 16, insert mine). His father cries over their conversation about corn and genetic engineering (17). This dialogue underscores an affective intelligence. Carballo explains that Nahuas have given maize "un valor cultural a su gran descubrimiento científico" (cultural value to their great scientific discovery; 17). The text touches upon mass media, maize, ancestors, language, and science. Carballo highlights how these areas intersect within an acoustic and visual ecology—a nonanthropocentric heterarchical land/visual/soundscape—where knowledge production is integrated within a relationality with one's surroundings.

This piece on maize is in a section focused on origins because maize is key to this relational knowledge production that opposes reducing the crop (and knowledge itself) to transactional exchanges. Carballo goes on to explain: "El conocimiento no tiene potestad. El conocimiento—esa otra forma de poesía—es patrimonio de la humanidad, nadie es su propietario" (Knowledge does not have legal custodians. Knowledge—that other form of poetry—is humanity's heritage, no one is its owner; 17). In the title "Padres de maíz" and the reference to *patrimonio* (patrimony/heritage), Carballo suggests a different form of *patria* (fatherland) away from this word's connotations bound up with the nation-state. Instead of allegiance to the nation-state, here the term is situated in close connection with the crop. In addition to their elaboration for deceased relatives, altars are erected for maize. Corn-based foods convene communities.[16] As a correlative, society must "exorcizar" (exorcise) the "soberbia" (arrogance) of Western perspectives that allow someone to "sentirse arriba cuando en realidad está abajo" (feel they are on top when in reality they are at the bottom; 17). Carballo refers to a cyclical time where nothing happens alone "en la metáfora constante de la espiral" (in the constant metaphor of the spiral; 17). This image gives a wider sense to the earlier statement "Todos somos Las Plumas de la Serpiente" (We are all the Serpent's Plumes). All people are interconnected. Carballo rejects the mistaken idea that Native histories are pertinent to only Native Nations. Their history is fundamental and interwoven with "mainstream" histories. Dates are not included in most episodes within *Las Plumas* to emphasize how their content continues to be relevant. These episodes are not ephemeral weekly updates; they touch upon lasting themes. The creation of the book *Las Plumas de la Serpiente* itself is a practice of revisiting the words from the radio program like one (re)turns to the maize harvest every year.

Heart/Seed/Prog Rock–Hard Affective Intelligence

The following sempoalxochitl-colored page, "Corazón piedra" (Heart Stone), transitions from the previous section focused on origins and maize to explore in depth an affective intelligence. "Corazón piedra" addresses this affective intelligence with numerous references to yolotl (heart). The text overlays heart, stone, and seed metaphors. One's heart should be firm like the maize seed or a stone to then hit Goliath-like colonial agents in the head. In this sense, the image of a stone on the cover of *Las Plumas* alludes to the semantic connection between the heart and maize seed. Carballo features Native Nations' strength and defense. The piece examines three common Nahuatl phrases: xiyolpaki (be happy of heart), ximoyolchikaua (be firm/strong of heart), and ximoyolzeui (be calm of heart). Carballo employs his idiosyncratic alphabet, writing these terms in the first part of the essay as "xi yolpaki," "xi mo yolchikaua," and "xi mo yolzeui" (18). The spacing is influenced by Castilian syntax ("que ría tu corazón," "que se haga fuerte tu corazón," and "que tu corazón se apague"). In Nahuatl, each phrase would usually appear as a single word, which is how Carballo writes them in the second half of the piece. He parses these phrases containing yolotl, such as "xi yolpaki, que ría tu corazón, como las piedras" (be happy of heart, let your heart laugh, like stones; 18). He goes on to state, "xi mo yolchikaua, como una piedra a Goliat" (be strong/hard of heart, like a stone aimed at Goliath; 18). Both aesthetically and conceptually, Carballo's code-switching resembles Gloria Anzaldúa's conceptualization of *la facultad*, an ability/gift that allows marginalized people to comprehend other people's suffering (60–61). This affective intelligence is developed by people living in the liminal spaces where translanguaging occurs. Like *la facultad*, Carballo's yolotl foregrounds personal knowledge rooted in observant feeling.

Moyolchikaua signifies to have a heart firm like a rock or seed, suggested in the wor(l)dplay within "Corazón piedra." Carballo calls this seed/stone a star or meteor fallen from the sky, with an inner heat and blazing energy concealed by a calm exterior. In relation to moyolchikaua and other phrases integrating yolotl, he illuminates the connection of the heart with maize seed, "hacer del *yolotl* una semilla que late incandescentemente" (to make of *yolotl* a seed that beats incandescently; 18). While a seemingly simple metaphor, yolotl carries profound meaning related to the landscape and maize. This nexus links people with their ancestors and the landscape. Carballo states that "la piedra es otro tipo de tierra" (stones are another type of earth; 18). He cites Serbian-American poet Charles Simic to speak of strength emerging from the ability to "frotar dos piedras y sacar chispas" (rub two stones and make sparks fly out; 18).[17]

This kindling is an apt metaphor for the *contrapunteo* throughout *Las Plumas*. Clashes and creative turns emerge from cultural confrontations and encounters without resolution, here symbolized as sparks or energy emerging from two stones. Moreover, the image plays with the pervasive mediatic trope of the Native "savage," behind on an evolutionary scale, who makes fire by rubbing two stones together. *Las Plumas* is premised on the aim to educate the public and correct erroneous depictions within mass media tropes about retrograde "dialects" and "indios." The heart-seed-rock is thrown at the eye of what Carballo describes as a cyclopes-like "Goliath," challenging a Western monocular view—what Linda Martín Alcoff terms an "epistemology of ignorance"—replete with miscues and misperceptions regarding Native Nations ("Epistemologies of Ignorance: Three Types" 39–41).

In an intricate transpoetic dialogue, Carballo alludes twice to Simic's famous poem "Stone" to reinterpret and transpose its verses through a Nahua context. By citing Simic, he breaks with the false portrayal of Native authors as insular and unaware of international literary currents. Carballo paraphrases Simic stating, "[S]ea usted feliz como una piedra" (May you be happy like a stone; 18).[18] He partially cites Simic, declaring, "Que otros se conviertan en palomas o rechinen sus dientes de tigre" (Let others turn into doves or gnash with tiger's teeth; 18).[19] The associative aesthetic common within Simic's work is apparent in Carballo's writing, as Carballo invokes various permutations of the heart in Nahuatl. A subtext intersects with genetically modified corn (since yolotl can signify maize seed), as in the previous piece "Padres de maíz," and the inability to store or replant it. By genetic design, GMO seeds must be purchased by farmers for every crop, and the kernels from that harvest cannot become firm like the stone/heart/corn described in "Corazón piedra."[20] Commercialized GMO maize literally breaks the system of reciprocity in which people and maize care for one another in a perpetual cycle.

"Corazón piedra" moves into a wider conception of text articulated in the radio short "Manos en armonía" (Hands in Harmony). "Manos en armonía" addresses the connection between the textiles and the text on the page, stating, "Así se teje un árbol" (Like this a tree is woven; 19). The essay elaborates on weaving as both medium and metaphor for writing and knowledge production, stating that the huipiles/embroidered blouses "tienen rostro" (have a face; 20). Wisdom in these threaded words produce chuj, the Maya Tzotzil word for textile (20). This piece joins a trans-Indigenous dialogue between Maya and Nahuatl. Carballo highlights that the experiential knowledge from these creations is "el *Curriculum Vitae* de los que no han sido tomados en cuenta" (the *Curriculum Vitae* of those who have gone unacknowledged; 20). The public must learn "de estos viejos que hicieron el camino bordándolo, *chapeándolo* o cardándolo—y por eso insisto en ello" (from these elders who made the path embroidering it, *weeding it*, or depilling it—and that's why I insist on it; 20). In this trans-Indigenous dialogue Carballo moves away from traditional ethnographic and anthropological studies where a privileged colonial agent investigates colonized communities. Instead, as Arturo Arias explains, the absence of colonial difference "implies that the relationship subject/otherness is distanced from abject manifestations of colonial violence" (my trans.; "Tramas y dramas de la descolonización" 203). As a Nahua researching Tzotzil cultural production, Carballo's observations do not carry the colonial baggage that a Western researcher may (un)wittingly bring to the foray.

Within "Manos en armonía," Carballo speaks of the need for "el otro México" (the other Mexico, i.e., non-Indigenous) to "reconocer la grandeza de estos artistas mexicanos" (recognize the greatness of these Mexican artists; 21). He repeats *reconocer*: "El reconocimiento entre los distintos nos hace reconocernos a nosotros mismos, simples seres humanos" (Recognition [literally "re-knowledge"] among different people makes us recognize ourselves, simple human beings; 20). Rather than the use of *reconocer* as *recognition*, in the sense of nation-state acknowledgment of Native peoples' existence and acceptance within Western systems of validation, here Carballo plays on the literal meaning of *reconocer*—re-conocer, "to become familiar with/know again" something or someone. With this move, Carballo's text avoids what Yásnaya Elena Aguilar Gil warns is the pernicious idea that Native movements must achieve validation according to Western standards centered on individual success ("Resistencia" 27). Nahua knowledges need to be revisited, **reconocidos**. The multiple words with the prefix *re-* connect with the metaphor of circular repetitions throughout *Las Plumas*, mirrored in the back-and-forth cross stitch, crop cycles, and the river's flow cited in "Manos en armonía." These text(ile)s situate the past in front. Carballo describes textiles as a path to help those who have migrated or died to *regresar* or *re*turn to their home communities and collective memory.

In this movement, Carballo proposes an alternative system of validation regarding what constitutes valuable texts. He concludes

"Manos en armonía" by linking land, textiles, maize, corporeality, and the *contrapunteo* of music: "Que sus manos sigan llevando la batuta del movimiento universal" (May their hands continue carrying the baton of the universal movement; 21). Reciprocity permeated these spaces, symbolized in the *manos* or hands invoking the *mano vuelta* ("returned hand" or collective work), a term used in Castilian and Nahuatl (often apocopated to manoj in Huastecan Nahuatl). Carballo comes back to the heart, stating, "Los dedicados al arte, tendremos que poner los ojos en la periferia, de ahí se alimenta el corazón—y el estómago—de esta nación mexicana" (Those of us dedicated to art, we must turn our eyes to the periphery, that is where the heart—and the stomach—of this Mexican nation is fed; 21). References to the heart and the stomach revisit maize-based foods. One's eyes should be on the periphery producing that sustenance and keeping the general populace alive both physically and epistemologically.

These textual landscapes transition into vertiginous inequities within the Mexico City metropolitan landscape in "Manos de Santa Cruz" (Hands of Holy Cross). The piece presents stunning vertical contrast between a high-rise building and people below on the street. The title's focus on *manos* relates to the Huastecan "mano vuelta" or "manoj" from previous pieces to denote people aiding one another within a system of reciprocity. Nonetheless, like the mother washing cars in the epigraph to this chapter, Indigenous workers are alienated from the skyscrapers they construct. Those who build these edifices and those who occupy them will rarely if ever come into meaningful contact with one another. Carballo crosses over the dividing line; he approaches Native workers in a building where he has a meeting. These workers take on precarious work to earn higher wages. From their location on a high-rise, they look down and see the Ángel de la Independencia (Angel of Independence), an iconic statue of Mexico City. Described by Carballo in a later piece, celebrations of the national soccer team's victories occur around this statue. The workers find themselves trapped within an inequitable system far from independence despite the monument's suggestion otherwise.

Through the initial pieces Carballo moves back and forth from Europe, then writes from Mexico City about the return to his Huastecan hometown. He speaks with his father about maize and then, in subsequent sections, addresses metaphors of the heart and Maya artisans.

Carballo engages in trans-Indigenous dialogues on the twenty-sixth floor of a skyscraper in downtown Mexico City. From there, he transitions to a musical landscape in "Músicas" (Types of Music). This episode is dedicated to Gonzalo Camacho, a professor of music at UNAM (25). Dedications initiate various essays to form a subtext of Indigenous and non-Indigenous alliances. "Músicas" focuses on music as a bridge to unite people, while simultaneously recognizing Native Nation's respective aesthetics. The initial verses mirror Carballo's contrapuntal style throughout the book. This style is described explicitly in verses visually leaping back and forth on the page: "El miedo preserva, construye y crea. / También mata. / Contraposición eterna. / Contrapunto necesario" (Fear preserves, constructs, and creates. / It also kills. / Eternal counterposition. / Necessary counterpoint; 25). These lines render vivid a continual death and rebirth. The poetic voice introduces a metaphor of musicians mixing gold with blood to underscore how this artistic production originates out of deep suffering, tying back to the previous piece with the construction workers. Gold mixed with blood can be read as a reference to precious metals stolen by colonial regimes and the systematic oppression left in their wake. The musicians play despite colonial traumas. Language breaks down into fragments, "Un pecho. Un dardo" (A chest. A dart), and then that pain bursts in a cathartic song and shout (25). Suffering makes for fertile soil, as tears fall to the ground. The piece describes musicians as Mesoamerican Prometheus-like possums who stole fire for humans and burned their tail in the process (25–26). Music possesses the power to kindle a spiritual flame inside people. Mixed metaphors weave back to the sparks and fire within the heart/seed's affective space. The knowledges that emerge from this space of affective intelligence are felt with the heart: "Del latido del corazón surge el cuero que da rienda suelta al tambor" (From the beating of the heart emerges the leather that gives free rein to the drum; 26). This beat in turn recalls "Corazón piedra" in which the heart is a rock thrown at "Goliath-like" threats.

In this process, music touches the landscape and is intoned before the altar during rituals for the earth. Carballo criticizes the tendency to view Native Nations' ceremonies and accompanying music, and by extension all aspects of these Nations, as a monolith, "[u]n tren de sonidos que uno escucha como si fueran todos uno a la vez" (a train of sounds that one hears as if they were all one and the same; 26–27). He responds, "No es así. Ni invisibles ni uno. Legión y con rostro los aludidos en la metáfora del cenzontle. Visible y muchos, y con rostro, y distintos entre sí" (It is not so. They are neither invisible nor one alone. Those alluded to in the metaphor of the cenzontle [mockingbird] are legion and they have faces. They are visible and numerous, and they have faces, and they are distinct from one another; 27). The face accentuates the experiential knowledges of those "invisibilized," or, as Shannon Speed posits, *vulneradas* (made vulnerable; *Incarcerated Stories* 3). They are real people with myriad voices, as suggested in the symbols of the centzontle ("bird of 400 voices") and the Serpent's diverse plumage.

Musical compositions carry what Carballo calls tziktli (gum, or what he refers to as a "gum ally"), a "glue bridge" that convenes people (27). According to this metaphor, from the encounter of the teeth with this gum emerges a counterpoint of conflict and sweetness described as "dulce, generoso vicio y pegamento" (sweet, generous vice and glue; 27). He locates this "stickiness" or bridge as a space "[p]ara cruzar, para salir, para llegar, para partir, para partir en uno y mil los prejuicios que nos separan" (to cross, to leave, to arrive, to depart, to split in one and a thousand the prejudices that separate us; 27). Carballo plays on *partir* as both "to leave" and "to part/divide." Within constant migrations immense creativity materializes to cross, leave, arrive, and separate into innumerable paths. Carballo code-switches stating, "Seamos el puente y el tziktli" (Let's be the bridge and the tziktli; 27). This description ties into the previous episode in which the workers construct bridges and buildings that simultaneously gather and segregate, as they the builders themselves are excluded from them. The episodes throughout *Las Plumas* serve as a different type of bridge where everyone crosses.

The episode "Músicas" concludes reiterating the verses with which it began, but with one additional line: "Otro mundo es posible, si cantamos" (Another world is possible, if we sing; 27). This phrase invokes EZLN's aim to create a "world where many worlds fit" ("La cuarta declaración de la Selva Lacandona"). This acceptance of alternative methodologies and epistemologies moves away from individual validation within Western systems. Through the previous three pieces, skilled hands combine to weave various types of texts—textiles, landscape/architecture, and music—all serving as inspiration for *Las Plumas*. Brought together in a *contrapunteo* of Mesoamerican and Western media, influences, and beats, these pieces move among multiple worldings through the text on the page, fabric, music, the body, and the earth itself as a surface to be read.

Serpents' Tongues Weave Language and Territory

In "Los idiomas tienen sus secretos" (Languages Have Their Secrets), Carballo addresses how attention to language uproots the pervasive notion that Indigenous peoples are stuck in time. Carballo speaks of "[h]ora de hacer una pausa. De volar como vuelan los que saben. Los que han hecho de los árboles lugar propicio para hacer nido" (time to pause. To fly like those who know how to fly. Those who have made of trees the favorable place to nest; 33). This motion intersects with the metaphor of the Serpent's avian flight to lay the nest to which Carballo alludes with Estados O*nidos* in this chapter's epigraph. The nest is high in the air, suggestive of far-reaching migrations, and deep knowledges communicated in that transit are reinforced through the tree, a Mesoamerican symbol of wisdom.

"Los idiomas tienen sus secretos" was written on 21 February 2012, the International Day of Maternal Tongues. Although this day commemorates an important cause, Carballo laments that it has fallen into a demagoguery oblivious to Nahua aesthetics, rhythms, and figures of speech. To explore those dynamics, he shares "consejo de mayores" (elders' advice; 33) and translanguages in verse between Castilian and Nahuatl:

> Que sea tu boca como una espina,
>
> > *Huitztli,* así le llaman.
>
> Que se haga tu boca de chuparrosa,
>
> de colibrí, para ser espada y para ser caricia.
>
> Que sea tu pico tu espada.
>
> > Colibrí.
>
> Que sea tu boca justa.
>
> > Y que sean bonitas tus palabras.
> >
> > Que tengan ritmo y música,
> >
> > que *Tzi, tzi, tzi* sea tu vuelo: *huitzitzilin.*

Onomatopeya de su vuelo y descripción poética al mismo tiempo.

> Los idiomas tienen sus secretos y sus interpretaciones.
>
> > Consejos de mayores para los tiempos nuevos. (33–34)

(May your mouth be like a thorn,

>> *Huitztli*, that is what they call it.

May your mouth become a florisuga's,

a hummingbird's, to be sword and to be caress.

May your beak be a sword.

>> Hummingbird.

May your voice be just.

> And may your words be pretty.

> May they have rhythm and music,

> may *Tzi, tzi, tzi* be your flight: *huitzitzilin*.

Onomatopoeia of its flight and poetic description at the same time.

> Languages have their secrets and their interpretations.

> Counsel from elders for new times.)

This subtle sonority is onomatopoeia and metaphor. The repetition of *tzitzi* in the Nahuatl word for hummingbird, huitzitzilin, is onomatopoeic in its imitation of fluttering wings. Close attention to sound resonates with an ecocentric comprehension in which other-than-humans speak. Concomitantly, huitzitzilin is a metaphor through its etymology comparing the hummingbird's beak with the root word "thorn" (huitz[tli]). Furthermore, this description encompasses writing itself both acoustically and figuratively, as the *tzitzi* resembles the sound of scribbling on paper and the hummingbird's beak recalls the tip of a pen.

Carballo uses huitzitzilin to underscore the Nahuatl language's aesthetic force (like a thorn) and beautiful complexities (the hummingbird and the flower from which it drinks). As seen in the introduction to this study, he insists that Nahuatl can be both beautiful and harsh. Like other younger authors, he stresses the need to denounce injustices. The hummingbird relates to the previous piece, "El regreso," in which Carballo's return to his hometown "irrupts like the stabs of a hummingbird's beak in one's chest" (13; 15). Carballo guards against people who exoticize Nahuatl and Nahua communities, and who proclaim how *bonito* or "pretty" they are. With that in mind, it is significant that the poetic voice declares,

"[Q]ue sean bonitas tus palabras" (May your words be pretty). This beauty is balanced with the call to be like a sword. Nahua voices should be piercing like flowers and their accompanying thorns. In these movements, rather than a lyric na (I), the poetic voice is a collectivity of elders. Carballo shares "[c]onsejos de mayores para los tiempos nuevos" (counsel from elders for new times; 34). The essay advises listeners/readers to wield the Nahuatl language and to bring out its potential in the present, to transform the elders' counsel *for new times*.

In "Otro calor de aliento" (Other Heat of Breath), this counsel is shared where "[a]lrededor del fogón, disfrazados de humo, llegan los cuentos" (around the fire, disguised as smoke, the stories arrive; 35). Nahua narratives and the epistemes they communicate are articulated around the tenamastli or hearth stones. Their language shapes dreams: "A golpe de palabra se esculpen los sueños" (With the blow of words dreams are sculpted; 35). Carballo concludes the piece with a stunning description of a dynamic circular/spiral temporality. Elders' wisdom narratives are the "revisited memories":

> La memoria revisitada hace de la vida un círculo y corre en espiral hasta nuestros tiempos, no hay error en ello. Se transforma: como la serpiente se quita escamas, se renueva reptando. Se hace en el camino otra serpiente y sin embargo es la misma siempre; así, hasta morderse la cola, otra vez. (36)

> (Memory revisited makes of life a circle and runs in a spiral into our times, of this there is no doubt. It transforms: like a serpent sheds its skin, it renews itself by slithering. Along the way it turns into another serpent and yet it remains its old self; so it goes on until it bites its own tail, once again.)

Biting the tale marks a circularity where people harm themselves and their own communities time and again. A revisiting of the past has the potential to strengthen or to fall into vicious cycles. Repetition of words with *re* emphasizes these patterns: **revisitada, corre, renovar, reptar,** and *siempre*. The serpent changes its skin in a continual becoming, while concomitantly there are positive and negative tendencies that resurface such as the (re)affirmation of Nahua perspectives or the recidivism of discriminatory practices. The serpent transforms in a dynamic present, but at same time elders identify patterns to emulate or to avoid across all aspects of life, ranging from the crop to human interactions. The circularity of memory can provide unity and renewal, but, if mishandled, thoughts can spin out into a destructive descent.

Within a section beginning with a sempoalxochitl-colored page that addresses the displacement of Native knowledges, Carballo returns to the EZLN in the episode "La otra campaña" (The Other Campaign). He denounces the oppression of Indigenous Nations and contrapuntally revisits the narratives he was told as a child in his hometown. For Indigenous peoples, the official history propagated by the nation-state "ha sido como esos zopilotes que vuelan por sobre las pirámides—cadáveres hermosos, pero cadáveres—volando siempre sobre restos de un pasado glorioso" (has been like those vultures who fly above the pyramids—beautiful cadavers, but still cadavers—flying always above the remnants of a glorious past; 53). Official history resembles vultures circling the pyramids in its treatment of Native Nations as carrion of a moribund past.

With a view rooted in tlaixpan, Carballo states that from a Western perspective, "para con los muertos no hay derechos que asumir, tampoco vergüenza" (for the dead there are no rights to assume, nor shame; 53). This Western framework contrasts dramatically with tlaixpan. In Nahuatl, the deceased possess rights like living people and the landscape, and they must be honored. A Western gaze sees Mexico "siempre en toma panorámica, siempre desde lejos" (always with a panoramic shot, always from far away; 53). Under that panoramic shot, the landscape and the deceased are exploited and dismembered in place of being remembered through a ceremonial repertoire.

The title "La otra campaña" invokes the EZLN's nonmilitarized campaign throughout Mexico from August to September 2005. The Other Campaign's main goal was to dialogue with marginalized communities in a heterarchical alliance against capitalism. Native peoples (the Serpent's Feathers), the EZLN among them, rewrite the official history: "Sin embargo estas plumas han escrito ya una historia nueva, una donde otro mundo es posible" (Nevertheless these plumes have already written a new history, one where another world is possible; 54). Carballo pursues this "other world" throughout *Las Plumas* (11, 12, 27, 42, 54, 95, 96, 109).

In response to colonial acts that thwart alternative worldings, the episode "Ida y vuelta: Jornaleros indígenas" (Round Trip: Indigenous Laborers) condemns the concrete effects of discrimination in Native lives. Carballo interviews Mè'phààs who have migrated from Guerrero to other regions of Mexico. The episode begins with the voice of a farm laborer named Fidel García: "En la carretera con los soldados que nos paran, con la policía que nos revisa como si fuéramos delincuentes, nos bajan de los camiones, nos dicen pendejadas, pues" (On the highway the soldiers stop us, and the police search us as if we're criminals, they pull us off the buses, they tell us a bunch of bullshit, yeah; 56). Carballo speaks of the knowledge gained from this harsh experience, similar to Anzaldúa's *la facultad*, as a "tristeza sabia" (wise sadness; 56). The laborers use the word *migrar* (to migrate) even though they travel within their country of birth to work in the fields of Sinaloa. Carballo mentions Fidel García by name to counter the anonymity commonplace in news reports. Guerrero has one of the highest rates of temporal migration, especially from the laborers' Mè'phàà community of Tlapa. Another farmhand, Joaquín Catalán, suffered wretched conditions and deception at the hands of *enganchadores* (recruiters who hunt low-wage workers; 57). In these contexts, Native workers are treated like foreigners, robbed, and forced to toil under horrific circumstances. The public ignores those conditions, "y nadie ve nada, / y una sociedad que ignora tozudamente, el camino que recorrió el jitomate para llegar hasta su mesa, / y nadie ve nada" (and no one sees anything, / and a society that stubbornly ignores, the path tomatoes traveled to arrive at their table, / and no one sees anything; 58). Alienation under the global capitalist system silences this exploited labor force hidden from public view. Carballo breaks that silence by bringing back these laborers' messages—as well as the Serpent-Plumed voices of numerous marginalized communities—to denounce social and economic inequities.

Reporting on the So-Called War: Denunciations of Massacres and Assassinations

With an untitled sempoalxochitl-colored page, Carballo opens a section focused on massacres and assassinations. The degradation of Nahua history, land, language, and affective spaces exerts a nefarious effect on Nahuas' everyday lives and renders their bodies disposable. Carballo denounces the rape of women from the community of Atenco, Estado de Mexico, by federal and state police in May 2006. He states that Atenco means "at the shore of the water;" he then quotes thirteenth-century Persian poet Rumi, "Toda sed es saciada salvo la sed de los peces" (All thirst is quenched except for the thirst of fish; 62).[21] Carballo cautions that "[t]arde o temprano la historia nos hará partícipes de su eco" (sooner or later history will make us participants of their [Atenco's] echo; 63). No one should feel unaffected by these losses; all should feel the responsibility to quench a thirst for justice. *Las Plumas* is like an altar on which Carballo places pictures of the many who have suffered human rights violations. This heartfelt reading recollects people who have suffered tragic deaths. Nonetheless, through remembrance, there is hope that these reports will elicit systemic transformation and, in that sense, those who have died will return to the present. *Las Plumas* keeps the memory of the deceased in front, sharing specific names and experiences of people with "[c]uerpo de *kuetlaxotl* y *omitl*" (body of *kuetlaxotl* [skin] and *omitl* [bone], "real-life people of flesh and bone") in the face of dehumanized statistics of the mounting death toll (62).

Dangers in reporting violent acts abound. "Periodistas en tiempos de crisis" (Journalists in Time of Crisis) bemoans how journalism seems to exert little impact. Entranced within a social bystander effect, people go about their lives and turn a blind eye to reported cases of human rights violations. In the essay, the oppressor is a "Giant;" the oppressor is also a woman who in her complicity ignores what occurs: "Y el Gigante ríe, su mano ostenta un puro que es a la vez garrote y macana y fusil y desprecio y es también, al mismo tiempo, una mujer que cierra una ventana para no mirar" (And the Giant laughs, his hand wields a cigar that's at once club and truncheon and gun and contempt and is also, at the same time, a woman who shuts her window so as not to see; 64). The Giant and the woman are willfully blind to knowledge rooted in personal observance suggested by ixtlamatilistli and the affective intelligence explored in earlier pieces. References to the Giant's derisive laughter contrast with heart-laughing or affective intelligence in "Corazón piedra." Under these repressive conditions, Carballo states that, according to Portuguese writer Fernando Pessoa, "si el corazón comenzara a pensar se detendría" (if the heart were to start thinking it would stop beating; 65). He avers that what Pessoa fails to address is "como parar lo que un corazón sensible causa en un cerebro, y por ende en una causa, y lo que nos causa" (how to stop what a sensitive heart causes in a brain, and hence in a cause, and what it causes in us; 65). This contemplation with the heart plays on the meanings of *causa* as both the (e/a)ffect developed (*what heart-thinking causes*) and social causes defended (*the causes heart-thinking creates*). "Periodistas en tiempos de crisis" concludes with a mix of hope and desperation. Carballo laments that "[g]olpeando al viento a nadie ponemos en jaque" (throwing punches at the wind we checkmate no one; 66). Concomitantly, the piece expresses hope that the public will develop a much-needed affective intelligence.

"Las postales invisibles" (Invisible Postcards) examines the yearning and anguish of reporting injustices across Native Nations in Mexico. Carballo recounts his travels throughout the country for his documentary series. He observes challenges in many locations, offering "invisible postcards" from places such as Sonora (the Tehono O'odham / Papago Nation's struggles against drug trafficking and state-sponsored violence in their region), Tabasco (two of the last speakers of a Native language are not on speaking terms), Sinaloa (wretched working conditions to which Native people migrate), and Chicontepec, Veracruz (a shortage of hospitals for Nahua communities). In Sinaloa, Indigenous laborers wear handkerchiefs on their faces to "protect" themselves from herbicides (68). The lines break off and pose the question, "¿Alguien gusta una ensalada?" (Would someone like a salad?; 68, 70). Like in "Ida y vuelta," Carballo awakens readers/listeners to unjust conditions and the alienation promoted by the global capitalist system.

"Las postales invisibles" features conflicting complexities within Native communities. There are Indigenous people who oppose Native rights movements. The EZLN has organized in Chiapas, but some Native people oppose the EZLN. The Tehono O'odham combat megaprojects; that does not mean they live harmoniously together. Isidro and Manuel, reportedly the last speakers of Ayapaneco, may never resolve their differences. A popular tendency extols Native Nations' resistance, but there are also members who acquiesce. Carballo states, "Postales del México indígena, olvidado, vilipendiado que se organiza (o no) pero aun así resiste los embates de una historia y una sociedad que no quiere voltear a mirar, a mirarse, a mirarnos" (Postcards from the Indigenous Mexico, forgotten, vilified, that organizes [or not] but that still resists the onslaught of a history and a society that does not want to turn to see, to see themselves, to see us; 69). After addressing these dire contexts, the piece suddenly asks, "¿Dónde están los diccionarios? ¿Dónde están los atentos y los encargados de desarrollar o registrar las culturas que están a punto de morir?" (Where are the dictionaries? Where are the attentive people and those in charge of developing or documenting cultures on the verge of dying?; 70). Defense of Native languages links with struggles for land, water, and improvement of overall conditions. Language constitutes a tool to change those contexts. The postcard, a recurring trope, emphasizes a type of reporting rooted in locality and the study of specific local concerns. Far removed from tourist posts, these figurative postcards are snapshots that mirror the brief format of Carballo's radio shorts; they are placed before the reader/listener like photographs on the altar to remind people of their lost loved ones.

In this way, within "Acteal," Carballo remembers those murdered in the Acteal massacre in Chiapas. In 1997 a paramilitary group raided the Tzotzil community of Acteal and killed members of the Abejas Civil Society, a nonviolent Maya-Tzotzil Christian organization that declared solidarity with the EZLN movement. The federal government claims that the massacre was an interethnic conflict. Nonetheless, evidence suggests that the perpetrators, also Indigenous, were a state-sponsored Priísta paramilitary group. To disrupt the reduction of people to statistics, Carballo gives the names of all forty-five Tzotziles killed. In a later episode, "Acteal y futbol, la noticia del día" (Acteal and Soccer, Today's News), the excruciating court proceedings for the Acteal massacre stand in stark contrast with a national soccer game occurring simultaneously. Carballo's contrapuntal observance of this context shifts among the court proceedings, the soccer game, and the protests denouncing the massacre. While Native people march, Mexico plays against "su par norteamericano" (its North American peer), the US national team (85). It is 2 p.m., 12 August 2009. The Supreme Court has acquitted the twenty-four Tzotziles accused of perpetrating the massacre. That they were also Indigenous underscores the complexities of this tragedy. In bringing out these nuances and inner divisions, Carballo eschews romanticization of Native communities.

Despite the ongoing court proceedings, the public fixates on the soccer game. Carballo is infuriated by the lack of attention to Acteal: "Los que *están pegados al balón* (metáfora cotidiana de la vida) seguro no se habrán enterado que mientras eso pasaba, algunos sobrevivientes de la masacre de Acteal, estaban bloqueando Pino Suárez, no están de acuerdo con el fallo" (Those *glued to the ball* [quotidian metaphor of life] are surely unaware that while the game was happening, some survivors of the Acteal massacre were blocking Pino Suárez Street, they oppose the verdict; 84). There pervades an affective deficit on the part of a public ensconced in a state-constructed patriotism reinforced by the national soccer team. Readers/listeners glean from this juxtaposition the nation-state's mistaken priorities; this polarity highlights how the focus on nation-state borders and rivalries b(l)ind people to the inner divisions and inequities within their own country. Carballo uses *par* (peer) rather than "rival" to accentuate the destructive nature of the state toward Native Nations in both the US and Mexico, to the extent that this oppression goes unreported and ignored in favor of a sports game centered on imagined communities.

The piece ends forcefully, stating, "La 'selección mexicana' acaba de ganarle a su par norteamericano, comenzarán a circular los coches, algunos pitarán como si la victoria les perteneciera" (The "Mexican team" just beat its North American peer, cars will begin to circulate, some will honk as if the victory were theirs; 85). As Yásnaya Elena Aguilar Gil asserts, these nation-state constructions act as "agentes aculturadores que integraran a sus comunidades a una nación monolingüe en español y monocultural" (acculturating agents that assimilate their communities into a monolingual and monocultural nation; *Ää: Manifiestos* 112). The losses at Acteal go unfelt by the public, even though those losses are more consequential than any patriotic win or loss at a soccer game.

After "Acteal," an untitled sempoalxochitl-colored piece breaks away from this nation(al)-state of obliviousness by observing the Day of the Dead. Despite its attention to death, this essay is one of the most hopeful in the collection. Carballo begins by listing various ways of addressing death in Mexico. He describes crossing the river Mictlan (Place of the Dead), a myth "revestido, revisitado por el humor, el albur, la claridad y el temor, así dijeron nuestros ante-pasados, los de antes y los contemporáneos"[1] (cloaked [literally "redressed"], revisited with humor, wordplay, clarity, and fear, like our ancestors said, those from before and the contemporary; 92). Carballo plays on the "ante" (before) in *antepasados* (ancestors) by referring to them as "los de antes y los contemporáneos" (92). Here they endure both temporally and spatially in front on the altar. They are *con*temporary, literally, and literarily, "with us in time." As reflected in the transformation of the word, written "ante-pasados" in the piece, ancestors are before us (*ante nosotros*). They are not relegated to a remote time before (*antes de nosotros*).

In "Maguey Maguaquite, 1980," Carballo similarly centers his home community and family, these *ante-pasados*. The meaning of his hometown Maguey Maguaquite appears in the glossary: "**Maguaquite**. Nauyaca. Cuatro narices. Serpiente" (**Maguaquite**. Nauyaca. Four noses. Serpent; 132). This potent snake embodies the community's strength. To project an analogous robustness in media outlets, Carballo's media team tasked with editing *Las Plumas*'s radio shorts is Nauyaca ("four noses" in Nahuatl) Productions. "Maguey Maguaquite, 1980" discusses mass media's influence in Carballo's life and throughout Mexico.

When his children moved away to Mexico City in the 1980s, Carballo's father could listen to traditional Nahua Huapango music and other radio programs in Nahuatl: "Pero de lo que no se quedó con ganas fue de escuchar la Xochipitzahuak o la flor menuda—para los que no hablen náhuatl—y tampoco se quedó con las ganas de escuchar voces en este idioma mexicano" (But what he didn't miss out on was listening to the Xochipitzahuak or little flower—for those who don't speak Nahuatl—nor did he miss out on hearing voices in this Mexican language; 106). The piece then shifts to the present: "pero ahora, siglo actual, México contemporáneo ni eso hay en la radio: No existen espacios para los indígenas en los medios de comunicación mexicanos" (but now, in the present century, in contemporary Mexico even that can no longer be heard on the radio: There are no spaces for Indigenous peoples in Mexican media; 106). Instead, the public is engulfed in discriminatory images where "[l]a imagen de *indias Marías* es la más socorrida, el indio sentado o dormido junto a un nopal o tirado de borracho" (the image of *indias Marías* is the most frequent one, the Indian sitting or sleeping by a cactus or collapsed on the ground drunk; 107). Carballo stresses that everyone, including Native communities, is complicit in these depictions.

The arc of this episode signals that, despite technological innovations, Native presence in mass media in many respects has waned. A person can no longer turn on the radio and listen to Nahuatl like in the 1980s. Carballo avers that Native media "coadyuva al proceso democrático. . . . Todo intento por crecerlo tendrá sin duda que sustentarse—como su raíz etimológica refiere, en el pueblo" (contributes to the democratic process. . . . Any attempt to grow it will no doubt have to be supported—like its etymological root suggests, in the community; 108). In other words, people must receive Native languages and perspectives to better understand themselves and their region's history. After advancing this etymology, Carballo mentions where he records this radio short: "Ciudad de México, delegación Cuauhtémoc, Colonia Roma, 2012" (108). The location is ironic, with its reference to the area of Mexico City named Cuauhtemoc, relating to an earlier comment that a romanticized Native past is tattooed on the people and surroundings (107). There is irony in the name of the neighborhood, the Colonia (colony) of Roma (Rome), both alluding to colonialism and imperialism. Colonia Roma is a neighborhood known for its fast-paced gentrification. While producing the radio shorts, Carballo occupies these spaces and centers the knowledges of his Huastecan community.[22]

The following piece, "Otro muerto..." (Another Dead), shifts from discussing the disappearance of Nahuas in mass media to addressing the thousands murdered and disappeared in the so-called War on Drugs.

"Otro muerto..." is dedicated to Mexican poet Javier Sicilia, who lost his son and subsequently became an activist. Carballo again puts faces on the ever-increasing statistic of those killed. He offers unusual statistics the public would never hear. He asks his audience to reconsider how dehumanizing tallies in the news reduce people to numbers and dissociate, dis-*member*, them from the kinship networks that feel these losses. The number of reported deaths at the time of this piece in 2011 was forty thousand deaths (and, as indicated in a note in *Las Plumas*, the number had grown to ninety thousand at the book's publication in 2012). Carballo states, "Ocho millones doscientos cuarenta mil huesos. Cuarenta mil corazones que dejaron de latir. Ochenta mil manos . . ." (Eight million two hundred and forty thousand bones. Forty thousand hearts that stopped beating. Eighty thousand hands . . . ; 125). By altering the usual drone of statistics in the news, Carballo brings humanity to every individual. He declares, "Con un muerto nos bastaba. Nos hemos muerto de a poquito" (One death was enough. We have died little by little; 126). Forty thousand final postcards highlight specific people's experiences. Carballo underscores the vision of each of these individuals in speaking of "[o]chenta mil niñas, corneas, pupilas . . . ochenta mil ojos" (eighty thousand apples of my eye, corneas, pupils . . . eighty thousand eyes; 126). He shares that, according to Mexican reporter Marcela Turati, "thanatologists [. . .] teach that for each violent death two hundred people are affected, as it alters all the settings in which the deceased developed [. . .] society is sick" (127). In this regard, mortality rates pass over a shared suffering where the effects of one death reverberate throughout society. Carballo concludes, "Cuarenta mil personas muertas x doscientos personas afectadas = 8,000,000 de personas tristes, enojadas" (four hundred thousand dead people x two hundred people affected = 8,000,000 sad, angry people; 127). This number would climb to eighteen million at the time of *Las Plumas*'s publication.

The penultimate essay, "¿Cuánto cuesta México?" (How Much Does Mexico Cost?), continues pondering the topic of statistics and connects back to earlier descriptions of the Mexican flag. Carballo inquires how much "bidders" would be willing to pay for Mexico: "Si México fuera una marca registrada, ¿Cuánto costaría?" (if Mexico were a registered brand, How much would it cost?; 128). There is irony in that Mexico is a Nahuatl word appropriated by the nation-state. Carballo poses the question, "¿Cuánto estaría usted dispuesto a pagar por un mito?" (How much would you sir be willing to pay for a myth?; 128). The formal *usted* stands out, as if selling to a client. Resembling the dismemberment in

"Otro muerto...," a figurative auctioneer asks, "¿Qué prefiere usted? ¿Espina, águila, escama, tuna, colmillo, pluma, serpiente, picos, garra o nopal? Dicen que de eso se compone el botín. Mito, nombre, escudo o bandera. ¿Qué prefiere usted?" (What would you prefer, sir? Spine, eagle, scale, prickly pear, fang, feather, serpent, beaks, claw, or cactus? They say the plunder consists of that. Myth, name, crest, or flag. What would you prefer, sir?; 128). Dismemberment and the auctioning of land to the highest bidder hark back to the settler colonialism examined particularly in chapter 2. Rather than a relational symbiosis among people and surroundings, the earth and its resources are reduced to transactional exchanges.

The final piece, "¿Cuánto pesa un muerto?" (How Much Do the Dead Weigh?), denounces the drastic increase in murders during the first decade of the federal government's "War on Drugs" campaign. "¿Cuánto pesa un muerto?" is the title of a song performed by Carballo's prog rock group $A^2 + C$ featuring portions of the *Las Plumas* essay.[23] This xochitlajtoli, an eclectic mix of radio short /essay / poem / song, asks the listener to contemplate the worth of each of the tens of thousands of individuals who has died in the "War on Drug Trafficking." The question "How much do the dead weigh?" refers to how much they weigh upon our consciences. In Carballo's prog rock performance of these words, the piece begins with a sampling from Gil Scott-Heron's "The Revolution Will Not Be Televised," which is fitting in its message that mass media excludes Afrodescendant and Indigenous perspectives that challenge the status quo. Scott-Heron's line is echoed in Carballo's repetition of "¿Cuánto pesan los muertos?"—death being the ultimate silencing of dissonant voices (130–31). The sampling common to hip-hop and rap functions as a contact zone for moving beyond expected borders to the creation of a solidarity network among those dissonant voices.

The first sentence begins: "Hace poco nos enteramos que en la llamada guerra contra el narcotráfico ha habido más de 90 mil muertos" (A short time ago we found out that in the so-called War on Drug Trafficking there have been more than 90 thousand killed; 130). The piece contests the effectiveness of this ever-increasing statistic. An impoverished affective connection, of not seeing other people as equals, permits such violence. "¿Cuánto pesa un muerto?" invites us to leave the statistics that reduce individuals to numbers; each loss must be felt with yoltlajlamikilistli or knowledge of the heart. Instead of data, the piece stresses materiality, stating, "Hay un ritual que es premonición, poema y augurio, que hacen las personas antes de morir" (There is a ritual that is premonition, poem, and omen, that people make before they die; 130). He describes "un barrunto" (a gut feeling) where "[a] la persona le entran deseos irrefrenables de recorrer caminos, lugares, amores, por donde ha sembrado gran parte de su vida" (the person has the uncontrollable desire to retrace paths, places, loves, where they sowed a large part of their life; 130). This practice consists of a person retracing their steps before they die, in Nahuatl literally to gather one's feet, as Carballo code-switches into Nahuatl: moijxipejpena (ijxi or ikxi, "feet," and pejpena, to "collect" or "choose").[24] His code-switching emphasizes the perspective of ixtlamatilistli and being familiar with one's surroundings: *"mo ijxipejpena, mo ijxi pej pen tinemi"* (*they collect their feet, they go around collecting their feet*; 130). As seen in earlier chapters, the suffix -tinemi contains the root nemi—from which the word nemilistli (philosophy / way or walk of life) is derived—and signifies going around doing something. *Las Plumas* is a dynamic revisiting of origins—such as the Nahuatl language itself—and these ancestral memories join a kaleidoscopic creativity, rather than "holding them back" in time as so often depicted in misrepresentations of Indigenous cultural production.

"¿Cuánto pesa un muerto?" counterpoints between a Nahua view and the dire situation in society. The deceased, without realizing it, "está recogiendo sus pies" (is collecting their feet; *Las Plumas de la Serpiente*, 130). Western technocracy reduces this suffering to calculations rather than a collective imaginary: "Hay sucesos que la ciencia explica de ciertas formas; al mismo evento revisitado o revestido por el imaginario colectivo, popular, se le llama de otro modo: ¿Ha sentido que se le sube el muerto alguna vez?" (There are events that science explains in certain ways; the same event, revisited and redressed by the collective, popular imaginary, is referred to differently: Have you ever felt that the dead rise up in you?; 131). An imaginary centered on collectivity moves beyond demography to revisit and "redress" those deaths, to truly sense them. We should be just as affected if one person dies as if many lose their lives—moving beyond what Seneca literary critic Mishuana Goeman calls the "mode of statistics" toward the power of individual stories ("Heteronormative Constructions"). To the final stanza in *Las Plumas*, the prog rock performance adds a one verse translation of Scott-Heron's song, "The Revolution Will Not Be Televised" ("La Revolución no será televisada"). Carballo denounces that Nahua perspectives go untelevised. Through *Las Plumas* he accentuates an affective space as part of a revolution—this moikxipejpena—as the word *revolution* itself means a return, a rolling back, a retracing of steps.

Through his art, Carballo retraces the steps of Nahua knowledges and underscores their applicability to a dynamic present and future.

The Serpent's Plumes: Conclusions and Native Horizons

The publication of *Las Plumas* in print form showcases the current relevance of these radio shorts. Pernicious cycles of colonial violence exposed in them repeat, as starkly evidenced two years after *Las Plumas*'s publication with the disappearance of forty-three students from the Teacher's College of Ayotzinapa in Guerrero and subsequently a pandemic that has affected Native populations disproportionately. Certain lives seem to weigh more heavily on the public's conscience than others. Carballo condemns an underlying illogic behind violence against Indigenous population that treats them as traces of the past, and therefore disposable. One still hears the refrain: "Hablan dialectos, no idiomas" (They speak dialects, not languages), in the mistaken sense of "dialect" as a stubborn remnant of what were great languages and civilizations. First Nations and their languages are physically and epistemically displaced.

In this chapter I have explored how Carballo invites readers/listeners/viewers to reflect on the struggles for sonic spaces in the fight against media colonialism. *Las Plumas* presses on the reader to hear and see Native peoples as real-life humans, "de piel y huesos" (of flesh and bones; 7; 35; 109) who claim their own territories, bodies, and minds, rather than as the stock images propagated through mass media. This move entails an assertion of intellectual production, agency, and the right to make mistakes and be enraged. Carballo's work entreats us to consider the ramifications of media colonialism on land rights and knowledge production. The perspectives of ixtlamatilistli, yoltlajlamikilistli, and tlaixpan foster an acoustic ecology framed around relational knowledge, reciprocity, and a circular/spiral temporality. Language serves as a nexus for assessing these spaces, and, although *Las Plumas* is mostly in Castilian, Carballo inserts nahuañol and Nahuatl to break with monolingualism. More than just language, this translingual space acts as a node to comprehend numerous contexts and debunk official nation-state history. It constitutes a call to view Mexico as plurinational. The deep link in *Las Plumas* among language, media, and territory projects out into Carballo's campaign "Las lenguas toman la tribuna" (Languages Occupy the Stand) from 2019 to 2020. This campaign welcomed forty-eight Native intellectuals from Nations across Mexico to defend their territorial rights and speak their Native languages in the Cámara de Diputados (House of Representatives) and YouTube broadcasts.[25]

Carballo's work advances discussions about Indigenous cultural production. The broader dissemination and reception of these literatures have significant implications in reconceptualizing borders, dismantling stereotypes, and foregrounding Indigenous theoretical approaches. Analysis of Mesoamerican authors' underrepresented texts shifts discussions from Indigenous peoples as informants toward a transformative space in which they figure as contemporary knowledge producers. Specific attention must be paid to literatures in Native languages and how these textualities reframe canons and fluid cultural identities. Carballo problematizes the categorizations of "traditional" and "modern" to imagine a space in which Indigenous knowledges are vital perspectives in contemporary intellectual production. As María Josefina Saldaña-Portillo and Silvia Rivera Cusicanqui posit, descolonization perceives ". . . not only the modernity of Indigenous people but also the fundamental role Indigenous peoples played in the formation of capitalism, contemporary culture, and modern politics" (Saldaña-Portillo, "Indians Have Always Been Modern" 228; see also Rivera Cusicanqui, *Ch'ixinakax*). Carballo underscores and underwrites the intersectionality of his xochitlajtoli with a wider a(r/c)tivism within contemporary politics. He raises pressing questions that should guide our discussions: How do Mesoamerican Nations articulate their subjectivities against prevalent ideologies? How do these Nations' narratives assert their respective aesthetics and theories? How do they broaden our conceptions of what constitutes text and close reading/listening/observation?

Las Plumas de la Serpiente is one of the most innovative developments in Nahua cultural production and kinship formation within urban areas such as Mexico City. The concepts of ixtlamatilistli, yoltlajlamikilistli, and tlaixpan elucidate how Carballo combats colonial practices through the takeover of airwaves and cyberspaces. These perspectives frame his journalistic methodology. Indigenous compositions in areas like news reporting subvert stereotypes imposed on their languages, among them the idea that they are not "modern." Through his untiring work to insert Nahua perspectives throughout all media, Carballo seeks to displace colonial practices and have a revolution—in the deeper sense of moikxipejpena—published, televised, sung, and shared.

This mediatic campaign materializes in Carballo's response to Article 230's prohibition of Native languages within mass media—230 being another number that could be added to the string of statistics Carballo mentions in *Las Plumas*. He started organizing events to oppose the article in December 2015. His deployment of a wide array of xochitlajtoli, mass media, and social media resists the monochrome of numbers; he promotes yoltlajlamikilistli's affective heart-space with images and audio media that challenge visual and acoustic colonialism. On Facebook, Carballo posted images that champion linguistic diversity. In an allusion to the Serpent of *Las Plumas*, one of the most shared posts was a drawing of two people facing one another with long serpentine-twisted tongues that spell out "Contra la discriminación lingüística" (Against language discrimination; see Coon, "Living Languages"). In their disregard for the mounting number of the disappeared without personal names or stories, the federal legislature perhaps hoped that Article 230 would go unnoticed—this was Article 230 buried within a more expansive law. Carballo organized an event in December 2015 with Indigenous rap and hip-hop artists to denounce language discrimination. His own works, among them *Las Plumas de la Serpiente in all its formats*, have appeared in these protests. Carballo's use of Nahua concepts such as moikxipejpena (retracing one's steps) defends the languages that Article 230 proposed to prohibit and silence.

The following year, 2016, in an effort to translate these efforts to the political sphere, Carballo assumed a position within Mexico City's Asamblea de Constituyentes (Constitutional Assembly)[26] to ensure Indigenous representation in the nascent constitution. He embodied the view of ixtlamatilistli, "knowledge with the face," as a person able to offer effective knowledges because he is personally involved. Carballo not only promotes Indigenous presence in mass and social media but also demands Indigenous land rights within Mexico City. It is a demand for virtual and physical spaces within urban areas. As he explained on Facebook, Carballo resigned from his position on the Constitutional Assembly in December 2016, because his participation was treated more as tokenism than valuation of a Native perspective. In contrast with this political landscape, Carballo has found the (a/e)ffective depth within social media, his family's restaurants, and his artistic productions like *Las Plumas de la Serpiente* to redress injustices such as Ayotzinapa and Article 230. The narratives generated in and through these spaces resemble what Françoise Lionnet and Emmanuel Bruno Jean-François describe as the "human interest stories that pull us into the concrete lives of individual migrants and their families" ("Literary Routes" 1223). Nonetheless, by leaving the Constitutional Assembly and exposing the racism within it, he brought visibility to the issue, and, in the end, no one voted against his proposals defending Indigenous rights within Mexico City (personal interview, 31 August 2017).[27] His activism vies for a real presence of Indigenous voices within mass media and in decisions made within politics and society at large.

Las Plumas de la Serpiente continues promoting systemic change. Carballo accepted the federal position of Director of Popular Cultures in 2018 with the stipulation that he be allowed to produce *Las Plumas* radio shorts. This program has accompanied Carballo over two decades of artivism, has survived two high-profile firings by radio stations of Carmen Aristegui's team, and continues strong as a firm mediatic weapon in Carballo's efforts. During the COVID-19 pandemic, *Las Plumas* has invited listeners to view the past in front, develop an affective intelligence, and value experiential knowledges. Like the circular/spiral temporality evident in *Las Plumas*, the essays analyzed in this chapter reappear in new episodes and still serve as inspiration for Carballo's works and fieldwork.

Chapter 6

Nahuatl Language and Territory as Coping Strategies in Ateri Miyawatl's *Neijmantototsintle* (2018) and *Tsintatak* (2020)

On 29 May 2015, a large crowd gathered in Acapulco at a federally sponsored event promoting "democracy and voting rights." The featured guest, Nobel Laureate Rigoberta Menchú, called for a moment of silence for the forty-three disappeared *normalistas* of Ayotzinapa.[1] As explored briefly in chapter 2, *escuelas normales* are teacher training colleges in rural areas of Mexico for students (*normalistas*) preparing to give instruction in the equivalent of K–12 institutions. One of the most well-known schools is the Escuela Normal Rural Raúl Isidro Burgos, commonly referred to as "Ayotzinapa" due to its location in Ayotzinapa, Guerrero. It is approximately two hours southeast by car from Nahua cultural promoter and artivist Ateri Miyawatl's home community. The majority of students are Native, and Ayotzinapa is known for advocating revolutionary changes to remedy economic and social inequities.[2] In late September 2014, a group of students from Ayotzinapa traveled to the city of Iguala, Guerrero, for annual protests denouncing the Tlatelolco student massacre perpetrated by the federal government in Mexico City shortly before the Summer Olympics on 2 October 1968. These protests have taken place since 1968 with banners declaring "el 2 de octubre no se olvida" (October 2nd will not be forgotten). Following a common practice during these demonstrations, the *normalista* students from Ayotzinapa commandeered commercial buses to travel to Iguala.[3] State police and federal troops attacked them and forcibly disappeared forty-three students. Their whereabouts are still unknown.[4]

Less than one year later, the National Electoral Institute (INE) invited Rigoberta Menchú to speak in Acapulco and encourage the public to vote in Guerrero state elections. She addressed the importance of never forgetting Ayotzinapa and stated, "Les pido y les suplico un minuto de silencio para conmemorar la vida de los cuarenta y tres estudiantes de la normal que están desaparecidos. Démosles un minuto de silencio" (I ask and plead for a minute of silence to commemorate the lives of the forty-three students from the teacher training college who are disappeared. Let's give them a minute of silence; "Irrumpe indígena de Guerrero en acto de Rigoberta Menchú"). As administrators were preparing to award Menchú a certificate of recognition, Ateri Miyawatl (Anna Yamel Gatica Matías) came forward from the audience and took the microphone:

> Hermana Rigoberta, admiro su lucha que he estudiado en muchos momentos, yo junto con varios colegas. Admiro que esté aquí. Y disculpe esta pregunta. No sé cómo nos pueden pedir que hagamos un voto, no sé cómo nos lo pueden pedir. Tengo 27 años. Me dedico a la gestión y la producción cultural desde los 14 años, con un colectivo en mi pueblo, en un pueblo nahua, de aquí de Guerrero en Acatlán. Tengo 27 años y desde 26 octubre del 2012 hasta 30 de mayo del 2015, puedo contar cincuenta desaparecidos, jóvenes. La primera, hija de mi prima, Gabriela Itzel Ortiz Vázquez, quince años; el último, Gilberto Abundis Sánchez, artista gráfico de treinta años. Lo levantaron afuera de su casa cuando estaba regando las plantas de su casa. Estudiaba en la escuela popular de Bellas Artes. Regresó a visitar a su familia. Lo levantaron afuera de su casa. Apareció el 27 de mayo. Le quitaron la cabeza. Su cuerpo estaba en descomposición absoluta y lo reconocimos por un tatuaje que tenía en la espalda. ¿Cómo, señor gobernador, me puede llamar a votar? ¿Cómo, partidos políticos del estado de Guerrero, nos pueden pedir a los jóvenes, que somos el más numeroso índice de población en México, cómo nos pueden llamar al voto? . . . Señora Rigoberta Menchú: la indignación y la rabia no se pueden acabar, y sé que usted lo entiende. Y una cosa más, no podemos seguir pidiendo un minuto de silencio por los desparecidos, porque pedir un minuto de silencio por cada desparecido y por cada asesinato en nuestro país, en

nuestro estado, es quedarnos callados eternamente. ("Irrumpe indígena de Guerrero en acto de Rigoberta Menchú")

(Sister Rigoberta, I admire your struggle which I have studied in many moments, I along with various colleagues. I admire that you are here. And pardon the question. I don't know how they can ask us to vote, I don't know how they ask us for that. I am twenty-seven years old. I have worked in cultural promotion and production since I was fourteen, with a collective in my community, a Nahua community, here in Guerrero in Acatlán. I am twenty-seven years old and, from October 26th, 2012, to May 30th, 2015, I can count fifty disappeared youth. The first, my cousin's daughter, Gabriel Ortiz Vásquez, fifteen years old; the last, Gilberto Abundis Sánchez, a thirty-year-old graphic artist. They abducted him outside his home when he was watering his plants. He studied in the Escuela Popular de Bellas Artes. He returned to visit his family. They abducted him outside his home. He reappeared on May 27th. They decapitated him. His body was completely decomposed, and we recognized him because of a tattoo he had on his back. How, Mr. Governor,[5] can you ask me to vote? How, political parties of the state of Guerrero, can you ask us young people, who make up the largest percentage of Mexico's population, to vote? . . . Ms. Rigoberta Menchú: indignation and rage cannot just go away, and I know you understand it. And another thing, we cannot keep asking for a minute of silence for the disappeared, because asking for another minute of silence for every disappeared person and for every murder in our country, in our state, is to remain silent forever.)

I begin the chapter with this conflict because it is key in understanding Miyawatl's artistic book *Neijmantototsintle / La tristesa és un ocell / Sadness Is a Bird* (2018), which adapts and illustrates an eponymous poem she wrote shortly after the Acapulco meeting. Videos disseminating a clip from the meeting went viral throughout social media and YouTube.[6] In fact, for the most part, this confrontation was the only portion of the event reported in the news. Stations edited and spliced the video, at times eliminating parts of Miyawatl's message solely to highlight that a Nahua student had dared to interrupt the event.⁷ The clip was shared with inaccurate headings such as "Ana Gatica [*sic*] criticizes Rigoberta Menchú for supporting Mexican electoral process and Mexican politicians." As seen in Miyawatl's own words, the brunt of her message criticizes the Mexican electoral process and politicians, and their appropriation of Menchú's image, rather than Menchú herself.⁸

Miyawatl received death threats after this event, and such threats appear in the comments section on YouTube. As the situation worsened, she was confined to her home in Acatlán for an extended period and subsequently forced to flee. After living in various locations, Miyawatl moved to Pátzcuaro, Michoacán. She wrote her xochitlajtoli "Neijmantototsintle" amid this deracination and confinement, an outwardly imposed "room of one's own" where away from her community she felt isolated.⁹ Miyawatl had no intention of publishing "Neijmantototsintle" until invited by longtime friend and illustrator Francisco Villa and the Catalan fine book printing house Elies Plana to share it in 2017.

In this chapter, I examine Ateri Miyawatl's trilingual Nahuatl-Catalan-English artistic book of poetry *Neijmantototsintle* and her short theatrical piece *Tsintatak* (2020). In *Neijmantototsintle*, Miyawatl represents the poetic word as a cathartic outlet to articulate the sorrows of her region of Guerrero, Mexico, which the poetic voice depicts as a quivering bird set upon her heart. She uses xochiameya (water springs up like flowers) to portray this catharsis in the tears streaming down the poetic persona's face and the subsequent healing achieved by pouring out words on the page. As seen in previous chapters, xochitl (flower) is the principal metaphor for poetry itself, xochitlajtoli (flowered words). I argue that, in Miyawatl's works, xochitl points toward Nahua spaces of ceremony, aesthetic, and affective intelligence as effective coping strategies to process trauma. Similarly, in her two-person theatrical piece *Tsintatak*, a grandmother deploys flowered words and ceremony to heal her granddaughter Tere from what she describes as neijmankokolistle, or "sorrow-sickness," reminiscent of the sorrow described in *Neijmantototsintle*. Deceased and yet present within an alternate dimension, the grandmother converses with Tere, who has returned to her Nahua community from a recent trip to New York City. Tere is infatuated with the big city, and her grandmother worries that the granddaughter has internalized a "modernizing"/colonizing discourse that depreciates Nahua practices. Like in *Neijmantototsintle*, Nahuatl language and land serve as conduits to comprehend the loss of loved ones and revered territory.¹⁰ Miyawatl's literary production claims territory in a wide conception encompassing land, water, Native bodies, soundscapes, spiritual territory, and communal governance. Miyawatl shares the goal with fellow Nahua authors to create a Serpent-Plumed acoustic ecology in which Native languages are treated as equal in value to hegemonic ones, and Nahuas are viewed as nothing less than full-fledged knowledge producers. Her *Neijmantototsintle* and *Tsintatak* join a larger effort for language strengthening—both encouraging the use of Nahuatl and utilizing the language as a medium to process the traumatic effects of colonialism.[11]

As a theoretical framework and a correlative to the tripartite perspectives of ixtlamatilistli, yoltlajlamikilistli, and tlaixpan, I build upon Luis Cárcamo Huechante's conceptualization of "acoustic ecology" explored in the previous chapter. Acoustic ecologies thrive on a multiplicity of perspectives and languages where, for example, one may turn on the radio and hear Nahuatl. Miyawatl seeks to open a space in which many voices occupy sonorous landscapes, as evidenced in the very structure of *Neijmantototsintle* and *Tsintatak*. Reflective of this polyphony, *Neijmantototsintle* is published in Nahuatl, Catalan, and English, with no translation into Castilian; *Tsintatak* appears in Nahuatl, Castilian, and English. An acoustic ecology counters the takeover of airwaves and the general mediascape by colonial regimes and their discursive tactics. Acoustic colonialism configures certain voices (and by extension lives) as disposable or of lesser importance.[12]

Miyawatl's poem and theatrical piece invite readers to ponder land acknowledgments, minutes of silence, and the ways in which we interact with and inhabit the earth. Along with language, land in her texts operates as a metaphor and a medium to process traumatic events, represented through the image of a buried seed that will subsequently return with strength. Land is linked with community and language, and inversely the language is rooted in a dynamic conception of territory and reterritorializations.[13] The term in Nahuatl for "poetry," xochitlajtoli or "flowered words," marks this close connection with the land; it is similar, in this sense, to Mapudungun's meaning as "language of the land" (Cárcamo Huechante, "Entre muros y cercados"). This notion is reinforced with the additional appellation of Nahuatl as maseualtlajtoli, the "language of *campesinos*" or the language of people who work the land.[14] I apply the framework of acoustic ecology and acoustic colonialism to address how territories of healing are either created or dispossessed. In Nahuatl, ejekatl or "air/wind" carries illness; it constitutes both metaphor and metonym in Nahua literature for psychological and physical ailments.[15] That air(wave) can carry mediatic transmissions aimed against minoritized populations, or, conversely, the languages transmitted through those frequencies can promote dialogue and trans-Indigenous networking. Media dominated by monolingualism resemble a monocrop with an increased susceptibility to illness and plagues, a sonorous pathology or "sorrow-sickness" diagnosed and treated within Miyawatl's works.

As copious studies have shown, the promotion of Native languages must be accompanied by support for the social and political spheres in which they are used. This idea is defended by the hashtags #NoHayLenguaSinPueblo and #NoHayLenguaSinPueblos (#ThereIsNoLanguageWithoutCommunities), which emphasize relationality and community rather than the preservation of Native languages merely for the languages' sake. The pressure to speak Native languages without that relationality—without kinship—can in fact diminish mental health.[16] Effective language revitalization recognizes language as one tool among many to fortify communal ties. Miyawatl advances this relationality through her writing. She does not write as a revitalization exercise to rescue the Nahuatl language, to ensure its prominence among national and international literary circles, or to receive Western validation that her language and cultural practices matter. She writes for herself and her community, and to process the trauma that temporarily separated her from kin. For this reason, when people request a Castilian translation of *Neijmantototsintle*, she replies, "If you don't understand it [the version of the poem as it is in Nahuatl], then the poem isn't meant for you" (personal interview, 8 November 2019). This remark resonates with Yásnaya Elena Aguilar Gil's analysis on an exclusive "we" in Ayuujk, mentioned in previous chapters (see "Ëëts, atom"). In Miyawatl's case, her reply intends not so much to exclude but rather to mark an inclusive and empowered "we Nahuas." I end this study with the present chapter because it moves from the forays into literary circles and mass media in previous chapters to a greater focus on local projects, on the specific experiences Mardonio Carballo showcases through the metaphor of the Serpent's Plumes. *Neijmantototsintle*, *Tsintatak*, and Miyawatl's other works are closely intertwined with local presses and workshops to strengthen community, be it in her hometown or in Pátzcuaro, Michoacán, where she resided for several years before returning to Guerrero in 2021.

Miyawatl's noncommittal stance toward being called a poet connects with this wider objective, as she considers herself first and foremost a cultural promoter for the works and knowledge production of her hometown of Acatlán and other Native Nations. She is concerned more with the distribution of other Native authors' works than with her own. This was evident in the publication of *Neijmantototsintle*. Miyawatl had first recommended that Elies Plana publish the text of another Nahua writer; it was not until the other author failed to send poems that Miyawatl decided to share "Neijmantototsintle." More broadly, Miyawatl focuses on Native promotion of Native works and performance in small local projects to break with traditional formulations of what constitutes the archive.

"I Am Not a Poet": Overview of *Neijmantototsintle, Tsintatak,* and Ateri Miyawatl's Trajectory

Why did Miyawatl's encounter with Rigoberta Menchú turn sensationalist in social media and news outlets? I contend that it is in part due to the colonial binary that places Native peoples at the extremes of "violent instigator" or *buen salvaje* (noble savage), gliding over complexities and nuances of specific individuals and Nations.[17] News headlines suggested Miyawatl had been violent and insolent. At a deeper level, these headlines are attributable to an expectation that there be no internal division among Native Nations—to the myth that all Indigenous people "get along" in a herd mentality.[18] Miyawatl's questioning of Menchú's participation in the event at Acapulco challenges that misconception.[19] She warns Menchú about being used in a long-standing nation-state apparatus that co-opts Native movements to weaken and destabilize them.[20] State-sponsored tokenistic gestures publicize Native languages and invite prominent figures such as Menchú to share their voices; however, this tactic lacks the deep relationality and long-term commitment needed for systemic change. Miyawatl also defies the expectation that Indigenous Nations will remain silent. How dare a Nahua woman interrupt a government event with the state governor in attendance? Miyawatl's intervention serves as a subtext of the xochitlajtoli *Neijmantototsintle* and embodies its main message that one must openly confront sadness and injustices. As analyzed in Martín Tonalmeyotl's xochitlajtoli, poets cannot always speak of laudatory "flowers and song." The poetic voice in *Neijmantototsintle* grapples with the traumas caused by injustices in her region.

Neijmantototsintle aids in scrutinizing the sensationalism in news outlets and colonial discourse that is apparent in the way events are reported. Miyawatl criticizes the media's tendency to focus on recent outrages or individual successes. News media overlook the *longue durée* of colonial practices and the need for systemic changes to dismantle those practices. The flipside of that colonial discursive double bind of "instigator" or "noble savage" surfaced when Miyawatl's *Neijmantototsintle* won the Judges' Choice award at the Oxford Fine Press Book Fair in 2018. Mexican news outlets declared she was one of the top Indigenous poets.[21] It was obvious none of them had read the book. Miyawatl was dismayed by this supposedly positive sensationalism and contacted news offices to get articles corrected (some even claimed that Miyawatl was a professional singer). For the most part, these news agencies were uninterested in hearing her complaints. In interviews, Miyawatl states that she is not really a poet since few of her poems have been published. Moreover, *Neijmantototsintle* is not even truly a book of poetry, since "Neijmantototsintle" is only one xochitlajoli stretched out across multiple pages with illustrations. Miyawatl clarifies that the Judges' Choice award was given in recognition of the book's aesthetic value and the collective effort with Elies Plana; it was not a literary prize exclusively for Miyawatl's poem. How this prize was reported and prior depictions of her encounter with Menchú reflect a pattern in journalism of seeing Indigenous people in an unrealistically positive or negative light.

Yásnaya Elena Aguilar Gil observes that Western forms of validation centered on the individual and the implicit bias bound up in those standards can be as dangerous as negative portrayals of Native peoples ("La validación como captura"). Western endorsement celebrates that someone "has made it" as an individual accomplishment, while simultaneously overlooking the systemic oppression against Native Nations and Native systems of validation. *Neijmantototsintle* invites readers to move beyond this commonplace toward the complexities and cultural specificities of Miyawatl's community of Acatlán, Chilapa, Guerrero.

In this context, rather than a poet, Miyawatl considers herself a playwright and actor. Her dramaturgy does not meet the general public's assumption that Native literature is limited to poetry.[22] Miyawatl works on numerous projects. Her writing has formed part of an effort since she was fourteen to promote the Nahuatl language and the knowledge production from her community. There are limited resources with information on her home region, and few dictionaries of the Nahuatl of this area.[23] Miyawatl marks this place of enunciation in using the name Ateri Miyawatl rather than Anna Gatica. Her legal name "Anna Yamel Gatica Matías" has always felt foreign to her as she only uses it within academic and government contexts. "Ateri Miyawatl" is not an artistic pseudonym but instead the name she is known by in Acatlán.

Nearly all projects on which she has worked have been in collectives to produce theater and *libros cartoneros*. These handmade books—literally "cardboard books"—are a sustainable practice that began in Argentina after an economic crisis in 2001 and quickly spread throughout Abiayala.[24] Although the official printing of *Neijmantototsintle* is a fine print book (priced at $250 US dollars), the large images combined with short selections of text are influenced by the *libro cartonero* genre. Miyawatl highlights that *Neijmantototsintle* was produced by a team, including Veracruzano illustrator Francisco Villa, with whom she has collaborated on multiple projects to make *libros cartoneros* with their artistic organization Laboratorios Tetl.[25] Beyond being a playwright and actor, Miyawatl has been a strong advocate of other authors' works, most recently with the Originaria series (the Native Women series). Located in Pátzcuaro, Michoacán, the Originaria printing house has published the texts of Native women throughout Mexico.

I offer an extended preface to Miyawatl's works because the circumstances under which Miyawatl wrote *Neijmantototsintle* showcase why the text has exerted such a profound impact. The official printing had a limited run of seventy-two copies, with only fifty placed in circulation. Publishing in Nahuatl and Catalan is an act of resistance. Catalan is a minoritized language that Miyawatl and Francisco Villa describe as "in the shadows of Castilian."[26] The inclusion of an English translation was at the request of the publisher to facilitate its entry into international book fairs. While a colonial language, English serves as a tool to access venues normally off limits to a Nahuatl text. Miyawatl created a facsimile or "pirated copy" that she distributed in Acatlán, Mexico City, and Michoacán. She reiterates that what matters are the networks and potential spaces for healing generated in these encounters, more than a large run of books or national attention.

In the following sections I first analyze Miyawatl's *Neijmantototsintle* to underscore how she copes with trauma. I then explore how the theatrical piece *Tsintatak* elucidates her approach. Both works invoke language and land to manifest how Nahua worldviews and healing can emerge from the fracture and disarray of colonial violence.

Sadness Perched on the Heart: The Articulation of an Affective Intelligence

The xochitlajtoli "Neijmantototsintle" is approximately one page long when brought together. The published book, *Neijmantototsintle*, contains a total of nine stanzas two to five verses in length each, in free verse, spread out over fourteen pages with the illustrations. Miyawatl recounts in interviews that the poem came to her in Nahuatl, and she refused to self-translate it into Castilian. Instead, her brother Omar Gatica did the translation into Castilian; this version was omitted from the publication. Within the published text, the Catalan version is based on Omar Gatica's translation.[27] Catalan expert D. Sam Abrams translated the poem into English based on the Catalan version, so the English text is a translation thrice removed.

The poem at first may seem deceptively simple. The poetic voice allows the "bird of sadness" to perch on her heart and body, to be observed and observe.[28] In summary, the poem narrates how sadness sits like a bird on different parts of the poetic persona's body. Her body sinks into the land, and flowers mend what is damaged inside her as the little bird watches and sings. The poetic persona observes and listens, letting a flowered fountain sprout within her. The bird of sadness tires and flies away, leaving the poetic voice in bloom.

Initiating this process, Miyawatl's poetic persona in the first two stanzas describes this sadness-bird suddenly perched on her heart:

> Ken se tototl ejko neijmantle
> patlantikisa niman notlalia ipan noyojlo.
>
> Notik chanchiwa
> Ompa nokwikacha, kolintika iakoko,
> kiminitocha ikxitsiwan. (5)
>
> (Like a bird sadness appears
> it flies suddenly and it perches on my heart.
>
> Inside me it nests
> There it sings, moves its throat,
> dances its little feet.)

This bird nests there, and its quivering throat and dancing feet move like a shudder through the poetic persona's body. These stanzas are accompanied by a linocut with the bird colored yellow (fig. 6.1). Significantly, the bird placed on the heart ties into metaphors of the corn fields; it represents a potential threat to the crop. The heart is like a seed, since, as noted in earlier chapters, the word for "seed" is the same as heart (yolotl). The

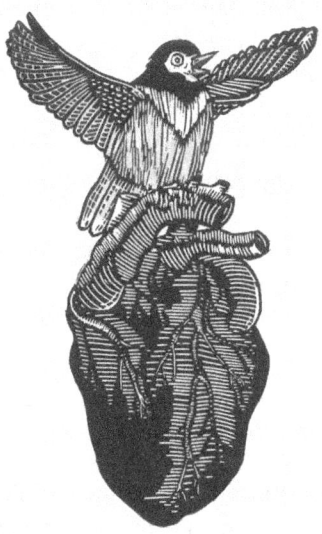

Figure 6.1. Linocut from *Neijmantototsintle* by Francisco Villa. *Source*: Published by permission of Elies Plana.

poem offers a healing from trauma that accepts (or "observes") sadness and, through this process of recognition, allows sorrow to transform into a renewed life force (rendered vivid by flowers growing from the seeds of sadness that the bird "plants" into the speaker's heart).

While the published English translation uses the word *sadness* for the Nahuatl neijmantle, this term has a broader meaning associated with drought. The threat posed by the bird is underscored more as Miyawatl translates "neijmantle" in another of her published poems as *hambruna* (famine).[29] This description carries significant meaning for the ritual context of Acatlán—like in Martín Tonalmeyotl's home community of Atzacoaloya only half an hour away by car—where the ceremony Atsajtsilistle (literally "the shout for water" or "water-shout") pleads for water in times of drought and famine.[30] Accordingly, this ceremony seeks protection and is a salient feature in Miyawatl's works.[31] As seen in the discussion of Tonalmeyotl's poetry, Atsajtsilistle includes violent punches and thus displays confrontation with pain as an integral part of any recovery. The speaker's healing and rebirth in *Neijmantototsintle* is better understood within a broader framework of Nahua beliefs and practices.

Miyawatl's poem does not explicitly mention this ceremony, yet there are allusions to it. The yellow hue used in *Neijmantototsintle* is the principal color employed throughout this practice; it appears in the regalia of the famed tekuanij or *tigres* (tigers). In the *peleas de tigres* (tiger fights), people dressed in tiger masks box to provoke rain.[32] The harder the blows are, the more plentiful the rain will be. Rather than flee conflict, this approach accepts it as a necessary part of life. A deep affective intelligence undergirds this space and avoids reducing anguish to the dry, coldhearted statistics criticized by Carballo in the previous chapter. This feeling cognition accepts a multivocality of experiences and perspectives. Resembling descriptions of *mindfulness*, the poetic persona speaks as if she were observing her body from the outside.[33] She does not reject sorrow or try to think positively, as is represented in her sustained observation of the sadness-bird. In effect, Miyawatl's poem—in dialoguing with the framework of planting (burial and renewal) while invoking the similar cycles of Nahua rituals—proposes a model for healing that grows from within her community's knowledges. Her model for renewal is thus not passive or imposed from without (as is the perfunctory moment of silence proposed at the electoral event in Acapulco for Ayotzinapa) but, instead, emerges from a core of Nahua values.

As examined at length in earlier chapters, the affective space of the heart within yoltlajlamikilistli views emotions and cognition as conjugated. I use "conjugated" because the word for "heart" in Nahuatl can be integrated in verbs, turning it into an adverb, seen for example in *Neijmantototsintle* with niyolyemania (I become soft with my heart). This affective connection is felt and assessed throughout the body. The poetic voice does not rationalize away feelings but rather takes the necessary time to process them.

Western views tend to push out those emotions as irrational.[34] In Miyawatl's poetry, knowledge and insight are gained through watching this viscerality. *Neijmantototsintle* eschews the silencing or dismissal of deep-rooted problems. The encounter with the bird brings grief but also words, such as those in the xochitlajtoli itself. This bird takes the place of any explicit mention of poem's subtexts, such as the encounter at the Acapulco meeting or the complicity of the nation-state in the violence engulfing Miyawatl's community. When Miyawatl wrote "Neijmantototsintle" while looking out her window, she saw birds and desired the freedom of their flight.[35] As stated previously, the bird can be both beautiful and a threat to the crop. Consequently, this depiction translates over into life in general, again returning to the importance of conflict and critical engagement instead of an uncritical nativism.

In the third stanza, the shudder caused by the bird travels throughout the poetic persona's body down to her toes. The bird possesses a fierce song:

> Kostiktototsintle, san tepitsaktsintle
> Ikamilak kualtsin nokwikacha,
> ikamilak kualtsin notlachalcha
> Onotlalia ipan nokxipil
> akotlacha niman ache chikawak nechtlakwikatlalia (6)

> (Little yellow bird, only small
> With much beauty it sings,
> with beautiful feathers
> It perches on my toes
> it looks up and somewhat fiercely places its song in me)

In addition to the visual representation within the book and cover, textual reference to yellow reinforces allusions to rain rituals. With these ceremonies in mind, the poetic persona switches from speaking of tototl (bird) to tototsintle (precious/little bird), with the reverential/diminutive -tsin. She observes this sadness-bird in turn observing her with the aforementioned tension between beauty and a fierce song. Relatedly, Miyawatl has suffered tragic events such as losing friends in the region. The forced disappearances of forty-three students from Ayotzinapa are part of a systemic problem. The bird's song reminds us of those who have died. The change from tototl to tototsintle demonstrates a certain reverence toward this sadness, allowing it to move through the whole body—the heart, toes, hands, feet—with a chikauak (fierce/strong/hard) song, the same word used to describe hardened maize.

In effect, the poem links this somatic process with agrarian cycles. In the fourth stanza, the tears sprouting from the poetic persona's eyes are like a flower beginning to bud and "ameya" (like water coming from a spring):

> Kwajon notiktopone xochitsintin
> niman nixtelolo ameya
> nixtelolo xochiameya. (9)

> (Then a precious small flower buds inside me
> and my eyes flow like a spring
> my eyes flow like a flowered spring.)

Growth, learning, strength, and creativity surface from the conflict that the poetic persona experiences. This renewal springs forth like the water and bursts like a fertile crop after a successful ceremony. "Notiktopone xochitsintin" (flowers blooming inside) and "nixtelolo ameya" (my eyes flow like a spring) render vivid the poetic persona's cathartic cries. These descriptions are a subtle allusion to the famous Pre-Columbian *flor y canto* (flower and song). Rather than representing a Pre-Columbian nostalgia, the poetic persona emphasizes the present-day observance of ixtlamatilistli; knowledge with the face is evinced in references, as seen also in Xochitiotzin's poetry, to vision and invoked visually like two eyes within the repeated *o* in nixtel*o*l*o*. Each little tear/flower rests on the poetic voice's skin, encompassing her body, hands, and feet in the fifth stanza:

> Sesentetl xochitsintin pewa wetse, wetse, wetse
> nomana itech nonakayo. (11)

> (Each precious little flower begins to fall, fall, fall
> they settle on my skin.)

These tears/flowers disseminate like seeds across the body and then bloom. In this process, the repetition of "wetse" is like the rain that falls after a ceremony. From traumatic experiences can come healing felt in both the heart and physically throughout the body.

Following this logic, descent into the land within the sixth stanza is central to understanding territory in *Neijmantototsintle*. The poetic voice sinks into the earth, and xochitl appears as a key metaphor encompassing ceremonial, artistic, sacred contexts:

> Pewa nitlakayopolake itik tlajle
> Xochijme xnotelcha kisa, kisa, kisa,
> netstlapanejktlalia. (12)

> (With time my body sinks into the earth
> The flowers do not come to an end, they bloom, bloom,
>   bloom,
> they mend what is damaged in me.)

The repetition of "kisa" (to leave / come out / bloom) parallels "uetse" (falls) from the previous stanza and points again to water ceremonies, as "uetse" is used to refer to rain. Miyawatl embraces a wider notion of text that includes ceremony as part of her affinity to performance and theater. Although *Neijmantototsintle* is a written poem, the text foregrounds performance and thus relates to Cárcamo Huechante's analysis of acoustic colonialism and the filling of airwaves with Native voices. With this poem, Miyawatl seeks to replenish soundscapes with Native perspectives. Language rooted in the land heals and offers strength to process traumas. Miyawatl's poetic persona's sinking into the ground parallels the rebirth of a successful crop (reinforced by the hair of the woman appearing like maize silk), after overcoming numerous threats. The flowers (xochitl) mend what is broken in her. Xochitl comprises multiple areas, similar to the Maya concept ts'iib (tentatively "literature") and its scope extending across artistic and sacred spaces.[36]

Within these procreant spaces, the bird continues to watch the poetic persona and to sing in the seventh and eighth stanzas:

Tototsintle sankan netstlakwikatlalia,
sankan netstlata.

Ijke kuak neijmantototsintle netsatlapalowa
Nejwa san nikaki, san ni yolyemania,
san ni tsinpolake itik tlajle,
san nixtololxochiameya. (14)

(The little bird does not stop placing its song in me,
it does not stop looking at me.

When the bird of sadness comes to visit me
I can only listen, I can only tremble in my heart,
I just join the earth,
I just spring like flowers in my eyes.)

The poetic persona carefully observes while suspending judgment. "I only listen" is very different from "quedarse callado" (staying silent) and the moments of silence Miyawatl criticized at the electoral campaign's meeting in Acapulco. To listen but not stay quiet. The poem itself is a product of this reflection. The stanza reiterates the descent into the earth: "san ni tsinpolake itik tlajle, / san nixtololxochiameya" (I just join the earth, / I just spring like flowers in my eyes). In discussions about her poem, Miyawatl expresses that she considers nixtololxochiameya (literally "I-eye-flower-spring") to be the least translatable word from *Neijmantototsintle*. Observation is underscored anew by the appearance on the page with the words nixtololxochiameya and tototl and the repeated *o*s resemblance to eyes. The text represents a deep processing of colonial traumas by first acknowledging the threat exists (like the threat to the crop). Moreover, the text states "I tremble in my heart," but "ni yolyemania" signifies a softening, like the softening of the earth for sowing.

In the final stanza, the bird tires and flies far away, leaving the poetic voice/body flourishing. Flowered words and empowerment emerge from this encounter with neijmantle (sadness or thirst) for justice:

> Kuak onsiewe tototsintle, kuajwon yo
> patlane wejka
> niman netskatewa nixochipontok
> netskatewa nixochipontok yejwin tototsintle. (16)

> (When the little bird tires, then
> it flies far away
> and leaves me as I bloom
> that little bird leaves me as I bloom.)

There is no mention of "longing" or "nostalgia" in the original Nahuatl as appears in the published English and Catalan versions (16). These translations in fact change the meaning and break with the perspective of tlaixpan. In effect, tlaixpan is not a backward-looking perspective of longing or nostalgia but instead a perspective that situates the past in front as a time/place of enunciation. The poetic voice does not yearn for some irrecuperable time. She heals in the act of *ar*ticulating, remembering, and establishing inter-generational kinships. *Nostalgia* in Catalan and English suggests a wistful gaze to the distant past, like the bird flying into the distance. Yet, the poetic persona does not flee. She is present in the moment, in the land on which she stands, and is now stronger after having processed trauma.

Miyawatl's poetic voice does not rationalize away feelings of sorrow. Through an affective intelligence articulated in Nahuatl, the poetic voice listens carefully, with experiential knowledge rooted in the heart. Her empowerment is accentuated in the Nahuatl "*I* bloom" as opposed to "leaves me blooming" in the published English rendition of the text (16). The poetic persona's transformation through this experience is stressed in the Nahuatl, as the original text literally means "the little bird *leaves me left*." Speaking Nahuatl and other Native languages is in and of itself an act of defiance due to a politics of linguicide propagated by the nation-state. As Yásnaya Elena Aguilar Gil argues, one cannot obviate resistance because one cannot obviate pervasive colonial structures.[37] Within *Neijmantototsintle*, the poetic persona comprehends structural oppression that inheres sadness and famine. She then reclaims language and land—a recovery that extends to psychological, spiritual, and physical territories with allusions to the crop cycle, ceremony, her homeland, her Nahuatl variant, the place where the disappeared reside, and the viewing of all these spaces as interconnected.

Re-membering Community Members: Processing Trauma through a Corporeal Art

Allusions to the disappeared suggest another reading of *Neijmantototsintle*. As stated earlier, in addition to "sadness," neijmantle can translate as "famine" in Miyawatl's poetry. In turn, that famine represents a thirst for justice for those who have been forcibly displaced. Seen in Tonalmeyotl's xochitlajtoli, starvation is a common metaphor to portray violence within Guerrerense Nahua literature. One of Miyawatl's Facebook posts from near the time she wrote her xochitlajtoli "Neijmantototsintle" ponders a corporeal expression (fig. 6.2). *Un arte del cuerpo* (an art of the body) makes the audience aware of losses, and then goes further in helping them feel those losses, like a hunger sensed throughout the body.

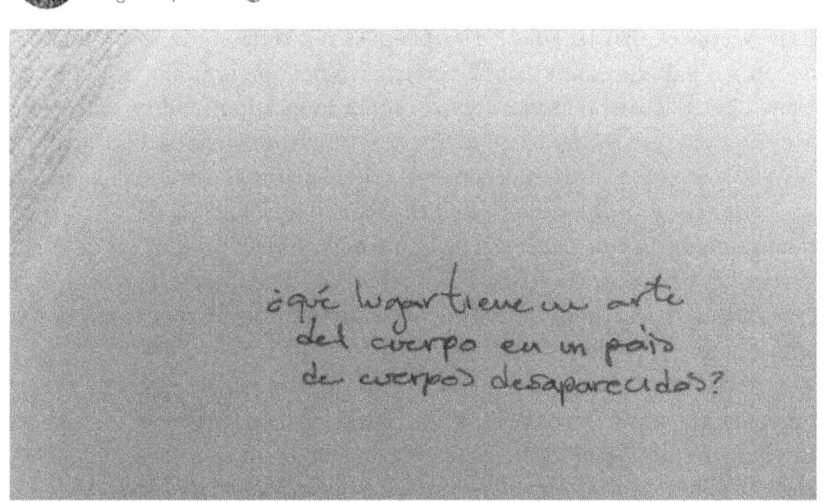

Figure 6.2. "¿Qué lugar tiene un arte del cuerpo en un país de cuerpos desaparecidos? / What place [or role] does an art of the body have in a country of disappeared [or kidnapped] bodies?" *Source*: Ateri Miyawatl's Facebook page, published with permission.

The concept *arte del cuerpo* comes from a well-known performance by Peruvian artist Emilio Santisteban. Audience members are blindfolded for an entire hour and led to reflect deeply on what it *feels* like to be disappeared.[38] In interviews, Miyawatl recounts how she was captivated by the word *performance* as a teenager, and this subsequently inspired her to study theater in Guerrero and abroad in Chile.[39] Diana Taylor's description of performance and archive no doubt apply to Miyawatl's work, as an epistemology and an embodied practice that, "along with and bound up with other cultural practices, offers a way of knowing" (*The Archive and the Repertoire* 3). The poem and images from *Neijmantototsintle* can be read as cues in a theatrical monologue as the bird moves from one part of the body. In fact, the descriptions in this text resemble plays for one or two actors like in some of Miyawatl's performances, among them *Tsintatak*. In this play, the young woman protagonist also sinks into the earth in potential rebirth or disappearance.

Miyawatl came home from her theatrical studies abroad in Chile with many proposals for her community. Nonetheless, she comments that she soon realized that Acatlán already had local forms and genres of performance. Her works, including *Neijmantototsintle* and *Tsintatak*, validate those unique modes of expression. Miyawatl emphasizes that *Neijmantototsintle* is a poem thought out—dreamed—completely in Nahuatl to underscore that the poem was conceived within the parameters and frameworks of that language. Her poem is not only a political statement denouncing disappearances in Guerrero; it is an ontological affirmation of Nahua perspectives that may be lost in the translation (and by extension, lost in society). By refusing to render *Neijmantototsintle* in Castilian, Miyawatl foregrounds Nahua concepts articulated in the original language.

The body of the disappeared in *Neijmantototsintle* is dismembered, then *re-membered* to return reconstituted. The poem focuses on different parts of the body, such as the heart, eyes, hand, and feet, represented in the images. These body parts are severed like the disappeared people, whose bodies, if found, are often mutilated (fig. 6.3).

Artistic production serves as a mode to help people remember their missing or deceased loved ones. While seemingly focused on an individual, the burying of the body in *Neijmantototsintle* connects to a homeland, and the common practice of burying one's umbilical cord at birth to mark one's native soil. As viewed previously, this sinking into the earth ties into the Nahuatl language rooted in that land.

Nahuatl Language and Territory as Coping Strategies | 241

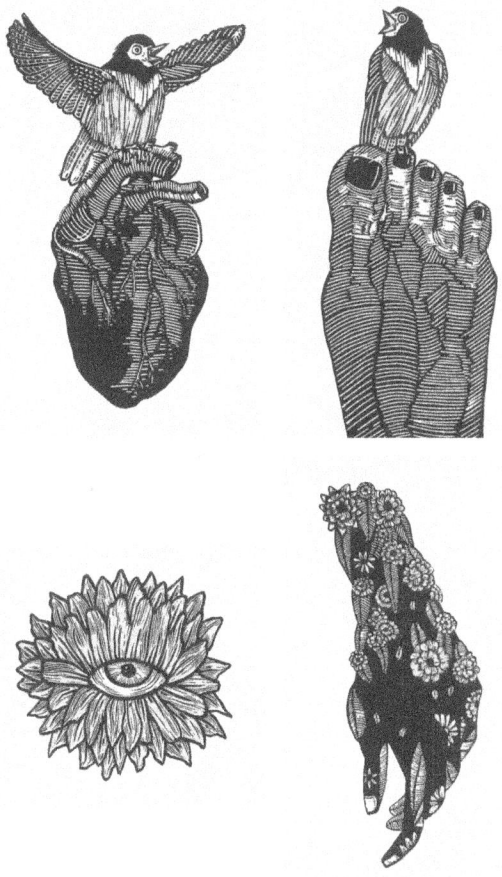

Figure 6.3. Linocuts from *Neijmantototsintle* by Francisco Villa. *Source*: Published by permission of Elies Plana.

The body shown in figure 6.4 is surrounded by Mexican marigolds and possibly maize seeds (suggested by the resemblance of the depicted woman's hair to corn silk). From challenges can emerge a rebirth. Ceremonial spaces are clearly marked with these allusions. The different parts of the body are reunited and transform into a flower (fig. 6.5). Flowers guide the wandering deceased to their homes during the Day of the Dead; they also draw the living back, affectively and physically, to their

Figure 6.4. Linocut from *Neijmantototsintle* by Francisco Villa. *Source*: Published by permission of Elies Plana.

Figure 6.5. Linocut from *Neijmantototsintle* by Francisco Villa. *Source*: Published by permission of Elies Plana.

communities of origin. Artistic production helps people collectively to feel the loss of loved ones and ponder that pain. What is it like to be disappeared? To be dis-membered, physically or epistemically (in the sense of being separated from one's community)? If those relatives go unremembered on the Day of the Dead (as well as throughout the year), they are left with no proper burial and wander the earth aimlessly seeking justice.

Ultimately, the body in *Neijmantototsintle* joins a larger collective that deeply values the life of every individual, like Mardonio Carballo's reiteration in *Las Plumas de la Serpiente* that "con uno basta" (one murder is too many). Miyawatl moves away from the mode of statistics recycled in newscasts in which large numbers of people, such as forty-three students, must die for the public to pay attention. Her own experience having to flee Acatlán was a type of forced disappearance that went unreported in such statistics. Her work illustrates the power of Serpent-Plumed specific histories and experiences. The poetic persona states with an active voice, "*I* sink with my body," underscoring her agency in the face of oppression. No adjectives describe the body, but rather the poem composes corporeality through active verbs in an attentive observance. Miyawatl alludes to her own surname (miyawatl as "corn tassel," called a flower in Nahuatl) with the concluding image of an optical flower emerging from the ground with an eye at its center. As seen in my analysis of Ethel Xochitiotzin Pérez's work in chapter 3, maize and its symbolism are often associated with men. Miyawatl overturns those masculine metaphors and claims the ability to create literature.

This reading brings together the three perspectives that have served as the crux of *The Serpent's Plumes*. Emphasis on observation highlights the face knowledge of ixtlamatilistli, accentuated in ixtololameya, the fountain streaming from the eyes. An intelligent affectivity rests on yoltlajlamikilistli (heart knowledge), both in description and visually with the bird set on the heart. The re-membrance of dead relatives insists upon tlaixpan in which kin are continually in front. *Neijmantototsintle* functions like an altar on which to honor the deceased with flowers. People today grow from what those kin have left, like a plant sprouting from the ground. This re-membrance is centered on the land and allows both humans and earth to be healed. Such empowerment gives flight to the Serpent's Plumes and counters a legacy of colonial practices manifested in present-day violence.

Curing the Colonial Itch in *Tsintatak*

Miyawatl's theatrical piece *Tsintatak* similarly addresses the loss of a loved one. Written after her grandmother Ana Alonso Flores died in 2016, *Tsintatak* intersects with several images that appear in *Neijmantototsintle*. Miyawatl created the piece as a medium to process her grief, after having already experienced the profound losses described earlier. Years later in 2020 she decided to share the work for publication. The online magazine *Strange Horizons* published *Tsintatak* in a trilingual Nahuatl-Castilian-English format. Although Miyawatl prioritizes the Nahuatl of some of her publications by choosing not to translate them into Castilian, she did self-translate *Tsintatak* into Castilian (and we worked together on an English translation). This decision allows her work to reach a wider audience, which is especially pressing given that the play touches upon themes of migration and movement to the United States. As her granddaughter Tere regales her with anecdotes from New York, the grandmother, Lamajtsin, performs a ceremony to cleanse Tere of what she terms neijmankokolistle or "sadness-sickness." Like the poetic persona who sinks into the ground in *Neijmantototsintle*, Tere gradually enters the earth as the grandmother performs the ritual with hopes of healing and renewing her granddaughter. Lamajtsin seeks to center her granddaughter on the Nahuatl language and land, which can strengthen her through the contexts of epistemic violence that target that very territory. According to the play, while it is perfectly fine to travel abroad, a person should keep sight of the linguistic roots and region that gave birth to them.

Parallelisms between *Neijmantototsintle* and the theatrical piece *Tsintatak* illuminate our understanding of both works. Within them the interplay of land, language, and kinship processes profound losses to confront colonial practices that threaten the poetic persona and main protagonists. In *Tsintatak*, the plot focuses on epistemic violence against Nahuas and their internalized discrimination. The play wryly describes this oppression as a "butt itch," a literal translation of the title. This term alludes to the granddaughter Tere's restlessness (in Castilian, *inquietud*), originating from a belief that large Western cities like New York are superior. Moreover, the onomatopoeia of "tsintatak" imitates the sound of wind instruments in Acatlán, Guerrero to suggest the curative power of communal art, ritual, and festivities accompanied by such music. The grandmother, Lamajtsin or "Woman Elder," attempts to cure the colonial itch that Tere feels after a trip to New York. Lamajtsin's repetition of the word "tsintatak" brings Tere back to Nahua language, ceremony, and kinship articulated on and through their community's land. The grandmother's subsequent ritual chants operate as flowered words to mend her granddaughter's damaged spirit.

The title *Tsintatak* is left untranslated in the Castilian and English versions, although footnotes explain the word's broader significance. As with *Neijmantototsintle*, Miyawatl refuses to self-translate the title. However, rather than exclusion, this gesture invites the audience to strengthen their use of the Nahual language. Resembling what literary critic Tiffany D. Creegan Miller argues regarding an onomatopoeic poem in K'iche' by Humberto Ak'abal, this choice welcomes Nahuatl speakers and non-Nahuatl speakers alike. For non-Nahuatl speakers, this is an appeal to engage "in linguistic revitalization efforts and to embrace cultural pluralism" (Miller, *The Maya Art* 143). For Nahuas it is a reminder of the need to accept "a wide berth of sonorities that we may all understand more semiotically than linguistically" (143). In this sense, like *Neijmantototsintle*, Miyawatl's theatrical piece is meant for people willing to learn the language, rather than those who simply demand a translation. That language pulls the granddaughter Tere back to Nahua territories. An examination of *Tsintatak* is a fitting way to round out the varied flights and landings of contemporary xochitlajtoli, as the interface between Tere and her grandmother encapsulates Mardonio Carballo's plumed metaphor and its foregrounding of experiential knowledge. Miyawatl's flowered words emerge with avian flight in both *Tsintatak* and *Neijmantototsintle* to soar with the Serpent's Plumes.

While Miyawatl has yet to put on a production of *Tsintatak*, the performance would last at most twenty minutes. There are significant differences between the published Nahuatl and Castilian versions. Miyawatl spent approximately two years, from 2016 to 2018, developing *Tsintatak* in Nahuatl before transcreating the work into Castilian. She expresses that the Castilian version fails to capture the essence of the original. The magazine *Strange Horizons* adapted this Castilian version into a short story format by removing protagonists' names (referred to as *Mujer Joven* [Young Woman] and *Anciana* [Elderly Woman] in the stage directions) and replacing them with quotation dashes. The Nahuatl maintains those stage directions. In my analysis, I read between the published versions in Nahuatl and Castilian, as well as unpublished drafts of the play from 2020 that we reviewed together while preparing the English translation. More broadly, the inclusion of *Tsintatak* in a magazine that labels it "speculative fiction" entails a certain degree of risk. The elements in the play are not speculative or fantasy.[40] This brings into question what the public reads as magic or exoticized "magical realism" within Latin America. While the popular genre of speculative fiction may reach a wider audience, Miyawatl warns that *Tsintatak* should not be read as "magical." For her, the work represents reality and the very tangible challenges faced in her region.

Tsintatak opens with the description "Onka miyek tlajle" / "Hay mucha tierra" (There is a lot of earth), marking from the first line that the land is vital to process pain and invoke a spiritual renewal. While singing tsintatak, "Tsin ta tak tsin ta tak tsin ta tak," Lamajtsin sits on a mound and cleans black beans on her lap. The text does not explicitly indicate that she has died. As the work progresses, there are increasing signs that Lamajtsin exists in the realm of the dead; for example, she sits on an earth mound that resembles a burial plot. An announcement over the community's megaphone informs the entire town that Señora Erlinda is selling fried pork rinds (*chicharrón* in Castilian). Lamajtsin wants to buy the pork rinds straightaway. She calls out for her granddaughter Tere, yet unseen, to go with her to purchase what she humorously calls "chicharrontlatlak" (burnt *chicharrón*). The grandmother stands up quickly and drops the beans onto the mound without realizing it. At this moment Tere emerges from the earth.

Tere's exhumation, which paradoxically inverts her grandmother's physical burial, symbolizes a spiritual death (and potential rebirth) to which she is oblivious. She has ceased to care for her Nahua lands. It is unclear whether Tere is physically present. She may have returned to her Nahua community in Guerrero, but it is also possible that she remains in New York and has transported herself in a dream state or by other supernatural means. Physically present or not, she is no doubt psychologically absent from Nahua territories. In *Tsintatak*, those territories constitute a magnetic force that draws the grandmother and granddaughter together in an alternate dimension to open space for healing.

A significant clue that Lamajtsin and Tere exist in alternate dimensions is the reversal of everything. The grandmother asks Tere to put out the candles, but instead the granddaughter lights them. This contradiction could be read as a representation of Tere's restlessness and rebelliousness, but also an indication that the granddaughter is quite literally in another dimension. Moreover, Tere's emergence from the earth constitutes entering the earth from the grandmother's perspective. The granddaughter has accessed the mound where her grandmother lies buried. Lighting the candles in the grandmother's land of the dead puts them out for the granddaughter, and, in turn, putting them out would signify lighting them. Candlelight is a common symbol for a person's tonal, or "spirit." Its extinguishment in this world manifests its kindling in the place of the dead. This meaning is reinforced by the play on Abuelita (Grandmother) and Velita ("Dear/Little Candle" or a shortened form of "Abuelita"). With her death, Lamajtsin passes on light to her grandchildren. Tere's unearthing alludes to Samuel Beckett's famous two-act play *Happy Days* (*Los días felices* in Spanish; 1961).[41] Beckett's main protagonist Winnie is gradually buried as a symbol of her being smothered by a factitious contentment with her husband, cosmetics, and Western lifestyle. She seeks happiness by convincing herself tautologically that she happy. A key difference in *Tsintatak* is the luminous presence of Tere's grandmother, who points to a space of kinship in contrast with the restlessness of Western perspectives for which New York is a metonym. The grandmother grounds Tere in practices that allow for a regeneration.

As Tere puts out the candles (actually lighting them), she asks why it is necessary. Lamajtsin's warning that otherwise the house may burn down is key to understanding *Tsintatak*. She explains that fire cannot be kept still, *quieto* in Castilian, from which *inquieto* or "restless" is derived: "Tlitl xwelis, maske tiknekisia, tikpiyase sanewatika" / "El fuego no se puede mantener quieto" (Fire can't, even if we wanted, be kept still / The fire can't be kept still). This image returns to the play's title, *Tsintatak*, and the granddaughter's restlessness. Lamajtsin signals that fire "kipiya iyolo, kwelita notlakwaltis, kwelita nemis. Kentla tejwame, kentla totlajtol" / "[t]iene vida, como nosotras, como tu lengua" (has a heart, they like to feed themself, they like to live, like you and me, like our language / has life, like we do, like your tongue). This description marks a relationality with surroundings. The intersection of language, kinship, and land is palpable, and the light emanating from those spaces may turn destructive if mishandled or neglected. The threat of candles destroying a house figuratively represents the disintegration of family and home. Like Tere, fire is restless, constantly moves, and likes to innovate. In *Tsintatak*, language flickers and moves like fire with paronomasias and neologisms. In effect, Lamajtsin's explanation plays on a phonetic similarity between vela (candle), kwelita (enjoys), and Velita ("Abuelita" or Grandma). The candles, the grandmother, and her own mischievous attitude toward language connect with Nahua territory and, while acknowledging the dynamic and unpredictable turns of life (and language), recognize the need to remember one's roots. As made evident in the play, the flame symbolizes multigenerational/dimensional kinship. Candles' light embodies relatives who have died and entered another realm, as the grandmother has done. If a person fails to care for the figurative fire of language, land, and kinship, their home may burn to the ground. The grandmother's alternate dimension draws Tere to a place where she can be reunited with her land, her language, and a personal growth in *compadrazgo*, or kinship.[42]

After explaining the responsibility associated with tending to the candles, Lamajtsin realizes that she has dropped her beans. She and Tere begin to retrieve them. The grandmother laments that they will not arrive in time to buy the chicharrontlatlak or burnt pork rinds. Tere replies that she does not like them, since they are just burnt anyway. They then hear the community announcement a second time. Tere asks her grandmother why she uses the word chicharrontlatlak. Lamajtsin replies that she likes the sound (mirroring her description of how fire likes to play). The grandmother's chicharrontlatlak encapsulates a dynamic space of change and challenges to traditional practices. Her comment that she likes the way it sounds points to the affective power of Nahuatl to strengthen, cheer, and heal in the face of dire contexts. In this process, humor serves as a coping strategy to cure the scars of colonial practices.[43] Moreover, tlatlak (burnt) is onomatopoeic, imitating the crackling sound of fire and touching Lamajtsin's description of flames. Nahuatl words are felt in performance, as the grandmother justifies her use of them with the pithy explanation that she enjoys their sonority.

No static stalwart of petrified cultural practices herself, the grandmother loves to eat the fried pork rinds so much that she quickly stands up and drops her beans. Pork, of course, is nonnative to Abiayala, as represented in Martín Tonalmeyotl's work (see chapter 2). Spaniards introduced both pigs and the practice of frying. This animal swiftly reproduced and ravaged Abiayalan ecosystems. Within *Tsintatak* and Miyawatl's work in general there are no pretensions of a "pristine" Nahuatl. Appropriated loanwords appear throughout the Nahuatl (and, in turn, Nahuatl loanwords appear in the Castilian version). The community announcement over the megaphone elucidates that this theatrical piece distances itself from a romanticized Pre-Columbian past. Megaphones and fried pork rinds are elements the public does not associate with their exotic imaginings of uncontacted Nahua tribes. Nahuas have appropriated both. As Zapotec linguist Ana D. Alonso Ortiz attests, within regions throughout southern Mexico, the widespread use of megaphones constitutes a communal tool that amplifies a town's cohesion and strengthens Native languages.[44] In regard to chicharrón, it is now a common dish. Nahuas refer to it in the community announcement as pitsonakatl (pig meat). Lamajtsin nahuañolizes *chicharrón* by adding tlatlak (burnt). The paronomasia between chicharron*tlatlak* and tsin*tatak* (restlessness) suggests that it is acceptable to introduce new practices and to travel afar; nonetheless, one should never forget one's home community in the process.

Significantly, the grandmother is referred to only as Lamajtsin (Woman Elder) in the stage directions and Velita in the dialogue in Nahuatl. She is *Anciana* and *Velita* in Castilian. Tere is only referred to as Ichpoxtli (Young Woman), until the grandmother mentions her name in dialogue. The protagonists' generic appellations of "Woman Elder" and "Young Woman" signal that *Tsintatak* reflects a situation common to families in the region. At the same time, the play points toward specific experiences. Autobiographical elements abound, like the resemblance of the name Tere to Ateri (aside from its similarity to *tierra* or "earth" in Castilian). Miyawatl's grandmother's name Ana is hidden in the word *anciAna* in Castilian.[45] The same year she started writing *Tsintatak* (2016), Miyawatl traveled to New York for a meeting on the protection and preservation of languages and cultures at the UN Division for Social Policy and Development, Secretariat of the Permanent Forum on Indigenous Issues.[46] Her article "Tokohkol xonomikileh" (2022), published in *Trece semillas*, begins with a poem to her grandmother. Miyawatl relates that she herself had internalized a discriminatory discourse about the inferiority of Nahua practices. During her studies in dramaturgy, she heard professors disparage "traditional" performances from the mountainous region of Guerrero. New York was a symbol par excellence of that destructive discourse. Like she does in *Neijmantototsintle*, Miyawatl uses *Tsintatak* as a medium to process loss in a transformation that hinges on language, kinship, and land. This sanative movement encapsulates the variegated Serpent-Plumed iterations of territory found in contemporary Nahua literature. Those Plumes span a diverse territory mapped and woven with the perspectives of ixtlamatlistli, yoltlajlamikilistli, and tlaixpan. The grandmother is in front like the light on the altar; personal knowledges take primacy, and the perspectives they articulate are bound up in a profoundly affective space.

After explaining why she likes the word chicharrontlatlak, Lamajtsin suddenly asks her granddaughter about New York (which she calls "Nuevayor"). Tere extols skyscrapers filled with lights, in contrast with the local candles that symbolize connection with kin and the Velita/Abuelita (Candle/Grandma). She comments that New York is pretty. Lamajtsin immediately responds, "Xilak, nikan milak tlakwaltsinkan" (That's not true, here it's truly beautiful). This exchange marks a telling disparity between the two. Tere agrees that their community is pretty, that one can "climb a hill and tickle the sky." The tall skyscrapers of New York contrast with the mountains/hills of Guerrero. People outside this mountainous region use the term *montañero* (hillbilly) to disparage its Native inhabitants. To provide context, Miyawatl comments that, when she talked about her community and they heard her "proper Castilian," people expressed surprise at "discovering" she was Nahua and stated (supposedly as a compliment) that she "did not sound like a *montañera*" (13 November 2018, Facebook). This context highlights the implications of references to mountains in *Tsintatak*. At first, Miyawatl disguised herself behind her Castilian name and her proficiency in Castilian. In her article "Tokohkol xonomikileh," Miyawatl shares three key words to find peace in this violent context that figures as central in *Tsintatak*: *cicatrices* (scars), *crianza* (nurturing), and Nahuatl. She writes that the Nahuatl language contains "las formas organizativas, el conocimiento y el sentido de lo justo a través del cual se ha hecho frente a las violencias que se viven en estos territorios" (the organizational forms, knowledge and sense of what is just through which violent acts experienced in these territories have been confronted). In *Tsintatak*, Miyawatl showcases defense of land and language as mutually dependent expressions. Through that land-language she has learned kinship (kompaliknitin) to heal harmful behaviors (the scars) originating from "the colonialist history of this country" and to prevent the transmission of those colonial practices to progeny ("Tokohkol xonomikileh"). The granddaughter Tere comments that New York was frigid, and the wind blew strong, symbolic of this threat that Western epistemicide poses to Nahua practices.

Upon hearing Tere's praise of New York, Lamajtsin brings Tere back to the land by shifting to the ethical imperative of picking up every bean off the ground. She explains that their flesh is made of this food to mark a relationality with surroundings. Nevertheless, Tere stops listening as "se regocija en sus recuerdos" (she rejoices in her memories) of New York. She reminisces over a visit to a fancy Italian restaurant in Brooklyn where they serve minestrone soup, wine, desserts, and spaghetti supposedly better than the food in her community. The grandmother asks if she craved tortillas, to which Tere replied, "¡Nin xonikilnamik!" / "¡Ni las recordé!" (I didn't even remember them!). Far from being a minor infraction, this dismissal of tortillas is an egregious oversight. As Miyawatl explains, unlike the candles that need to be put out, the fire at the tenamastle (hearthstones where tortillas are cooked) must burn continually. Tere's abandonment of tortillas is symbolic of a grim distancing that carries with it the many meanings of maize explored throughout this study. The increasing cold she feels owes itself to her separation from the hearth of kinship.

Lamajtsin and Tere continue retrieving the beans, and the grandmother repeats, "tsin ta tak tsin ta tak tsin ta tak." The granddaughter inquires why she sings it, to which Lamajtsin gives a nearly identical answer as for chicharrontlatlak, that she likes the sound. To be sure, Lamajtsin sings "tsin ta tak" at the play's opening, and then again near the end, as if the word attracted Tere to then send her back into the living world. Lamajtsin asks Tere if she likes the word, to which Tere replies that it makes her laugh. Tsintatak, a butt itch, humorously refers to the granddaughter who cannot stay still. As mentioned previously, humor serves as a strategy to confront injustices and heal from them. Like earlier descriptions of the tongue constituting a dangerous fire if mishandled, it is vital to find a balance in which inevitable change does not smother a person's communal roots. In *Neijmantototsintle*, an external threat pushed the poetic persona to flee and then come to terms with an oppressive situation. In *Tsintatak*, the granddaughter has internalized the depreciation of her region. Within both works, food, music, language, and territory are fundamental elements in healing or else in causing harm.

Before Lamajtsin begins to chant a healing ceremony, the text states twice in Castilian, "Parece no estar ahí" (She seems not be there) to suggest the grandmother's presence in a different dimension. Parallels arise between the repetition of the announcement for fried pork rinds and Lamajtsin's subsequent invocation for her granddaughter. The grandmother observes Tere and repeats the same ritual litany three times, in contrast with the earlier announcement for fried pork rinds, which is approximately the same length and repeated twice. She calls on various animals to take away her granddaughter's neijmankokolistle, "sadness-sickness":

> Mixtontstintin, chichijtsintin, tekolome, tsikatsitsintin, tojtotsintin, kojlotsintin, xwajlian xkoajkike ikokolis yejwin ichpoxtle, xkanake ineijmankokolis, xkwikakan wejka, ne ipan tepetsintle xmakawate. Mixtontsintin, wiwitsakatsintin, chichitsintin, tojtotsintin, pitsotsintin xkanake yejwin ikokolis, xkwikakan wejka xkwikakan yejwin neijmankokolistle kampa achopawalko ...

> (Come, cats, dogs, owls, ants, birds, scorpions, come bear away this young woman's sickness, her sorrow-sickness, carry it far, and set it free at the top of those mountains. Come, cats, swallows, dogs, birds, pigs, come bear away her illness, carry it far, take this sorrow-sickness far away to where there is pure water ...)

Pitsotsintin (*marranitos* in Castilian), or little pigs, are mentioned in the prayer, recalling references to chicharrontlatlak. Lamajtsin invokes the animals to take sadness-sickness to achopawalko, "where pure water grows," a specific lagoon in Miyawatl's home region. There her grandmother would invoke animals to consume afflictions and deposit them at the water, where they can transform. Neijman (sadness) is the same word used in Neijman-tototsintle (sadness-bird). This curative space ties back to rain ceremonies to overcome droughts alluded to in *Neijmantototsintle*.

As Lamajtsin proceeds, Tere shivers, breathes heavily, and now seems fragile, "saken se pitentototsintle wan xok wejle patlani" (like a little bird unable to fly). Like the beans that fall to the ground, the granddaughter can regenerate and resurface, or, in reference to the avian metaphor, emerge with flight like the bird in *Neijmantototsintle*. The grandmother grounds Tere in a Nahua ethic so that she can learn to fly without forgetting her community. Tere asks again why her grandmother sings "Tsintatak." This time the grandmother does not respond; she instead repeats the same chant. Lamajtsin tenderly places ceremonial basil on the ground and tosses dirt on her granddaughter. This burial resembles images in *Neijmantototsintle* when the poetic persona sinks into the earth. Tere pleads with her grandmother, "Velita, xnetsintlikwiltile kantelajtin, etlayowatika" (Abuela, light a candle for me, it's getting dark). The granddaughter curls up in a fetal position; she "se ovilla sobre la tierra" (curls up into a ball on the earth). Winding up into a ball, *ovillarse*, is a term associated with wool balls (*ovillo*) to make textiles and hints at the procreant possibilities that may mend this traumatic moment. Lamajtsin recites the litany once more. Tere weeps uncontrollably as she sinks into the earth and "nonapalowa itik tlajle sanken sepitenkonetl" (hugs herself beneath the earth like a small child). Lamajtsin then puts out the candles, which in fact lights them for Tere since their realities are flipped in this alternate dimension. She takes her time and respects them, "Apaga su luz con mucho cuidado, como si las besara" (She puts out their light with great care, as if kissing them). The grandmother passes on light to her grandchild. Without this identifying element, the play could be misread as an insensitive grandmother who eliminates warmth as her granddaughter desperately pleads for candles to be lit. Unlike the poetic persona's mindful attention in *Neijmantototsintle*, Tere appears oblivious to her plight and lost in reminiscences of New York. Lamajtsin recognizes this ailment and deploys Nahua language and territory to heal her.

Tsintatak leaves the viewer/reader in a limbo. We do not know if Tere heals and recovers. She sinks into the earth, with the potential of renewal, or the risk of being lost. The granddaughter's reentrance into the mound is perhaps her return to the land of the living. Lamajtsin hopes that Tere arises healed with the remembrance of her community, to view it as attractive and eminent as New York. Tere may emerge healed and able to soar like the Serpent's Plumes and like the avian flight in *Neijmantototsintle*. In her article on the importance of *crianza* (nurturing), "Tokohkol xonomikileh," Miyawatl explains the centrality of land rights in raising children: "Hay un discurso permanente y totalitario que narra a las ruralidades como un sitio del cual hay que alejarse para estar 'bien,' para 'ser mejor,' para poder 'lograr' estabilidad económica" (There is permanent and totalitarian discourse that narrates ruralities as a site from which one must distance oneself to be "well," to "be better," to be able to "achieve" economic stability). She confesses that she was not immune to this discourse and had failed to realize that not having the option to study in Nahuatl was "una de las formas de violencia estructural hacia mí, mi familia y mi comunidad" (one of the forms of structural violence toward me, my family, and my community). Miyawatl explains that many Acatlán youth have migrated, pursuing the "university dream." *Tsintatak* never states explicitly where Tere and her grandmother are located, but pieces such as the megaphone, the Nahuatl variant used, and references to the mountains clearly situate them in Acatlán. The play never mentions why Tere has gone to New York, but the dialogue reveals that she traveled by plane with resources. Her hosts took her out to eat at a nice restaurant in Brooklyn. The trip could be for Tere's university studies, or, ironically, as was the case in Miyawatl's own life, a UN meeting to defend Native rights and languages.

Tsintatak embodies a Nahua community that Miyawatl describes as an alternative educational space, a "comunidad-escuela que no toma asistencia ni hace exámenes, que sucede. Son quienes nos han permitido a cada cual, a su tiempo y posibilidades, integrarnos a esa estructura colectiva" (a community-school that does not take attendance or give exams, that happens. They are those who have allowed each of us, according to their time and means, to join that collective structure). She speaks in language echoing *Neijmantototsintle* and *Tsintatak*, of an "espacio-tiempo en el cual también logro ver hacia dónde avanzar con esas heridas y cómo hacerlas florecer" (space-time in which I also succeed in seeing in which direction to advance with these wounds and how to make them flourish). *Tsintatak* and *Neijmantototsintle* bring together language, territory, and kinship rooted in a past-present, experiential observation, and affective intelligence to heal the external and internal wounds of colonial violence.

Re-membered: Beyond Rote Minutes of Silence

What is at stake in only one poem and a short theatrical piece? Miyawatl's *Neijmantototsintle* and *Tsintatak* underscore an affective intelligence, moving beyond rote minutes of silence or land acknowledgments, to feel losses. Land recognition is salient in the use of the Nahuatl language combined with a translation into Catalan and publication in Barcelona to recognize a global struggle for autonomy and self-determination.[47] Miyawatl's texts are intertwined with the land, in her case specifically Acatlán, Guerrero. Her use of the Nahuatl variant unique to her community suggests an autonomy focused on the experiences of Nahuas in Guerrero, against a nation-state that manipulates and disposes of them. This language is restorative. In that recovery, as Cárcamo Huechante highlights, the intersection of soundscapes in territorial demands eschews the tendency to compartmentalize land rights, language revitalization, and violence inflicted on the body.

Miyawatl's claiming of the body from assimilation into nation-state narratives is evident in her use of the name Ateri Miyawatl. Anna Yamel Gatica Matías is her legal name before the nation-state. Conversely, her name Ateri Miyawatl (*Ateri* is from the Purépecha language and *Miyawatl* from Nahuatl) points toward a wider alliance—an acoustic ecology—among Native Nations. This trans-Indigenous interconnection is showcased in the introduction to *Neijmantototsintle*, which states that "Nahuatl belongs to a family of at least 61 different languages that are commonly used in areas from the United States to El Salvador" (2). This language family includes Hopi, Shoshoni, Ute, and Comanche and opens to a rebordering that transcends nation-state boundaries. Miyawatl has studied and collaborated in projects across Abiayala from Chile to New York as part of this wider effort.

As seen in previous chapters, territorial claims are not an abstract longing within Miyawatl's region of Guerrero. Struggles for autonomy combat linguicide, mining companies, megaprojects for dams, and government collusion with organized crime. In response to this situation, communities have formed *policías comunitarias* (community-led police), organized protests in which they have expelled federal and state officials and transnational company representatives, and created communities without political parties.[48] Within these struggles, Miyawatl's works point to the Nahuatl language as a coping strategy to process colonial traumas and, in turn, as a source of xochitlajtoli to assert territorial autonomy in the wider sense explored here. It is perhaps in part due to this history that when someone is in dire distress, in Nahuatl they say mokokoa (to get sick/hurt), which shares a root with kokolistli (illness); kokolistli denotes the diseases brought by Europanes, and the grandmother deploys this word to describe her granddaughter's neijman*kokolistle* (sadness-sickness), resembling the title of the poem "Neijman*tototsintle*." This language points to a ceremonial space in which there can be healing to then set in motion the Serpent Plumes' flight. It foregrounds a situated affective intelligence in which one pays close attention to the language of those feelings. As seen in this study, *Neijmantototsintle* and *Tsintatak* hinge on Miyawatl's community of Acatlán projected out to a broad audience.

In "Painting the Archive," Pamela McCallum ponders the sacredness of objects in Ojibwe author Louise Erdrich's novel *The Painted Drum* (2005). This novel insists on the role of performance in preventing the theft of life from an object and its removal from a situated interconnection with community. Erdrich recalls a federal agent who acquired a drum as part of a collection of artifacts: "[H]e removed it from people who respected its sacredness and understood its communication with the spirit world; he literally imprisoned the drum in his attic, where it remained, forgotten and neglected" (McCallum 239). I posit that, in a similar manner, Miyawatl's emphasis on local projects circumvents the loss of that affective connection—to keep her xochitlajtoli and Nahua knowledge production from being displayed as an "artifact" divorced from performance and the everyday lives of Nahuas. Those specific, situated experiences are the many Plumes of the Serpent featured throughout this study. Miyawatl's attention to nuance relates to Martín Tonalmeyotl's reflections on poetry's effectiveness and the potential risk of forming a literary elite distanced from Nahua communities' pressing concerns. She cultivates sacred spaces that process traumatic events through a genuine engagement with language and community. Such is the difference between Western language revitalization and true strengthening through both language and territory.

Conclusion

Slinging Xochitlajtoli at Dams

A Prismatic Project(ion) of Contemporary Nahua Literature

> What good does it do—as the Cherokee author Marilou Awiakta once put it—to "sling a poem at a dam"?
>
> —Melanie Benson Taylor, "Indigenous Interruptions in the Anthropocene" (10)

Above Nahua communities in the Balsas region of Guerrero, approximately two hours northwest by car from Miyawatl's and Tonalmeyotl's hometowns, towers the Mezcala-Solidaridad Bridge. When completed in 1993, it was the tallest bridge in the world. This elevated structure anticipated a megaproject for a dam that would have flooded out Nahua communities located below. Nonetheless, Nahuas organized protests and, as part of these demonstrations, they created art in the amate tradition for which this region is well known.[1] After a selection of these works was displayed at the Mexican Fine Arts Center Museum in Chicago, protesters began to receive international support. Combining grassroot movements and artwork, the protests were successful, and the dam construction was canceled in 1993. The Mezcala-Solidaridad Bridge still hangs above these communities as a constant reminder of the power of artistic production—like poems hurled at a dam—and as an ominous warning of the destruction that could still occur. It is simultaneously a Serpent-Plumed symbol of Nahua empowerment and a potential harbinger of territorial devastation and appropriation.

Regarding the role of literature within such struggles, I have argued in *The Serpent's Plumes* that contemporary Nahua cultural production highlights three transformative Nahua perspectives that encompass the past in front (tlaixpan), the value of personal knowledge (ixtlamatilistli), and emotions as conjugated with one's cognition (yoltlajlamikilistli). Care has been taken to emphasize their connection with territory. In a decade that has initiated with increased protests over megaprojects and police brutality, and a pandemic that has disproportionately affected Native Nations, these perspectives are acutely vital. Colonial practices are a structure that literary imaginaries underwrite or potentially undermine. Within his critical analysis of Maya poetry, Emil' Keme underscores "the role that literature plays in processes of linguistic, cultural, political, and social decolonization" (*La Maya Q'atzij* 10). He cites Angela Davis's statement that art has the charge to see "the future in ways that the rest cannot see; it can express what has not yet been expressed. If we want to create a new world, we must be capable of imagining it. Because of that, political activists and intellectuals must recognize the role of the artists because they develop a radical and revolutionary consciousness" (qtd. in Keme, *Le Maya Q'atzij* 10). Far from delivering romanticizations and overgeneralizations, Nahua perspectives offer strategies for a descolonized world. As literary critic Melanie Benson Taylor asserts, while Native Nations do not have the definitive answers, the result will no doubt be more just if they are at the table making decisions and proposing responses to ever-changing circumstances (14).

The Serpent's Plumes offers a prismatic approach to contemporary Nahua literature. Diverse Nahua publications and mediatic incursions give glimpses of multiple refractions linked to the dynamic moniker *Nahua*. These various nodes in literary production point to an ethical coexistence among Nahuas and numerous Native Nations. The three perspectives that have served as the theoretical framework of this study center upon relationality as essential to mental health. The past in front emphasizes a relationality of the dead with the living, as well as an evolving scaffolding that convenes the living. Knowledge with the face showcases wisdom gained from a cultivated relationship with one's surroundings in the wide sense of both humans and other-than-humans. An affective intelligence represented with the heart signals deep bonds forged with these perspectives and the viewing of emotions as intelligent responses to challenges one may *face*. A person must be attuned to those circumstances, and, as seen especially in Miyawatl's works, can confront dire situations to emerge with a reforged agency and strength.

In chapter 1, we saw how Natalio Hernández counters stereotypical portrayals of Indigenous peoples. The three perspectives that serve as the theoretical framework for this study are readily apparent. An examination of *Xochikoskatl* and *Patlani huitzitzilin* traced Hernández's literary trajectory and his importance in discussions surrounding interculturality. Chapter 2 explored the xochitlajtoli of Martín Tonalmeyotl, who is representative of a younger generation of contemporary authors. His work deploys ixtlamatilistli, yoltlajlamikilistli, and tlaixpan to break with idyllic descriptions and battle injustices. Chapter 3 closely observed Ethel Xochitiotzin Pérez's *Tlaoxtika in tlajtol* and her transformation of traditional Nahua metaphors to empower Nahua women writers. This effort is pressing given the obstacles these writers have faced in publishing their texts. Chapter 4 addressed Judith Santopietro's *Palabras de agua* and her questioning that one must speak Nahuatl to be Nahua. This position has the potential to overturn how, within nationalist discourse, Indigenous language proficiency is the principal determiner of who is Indigenous and language loss is treated as a sign of the "vanishing Indian." Chapter 5 reviewed the mix of multiple genres in Mardonio Carballo's essay collection *Las Plumas de la Serpiente*. Carballo stresses the power of mass media in disseminating Native perspectives and disassembling the visual and acoustic colonial misrepresentations of Native Nations. Chapter 6 foregrounded local efforts led by Ateri Miyawatl and assessed how her book *Neijmantototsintle* and play *Tsintatak* serve as nodes in projects to repair the disastrous effects of colonialism. In her works, the Nahuatl language is a medium through which to process historical and present-day traumas. Taken together, the flowered words analyzed in *The Serpent's Plumes* sling a powerful message at threats to Nahua territory in all its dimensions.

Remapping toward the East: Inconclusive Conclusions and New Horizons in Nahua Cultural Production

In his famous drawing titled "América invertida" / "Inverted America" (1943), Uruguayan artist Joaquín Torres García flips a map of the Americas on its head to situate it toward the South.[2] Such a move suggests a different framework in which the global South takes center stage in knowledge production. More recently, Nahua artist Eneida Hernández completed the artwork on the cover of *The Serpent's Plumes*. Titled *Universo de las hilanderas* (Universe of Women Spinners; 2010), this work reorients space toward the East. This image touches upon main themes explored in *The Serpent's Plumes*. Hernández's embroidered painting renders vivid the five cardinal directions in Mesoamerica: East, North, West, South, and the fifth point where a person stands. The central point is the East, since that is where the sun rises. As opposed to a hierarchical perspective with a North or South above in competition for hegemony, such a view places the world map horizontally "on its side" in what can be described as a heterarchical conceptualization.[3] As a Nahua female artist, Hernández associates the sun with women and their power to observe and create texts. Her alternative cartography confronts male-dominated nation-state discourses and their distortion of the land and knowledge production under conquest and invalidation of supposedly inferior "Others." According to a colonizing logic of national elites, subalternized and racialized populations who put in question the territorial and conceptual borders of the nation-state are deemed anathema. Implicit within "all-inclusive" nationalist discourses is the exclusion of certain sectors of society—historically Indigenous populations among others.

Although a seemingly inconsequential shift, Hernández's turning of the map communicates that there are no superior epistemes but rather numerous nodes of knowledge production—symbolically spinning—along a network in which Nahuas are as significant as other actors. Her art(net)work addresses one of the principal objectives of *The Serpent's Plumes*, which has been to foreground Nahua perspectives. It is to place these epistemes in a cultural midpoint, while challenging the rigid centers and borders that nation-states impose. The desire to situate Nahua intellectual contributions in the present constitutes an aim throughout the texts of the authors in this study.

Eneida Hernández's embroidered painting gestures toward the heterogeneity and tensions within Nahua cultural production. Issues of contention abound within Nahua communities, foregrounding the need to avoid treating "Nahua literary production" as a monolith. *The Serpent's Plumes* has highlighted the diversity within this literature to debunk stereotypical depictions of Nahuas and Indigenous Nations in general as homogeneous. Attention to these divisions breaks down attempts to "other" Nahuas as outside "Modernity," subsumed within a prehistory, and devoid of individual subjectivities. *The Serpent's Plumes* has shown Nahuas in flux to disrupt static portrayals.

Migration and movement constitute pivotal experiences that unsettle these static views. Natalio Hernández authored *Xochikoskatl* over a period of nearly five years as a means of coping with the social and epistemic cacophony of Mexico City; Martín Tonalmeyotl wrote in Mexico City while completing his MA and subsequently in Puebla while pursuing a PhD; Ethel Xochitiotzin Pérez left her home community to complete a bachelor's at the University of Tlaxcala; Juditzin Santopietro left her city due to death threats and has resided in areas throughout Abiayala; Mardonio Carballo relocated from the Huasteca to Mexico City as a teenager to attend high school; Ateri Miyawatl fled her home community in Guerrero and lived for years in Michoacán. Writing has served as a cathartic outlet for these authors to come to terms with an urban milieu that erases their very existence. They network across rural, urban, and in-between spaces; they refute the view that there is an "outside" and "inside" to Indigenous communities and that these communities are isolated within rural areas. Instead, ruralities extend and enhance alliances past state, national, and international boundaries. Demands for land rights coexist with the strengthening of Nahua communities beyond their lands.

Rather than assimilate into supposedly superior urban centers in the United States or Mexico, Nahua artists showcase the innovative strategies that Nahuas employ to protect their practices and worldviews. Mardonio Carballo's multitude of "mis"-pronunciations (e.g., the transformation of "Estados Unidos" into "Estados Onidos") satirizes nation-state assimilationist education and dismantles the "national" language that figures at the center of its projects. Martín Tonalmeyotl through *Tlalkatsajtsilistle* protests economic and social inequities masked by state developmentalism. Nahua female authors such as Ethel Xochitiotzin Pérez call into question male-dominated discourses that pervade both nation-state discourse and Indigenous movements. Thus, taken as a whole, Nahua authors bring attention to the complexities and nonconformities that make the nation-state uneasy.

Nahua writers' travel toward urban centers reverses the order by which knowledge is thought to travel from north to south. *The Serpent's Plumes* has applied the perspectives ixtlamatilistli, yoltlajlamikilistli, and tlaixpan as the theoretical footing for an analysis of contemporary Nahua cultural production. These perspectives renew Indigenous empowerment within Abiayala—that is, within Indigenous societies that deconstruct Latin America epistemically speaking, offering innovative theoretical and aesthetic approaches to continental challenges. Tlaixpan (that which is in front or altar) is tied to a conceptualization of space and time reflected in Nahua authors' texts. Altars face toward the East to greet the morning sun. The arc over the altar represents solar passage across the sky.[4] As the movement of the sun itself, the care for ancestors' knowledges displayed upon the altar is not at all static—a theme that is reflected in Eneida Hernández's innovative use of traditional designs on her embroidered painting as well as within the unexpected turns of the literature examined in this study.

La bodega / The Warehouse: A Question of Readership

There is a large body of contemporary Nahua literature, but where do these texts get distributed? Who reads them? What is the size of this readership? In response to these questions, Mardonio Carballo remarks, "I have books with print runs of one hundred thousand, thirty thousand, seventy thousand copies, but if you try to track them down you won't find them. You won't find them in libraries or in schools. 'Where are they?' you ask: in a warehouse" (my trans.; qtd. in Sánchez de la Rosa).[5] While emphasis has been placed on the publication of Indigenous literatures, efforts to expand distribution and form a new public for these works are scarce by comparison. In his article "Textos con pocos lectores: En busca del libro perdido," journalist Jaimeduardo García investigates how the Consejo Nacional para la Cultura y las Artes (CONACULTA) does not function like a publishing house. One of the administrators of this program, Felipe Garrido, explains that CONACULTA (renamed the Secretaría de Cultura in 2015) "is not a publishing house, although it publishes books. Its most important task is to support the work of editors who are working in Mexico" (my trans.; qtd. in Jaimeduardo García). The circulation of these books is limited and concentrated in Mexico City. Carballo is probably the most active author in promoting a fan base for his works. Nevertheless, he admits that it has been difficult to bolster circulation despite his efforts. Considering the reduction in the number of readers in general, print publications may even partially reinforce a stereotype of Native peoples as stuck in older, "analog" mediums.

With the great influence visual media has in the public imaginary in contrast with a limited audience for print media, why do Nahua authors continue to write? Literature constitutes a powerful means to reimagine a society that respects Nahua practices. Writing offers a way to work through the discrimination that these authors have faced. While the readership may be limited, the text is often as much for the writer as for the reader. Their texts foment dialogue among the authors themselves, who represent the audience most attentive to these publications. They find in it a means to question official narratives, such as the accounts surrounding Ayotzinapa. Against a backdrop in which there are few readers, Mardonio Carballo describes continuing to write as falling from a high-rise building and trying to build something during the descent (qtd. in Sánchez de la Rosa). The hope is that Nahua authors will build up enough of a readership to stop that fall.

Another issue that arises in relation to Indigenous publications is that many are funded by government programs, principally scholarship programs administered by the Secretariat of Culture and the National Institute of Indigenous Languages (INALI). This type of funding began in the early nineties amid protests against quincentennial celebrations of Christopher Columbus and increased exponentially after the Zapatista uprising in 1994. The Mexican government sought to co-opt Indigenous movements through developmentalist programs and scholarships to show that they were ameliorating the "problema indio." Although federal funding for CONACULTA and subsequently the Secretariat of Culture started to drop at an alarming rate under Felipe Calderón's administration (2006–2012) and Enrique Peña Nieto's administration (2012–2018), and has continued to fall during Andrés Manuel López Obrador's presidency, government programs still constitute one of the principal sources for grants to publish Native works.[6] This context creates an ambivalent relationship since, despite their criticism of government actions, authors rely on government funding to give voice to their denunciations. Despite their texts' criticism, "CONACULTA" or "Secretaría de Cultura" appear in bold letters on the covers and could be perceived as validating the very nation-state that Native Nations challenge. Why then do authors accept the funding? For one, major publishing houses disregard Indigenous literatures as unmarketable, and major distributors avoid them for the same reason.[7] State-funded editorial houses are one of the few outlets available to release their works. The general sentiment is "We take the funding, but not the recognition." In other words, they take the money but deny they need government recognition to exist. Nahuas regard the funds as long overdue—and excessively limited—reparations for the damages inflicted against Indigenous peoples over centuries.

Concerning the politics of publication, another debate addresses whether Nahua writers risk becoming an uncommitted intellectual elite.

Within the confines of the Mexican state, such a privileged group could be viewed as favoring Western forms to gain acceptance at the cost of Indigenous expressive forms that transgress the nation-state. In this sense, they are recolonized or, even worse, they recolonize themselves. These authors can find themselves stigmatized by the mainstream literary market, since they do not write primarily in Castilian. This happens even though, with few exceptions, the publications are bilingual, so that a Castilian-reading public can access them. At the same time, authors potentially alienate themselves from their own Nahua bases and their communities' concerns.[8] This split no doubt poses a risk if written literature is displayed as a "higher" form in comparison to other artistic media. Nonetheless, rather than an elitist aspiration, this literature is a node in a network of multiple expressive forms. Nearly all Nahua authors collaborate in myriad projects beyond their written texts, and these undertakings are vitally important to them in affirming that they are community participants. All the authors in this study have led strengthening/revitalization projects for the Nahuatl language and cultural practices. In fact, Tepeko community members know Natalio Hernández more for these efforts than as a writer. Different media, from oral narratives to Nahua television programs, should be seen as being on equal footing. Such a perspective avoids the construction of an elite *letrado*.

Crossing Borders:
New Horizons in Contemporary Nahua Cultural Production

The Serpent's Plumes points toward future approaches to contemporary Nahua cultural production and Native cultural production throughout Abiayala. I have focused on what would more commonly be termed "poetry," with the exception of Mardonio Carballo's transgenre essay collection and Ateri Miyawatl's *Tsintatak*. I have proposed the term xochitlajtoli as a more accurate way to refer to this literary production and its move beyond the borders of Western genres. Rather than constituting art for art's sake, these flowered works function as nodes in larger, multimedia projects that defend Indigenous rights. This range of expression is underscored in Mardonio Carballo's book/DVD/CD *Las horas perdidas* (2014). This collection mixes multiple genres: diary, poetry, prog rock, and documentary. The transgression of genre borders highlights the creative potential in breaking with traditional categorizations. *Las horas* represents one of the most innovative developments in contemporary Nahua cultural production and is a promising area of study.⁹ Texts such as this one signal new horizons in Nahua cultural production where Indigenous artists fight visual and acoustic colonialism through a diverse array of Serpent-Plumed media.

The dynamic transit apparent in Nahuas' texts clashes with colonial conceptions of the land and closed cultural systems. Within a colonized cartography, the mapping process authorizes certain frameworks while denying others. This logic sets its conditions through everyday practices that seem natural and go uncontested. The authors in this study question the strict boundaries of nationalist discourse that relegate them to the ungrammatical and unintelligible, outside "Modernity." Nahuas vie for an intellectual sovereignty that is not founded on the conquest and dismissal of alternative knowledges.¹⁰ It is a context in which their knowledge production possesses the same validity in relation to other epistemes. I have heard authors express their intent to compete for awards outside the category of "Indigenous literatures." Huastecan Nahua poet Juan Hernández half-jokingly said, "Quiero un Nóbel," referring to the Nobel Prize for literature.¹¹ He, along with fellow writers, seeks to Nahuatlize not only Western genres but also the Nobel. They battle the "othering" of Native authors and the false notion that they are unable to compete with "mainstream" literary production.

An important gap in my analysis concerns Nahua communities' experiences in the US. It was in Southern California where I started to learn Nahuatl twenty years ago. Attention to Nahua and Southern Abiayalan Indigenous artists in the US promises to disrupt the dominant gaze of the US toward the South, in which "North American" researchers travel *down* to investigate "primitive" cultures. Conversely, attention to Southern Abiayalan artists in the US and their views flips the exchange of ideas in such a way that Native intellectuals evaluate US populations. This shift engages strategies that strengthen transnational networks and dismantle the stereotypical depiction of Indigenous peoples as stuck in place.

Another promising approach is to examine contemporary Nahua artistic production from the perspective of environmental justice. Natalio Hernández comments that Nahuas spoke about Mother Earth long before it became fashionable within global environmental movements.¹² He recounts that when Nahuas spoke of Mother Earth in the 1950s and 1960s, people thought they were crazy. Nahua texts convey reciprocity, close relationships with the land, and respect for the earth as a living entity with rights. Especially intriguing is an analysis of Nahua collaborations with other Native Nations. Protection of natural resources has sparked the formation of Indigenous and non-Indigenous alliances across the globe.

Queer studies offer additional innovative approaches to this Nahua cultural production. Works related to LGBTQ Nahuas and Indigenous peoples across Abiayala are increasing rapidly.[13] Mardonio Carballo's texts have much to say about approaches within Queer studies. He overturns heteronormativity through his art, as evidenced in his documentary program *De raíz luna*. In a historic episode of this nationally televised show, Carballo interviews Felina Santiago, a Zapotec *muxe* (an identity outside the Western gender binary) from Oaxaca. Santiago speaks of the discrimination she has experienced outside of her community since she was assigned male at birth but identifies as female.[14] The broadcasting of this episode was a courageous act, due to the threats faced by nonheteronormative people. Carballo's works span various types of media to overturn the hierarchical, heteronormative map in favor of fluid conceptions of gender. His art is especially rich from the angle of media studies, as he has films, documentaries, music albums, an active Facebook page, radio programs, podcasts, and a nationally televised show. Carballo's efforts underscore a principal objective of this study: to situate Nahuas as key actors who offer valuable perspectives in unexpected places.

I have sought in the present analysis of Nahuas' literary production to "take their word for it"—that is, to engage seriously with their literature, which is often framed within the "marginality of marginality." Indigenous peoples are placed in what some problematically refer to as a "fourth world," which suggests they are located even further "down" south from the global South. Conversely, Nahua authors propose a horizontal frame of knowledge production that positions them as equal players in what Natalio Hernández aptly depicts in his xochitlajtoli as multiple furrows within fields of knowledge. Like tlaixpan (the altar), which directs one's view toward ancestors, the authors within this study turn toward their ancestral knowledges and insist upon their value, which transcends beyond their communities. This ancestral *forward observance* orients us toward the Serpent-Plumed turns, spirals, and bridges across contemporary Nahua flowered words.

Notes

Introduction. The Serpent's Quills, Keyboards, and Touchscreens: Writing, Not Being Written

1. Personal interview, 9 June 2013. Carballo has voiced this criticism on multiple occasions, in personal interviews and on his radio and television programs. See Andrea Rodés, "Las lenguas suenan." Unless otherwise indicated, translations from Nahuatl and Castilian into English are mine. Additionally, unless otherwise indicated, all cited interviews are formal meetings conducted after completion of the my university's Institutional Review Board process.

2. Regarding the use of general terms such as *Native* and *Indigenous*, I follow *NAIS Journal* guidelines. Whenever possible, the *NAIS* editorial board recommends specifying Nations with their endonyms. General terms vary by region, and *Indigenous*, *Native*, and *First Nation* are common where I work (alongside *pueblo originario* and *indígena* in Spanish, and *maseuali* in Nahuatl). I use these terms interchangeably when not referring to a specific Nation.

3. Like many Nahua authors, I often use Castilian (*castellano*) to highlight that it is one of numerous languages spoken in Spain, and in that sense provincialize it as coexisting with them rather than occupying a superior status. The importance of the parallel between linguistic discrimination in Spain and Mexico is especially apparent in the sixth chapter focused on Ateri Miyawatl's *Neijmantototsintle*, a work published in Nahuatl and Catalan. That said, I use Castilian and Spanish interchangeably, much like authors do in their own works (*castellano* or *kaxtilan* is more common in texts in Nahuatl; *español* more so in texts in Spanish).

4. Xochitlajtoli can also be written xochitlahtolli, xochitlahtoli, xōchitlajtōli, and xoochitlajtooli. There are competing alphabets in Nahuatl, and heated discussions have arisen as to which system is "correct." Nahua playwright Ildefonso Maya even invented his own system of hieroglyphics. Unless quoting directly from a text with a different orthography, I use the system developed by Nahua teachers in the 1970s, which was later adopted by the Secretariat of Public Education (SEP) for

bilingual education in Veracruz. Rather than privilege a particular writing system, my principal aim in standardizing the orthography outside of direct citations is to increase readability and consistency in analyzing Nahuas' works. Moreover, there are disagreements over Classical Nahuatl orthography. In this study, for words in Classical Nahuatl, I use either the system proposed by Frances Karttunen, R. Joe Campbell, and J. Richard Andrews (inspired by seventeenth-century Jesuit father Horacio Carochi's work) to emphasize vowel length (marked with a macron) or the more common standardized orthography that excludes vowel length. See José Antonio Flores Farfán, *Variación, ideologías y purismo lingüístico*; Frances Karttunen, *An Analytical Dictionary*; and Adam W. Coon, "To *In* or Not to *In*."

5. Following the editorial norms of the Native American and Indigenous Studies Association (NAISA), I avoid the italicization of words in Native languages since this practice tends to reinforce the othering of them. I only italicize Nahuatl words when necessary for clarity or when italicized in citations. I thank Ojibwe historian Jean O'Brien for this suggestion. No doubt the same argument could be made regarding the othering colonial relationship of English toward Castilian. Nonetheless, Castilian is italicized because of its diglossic relationship to Nahuatl.

6. In using "archive and repertoire," I allude to performance studies scholar Diana Taylor's use of *archive* as constituting "materials that seem to endure" and "exceed the live," and *repertoire* as enacting "embodied memory: performances, gestures, orality, movement, dance, singing—in short, all those acts usually thought of as ephemeral, nonreproducible knowledge" (*The Archive and the Repertoire* 19–20). In this study I propose that Nahua artistic production moves beyond the privileged status of written texts in the sense of graphemes on paper, to open toward a wide array of performative/archival strategies that both embody and endure. These strategies encompass ceremony, music, and tending to the land.

7. *Modernity* is a highly fraught term often conflated with "modernization." By *(M/m)odernity* I refer to a Western project that champions an exclusive modernity based principally on the discrediting of its Other's knowledges as inadequate and superstitious in comparison with the supposed superiority of Western technological and scientific advancements. I capitalize *Modernity* to expose its pretentions toward such exclusivity. Its buzzwords are *Progress* and *Development*. The term *modernity* suggests that there are people somehow located "outside" the present—othered both physically and temporally instead of representing alternative proposals for moderni*ties*. For a greater discussion of this topic, see Walter Mignolo, *The Darker Side of Western Modernity*, and Graciela Montaldo, "Modernity and Modernization."

8. Copious research addresses this topic. See Guillermo Bonfil Batalla, *México profundo*, and Patricio Solís et al., *Por mi raza hablará la desigualdad*.

9. One could possibly argue that this is reactive as a *counter*discourse to colonialism. Ayuujk theorist Yásnaya Elena Aguilar Gil examines this paradox in her essay "Resistencia: Una breve radiografía." She argues that it is impossible to

obviate resistance because it is impossible to obviate the far-reaching and disastrous effects of colonialism (21). In other words, opposing the perpetual depiction of Native movements as only "resistance" is a form of resistance. Aguilar Gil underscores the creative solutions of Native Nations in the face of colonial oppression; such Native innovation and empowerment are often lost in mainstream portrayals of Native movements as always reactively resisting.

    10. I use Abiayala instead of "Latin America" to highlight the networks among Afrodescendant and Native Nations throughout the continent. Abiayala (also spelled Abya Yala) is a Gunadule term that means "Land in Fruition," "Land of Plenitude and Maturity," "Land of Fullness," "Land of Blood," and "Saved Territory." As part of trans-Indigenous movements, Aymara activist Takir Mamani proposed this term as an alternative for "the Americas" in the 1970s. Since then, this appellation has become increasingly common. In its gesture toward a flowering abundance, "Abiayala" defies colonial discovery narratives that describe the land as empty, undeveloped, and open for conquest. For an in-depth exploration of this term's history, see Emil' Keme, "For Abiayala to Live, the Americas Must Die"; Sue Patricia Haglund, "A Selection of Contemporary Gunadule Literature"; Hannah Burdette, *Revealing Rebellion in Abiayala*; and Diana Gómez Correal, "Améfrica Ladina, Abya Yala y Nuestra América."

    11. For overviews of contemporary Nahua literary production, see Martín Tonalmeyotl, "Poesía contemporánea en lengua náhuatl"; Hermann Bellinghausen, "Un viaje por la poesía contemporánea náhuatl"; Kelly McDonough, *The Learned Ones*; Miguel León Portilla, "Yancuic tlahtolli"; Adam W. Coon, "To *In* or Not to *In*"; and Adam W. Coon, "Living Languages as the Acoustic Ecologies."

    12. In xochitl in cuicatl (*flor y canto* / flower and song) is one of the most well-known expressions in Nahuatl. Often described as the Nahua term for "poetry," although encompassing other creative forms, *in xochitl in cuicatl* within nationalist discourse refers to Pre-Columbian and early Colonial Nahua artistic production. Nationalist discourse celebrates this genre as uniquely Mexican and as evidence that there was already valuable knowledge production when Europeans invaded. This much-vaunted history of ancient Native civilizations, particularly of Nahuas, was exalted after the Mexican Revolution to assert the uniqueness and legitimacy of the Mexican nation-state. Within an (a)temporal paradigm, the post-Revolutionary state appropriated the works of figures such as painter Diego Rivera and UNAM professors Ángel María Garibay and Miguel León Portilla, despite Garibay and León Portilla's insistence on the importance of studying contemporary Nahuatl and their support for Nahua authors. For more on in xochitl in cuicatl and debates surrounding its presence in nationalist discourse, see Jongsoo Lee, *The Allure of Nezahualcoyotl*.

    13. Numerous scholars address this discourse of ancientness. For example, in *A Finger in the Wound*, Diane M. Nelson considers how people commonly talk about the Maya as the builders of Tikal, but they are shocked to learn that

there are Mayas today. For in-depth criticism of this romanticization, see Miruna Achim et al., *Museum Matters*; Natasha Varner, *La raza cosmética*; and Jongsoo Lee, *The Allure of Nezahualcoyotl*. The obsessive idealization of Quetzalcoatl and Mexica symbols plays out in English as well, from D. H. Lawrence's strange novel *The Plumed Serpent* (1926) to video games like *Freedom Force vs. the 3rd Reich*. In his novel, Lawrence imagines a resurgence of Quetzalcoatl followers among "the silent, serpent-like dark resistance of those masses of ponderous natives whose blood was principally old, heavy, resistant Indian blood" (49).

14. Other terms in Nahuatl for the language are mejikanoj (Mexican), mexikatl, nauatlajtoli (Nahuatl language / discourse / words), and maseualtlajtoli (Maseuali / Indigenous language / discourse / words). Mejikanoj, in some regions, used to be the prevalent way for Nahuas to refer to their own language. Academia popularized the term Nahuatl, particularly in the mid-twentieth century, to such an extent that it has become increasingly common within Nahua communities.

15. I use the present tense *speak* because there are people who self-identify as Mexica today, notably Chicanxs in the US, to debunk the vanishing Indian narrative propagated by the state.

16. Some of the most well-known loanwords are avocado, axolotl, chili, chipotle, chocolate, cocoa, coyote, guacamole, Guatemala, mesquite, tamal, tomato, and xoloitzcuintli. For additional examples, see Jason D. Haugen, "Borrowed Borrowings."

17. See David Carrasco, "Aztec."

18. The official census of the Mexican federal government calculates a population of approximately 1.5 million Nahuas. Nahuas are principally in the federal entities (states) of Veracruz, Guerrero, Puebla, Mexico City, Estado de México, Morelos, Hidalgo, and San Luis Potosí. Natalio Hernández suggests there are at least three million (N. Hernández, personal interview, 22 Sept. 2012). He argues that in the census many—especially those in urban areas—avoid stating that they are Nahua due to discrimination. Moreover, the Mexican census misses the hundreds of thousands who live outside of Mexico or those who identify as Nahua but do not speak the Nahuatl language. See INEGI, *Censo de Población y Vivienda 2020*.

19. In *Death of a Discipline*, Gayatri Chakravorty Spivak addresses the implications of readings from different parts of the world and calls for a "New Comparative Literature" that does not depend on market appeal.

20. Alluding to a heated exchange with a non-Indigenous scholar within the prominent journal *American Historical Review*, Jean O'Brien condemns this tendency. She lays bare a "long-standing and damaging critique" that Native American and Indigenous studies are biased and "that we Indigenous scholars cannot be 'objective' because we are too close to the subject, and thus our work distorts the past" ("Animating Box 331" 371). For a detailed response to this critique, see Jean O'Brien, "What Does Native American and Indigenous Studies (NAIS) Do?"

21. As a case in point, regarding debates over novels by Mesoamerican authors, Gloria Elizabeth Chacón questions literary critics' assumption that these authors are "tainted by a mestizo worldview" within a teleological framework where "an education taints an individual and dilutes indigeneity into a mestizo identity" (*Indigenous Cosmolectics* 128).

22. See McDonough, *The Learned Ones*; Lisa Brooks, *The Common Pot*; Robert Warrior, *Tribal Secrets*; Daniel Heath Justice, *Why Indigenous Literatures Matter*; and David Chang, *The World and All the Things upon It*.

23. I use "translingual poetics" in the sense theorized by Sarah Dowling in *Translingual Poetics* to accentuate the "capacity of languages to interact, influence, and transform one another" and call for scholars "to move away from the monolingual/multilingual binary to recognize a range of competencies across, as well as within, languages" (4–5). According to Dowling, translingual poetries signal that "there are always alternative structures of thinking and doing, always other stories to be told, and always other ways to describe the relationships between present and past" (169).

24. In *Revealing Rebellion in Abiayala*, Hannah Burdette warns: "Yet much like 'revival,' 'resurgence,' and 'awakening'—all terms variously used to describe the same phenomenon—the concept of revitalization can also problematically evoke the idea of a 'pure' or 'authentic' model of indigeneity from the past that contemporary movements aim to reconstruct" (7). Terms like *revitalization* and *Native American Renaissance* can mistakenly lead people to believe that Native Nations have been dormant or on the verge of extinction for the last five hundred years.

25. Mè'phàà author Hubert Matiúwàa published an article calling into question the effectiveness of such declarations. See "El día bajo la sombra."

26. For additional examples, see Paul M. Worley, *Telling and Being Told* (2013); James H. Cox and Daniel Heath Justice, *The Oxford Handbook of Indigenous American Literature* (2014); Emil' Keme, *Teorizando las literaturas indígenas contemporáneas* (2015); Gloria Elizabeth Chacón, *Indigenous Cosmolectics* (2018); Luz María Lepe Lira, *Relatos de la diferencia y literatura indígena* (2018); Daniel Heath Justice, *Why Indigenous Literatures Matter* (2018), Thomas Ward, *Decolonizing Indigeneity* (2018); Jennifer Gómez Menjívar and Gloria Elizabeth Chacón, *Indigenous Interfaces* (2019); Hannah Burdette, *Revealing Rebellion in Abiayala* (2019); Inés Hernández-Ávila, "La literatura Indígena" (2020); Víctor Montejo, *Mayalogue* (2021); Miguel Rocha Vivas's *Word Mingas* (2021); and Tiffany D. Creegan Miller, *The Maya Art of Speaking Writing* (2022).

27. There are significant efforts to promote continental Abiayalan dialogues and overcome this divide. A notable example is the Abiayala Working Group within NAISA. Within LASA, the sections Otros Saberes and ERIP-LASA nurture trans-Indigenous exchanges across the continent.

28. For more on the harmful tendency within the US to fold Native migrants from Latin America into the categories *Latino* and *Hispanic*, see Shannon Speed, *Incarcerated Stories*.

29. Paul M. Worley and Rita M. Palacios address this issue in a Castilian synopsis of their academic publication, *Unwriting Maya Literature*. They argue that reading Native literatures demands a dialogue that "allows the written word to jump from the page and confront the reader and his position, which very likely is colonial" (my trans.; 2). See Worley and Palacios, "Des-escribir la literatura maya," 2–4.

30. For examples, see Wilson-Hokowhitu, *The Past before Us*, in which Hawaiian intellectuals explore a theoretical framework, moʻokūʻauhau, that resembles tlaixpan by orienting the past in front for a wide array of activism. See also Victor Montejo, *Mayalogue*; Lisa Kahaleole Hall, "Navigating Our Own 'Sea of Islands'"; Arturo Arias, *Recovering Lost Footprints*; Paul M. Worley and Rita M. Palacios, *Unwriting Maya Literature*; and Robin Wall Kimmerer, *Braiding Sweetgrass*.

31. On his radio programs, Mardonio Carballo has probed the politics of citation and intellectual theft, in particular the plagiarism of Native textile designs. For example, consult the episode of *Xochikozkatl* with Nancy Vázquez and Stephani Delgado on 11 October 2021.

32. See Lisa Kahaleole Hall, "Navigating Our Own 'Sea of Islands.'"

33. Discussed for instance on Mardonio Carballo's radio program *Xochikozkatl* on 6 December 2021 in an interview with Gloria Palacios and Gabriela González.

34. In her article "Ixtlamatilistli: Las mujeres en la formación de la niñez de Tepenahuac, Veracruz," Nahua historian Jacinta Toribio Torres defines knowledge as "algo que viene y se construye con el sentido de la vista; luego entonces, el conocimiento es algo concreto y no abstracto" (something that comes and is constructed with one's sight; thus, knowledge is something concrete and not abstract; 36)

35. Similar temporal views, with specific nuances, are shared across many Native languages. For example, when speaking Aymara, people signal with their hands in front when referring to the past. See Rafael E. Núñez and Eve Sweetser, "With the Future behind Them."

36. In Nahuatl, each day is measured by tonatij (suns).

37. Epistemologies and ritual symbolism are rarely explained explicitly. See Arturo Gómez Martínez, *Tlaneltokilli*; Alan Sandstrom, *Corn Is Our Blood*; Alan Sandstrom and Pamela Effrein Sandstrom, *Pilgrimage to Broken Mountain*.

38. This view of the past resembles the conceptualization of history in the Aymara language. The word for "FRONT (*nayra*, 'eye/front/sight') is also a basic expression meaning PAST, and the basic word for BACK (*qhipa*, 'back/behind') is a basic expression for FUTURE meaning" (Núñez and Sweetser 402). Silvia Rivera Cusicanqui traces this view forward to the past in the terms nayrapacha (past-as-future) and pachakuti (overturning of time). See *Violencias (re)encubiertas en Bolivia* 39–51.

39. Kaqchikel scholar Irma Otzoy analyzes textiles as a "visible language" and a "language of silence." See Otzoy, *Maya' b'anikil*. In *Word Minga*, Miguel

Rocha Vivas considers at length a "pluriscriptual minga map" communicated through textiles and numerous other types of texts (43–92).

40. Copious research examines the significance of maize-centered symbolism. See Alan Sandstrom, *Corn Is Our Blood*; Arturo Gómez Martínez, *Tlaneltokilli*; Arturo Arias, "Indigenous Literatures?"; and Paul M. Worley and Rita M. Palacios, *Unwriting Maya Literature* 31.

41. *Priístas* (members of Partido Revolucionario Institucional [PRI]), *panistas* (members of Partido de Acción Nacional [PAN]), *perredistas* (members of Partido de la Revolución Democrática [PRD]), and, since 2015, *morenistas* (members of Movimiento Regeneración Nacional [MORENA]) constitute the four largest political parties in Mexico.

42. I use *worlding* in the sense expressed by Marisol de la Cadena and Mario Blaser in *A World of Many Worlds*. That is, "knowledges are world-making practices, they tend to make the worlds we know" (6).

43. The term macehualli/maseuali has a varied history from the colonial era. Macehualli (commoner) had been used precontact to denote a social class separate from pilli (noble). It signified "vassal" or a position of subservience to an individual with greater authority. Through the sixteenth and seventeenth centuries, macehualli gradually became synonymous with *indio* (Indian), regardless of one's social position among Indigenous populations. In the Huasteca Veracruzana, maseuali came to signify less "indio" and referred instead to Nahuas who speak Nahuatl, know how to personally work the land, and follow cultural practices for a successful crop. Rather than self-identify as *indio* (Indian), *indígena* (Indigenous), or even *nahua*, maseualmej usually self-identify according to their specific communities and the location of their homes (e.g., by the river, near the hill, and so forth). With the emergence of national and international Indigenous movements in the 1970s, *Indigenous* or *indígena* became the widely accepted legal term in international courts and organizations such as the United Nations. Within Nahuatl translations of their proceedings, *indígena* is *maseuali*. This general association of maseuali with *indígena* or *nahua* has become increasingly common within Native communities. Nonetheless, the term tends to be employed with this wider meaning when used in state, national, or international politics. For an extensive discussion of these terms, see Mercedes Olivera, *Pillis y macehuales*.

44. Cusicanqui self-identifies as *chola*. I use *Aymara* due to the significantly different meanings of *chola* in Mexico and the United States. Cusicanqui defines *cholo/a* in Bolivia as "indigenous people who have emigrated to urban areas and live somewhere between the cultural spaces of mestizo and indigenous identity" (Rivera Cusicanqui, "The Notion of 'Rights'" 51).

45. The *s* represents El Sur or Southern Abiayala in South-South dialogues. I am cognizant of the contradiction of this gesture in a study written in English from the northern academia Cusicanqui critiques. Nonetheless, by employing Abiayalan theoretical frameworks as full-fledged heuristics rather than "raw material," *The Serpent's Plumes* seeks to break with a long tradition of what Antonio Cornejo

Polar denounces as "el excesivo desnivel de la producción crítica en inglés que parece—bajo viejos modelos industriales—tomar como materia prima la literatura hispanoamericana y devolverla en artefactos críticos sofisticados" (the excessive unevenness of critical production in English that appears—under old industrial models—to take Hispanic American literature as raw material and render it sophisticated critical artifacts; "Mestizaje e hibridez" 343).

46. From Nauanechikolistli meeting in Tepeko (Lomas del Dorado), Ixhuatlán de Madero, Veracruz, Mexico on 29 September 2020.

47. For examples, see Yásnaya Elena Aguilar Gil's essay "Jajajatl: ¿Es para reírse?" 57–61. Mardonio Carballo exposes the invented origins of a viral meme purporting that *apapachar* derives from a Nahuatl word meaning "to caress with the soul." See Darinka Rodríguez, "Apapachar."

48. For further discussion of this expansion, see Justyna Olko, "Aztec Universalism," and Laura E. Matthew, *Memories of Conquest* 37–50.

49. See Alexander Koch et al., "Earth System Impacts of the European Arrival."

50. See *Language Contact and Change in Mesoamerica and Beyond*, edited by Karen Dakin, et al.

51. For a more detailed discussion of this context, see Laura E. Matthew, *Memories of Conquest* 16, and Jane H. Hill and Kenneth C. Hill, *Speaking Mexicano*.

52. See Justyna Olko et al., *The Insignia of Rank in the Nahua World*, and Olko, *Dialogue with Europe*.

53. *Nobility* refers to families who descended from city rulers' dynasties or who laid claim to special rights due to their ancestors' aid toward Spanish conquistadores. Noble status afforded a person land rights, exemption from certain taxes, permission to wear unique apparel, and so forth. See Justyna Olko, *Dialogue with Europe*, and Olko et al., *The Insignia of Rank in the Nahua World*.

54. This large corpus of documents was a stimulus for the New Philology movement in Nahuatl studies, based primarily in US academia. This movement stressed the need to study Native-language sources for a better understanding of Native societies. See Matthew Restall, "A History of the New Philology." After Mexican nation-state independence, the practice of proceedings in Native languages nearly disappeared, with limited exceptions.

55. See McDonough, *The Learned Ones*.

56. Debates abound over authorship of these texts from the sixteenth and seventeenth centuries. See Susan Schroeder, "The Truth about the *Crónica Mexicayotl*."

57. Studies of these texts have increased exponentially over the last decades. Excellent examples include Jonathan Amith's *The Möbius Strip* (2005); David Tavárez's *The Invisible War*; Molly H. Bassett's *The Fate of Earthly Things* (2015); James Maffie's *Aztec Philosophy* (2015), Barbara Mundy's *The Death of Aztec Tenochtitlan* (2015); Justyna Olko et al.'s *Dialogue with Europe, Dialogue with the Past* (2018); Jonathan Truitt's *Sustaining the Divine in Tenochtitlan* (2018), Angela

Herren Rajagopalan's *Portraying the Aztec Past* (2018); Jeanette Favrot Petersen and Kevin Terraciano's *The Florentine Codex* (2019); Ben Leeming's *Aztec Antichrist* (2022); Getty Research Institute's *Digital Florentine Codex* (2023). In 2020, the NEH Summer Institute offered a course, Worlds in Collision, that focused on sixteenth-century Spanish and Nahua documents.

58. For more on these literary traditions, see McDonough, *The Learned Ones*; Miguel León Portilla, *Literaturas indígenas de México*.

59. Debates surround Ignacio Manuel Altamirano's origins. The scarcity of information about Altamirano and other writers reflects the assimilationist campaigns of a nascent nation-state in which approximately two-thirds of the population spoke a Native language. See Rocío González, *Literatura zapoteca*.

60. See McDonough, *The Learned Ones* 88–115, and Baruc Martínez Díaz, "Un intelectual indígena del México decimonónico."

61. See Miguel León Portilla, *Los manifiestos en náhuatl de Emiliano Zapata*.

62. Brandon Archambault is writing his doctoral dissertation on Nahua authors from the 1940s (such as Pedro Barra y Valenzuela and Mariano Jacobo Rojas).

63. See Miguel León Portilla, *Literaturas indígenas de México* 325–26.

64. For an in-depth analysis of Jiménez's works, see Natasha Varner, *La raza cosmética*, and Kelly McDonough, *The Learned Ones*.

65. This categorization is evidenced in *Acción indigenista*, the monthly bulletin of the INI from 1953 to 1976, in which Indigenous languages constitute a determining factor for naming the communities to which the INI administrated various projects, particularly with government health campaigns.

66. The Secretaría de Educación Pública (SEP) was created by the Mexican Congress in 1921, with the express goal of complying with the Mexican Constitution's Third Article and its promise to offer free, secular compulsory national education. Since its inception, through programs of varying names, the SEP has continued the project of constructing a "national unity" of model citizens. Though SEP terms like *educación indígena*, *bicultural*, *pluricultural*, and *intercultural* seem to suggest otherwise, Nahua professors from the period, among them Natalio Hernández, indicate that these are hollow terms that in many instances have done more to erase Indigenous knowledge production than did programs with explicit assimilation and "Mexicanization." For studies on SEP history, see María Luisa Escalante Correa, *Utilización de algunos medios*, and Fernando Solana, *Historia de la educación pública en México*.

67. This of course resembles Spivak's concept *strategic essentialism*. For more on the creation of OPINAC and Indigenous teachers during this period, see Natalio Hernández, *Forjando un nuevo rostro*, and Nechikolistli tlen Nauatlajtouaj Maseualtlamachtianej, *Neluayotl tekiyotl uan tlajtoltlanauatili*.

68. For a history of these organizations, see Natalio Hernández, *Forjando un nuevo rostro*.

69. In *Forjando un nuevo rostro / Yancuic ixtlachihualistli* (Forging a New Face; 2016), Natalio Hernández corrects the erasure of Nahua professors' role within Indigenous education.

70. I use "disappeared" as opposed to "kidnapped" to refer to the governmental crime throughout Latin America of abducting and eliminating political threats, *los desaparecidos*. For more on Víctor Pineda Henestrosa, see Francisco López Bárcenas, "¡Y eso no es todo . . . falta Víctor Yodo!"

71. See Irma Pineda, "Palabra de nube entre flores y piedras," and Rocío González, *Literatura zapoteca*.

72. Among the most prominent poets are Andrés Henestrosa, Enrique Liektens, Gabriel López Chiñas, and Pancho Nácar.

73. Indigenous farmers have been some of the hardest hit by NAFTA (now replaced with USMCA), as they cannot compete with subsidized surplus corn that pours into Mexico from the United States. See Ramón Eduardo Ruiz, *Mexico: Why a Few Are Rich and the People Poor*, chapter 10.

74. For an excellent analysis of the Zapatista movement, see Bruno Baronnet et al., *Luchas "muy otras"* (2011).

75. In 2013, Pluralia published bilingual books of poetry by Irma Pineda, Ruperta Bautista, Celerina Patricia, Enriqueta Lunez, and Juana Karen Peñate Montejo.

76. Additional anthologies of Native Nations' literatures include *Like a New Sun: New Indigenous Mexican Poetry* (2015) and *Chiapas Maya Awakening* (2017).

77. *Espanahuatl* and *nahuañol* are used in Nahuatl and Castilian to name this translanguaging.

78. Personal interview, 12 December 2019.

79. Numerous sources address the biases present within Western-led language revitalization movements. See Hannah Burdette, *Revealing Rebellion in Abiayala*, and the volume *Indigenous Languages and the Promise of Archives* edited by Adrianna Link et al.

Chapter 1. More Mexican Because We Speak Mexican: Natalio Hernández Transgressing the Borders of Nationalist Discourse

1. Personal interview, 26 August 2012. Also told in Hernández, *De la exclusión* 59–60. The endonym mejikanoj is more common in many Nahua communities, to the extent that there are Nahuas who enter urban universities unaware that they speak "Nahuatl."

2. *Castellanización* refers to SEP and INI educational programs that sought to assimilate Indigenous youth into the "national" Spanish language; any classroom use of undesirable Indigenous "dialects" served only as a means to this end.

Although the term gradually fell out of favor in the 1970s, the concept remained strong and pervades today.

3. Nahua sociologist Catalina de la Cruz and Nahua historian Ofelia Cruz Medina note that mejikanoj carries this meaning in Tecomate, Chicontepec, in the Huasteca Veracruzana.

4. For more on this topic of self-translation and untranslatability, see Arturo Arias, *Recovering Lost Footprints*; Paul M. Worley, "*Maseual excluido/indio permitido*"; and Tiffany D. Creegan Miller, "'Kixinto', k'u xa jub'iq' ('I give, but just a little')." *Transcreation* was originally coined by Haroldo de Campos. See "Translation as Creation and Criticism" in *Novas: Selected Writings*. Arias innovatively adapts the term for Native literary production and authors' self-translations.

5. Personal interview, 22 September 2012.

6. Throughout *The Serpent's Plumes*, poetry citations conform to the way original poems are presented on the written page.

7. As Aníbal Quijano theorizes, economic subalternity is intrinsic to a colonial system of racism that has outlived the era of colonialism. This *coloniality*, as he terms it, associates "races" with "social roles and geohistorical places" (Quijano 3). Colonial society "naturally" associated Indigenous peoples and other subalterns with manual labor. For the most part, administrators prohibited them from participating in knowledge production or "higher" professions. This division of labor was transmuted into the social classification of the world's population under global capitalism.

8. In his 1999 essay "Del indigenismo," Hernández stresses that in the late 1970s "[c]ambió el discurso, es cierto, sin embargo, en la realidad nada cambió" (the discourse changed, true, but in reality nothing changed; *De la exclusión* 24). Altering the names of this praxis did not end centuries of deeply entrenched discrimination, especially when the name change came from the proponents of the former discourse. For examples of debates surrounding SEP and INI educational programs, see Aguirre Beltrán, *Teoría y práctica de la educación indígena*; SEP, *Delegaciones estatales*; INI, *¿Ha fracasado el indigenismo?*; SEP, *Organismos*; SEP, *Política educativa*.

9. Personal interview, 22 September 2012.

10. Personal interview, 31 August 2012. Hernández also addresses this intuitive process in *De la exclusión* 176.

11. Personal interview, 31 August 2012.

12. Anthropologist Claudio Lomnitz-Adler argues that by the late 1960s the complicity between "Mexican anthropology and official nationalism" had reached its apex ("Bordering on Anthropology" 349). Mexican anthropology provided the tools to forge "a modernist aesthetics" of Mexican citizenship by "'indigenizing' modernity and by modernizing the Indians" (349). This complicity incited virulent denunciations of nationalist *indigenismo*.

13. Personal interview, 31 August 2012.

14. For more information on *campesino* uprisings in the Huasteca during this period, see Rafael Nava Vite, *La Huasteca / Uextekapan*, and Frans J. Schryer, *Ethnicity and Class Conflict in Rural Mexico*.

15. Personal interview, 31 August 2012.

16. Personal interview, 31 August 2012. Within Aldous Huxley's futurist novel, the protagonist, John "the Savage," is removed from one of a few remaining Native American reservations, preserved as voyeuristic honeymoon destinations. He is relocated to a so-called "civilized" society of upper-class Alphas.

17. See Garibay, *Poesía indígena de la altiplanicie* (1940) and *Poesía náhuatl* (1964–1968); León Portilla, *Visión de los vencidos* (1959), *Los antiguos mexicanos a través de sus crónicas y cantares* (1961), *Trece poetas del mundo azteca* (1967), and *Quince poetas del mundo náhuatl* (1994).

18. See Concepción García Moral, *Antología de la poesía mejicana* (1975); Gabriel Zaid, *Omnibus de poesía mexicana* (1980).

19. Consultation of Natalio Hernández's home library, 30 August 2012.

20. This entrance into the "lettered city" raises the question of whether it privileges Western genres over Indigenous forms of expression. In his article "Kotz'ib: The Emergence of a New Maya Literature," Arturo Arias asks whether "these scriptural processes could be read also as a belated embrace of *The Lettered City*" (23). What are the implications of being marginalized by the hegemonic Other outside of mainstream publications, and simultaneously away from Indigenous communities' narrative practices? Instead of taking sides in this dichotomy, I observe how Hernández negotiates between Western literary forms and the aesthetics from his Huastecan community. Like the Maya authors analyzed in Arias's study, Hernández confronts colonialism and Western essentialisms with innovative rhetorical devices.

22. Hernández has published various single-authored essay collections. See *In tlahtolli, in ohtli / La palabra, el camino: Memoria y destino de los pueblos indígenas* (1998), *El despertar de nuestras lenguas* (2002), *De la exclusión al diálogo intercultural con los pueblos indígenas* (2009), *Tamoanchan: La tierra originaria* (2017), *Forjando un nuevo rostro / Yancuic ixtlachihualistli* (2018), and *De la hispanidad de cinco siglos a la mexicanidad del siglo XXI* (2020).

22. This publication of the first part is more readily accessible than the full text of *Xochikoskatl*, especially with an electronic copy that was publicly available online through UNAM until 2022.

23. Stated in an email from Natalio Hernández, 21 December 2013.

24. A case in point, a tlamatini (ritual specialist) who has visited Hernández's community for the last four decades is Ñhähñu (Otomí).

25. See Lomnitz-Adler, *Exits from the Labyrinth* 321.

26. Other Huastecan Nahua artists include Eneida Hernández, Norma Martínez Martínez, Juan Hernández Ramírez, Ildefonso Maya, Alberto Becerril Cipriano, Crispín Amador Ramírez, Crispín Martínez Rosas, and Mardonio Carballo.

27. These ceremonial aspects are based on firsthand participation while I conducted research in Natalio Hernández's hometown, Tepeko, for two years. Published sources touch upon these elements, though often with features unique to communities near Tepeko. For discussions of these ceremonies, see Arturo Gómez Martínez, *Tlaneltokilli: La espiritualidad de los nahuas chicontepecanos*; Alan Sandstrom, *Corn Is Our Blood*; Alan Sandstrom and Pamela Effrein Sandstrom, *Pilgrimage to Broken Mountain*.

28. On the role of storytelling and territory in Indigenous literatures, see Keith H. Basso, *Wisdom Sits in Places*, and Lisa Brooks, *The Common Pot*.

29. I use *contact zone* in the sense defined by Mary Louise Pratt: "social spaces where cultures meet, clash, and grapple with each other, often in contexts of highly asymmetrical relations of power, such as colonialism, slavery, or their aftermaths as they are lived out in many parts of the world today" ("Arts of the Contact Zone" 34). This concept challenges the tendency to see languages, communication, and cultures as "discrete, self-defined, coherent entities" (37).

30. For an incisive examination of maseualtlatsotsontli (Nahua music), see Jesús Alberto Flores Martínez, "Resistencia cultural y lingüística a partir de la música tradicional."

31. Tepetl in Nahuatl refers to both "hills" and "mountains."

32. For in-depth analyses of the Chikomexochitl ceremony, see Abelardo de la Cruz de la Cruz, "The Value of *El Costumbre*"; Rafael Nava Vite, "El costumbre"; Eduardo de la Cruz Cruz, *Cenyahtoc cintli tonacayo*; Sandstrom, *Corn Is Our Blood*, chapter 6.

33. I thank John Sullivan for this observation.

34. This continuity is apparent in parallel structures and repetitions, as in "Xopancuicatl otoncuicatl tlamelauhcayotl": "**oncan** ahuachtonameyoquiauhtimani, / **oncan** cuicuica in nepapan tlaçototome, / **on**cuicatlaça in coyoltototl" (**where there** is rain with shining dew, / **where** various precious birds sing continually, / **toward there** the coyoltototl bird launches his songs; León Portilla, *Cantares mexicanos* 22; emphasis added).

35. To appreciate this proximity between the language in "Iknotlajtoli" and Huastecan ceremonial language, see Nahua scholar Manuel de la Cruz's "El paralelismo semántico-gramatical."

36. Hernández shares an example of ceremonial language in "Presencia contemporánea de los nahuas" 54.

37. Common to Mesoamerican literatures, such reiterations sometimes receive criticism as simplistic. In part because of this misreading, it is not unusual for people to ask Indigenous authors if their literature is for children. For an account of renowned K'iche poet Humberto Ak'abal being asked this, see Rogachevsky, "La voz de la naturaleza" 24. Mardonio Carballo comments on how his texts are displayed in the children's section of bookstores.

38. Personal interview, 31 August 2012.

39. See Sandstrom, *Corn Is Our Blood* 235–37. For more on this ceremony, see also Arturo Gómez Martínez, *Tlaneltokilli*.

40. On the use of the term *Modernity* within this study, see note 7 in the introduction.

41. In personal interviews conducted from 2012 to 2013 with individuals from Hernández's home community as well as Hernández himself, pinaua repeatedly emerged as the term used to describe why people avoided speaking Nahuatl.

42. For an analysis of terms like *toindioma* to combat *dialecto* and *indialecto*, see Flores Farfán, "Efectos del contacto nahuatl-español."

43. I thank Arturo Arias for this observation.

44. This discrepancy appears in Hernández's translation of Article 27: "La propiedad de las tierras y aguas comprendidas dentro de los límites del territorio nacional, corresponde originariamente a la Nación, la cual ha tenido y tiene el derecho de transmitir el dominio de ellas a los particulares, constituyendo la propiedad privada" (18). Hernández translates *Nación* as totlalnantzin (our earth mother): "In axcayotl tlali ihuan atl mani ipan iitihco anahuac tlaltipactli, achtohui iaxca totlalnantzin, tlen yehua mopialihtoc ihuan quipia itechpohui quinmactilis san tlacameh, tlen ica mochihuas sentlapiali" (Property over land and water lying within the land of Anahuac, first and foremost is the property of our earth mother, who has held and who holds the right to confer it to people, with which is created all ownership; 49).

45. Resembling tlaixpan, Pachakuti implies a temporal perspective in which the past is intimately tied to a dynamic present and future. See Rivera Cusicanqui, *Violencias* and *Pachakuti*.

46. A term coined by Ángel María Garibay, *difrasismo* "consists in pairing up two metaphors that, together, serve as the symbolic medium to express a single thought" (my trans.; *Historia de la literatura náhuatl* 19). In xochitl in cuicatl (flower and song) is one of the most well-known *difrasismos* and this pairing evokes ceremonial music and art.

47. In "Stratification by Skin Color in Contemporary Mexico," Andrés Villarreal gives overwhelming statistical data confirming white privilege. He concludes that "dark-brown individuals" have "50.9 percent lower odds than whites of being affluent" (670). These findings quash popular claims that racism is nonexistent.

48. I use *survivance* as coined by Gerald Vizenor to denote survival + resistance. He underscores that "Native survivance stories are renunciations of dominance, tragedy, and victimry" (*Manifest Manners* vii).

49. See *Xochikoskatl*, 52, 60, 72.

50. Personal interview, 22 September 2012.

51. Anthropologist Brigitte Bonisch-Brednich problematizes *community* for the reductive baggage it carries "from past academic frameworks" (Bonisch-Brednich and Trundle 5–6). Within this old framework, researchers "praise the little community and strip it of its history" (5).

52. The etymology of altepetl connotes a proximate relationship with the landscape, composed of atl / water and tepetl / hill, mountain. Chinanco is deep-seated in the landscape and comes from chinamitl, a parcel of land set off by a fence of cornstalks or canes and from which the famous *chinampas* (floating land plots constructed on the lake surrounding Tenochtitlan) derive their name. These significations of altepetl and chinanco provincialize Mexico City residents, who alienate themselves from the landscape and hence lack a properly organized city.

53. Hernández defines tonal in his book of poetry *Semanca huitzilin* (39).

54. In *Indigenous Dispossession*, M. Bianet Castellanos examines how Native lands were declared *terra nullius* and distributed to non-Indigenous settlers (5).

55. As M. Bianet Castellanos posits in her study on Native urban planning in Cancún, we must move beyond the binaries that ignore Native agency and creativity within settler colonial spaces (18).

56. For an example of this criticism, see Miriam Hernández Reyna and Juan A. Castillo Cocom, "Ser o no ser indígena." For an overview of intercultural universities, see Laura Selene Mateos Cortés and Gunther Dietz, "Universidades interculturales en México."

Chapter 2. Ritual Shouts of the Forgotten: Anti-colonial Protest in Martín Tonalmeyotl's *Tlalkatsajtsilistle*

1. Tonalmeyotl made this remark at the Macehualnechicoliztli (Nahua Meeting) in San Miguel Xaltipan, Tlaxcala, Mexico on 26 August 2017. Natalio Hernández has a poem with this title, "Padre Sol" / "Totahtzin Tonati," in a collection that includes a poem from Tonalmeyotl. See Ana Matías Rendón, "Panorama de poesía en lenguas originarias," *Círculo de traductores*, 9 August 2016.

2. Within Guerrero, Nahua author Araceli Patlani, Mè'phàà author Hubert Matiúwàa, and Ñuu Savi author Florentino Solano are representative of this movement. Beyond Guerrero, Irma Pineda and Mikel Ruiz defy a general public's expectations regarding "flowery" Native literature. Nahua author Gustavo Zapoteco Sideño's (Topiltepec, Zitlala, Guerrero) earlier works beginning in 2005 also resemble this style. Tonalmeyotl and Matiúwàa have written extensively on an aesthetic of violence. See Tonalmeyotl, "Guerrero: Autores en lenguas originarias."

3. Tonalmeyotl made this clarification regarding *poesía insurrecta* in a personal interview, 6 November 2019. This view is expressed in the anthology of poetry in Native languages, *Insurrección de las palabras: Poetas contemporáneas en lenguas mexicanas* (2018), in which he participated. For more on insurgent poetics, see Hannah Burdette, *Revealing Rebellion in Abiayala*.

4. Charles Hale warns that the celebratory multiculturalism that surged in the 1990s under neoliberal regimes is trapped within a politics of recognition that overinvests in cultural revindication at the cost of systemic change. This

neoliberal multiculturalist discourse tends to reify the power of the nation-state by directing people's focus to remediation through the state. See Charles Hale, *Más que un Indio*.

5. For numerous examples of such megaprojects, see the websites *Flores en el desierto* and *Derecho de Réplica. Hablan los pueblos*, coordinated by Gloria Muñoz Ramírez.

6. Settler colonialism is tied to a way of taking the land by "legal" (i.e., by the standards of the inner logics within the nation-state's legal system) and illegal means. State clout and authority give an aura of legality to what would otherwise be deemed criminality. A signed document, a title, restraining orders, police presence, and so forth, are supposed to somehow make unjust circumstances binding. Anthropologist Maurice Rafael Magaña similarly terms this context *neoliberal militarization* (*Cartographies of Youth Resistance* 3).

7. For more details regarding this debate, see M. Bianet Castellanos, *Indigenous Dispossession*; Kelly S. McDonough, "Settler Colonial Mexico"; Shannon Speed, *Incarcerated Stories*; Diana Negrín, *Racial Alterity*; and Jessica Hernández, *Fresh Banana Leaves*.

8. In addition to Shannon Speed's *Incarcerated Stories*, see Maylei Blackwell, "Geographies of Indigeneity."

9. For an in-depth study of the origins of these terms, see Joanne Rappaport and Tom Cummins, *Beyond the Lettered City*.

10. For additional sources on this topic of dispossession and settler belonging, see María Josefina Saldaña-Portillo, *Indian Given*, and Estelle Tarica, *The Inner Life of Mestizo Nationalism*.

11. Patricio Solis et al.'s study, *Por mi raza hablará la desigualdad* (2019), can be consulted at Red de Desarrollo Social de América Latina y el Caribe.

12. In interviews, Tonalmeyotl comments that he did not discover until later that he was writing poetry. He had not set out explicitly to create poetry but rather the xochitlajtoli grounded in genres and expressions of his home community. Personal interview, 6 November 2019.

13. See Cárcamo-Huechante, "Indigenous Interference" and "Entre muros y cercados."

14. In his article on Tonalmeyotl's *Tlalkatsajtsilistle*, Matiúwàa emphasizes the social commitment needed in literary production in Native languages. See Matiúwàa, "Los hombres zanate en *El ritual de los olvidados*."

15. For more on ceremonies in this region and the Nahuatl from Tonalmeyotl's community of Atzacoaloya, see *Los pueblos indígenas de Guerrero* and Martín Tonalmeyotl's (Martín Jacinto Meza) master's thesis, *Documentación lingüística de la variante náhuatl de Atzacoaloya, Guerrero*.

16. For more on the "pelea de tigres," see Samuel Villela F., *Los pueblos indígenas de Guerrero*.

17. See Martín Tonalmeyotl, "Poesía indígena sufre de 'inexistencia,'" and Yásnaya Elena A. Gil, "La literatura indígena no existe," 54–56.

18. See Eduardo Sabugal, "Pensar y escribir doble."

19. See Martín Tonalmeyotl, "Literaturas en lengua náhuatl." For more on generational tensions, see also Adam W. Coon, "*El rescoldo del tlicuil.*"

20. Particularly in the state of Guerrero, this war did not begin in 2006 but stretches back years prior (see Lynn Stephen, "The Construction of Indigenous Suspects"). Anthropologist Maurice Rafael Magaña explores what he terms the "2006 Generation" marked by the intense militarization throughout Mexico that resulted in greater instability and mistrust in the nation-state government (*Cartographies* 7).

21. There are notable exceptions to this, particularly literary workshops led by Nahua author Juan Hernández Ramírez.

22. For more on Native deployment of social media, see the edited volume Bronwyn Carlson and Jeff Berglund, *Indigenous Peoples Rise Up*; Jennifer Gómez Menjívar, "Indigenous Online"; and Adam W. Coon, "From Facebook to Ixamoxtli."

23. I avoid using "violent opposition" or "violent protest," since community-led police and demonstrators respond to violence rather than instigate it. As Maurice Rafael Magaña explains, property-damaging protest is not comparable to state-sponsored terror imposed on communities. Moreover, the armed resistance of community-led police is out of self-defense. For more on these movements, see Francis Mestries and Enrique Victoria, "Extractivismo, territorio y narcotráfico"; "PBI México"; and Centro de Derechos Humanos de la Montaña Tlachinollan at tlachinollan.org.

24. This optic resembles Javier Sanjinés's "bodily metaphor" of *viscerality* (*Mestizaje Upside-Down* 5, 11). Sanjinés's approach to this issue with the concept of "both eyes" arises from criticism of twentieth-century Marxist movements within Latin America. In the name of the working class, these movements gave a blind eye to ethnic discrimination and instead centered on social class and economic inequality. For in-depth discussions of these critiques, see Charles Hale, "Between Che Guevara and the Pachamama"; Arturo Arias, "*Tzitzi'n* for the *Poxnai*"; and Emil' Keme, *Maya Nationalisms*.

25. I heard this explanation on repeated occasions both with Nahua authors and generally within Nahua communities. In a personal interview with Gustavo Zapoteco Sideño, 20 June 2010.

26. Coined by Silvia Rivera Cusicanqui, *indio permitido* refers to, in the words of Charles Hale and Rosamel Millaman, the "identity category that results when neoliberal regimes actively recognize and open space for collective indigenous presence, even agency" (Hale and Millaman, "Cultural Agency" 284). The use of the word *indio*, to which those in the dominant culture who work with these Indigenous subjects might object (preferring the less controversial term *indígena*), highlights that "this newfound respect may be only skin-deep" (284).

27. For more details regarding the community of Atzacoaloya, see Tonalmeyotl's (Martín Jacinto Meza) master's thesis, *Documentación lingüística de la variante náhuatl de Atzacoaloya, Guerrero.*

28. In addition to *Tlalkatsajtsilistle* and *Nosentlalilxochitlajtol*, he is the author of *Istitsin ueyeatsintle / Uña mar* (Cisnegro, 2019). He coordinated the poetry anthologies *Xochitlajtoli* (Círculo de Poesía Ediciones, 2019), *Flor de siete pétalos* (Editorial El Espejo Somos, 2019), and *In xochitl in kuikatl* (UDLAP, 2020). Selections of his work have also been published in *Sinfín, Rojo Siena, Revista Electrónica Luz desde el inframundo, Revista Circe, Revista Colibrí, Poesía Mapuche, Latin American Literature Today, World Literature Today*, and the newspaper *La Jornada*.

29. *Xochitlajtoli* is written *xochitlájtoli* with a diacritic because some Nahuatl variants in Guerrero and elsewhere have a unique pronunciation in which the stress is transferred to the antepenultimate syllable in certain words.

30. *Tlalkatsajtsilistle* is available in pdf format at Gusano de la Memoria, https://www.gusanosdelamemoria.org/nahualt. A small run of one thousand copies was printed, and they are not sold in bookstores. Rather, copies were sold at book presentations and directly by the publisher and Tonalmeyotl.

31. To describe catachresis, Javier Sanjinés shares the Quechua term lloqla, used by a migrant to describe the city in one of José María Arguedas's novels (Sanjinés, *Embers of the Past* 54). Indigenous migrants in the position of exteriority/interiority can view and name what seems oblivious to people in the interior. In other words, you cannot observe a "black hole" (a classic example of catachresis) if you are inside it.

32. This poem has also been published in the *Ojarasca* section of the newspaper *La Jornada* (14 January 2017).

33. "Emotional intelligence" is tightly bound up as a corporate management tool within neoliberal ideology's focus on individual costs and benefits, and the optimization of human resources. As literary scholar Merve Emre explains, "Emotional intelligence, in other words, is a self-help doctrine deeply indebted to the moralizing ideology of neoliberalism" ("The Repressive Politics of Emotional Intelligence"). Michel Foucault posits that this brand of intelligence is wrapped up in neoliberal aspirations to manage individual laborers' emotions with the aim of maximizing production. See Foucault's 1978–1979 lectures, *The Birth of Biopolitics*, and Daniel Zamora and Michael C. Behrent, *Foucault and Neoliberalism*.

34. This poem can also be found in *La Jornada del Campo*, num. 90, 21 March 2015.

35. For more on the nation-state sponsored celebratory tradition surrounding Nezahualcoyotl, see Jongsoo Lee, *The Allure of Nezahualcoyotl*.

36. See Alberto Nájar, "Los crueles rituales de iniciación del narco en México," and R. V. Gundur, "Negotiating Violence and Protection in Prison and on the Outside."

37. Three of Tonalmeyotl's poems, including "Las arañas," are published in *Latin American Literature Today*.

38. *Comunalidad* ("communality") is a Mixe and Zapotec concept that elucidates Nahua kinship ties. Zapotec anthropologist Alejandra Aquino Moreschi identifies *comunalidad* as a grassroots theoretical approach to community creation in rural or urban areas (Aquino Moreschi 8). It constitutes a community-centered approach based on reciprocity and participation within institutions such as *la Asamblea* (Assembly), *el Tequio* (altruistic action taken on behalf of the community), and *el sistema de cargos* (system of community posts and tasks). The principal proponents of this concept, Ayuujk (Mixe) sociologist Floriberto Díaz Gómez and Serrano Zapotec anthropologist Jaime Martínez Luna emphasize specificities; this term was not meant to describe all Indigenous Nations as a monolith. For an excellent analysis of *comunalidad* in the works of Martín Tonalmeyotl and Gustavo Zapoteco Sideño, see Osiris Aníbal Gómez Velázquez, "Tierra."

39. English translation by Clara Martínez Zuviria.

40. In Castilian, *desaparecer* as a transitive verb is associated with a state strategy of eliminating opposition by secretly abducting people and disposing of the bodies. I use *disappear* in English with this sense.

41. Personal interview, 6 November 2019.

42. In personal interviews, Tonalmeyotl explains that the ambiguity present in many poems is intentional. In part, this reflects his own inner debate as to what good poetry can do in the face of such stark challenges. Personal interview, 6 November 2019.

Chapter 3. Grinding Words: Ethel Xochitiotzin Pérez's Subversion of Nahua and Nation-State Patriarchy in *Tlaoxtika in tlajtoli*

1. For example, at that time Irma Pineda and Natalia Toledo, among many other authors, were publishing in Diidxazá; Mikeas Sánchez in Zoque; Celerina Sánchez in Tu'ún ñuu savi; Juana Karen in Cho'ol; Enriqueta Lunez in Tsotsil; Briceida Cuevas Cob and Marisol Ceh Moo in Yucatec Maya.

2. By "author" I do not mean solely authors of written texts. An excessive focus on the written word resembles the formation of a cultured elite—predominantly men—critiqued by Ángel Rama in *Ciudad letrada*. Such a framework encourages the creation of a privileged class with the goal of inscribing itself in the upper echelons of intellectual production. Linda Tuhiwai Smith addresses the idea of "Native intellectuals" in *Decolonizing Methodologies* and warns: "What is problematic is that this group of men have been named by the dominant non-indigenous population as individuals who represent 'real' leadership. They have been idealized as the 'saviours of the people' and their example remains as a 'measure' of real leadership" (73). Rather than challenge patriarchal hierarchies, this approach reiterates male-dominated knowledge production and constitutes

gaining a space within the present system instead of transforming it. A focus on written texts excludes the intellectual production of Nahua women through other mediums such as textiles, visual art, oral narratives, music, and ceremony. Creator of the textile-painting *Universo de las hilanderas*, Nahua artist Eneida Hernández prefers the terms *saberes* (knowledges) and *valores* (values) to refer to Nahua cultural production in general and avoid a privileging of Latin script (see "Xochiohtli").

3. For more on this stigma, see Delfino Carro Muñoz, *El estigma de los tlaxcaltecas* (2012).

4. Tetepetla is a small archaeological zone located to the northeast of Xochitiotzin's home municipality of Contla. The site is most well known for the extended fortifications surrounding it, with walls and ditches constructed on the northeastern side of the Malinche volcano. The size of this site suggests that the area near Contla at one point held an expansive population, in the early postclassic period between 900 and 1100. Within the symbolism of Xochitiotzin's poetry, these fortifications at the foot of the Malinche represent strength and active resistance in the historical figure Malinche, in contrast to Paz's depiction of her as delivering herself to the Spanish conquistadors. See Ángel García Cook and Raziel Mora López, "Tetepetla: Un sitio fortificado del 'clásico' en Tlaxcala."

5. Isabel Ramírez Castañeda wrote a paper in 1912 on the cultural practices of Milpa Alta. This paper was published in the *Proceedings* of the Eighteenth International Congress of Americanists. That same year, Ramírez Castañeda shared Nahuatl texts with Frans Boas, and Boas published these texts in the 1920s. He describes Ramírez Castañeda along with another author as "informants" (Karttunen, "Indigenous Writing" 438). Luz Jiménez worked as an "informant" for Benjamin Lee Whorf in the 1930s, Robert Barlow in the 1940s and early 1950s, and Fernando Horcasitas in the 1950s and 1960s. See Karttunen, "Indigenous Writing" 338–440.

6. Patriarchal hierarchy is deeply rooted in colonial regimes, and Nahua women experienced a decline in their authority in politics, law, and religion (see Truitt, "Courting Catholicism" 416–17). Nevertheless, these women created spaces of empowerment within colonial systems. See Susan Kellogg, *Law and the Transformation of Aztec Culture, 1500–1700*; Stephanie Wood, "Gender and Town Guardianship in Mesoamerica"; Karen Vieira Powers, *Women in the Crucible of Conquest*; William B. Taylor, *Drinking, Homicide, and Rebellion in Colonial Mexican Villages*.

7. I alternate between the words ixtlamatini or ixtlamatketl (knowers with the face) and *intellectual* because of the problematic connotations *intellectual* carries of one separated objectively from the subjects studied. *Intellectual* overemphasizes cognition at the cost of affect. While there are notable attempts to shift this meaning, such as Antonio Gramsci and the concept of an *organic*

intellectual, ixtlamatketl effectively points toward a descolonizing notion of who constitutes a knowledge producer and opens to a wider conception of what constitutes "text"—music, artisan work, dance, and so on.

8. I heard this repeatedly during fieldwork from 2010 to 2013.

9. This insistence on observation reflects studies regarding "observational learning." Such studies have shown that Native Nations of Abiayala have a greater capacity for experiential learning. See Barbara Rogoff, "Learning by Observing"; Andrew D. Coppens et al., "Children's Initiative in Family Household Work in Mexico"; Suzanne Gaskins, "Open Attention as a Cultural Tool for Observational Learning."

10. Personal interview, 10 February 2013.

11. Although this is generally the case, the dynamic exchanges between Castilian and Nahuatl have introduced plural markers for inanimate objects (such as tlajtoli or tlajtolmej for languages/words; amochtli or amochmej for books). Moreover, it is important to note that there are entities Nahuas consider animate that a Western perspective deems inanimate (such as hills, tepemej, and winds, ejekamej). For more details regarding debates over linguistic purism, see José Antonio Flores Farfán, *Variación, ideologías y purismo lingüístico*, and Adam W. Coon, "Los ojos de la cara, la cara de las hojas."

12. For more on Indigenous feminisms and debates over use of the term, see Yásnaya Elena Aguilar Gil, "Mujeres indígenas, fiesta y participación política"; Aura Cumes and Yásnaya Elena Aguilar Gil, "Entrevista con Aura Cumes: La dualidad complementaria y el *Popol vuj*"; Aura Cumes, "Multiculturalismo, género y feminismos"; "Las mujeres indígenas: Defensoras de la vida y los territorios"; Paul M. Worley, "U páajtalil maaya ko'olel," 141–44.

13. bell hooks addresses a similar problem within feminisms and ethnic vindications, critiquing racism inside feminist movements and sexism inside ethnic movements. See bell hooks, *Feminist Theory from Margin to Center* (1984). See also Cheryl Suzack and Shari M. Huhndorf, "Indigenous Feminism"; Emma LaRoque, "The Colonization of a Native Woman Scholar"; Andrea Smith, "Indigenous Feminism without Apology." On the politics of citation, see Zoe Todd, "An Indigenous Feminist's Take on the Ontological Turn."

14. For excellent analyses of the conflation of masculinity with nationalist discourses in Mexico during the late nineteenth century and throughout the twentieth century, see Héctor Domínguez Ruvalcaba, *Modernity and the Nation in Mexican Representations of Masculinity* (2007); Samanta Ordóñez, *Mexico Unmanned* (2021); and Nicole M. Guidotti-Hernández, *Archiving Mexican Masculinities in Diaspora* (2021). Joyce Green and contributors contend that feminism is entwined with struggles against colonialism and nation-state models that inherently create marginalized communities. See *Making Space for Indigenous Feminism* edited by Joyce Green.

15. See Paja Faudree, "What Is an Indigenous Author?" 19–20.

16. See Pablo Yanes, "Mexico's Targeted and Conditional Transfer" (2011). Oportunidades (previously called Progresa and subsequently Prospera) was a social program that operated from 1997 to 2019. Its express goal was to reduce extreme rural poverty through direct payments contingent upon participation in preventive medicine, nutrition, and hygiene workshops. See Gerardo Manuel Ordóñez-Barba and Aída Lilia Silva-Hernández, "Progresa-Oportunidades-Prospera."

17. These writings are compiled in the publications *Bajo la sombra del guamúchil*, *Bitácora del destierro*, *Divinas ausentes*, and *Libertad anticipada*, among others. To access these works, see https://hermanasenlasombra.org/books/. For more details regarding Hermanas en la Sombra, see R. Aída Hernández Castillo, *Multiple Injustices*, 57–66; 190–228.

18. See Escritores en Lenguas Indígenas, *México: Diversas lenguas una sola nación. Antología de poesía en lenguas mexicanas* (2008).

19. Personal interview, 5 April 2014.

20. For example, tlajtoli (word) and tlaxkali (tortilla) are pronounced tláhtolli and tláxcalli.

21. For example, Mardonio Carballo and Martín Barrios have both produced music in these genres. For more on Native deployment of these genres, see Alicia Ivonne Estrada, "YouTubing Maya Rock."

22. This short story was published in the anthology *Pensamiento y voz de las mujeres indígenas* (INALI, 2012). Her publications include *San Pablo del Monte Cuauhtotoatla, una historia a través de los estratos de la toponimia náhuatl* (2012); the anthology *In xinachtli in tlahtolli* (2014); and *Yei xinachtli, Yei tlahtolli. Tres semillas, tres palabras* (2015). She is coordinator of the book project *Toconehua* (2016).

23. The digital version of this edition can be found at https://culturalcontinuity.al.uw.edu.pl/wp-content/uploads/2020/08/Ethel-Xochiotzin.pdf. As part of the University of Warsaw Press's language revitalization efforts, Xochitiotzin's translation (or transcreation) into Castilian was removed and the text was adapted to the orthography proposed by Frances Karttunen, R. Joe Campbell, and J. Richard Andrews. For the purposes of this study, I cite the original Nahuatl-Castilian manuscript (2012) with Xochitiotzin's transcreations to highlight valences and word plays evidenced in a translingual reading between the Nahuatl and Castilian texts.

24. Personal interview, 10 February 2013.

25. While they still maintain contact, this collective has been unable to continue meeting due to the costs of travel to the city of Tlaxcala.

26. Personal interview, 10 February 2013.

27. Personal interview, 10 February 2013.

28. The root of this word is oya. Koya would specify an object (to shell *it*) whereas tlaoya uses the unspecified tla (simply "to shell").

29. Xochitiotzin's shifts between Castilian and Nahuatl resembles Spivak's consideration of "the role played by language for the *agent*, the person who acts, even though intention is not fully present to itself" (398). Spivak argues that "the task of the feminist translator is to consider language as a clue to the workings of gendered agency" ("The Politics of Translation" 397–98). Xochitiotzin, as both author and translator, exercises multiple layers of agency in writing; she does not have the same ethical bind to be loyal to her own "original." Reading between the differences in the Castilian and Nahuatl versions reveals "workings of gendered agency" in Xochitiotzin's translation.

30. In *Speaking Mexicano*, Jane Hill and Kenneth Hill recognize the stigma both from Nahuas and non-Nahuas against supposedly "corrupt" Nahuatl (1–3). The imposed standard of an "authentic," "pure" form often causes greater harm than good, leading to a synthetic form of the language mastered by only a handful of speakers.

31. Personal interview, 10 February 2013. Xochitiotzin also comments on this context in an interview on the program *Las Hijas de la Malinche*, 18 February 2022.

32. *Shelling* is technically the correct term, but this word has mostly fallen out of use for corn along with the practice of drying out maize in the United States. In fact, Nahuas in the Huasteca refer to US GMO corn as "puro elotl" (just soft corncob) because it cannot be stored as sintli (hardened maize). See "shell, v.," *Oxford English Dictionary*.

33. Alonso de Molina includes both cihuatl and zouatl in his dictionary. Karttunen specifies that cihuatl is "the standard form for the valley of Mexico" ("cihuatl," *Online Nahuatl Dictionary*).

34. Xochitiotzin describes these two elements as giving her strength to write poetry. Personal interview, 10 February 2013. In regional narratives transcribed by Xochitiotzin for a book to teach Nahuatl, she shares a story titled "In ueuetonaltsin uan tlakuatsin" (The Old Sun and the Possum) in which the rainbow represents literary production: "kinkaua kimauiltiaj ika itlapal in kosemalotl, kitlakuiloa ixayak in tlapoualis, tlen kitlapoa yej" ([the sun] lets them play with the colors of the rainbow, they write/paint the face of his stories, which he tells; *Ameyal tlajtolistli* 73).

35. See Susan Schroeder, "The Annals of Chimalpahin" 3.

36. The female gender of the *huesuda* in Castilian indicates that she directs herself to a woman.

37. See Hugo Gino Nutini, *Todos Santos in Rural Tlaxcala* 116.

38. These kinships encapsulate the concept of *comunalidad* (communality) as a system of social relations outside the bounds of the nation-state. Zapotec anthropologist Alejandra Aquino Moreschi highlights the tensions between the neoliberal government and proponents of *comunalidad*, who "against the prevailing individualism have placed their bets on communal work of the common

good" (my trans.; 12). Echoing Aymara feminists, Aquino cautions against the idealization of Indigenous communities. She emphasizes the need to criticize the "patriarchal junction" (*entronque patriarcal*) of unjust exchanges between men and women in both Pre-Columbian and Western patriarchies (15). Xochitiotzin similarly stresses the importance of kinship within her community, but not at the cost of ignoring sexism.

39. Castilian version titled "Donde nace el arcoíris": "Ethel Xochitiotzin Pérez / Tierra morena. / El arcoíris nace en tu urdimbre / hilos que tejen mi huipil y llenan de luz mi cuerpo. / ¡Hazme un ceñidor, / dale fuerza a mi vientre! / Sé semilla, / sé manantial / al pie de la Malintzi. / Tetepetla lugar donde nace tu rostro. / Hace siglos nuestros ancestros construyeron tu historia, / diseñaron ollas, / cada una lleva el color, el sabor y el aroma de esta tierra. / Cuando llegaron los españoles, fueron quebradas, / quedaron esparcidas en tu cuerpo. / Se funda el pueblo de Contla / ahora tu cuerpo se forma de hilos, / hilos que llevan tu raíz. / Juárez, / Aztatla, / Tlacomulco, / Xelhua, / Xicotenco, / Xochayatla / Cuatzincola, / Acuic, /Axolhuaca. / Hilos que tejen cobija, saltillo, ceñidores, / hilos que desprenden el aroma del mole prieto, / hilos que se mueven al son del *Xochipitzahuatl*, y de los *Catrines*, / hilos que tejen el corazón del conteco y la conteca" (9–10).

40. Personal interview, 10 February 2013. When I visited Xochitiotzin in Tlaxcala, we went through an open-air market where whitening cream was sold. She complained of how people with darker skin use cosmetics to whiten their skin.

41. Literary critic Jahan Ramazani comments on the tendency of writers fighting colonial practices to list names of cities and geographical features: "Consequently, imaginative writers often make use of the decolonizing list to invert this process, repossessing multinationed regions through toponym-studded poems" (*A Transnational Poetics* 144). Particularly through the poem "Donde nace el arcoíris," Xochitiotzin makes a descolonizing turn by referring to the municipality only by its Nahua name (rather than the full name with its patron saint, San Bernardino Contla) and by including the Nahua toponyms of its nine communities (with the exception of Juárez, named in honor of Binnizá/Zapotec President Benito Juárez).

42. Xochipitzahuatl (Precious Little Flower) is a traditional melody played on special occasions such as weddings. See Juan Luna Ruiz, *Tlaxcala*.

43. For details regarding these depictions, see Jacqueline Messing, "Multiple Ideologies and Competing Discourses" 556. If the capital city of Tlaxcala is considered inconsequential in national perceptions of the state, Contla is even more so, as residents of the capital of Tlaxcala consider it excessively provincial.

44. In the poems one can see the influence of Castilian in the spacing of words (such as the separation of the subject and object markers from the root of the verb, seen in the alternation between the spelling niknekiskia and nik nekiskia. Nik nekiskia resembles Spanish syntax *Yo quisiera*).

45. Xochitiotzin gives the approximate translation of "tu mirada" (your look) in Castilian. The word motlachilis conveys "close observation" or a "watchful look." In interviews, Xochitiotzin states that all people should possess this ability to observe carefully, but many are too distracted.

46. Personal interview, 10 February 2013.

47. I thank Clara Martínez Zuviria for this observation.

48. See Alan Sandstrom, *Corn Is Our Blood* 122.

49. In orthographies that do not mark long vowels, such as Xochitiotzin's, "onijtlati[j] notlajtol" can also mean "I burned my words." Onijtlātij with a long ā is "I hid" and onijtlatij is "I burned."

50. Tlaxcalan Nahuatl uses tlajtol without the absolutive ending -li, hence the title of Xochitiotzin's book *Tlaoxtika in tlajtol*.

51. Personal interview, 10 February 2013.

52. In interviews, Xochitiotzin addresses not being able to conceal that history and those roots, that they can be seen on the skin. Personal interview, 10 February 2013.

53. See Karttunen, "Rethinking Malinche" 302.

54. Personal interview, 10 February 2013.

55. Personal interview, 10 February 2013.

Chapter 4. Words of Water: Fluid Nahua Identities in Judith Santopietro's *Palabras de agua*

1. I employ *history* with the connotations that this word carries in Castilian and Nahuatl. In Castilian, *historia* can signify both "history" and "story." In Nahuatl, the binary of "history" and "tale" disappears altogether. Rather than a noun to refer to narratives, the verb nimitspouilis (I will relate to you) is more common in the Huasteca Veracruzana. As Alan Sandstrom and other researchers attest, variations exist within Nahua narratives, which are replete with seeming contradictions and temporal jumps. Unconcerned with exactness, these stories compose an assemblage of moving and varied parts that communicate ethical perspectives of reciprocity, a nonanthropocentric positionality, and mnemonic devices to recall ancestral teachings. See Alan Sandstrom, *Corn Is Our Blood*, and Sandstrom and Sandstrom, *Pilgrimage to Broken Mountain*.

2. Personal interview, 9 December 2013.

3. Part of this suspicion arises from the increase in scholarships, grants, and awards designated for Native peoples. The concern is that someone may fake Native heritage to steal these benefits. Juan Gregorio Regino criticizes the texts of Native authors who are not fluent in their respective Native languages. He avers that lower-quality works achieve publication due to a lack of critical engagement

with them (see Paja Faudree, "What Is an Indigenous Author?" 19–20). Debates over this issue invite appreciation of the complexities among Native authors. While no doubt there are writers and students who claim Native heritage disingenuously, at the same time this can be a two-edged sword in which state-run categories of competition divide Native communities. The state imposes an artificial binary that elides nuance. Many Native authors who do not speak Native languages have "Indigenized" the colonizers' languages. Similar debates over Native scholarships and awards occur in Northern Abiayala. See "Open Letter from Indigenous Women Scholars," and Joseph Pierce, "In Search of an Authentic Indian."

4. María de Jesús (Marichuy) Patricio Martínez made this point in an online meeting with the Red de Solidaridad con Chiapas de Rosario on 26 December 2020.

5. For a critical analysis of this context, specifically in relation to Alfonso Cuarón's *Roma*, see Joseph Pierce, "Roma Is a Beautiful Film of Indigenous Erasure."

6. For example, in the 1940s, President Ernesto Cárdenas's talks were translated into Nahuatl. During his 2012 presidential campaign, Enrique Peña Nieto used Nahuatl to appeal to Nahuas in the Huasteca Veracruzana (mistakenly telling the people "tlaxkali miak" [many tortillas] instead of "tlaskamati miak" [many thanks]). In Yucatán, owners of large estates spoke Yucatec Maya in the nineteenth and twentieth centuries.

7. The preconception that people only speak contemporary Nahuatl if they grew up with it contributes to language loss. Learning contemporary Nahuatl is depicted as a backward step on the ladder of social evolution. This is very different from learning Classical Nahuatl. Many programs and clubs study Nahuatl documents from the sixteenth and seventeenth centuries. With notable exceptions, programs studying contemporary Nahuatl are scarce.

8. Personal interview, 9 December 2013.

9. For discussions on the role of Native languages, see Robert Warrior, *The People and the Word* 137, and Teresa L. McCarty et al., "Hear Our Languages, Hear Our Voices."

10. For analyses of how Mexican *albergues* or *internados* resembled the American Indian boarding schools, see M. Bianet Castellanos, *Indigenous Dispossession*, and Diana Negrín, *Racial Alterity*.

11. See Yásnaya Elena Aguilar Gil, *¿Nunca más un México sin nosotros?*

12. As explored in depth in chapter 6, newer research on language revitalization favors a holistic approach to Native languages that encompasses community formation and strengthening. See Justyna Olko et al., "The Positive Relationship."

13. Santopietro's MA thesis, *Migrantes nahuas celebran a Santiago Apóstol: Un ejercicio de comunalidad en Nueva York*, is available in the University of Texas at Austin repository. An article based on this study was published in the edited volume *Transfiguraciones de danzas tradicionales* (2017).

14. See Judith Santopietro, "Iguanazul." *Palabras de agua* is available online in PDF format at https://reddoormagazine.files.wordpress.com/2011/12/judith-santopietro-palabras-de-agua-1.pdf.

15. Personal interview, 9 December 2013.

16. Addressed in chapter 6, Ateri Miyawatl's book of poetry *Neijmantotot-sintle* was also translated into Catalan.

17. *Se incendia la palabra* (2008) was published by the Instituto Municipal de Arte y Cultura de Puebla.

18. This symbol is *voluta* in Spanish and English because of its similarity to a shape within architectural columns.

19. My use of "remediation" draws on Tiffany D. Creegan Miller's deployment of this term to signal a rich Native media landscape where older and newer forms coexist and "challenge distinctions between 'old' and 'new' media and narratives about the deprecation of orality in favor of inscribed forms" (*The Maya Art of Speaking Writing* 4).

20. In Nahuatl, rain "comes from below," as the water is said to originate from under hills/mountains.

21. A statistical increase in the Native population would not only challenge nation-state rhetoric. It also has economic implications regarding where funds are allocated and exposes how government officials' backgrounds fail to represent the general population. According to the 2020 census, 6.1 percent of the Mexican population speaks an Indigenous language (down from 6.6% in 2010) and approximately 15 percent of the population identifies as Indigenous (without necessarily speaking an Indigenous language). See IWGIA, *El mundo indígena 2021: México*; INEGI, *Censo de Población y Vivienda 2020: Marco Conceptual*; INMUJERES, *Población indígena*; Armando Martínez, "¿Cuánta población indígena y afrodescendiente hay en México?" It must be noted that census data misses the hundreds of thousands of Nahuas who reside in the US and Canada. Speaking a Native language continues to be a determining factor in deciding who is Native. See Karla Sánchez, "Entrevista a Yásnaya Elena A. Gil: 'La lengua tiene una carga política.'" I would be remiss not to mention that the census itself is a tool implemented by the nation-state to assert its validity. While statistics can be useful as a general guide of how the population self-identifies, the imposition of the nation-state itself is questioned by many Native intellectuals. See Yásnaya Elena Aguilar Gil, "Nosotros sin México." I reflect on this issue of the census at length because it came up repeatedly when interviewing Santopietro. Statistically, nationally, and socially in day-to-day activities—and within her own family—she is pressured to deny that she is Nahua.

22. This context was examined within the introduction.

23. Cabrera González's books of poetry include *Vestigios incipientes* (1996), *Xantiltlakuikal / Canto de piedra* (2010), *Xochitlikonex tlauil / Polen de luz* (2012), and *Iknoxochitlakuikaltij / Poemas huérfanos*.

24. Personal interview, 9 December 2013.

25. Ibid.

26. For more on this narrative in the Huasteca Veracruzana, see Adam W. Coon, "Down the Rabbit Hole and into the Moon."

27. Regarding *usos y costumbres* in Mexico, see Isabel Altamirano-Jiménez, "The State Is Not a Saviour."

28. This representation of the literate power of dance resembles Cutcha Risling Baldy's description of healing, where "[o]ur landscapes once more feel the stomp of our feet and the warmth of our fires . . . as we continue to (re)write, (re)right, and (re)rite history through songs, laughter, food, and ceremony" (*We Are Dancing for You* 72).

29. For more on the persecution of nahuales, see Laura A. Lewis, *Hall of Mirrors* 152–53, 201–02, 230; Danièle Dehouve, *Entre el caimán y el jaguar*; Gonzalo Aguirre Beltrán, *Medicina y magia* 97–112; Gerardo Lara Cisneros, *¿Ignorancia invencible?* 376; Félix Báez-Jorge, *Entre los naguales y los santos*; Lisa Sousa, "The Devil and Deviance"; Alfredo López Austin, *The Human Body and Ideology*, volume I; Roberto Martínez González, *El nahualismo*; David Tavárez, *The Invisible War*; Anderson Hagler, "Exhuming the Nahualli."

30. Cited by Martín Tonalmeyotl on his radio program *Ombligo de tierra*.

31. For a discussion of an exclusive versus inclusive *we*, see Yásnaya Elena Aguilar Gil, "Ëëts, atom."

32. For more on these stereotypes propagated through mass media, see John Lutz, *Makúk: A New History of Aboriginal-White Relations* 31–46 and Ana Matías Rendón, *La discursividad indígena* 214–15.

33. For a detailed analysis of Mesoamerican maps, see Barbara E. Mundy, "Mesoamerican Cartography."

34. Led by James Lockhart, the New Philology movement studied "mundane texts" from legal proceedings in which Native people defended their rights. See J. O. Anderson et al., *Beyond the Codices*.

35. See Mariana Mora, "Asesinatos y violencia (neo)colonial."

36. Personal interview, 9 December 2013.

Chapter 5. Redressing the Eagle and Feathered Serpent: Mardonio Carballo's Trans-Indigenous Dialogues and Descolonizing *Contrapunteo*

1. This poem was published earlier in 2004 in *La Jornada*. See *Ojarasca* 86 (June 2004).

2. In his article, "Indigenous Interference" (2013), Cárcamo Huechante develops the concept "acoustic colonialism." Cárcamo Huechante spoke of "visual colonialism" in the Fall 2014–Spring 2015 Mellon-Sawyer Faculty Seminar at the University of Texas at Austin.

3. Proposed by the executive branch under President Enrique Peña Nieto, the Ley de Telecomunicaciones was enacted on 14 July 2014 (Secretaría de Comunicaciones y Transportes, *Ley Federal*). Carballo successfully had the article struck down as unconstitutional on 1 June 2016 (see Secretaría de Comunicaciones y Transportes, *Decreto*). See LXIII Legislatura, "LEY federal" n.d., for access to all changes made to this law.

4. For more on the history of the term *transculturación*, see Jossianna Arroyo, "Transculturation, Syncretism, and Hybridity"; Mary Louise Pratt, *Imperial Eyes* and "Arts of the Contact Zone"; and Ángel Rama, *Writing across Cultures*.

5. While positivism is most associated with the Porfiriato, positivist perspectives took on meaning in Mexico after the Mexican Revolution, in which, on a scale of social evolution, "[a] government as corrupt and decrepit as Porfirismo in its latter years had to be replaced by a young and vigorous government" (Zea, *Positivism in Mexico* 19). As Leopoldo Zea attests, positivism continues to influence Mexico.

6. I use "site of memory" (*lieu de mémoire*) in the sense conceptualized by Pierre Nora as "any significant entity, whether material or non-material in nature, which by dint of human will of the work of time has become a symbolic element of the memorial heritage of any community" ("Preface" xvii).

7. In a more recent interview, Carballo reiterated this inspiration for his work. Personal interviews, 9 June 2013 and 30 August 2017.

8. It is common to refer to Facebook as Ixamochtli, Ixamoxtli, or simply Face in Nahuatl.

9. Personal interview, 9 June 2013.

10. To highlight the text's movement among numerous media, I also refer to the essays in *Las Plumas* as xochitlajtoli, radio shorts, episodes, compositions, and pieces.

11. In the presentation "Nuevos formatos, soportes y cantos en lenguas indígenas" [13'38"], on 22 November 2013 at the Biblioteca Vasconcelos.

12. For more on the politics of translation and the choice not to translate, see Tiffany D. Creegan Miller, "'Kixinto', k'u xa jub'iq' ('I give, but just a little')."

13. This system resembles the orthography most used among Nahuas in the Huasteca Veracruzana with the graphemes *k* and *j*. The idiosyncratic exception is Carballo's use of *z* to the near exclusion of *c* or *s* (for example, zintli [maize] and zempoalxochitl [Mexican marigold]).

14. A case in point, in presentations Carballo sometimes asks audiences to raise their hands if they have parents or grandparents who speak a Native language. The majority of hands go up.

15. Carballo addresses this tension in a powerful reading on YouTube of a poem titled "Dejar en paz a los muertos" (see "Dejar en paz a los muertos"). Yásnaya Elena Aguilar Gil published the verses on her Twitter feed (see Yasnaya Elena [@YasnayaEG], "No estoy llorando").

16. On his radio interview program *Xochikozkatl*, Carballo showcases maize's role in strengthening kinship. The choice corncob is given to one's godparents and used for the next harvest.

17. The original is "I have seen sparks fly out / When two stones are rubbed, . . ."

18. The original is "I am happy to be a stone."

19. The original is "Or gnash with a tiger's tooth."

20. For this reason, Huastecan Nahuas refer to GMO corn as "puro elotl" (*puro elote* or "just soft corn on the cob").

21. The search for social justice as an unquenched thirst and famine in Carballo's text resembles metaphors in the works of Guerrerense Nahua authors such as Ateri Miyawatl and Martín Tonalmeyotl.

22. Carballo's family runs three different restaurants in this Colonia, in a way literally placing pieces of the Huasteca within this urban space.

23. For a study of Carballo's prog rock group, their book *Las horas perdidas*, and Carballo's social media activism, see Coon, "From Facebook to Ixamoxtli."

24. *Pejpena* as a loanword in Castilian, *pepenar*, has negative connotations—to scavenge for trash—that are absent in the original language. In Nahuatl, pejpena denotes the gathering of precious corn kernels from the ground.

25. For more on this campaign, see "Las lenguas toman la tribuna (Del 21/02/2019 al 20/2/2020)."

26. In January 2016, Mexico City became a federal entity (*entidad federal*) like Mexico's other thirty-one states. As part of the transition from federal district to entity, a constitutional assembly was formed to draft the Mexico City Constitution. See *Gaceta Oficial de la Ciudad de México*.

27. Among other demands, the Mexico City Constitution assures that Indigenous communities "tienen derecho a establecer sus propios medios de comunicación en sus lenguas. Las autoridades establecerán condiciones para que los pueblos y las comunidades indígenas puedan adquirir, operar y administrar medios de comunicaciones en los términos que la ley de la materia determine" ("Constitución Política de la Ciudad de México" 101).

Chapter 6. Nahuatl Language and Territory as Coping Strategies in Ateri Miyawatl's *Neijmantototsintle* (2018) and *Tsintatak* (2020)

1. I use *disappeared*, although not widely accepted, in English to signal the connotations *desaparecido* carries in Castilian of a governmental strategy, complicit with organized crime, to eliminate political dissidence by abducting and killing opposition. "Kidnapped" or "abducted" do not necessarily connote

this systemic problem. For analysis of the term *desaparecido*, see Lynn Stephen, *Transborder Lives* xiv–xv.

    2. The formation of "normal schools" stretches back several centuries. They began to emerge in full force throughout nascent nation-states in the nineteenth century as part of a campaign to educate future voters. For more on the history of normal schools and their conflation with nationalist *educación*, see Thomas Genova, *Imperial Educación* 8–9, 88–89. It was not until the 1920s that the Escuelas Normales Rurales arose in Mexico as part of the post-Revolutionary campaign to assimilate rural areas into the nation-state. Under a semi-Marxist rhetoric, this project sought to educate and prepare citizens for integration into the capitalist system. Today in Mexico, *escuelas normales* usually refers to these rural teacher-training colleges. For more on the complex history of the *escuelas normales* after the Mexican Revolution, see Raúl Olmo Fregoso Bailón, "Los Normalistas en el pensamiento latinoamericano," and Tanalís Padilla, *Unintended Lessons of Revolution*.

    3. News outlets often label such protests as "violent." As Maurice Rafael Magaña posits, it is important to avoid language that treats property damage as equivalent with a state apparatus taking someone's life or disappearing them. The state-sponsored response is violence unwarranted by the supposed "violence" of protesters. See Maurice Rafael Magaña, *Cartographies of Youth Resistance*.

    4. Numerous sources have reported on the forty-three disappeared students of Ayotzinapa. See Ximena Antillón Najlis, *Yo sólo quería que amaneciera*; Mariana Mora, "Ayotzinapa and the Criminalization of Racialized Poverty" and "Desaparición forzada, racismo institucional y pueblos indígenas"; *Ayotzinapa: Una cartografía de la violencia*. Miyawatl stresses that the disappearances of the forty-three students form part of a systemic problem. Forty-three is a metonym for many more people.

    5. Interim Governor Rogelio Ortega Martínez sat in the audience near the front. He was appointed interim governor on 27 October 2014, following Ángel Aguirre Rivero's resignation due to outrage over his involvement in the forced disappearances of *normalistas* from Ayotzinapa. Miyawatl criticizes a discourse of "transition to democracy" into which the Tlatelolco massacre was also co-opted, the idea of a "post-1968" that achieved democracy. In a similar fashion, public officials in Guerrero called for a meeting about "democracy and voting rights," rather than a deep analysis of the systemic problems that have led to forced disappearances. For more on this "transition to democracy" trope in Mexican politics, see Susana Draper, *1968 Mexico*.

    6. See "Réplica de una joven a Rigoberta Menchú"; "Interrumpen a Rigoberta Menchú"; "Irrumpe indígena de Guerrero en acto de Rigoberta Menchú"; "Joven increpa a Rigoberta Menchú y al gobernador de Guerrero"; "Cómo nos puede llamar al voto; indígena irrumpe en acto de Menchú en Acapulco"; Javier

Trujillo, "Mujer irrumpe en evento de Rigoberta Menchú en Acapulco"; and Myriam Corte, "La indignación y la rabia no se acaban con la acción de votar." For a detailed account of the context surrounding Miyawatl's intervention in this event and the consequences, see Daniela Pastrana, "Ayotzinapa, un año después: ¿Qué hemos hecho?"

7. Univisión, for example, spliced the video into many parts. See "Joven cuestiona a Rigoberta Menchú sobre elecciones en Guerrero." Evidence of the mediatic sensationalism, no full recordings of this event or Rigoberta Menchú's full talk are publicly available. See also "Ana Gatica Criticizes Rigoberta Menchú" and "Ana Gática irrumpe ante Rigoberta Menchú en Guerrero, México."

8. This is of course within a wider context in which Menchú has exerted an enormously positive influence. The problem is more an issue of how media and academia, principally within the US, have portrayed Menchú. Within Maya studies, there have been objections to how her presence dominates within media outlets and eclipses a myriad of Maya voices. For more on Menchú, see Emil' Keme, *Le Maya Q'atzij* 71–74, and *The Rigoberta Menchú Controversy* edited by Arturo Arias.

9. What Miyawatl defends is "a *community* of one's own" in a move away from the individualism within mainstream feminism. Generally, this communal focus appears throughout Native feminisms (or else the term *feminist* is rejected due to its associations with bourgeois individualism). See Yásnaya Elena Aguilar Gil, "Mujeres indígenas, fiesta y participación política"; Aura Cumes and Yásnaya Elena Aguilar Gil, "Entrevista con Aura Cumes: La dualidad complementaria y el *Popol vuj*"; and Aura Cumes, "Multiculturalismo, género y feminismos." Rather than the nation-state imaginings that Benedict Anderson terms *imagined communities*, the community Miyawatl promotes foregrounds deep affective connections.

10. Miyawatl signals the importance of the Nahuatl language and territory in processing trauma and finding peace in her poem/article "Tokohkol xonomikileh. Totik noyolicha / Nuestra abuela no ha muerto. Vive dentro nuestro" (Our Grandmother Has Not Died. She Lives Inside Our Hearts; 2022).

11. As in previous chapters, I mostly use *strengthening* instead of *revitalization* to avoid the connotations of an agonizing language on the verge of extinction intimated by the latter.

12. Critical studies on the role of Native languages in processing trauma include Paul V. Kroskrity, *Telling Stories in the Face of Danger*; Josep Cru, "Language Revitalisation from the Ground Up"; Justyna Olko and Julia Sallabank, *Revitalizing Endangered Languages: A Practical Guide*. For the purposes of this study, an essential aspect in healthy language strengthening/revitalization is the centrality of community formation and kinship. Linda Tuhiwai Smith addresses the role of language as a methodology for decolonization and healing in *Decolonizing Methodologies*.

13. For more on this symbiosis between language and the land in Native movements, see Cárcamo Huechante, "Indigenous Interference."

14. When speaking in Nahuatl, Miyawatl refers to the Nahuatl language (and Native languages in general) with the term maseualtlajtoli. She used it in a December 2021 meeting with Nahua activists from Tepeko, Veracruz.

15. For more on Nahua conceptions of ejekatl/air (not specific to Guerrero), see Alan Sandstrom, *Corn Is Our Blood*.

16. The findings of a collaboration among Nahua and Polish researchers suggest the indispensable role of community. During the pandemic, they administered a survey to gauge the well-being of people who spoke Native languages. The survey found that those who used the language as part of a community reported higher levels of happiness than average; conversely, those who felt isolated from community reported reduced levels of happiness when they spoke a Native language. This in part may explain why several previous studies have found no measured benefit to mental health when speaking a Native language. This research was discussed at a book launch for the edited volume *Revitalizing Endangered Languages: A Practical Guide* on 14 May 2021. See Justyna Olko et al., "The Positive Relationship."

17. For sources on this double bind and "indigeneity" in a global context, see Francis Ludlow et al., "The Double Binds of Indigeneity."

18. Leanne Betasamosake Simpson addresses this myth in *As We Have Always Done*.

19. At least in the sensationalist way it was reported, Miyawatl's questioning of Menchú is reminiscent of the widely published news that US anthropologist David Stoll had discovered Menchú's "lies." Nonetheless, Miyawatl's engagement differs vastly from David Stoll's accusations. Rather than being engrossed with US academic debates, Miyawatl focuses on the political and social ramifications of Menchú's visit and seeks to engage seriously with her. For more on (mis)representations of Menchú in the US and Latin America, see Arturo Arias, "Enunciating Alleged Truths."

20. For sources on this land-standing strategy of state co-optation, see Claudio Lomnitz-Adler, *Exits from the Labyrinth*.

21. See Marcela Vargas, "10 poetas en lenguas indígenas que necesitas conocer." This same news piece was published in *AGlo: Anuario de Glotopolítica*, among other news outlets. See also "La escritora y actriz nahua Ateri Miyawatl es premiada en Inglaterra por su libro-arte"; Omar Porcayo, "Premian en Inglaterra a indígena mexicana por bello poema escrito en náhuatl"; "Artista nahua gana reconocimiento en Inglaterra." Miyawatl jests at how news outlets began to promote her as one of the foremost Indigenous poets. Personal interview, 8 November 2019.

22. There are no articles declaring the top Native novelists, essayists, or playwrights. The prominence of poetry attributed to Nezahualcoyotl is most salient in the nation-state imaginary. In part tied to this expectation, when they hear Nahuatl, the public often declares that "the language is so poetic." This comment relates to Carballo's criticism shared at the beginning of this study regarding

people who admire "the dialects' beauty" and wonder how difficult it might be to learn them. Miyawatl's publications include the poem "Se weyi ostotl notik onka" (2018) in the newspaper *ContraRéplica*; the poem "Tokohkol xonomikileh" (2022) in *Tzam Trece semillas*; and two poems in the literary anthology *Raíces a una sola voz*. Miyawatl participated in the 2022 Festival de Poesía: Las Lenguas de América Carlos Montemayor; her reading of "Neijmantototsintle" and additional poems are available on YouTube. See "IX Festival de Poesía." She completed an audio recording of nine poems, including "Neijmantototsintle," for the Library of Congress in 2023. See Miyawatl, "Nahua Poet Ateri Miyawatl Reading from Her Work." In addition to *Strange Horizons*, her play *Tsintatak* appears in the magazine *Shilaa'*. See Miyawatl, "Tsintatak (Náhuatl)." Within this chapter, I cite the version published in *Strange Horizons*. Note that Miyawatl's *Tsintatak* was named to the honor list for the Premio Imaginación y Futuro Award, but has received nowhere near the same attention as *Neijmantototsintle*.

23. For more on Acatlán, Chilapa, Guerrero, and the surrounding region, see Samuel Villella F., *Los pueblos indígenas de Guerrero: Atlas etnográfico*, and Marcos Matías Alonso, "Tlayolli: El pan de los indios en Acatlán."

24. For more on the history and practice of creating *libros cartoneros*, see Lucy Bell et al., *Taking Form, Making Worlds*; Adrián R. Vila, "Ediciones cartoneras latinoamericanas"; and the University of Wisconsin–Madison Libraries research guide "Cartonera Publishers / Editoriales Cartoneras."

25. This artistic organization based in Acatlán has created *libros cartoneros* such as *Atsajtsilistle*.

26. Stated at "Presentación de libro *Neijmantototsintle* con y de Ateri Miyawatl y Francisco Villas" on 29 August 2018 in Patzcuaro, Michoacan.

27. Maria Mercè Padrosa and Miquel Colomer rendered the translation from Castilian into Catalan. For more on the politics of translation and publication in Cataluña, see Steven Byrne, *Identity and Nation in 21st Century Catalonia*.

28. This observation resembles the concept of *mindfulness*, but with key differences. While mindful awareness of the situation is fully present in the text, the mindfulness in Miyawatl's work is closely tied to land claims, community belonging, and the language as conduits of that mindfulness, very much situated in Acatlán. In that sense, this approach fundamentally differs from the more individual-centered practice of mindfulness that has come into vogue. For more on the topic of mindfulness and Native frameworks, see Michael Yellow Bird et al., "Defunding Mindfulness: While We Sit on Our Cushions, Systemic Racism Runs Rampant." In this article, Yellow Bird argues that "Western mindfulness has been much more about healing the individual than the healing of society."

29. See Ateri Miyawatl, "Se weyi ostotl notik onka," in the newspaper *ContraRéplica*.

30. For more on this ceremony, see Villela F., *Los pueblos indígenas de Guerrero*.

31. Miyawatl collaborated in the creation of a *libro cartonero* titled *Atsajtsilistle* in which this ceremony is represented.

32. See the documentary *Tigres en la montaña*, and Villela F., *Los pueblos indígenas de Guerrero*.

33. For more on how Miyawatl's *Neijmantototsintle* resembles and differs from *mindfulness*, see note 28 in this chapter.

34. For more on affective intelligence, see Martha Nussbaum, *Upheavals of Thought*, and Robin Wall Kimmerer, *Braiding Sweetgrass*.

35. Personal interview, 8 November 2019.

36. See Paul M. Worley and Rita M. Palacios, *Unwriting Maya Literature*.

37. See Aguilar Gil, "Resistencia: Una breve radiografía."

38. For more on Emilio Santisteban's works, see Mihaela Radulescu de Barrio de Mendoza, "El cuerpo ausente en las performances de Emilio Santisteban," and emiliosantisteban.org/performance.

39. See "Ateri Miyawatl," *Ombligo de tierra*, 30 July 2018.

40. Miriam C. Brown Spiers similarly warns of this risk in *Encountering the Sovereign Other: Indigenous Science Fiction* xv–xvi.

41. In a meeting on 2 March 2023, Miyawatl expressed that Samuel Beckett was an inspiration for the overall structure of *Tsintatak*.

42. Miyawatl addresses this connection explicitly in her poem/article "Tokohkol xonomikileh."

43. For more on the power of Native humor, see Paul Chaat Smith, *Everything You Know about Indians Is Wrong*, and Diana Taylor and Sarah J. Townsend, *Stages of Conflict* 318–20.

44. Presentation at ERIP-LASA in Mexico City on 28 October 2022.

45. In the poem that opens her article "Tokohkol xonomikileh," Miyawatl speaks to her daughter about their (great)grandmother Anita.

46. For an interview of Ateri Miyawatl at this event, see UN DESA, "Protecting Languages, Preserving Cultures."

47. This is not to suggest that Nahuas and Catalans share the same history or engage analogous situations. They coincide in their demands for increased autonomy in (or outside) a nation-state, and sociolinguistically Nahuatl and Catalan persevere under the "shadow" of Castilian. Dialogues between Cataluña and Native Nations in Abiayala became prevalent with the EZLN uprising. See Jennifer Seefoo, "Escuadrón 421 llega a Cataluña y la bautiza como 'Tierra insumisa.'"

48. For more on these movements, see Francis Mestries and Enrique Victoria, "Extractivismo, territorio y narcotráfico"; "PBI México: Los pueblos indígenas se oponen a la explotación minera en la Costa Chica y la Montaña de Guerrero"; and Centro de Derechos Humanos de la Montaña Tlachinollan at tlachinollan.org.

Conclusion. Slinging Xochitlajtoli at Dams: A Prismatic Project(ion) of Contemporary Nahua Literature

1. The exhibition was titled *The Amate Tradition: Innovation and Dissent in Mexican Art*. For more on this artwork and the exhibition, see *La tradición del amate*, edited by Jonathan D. Amith. The hydroelectric dam would have destroyed over twenty communities and displaced forty thousand people.

2. For an in-depth analysis of this image, see Rachel Adams, *Continental Divides* 11, and Miguel Rocha Vivas, *Word Mingas* 43–92.

3. Similarly, in his article "Los mapuche antes de la conquista militar chileno-argentina," Mapuche historian Pablo Marimán Quemenado includes two drawings in which the map of Wallmapu (Mapuche territory covering large portions of Chile and Argentina) is "turned on its side" and reoriented toward the East (60, 77). Although a seemingly minor alteration, this recalibration points toward a wider questioning of Western conceptions of land, sovereignty, and space. Such a remapping resembles what Santiago Castro-Gómez and Ramón Grosfoguel term "heterarchical thought." This heterarchical reconceptualization creates a network "in which no basic level governs over everyone else, but rather all levels exercise some degree of mutual influence in different aspects and in accordance with specific historical circumstances" (my trans; 18).

4. As stated in chapter 3, each day is in fact measured by tonatij (suns) in Nahuatl.

5. Original quote: "Yo tengo libros con tirajes de cien mil, treinta mil, setenta mil ejemplares, pero si uno los intenta rastrear no los encuentra. No los encuentras en las bibliotecas, en las escuelas, ¿Dónde están?, te preguntas: en una bodega."

6. See Roberto Garduño and Enrique Méndez, "En dos años se reducirá 42% el presupuesto de Conaculta." Funding for the arts has been cut by half annually so many times (an issue by no means limited to Mexico) that the situation is becoming like Zeno's paradox where the trajectory of an arrow is cut in half so many times that it never reaches its target.

7. In his investigation of the distribution of Indigenous literatures, Alejandro Sánchez de la Rosa observes: "[L]ack of funding, limited distribution, and publishers' zero interest in publishing them is the situation faced by Indigenous writers in Mexico" (my trans.; "Entre la espada y la pared").

8. I thank Arturo Arias and Luis Cárcamo Huechante for their insights on Indigenous *letrados* at the Mellon-Sawyer faculty seminar Territorial Roots and Diasporic Routes, 30 January 2015.

9. For an analysis of *Las horas perdidas*, see Adam W. Coon, "From Facebook to Ixamoxtli."

10. Reflective of this approach, Nahua anthropologist Abelardo de la Cruz argues that Nahua religious practices are sympathetic toward other religions and adopt/adapt aspects from them. See "The Value of *El Costumbre*."

11. Personal interview, 15 February 2013.

12. Personal interview, 12 August 2012.

13. Studies that address this topic in Southern Abiayala include the Quo-Li Driskill's edited volume *Queer Indigenous Studies: Critical Interventions in Theory, Politics, and Literature*; the chapter "Maya Feminism and Queer Poetics" in Emil' Keme's *Le Maya Q'atzij*; the chapter "A Politics of Creation" in Paul M. Worley and Rita M. Palacios's *Unwriting Maya Literature*; Tiffany D. Creegan Miller, "Queering Abiayala." Within Native studies, see also Scott Lauria Morgensen, *Spaces between Us*; Ma-Nee Chacaby, *A Two-Spirit Journey*; Andrew Farrell, "The Rise of Black Rainbow" in *Indigenous Peoples Rise Up*; Qwo-Li Driskill, "Doubleweaving Two-Spirit Critiques"; Michael Hames-García, "What's After Queer Theory."

14. Interview conducted for the 2012 season of *De raíz luna*. See "Felina Santiago, activista muxe."

Bibliography

Achim, Miruna, et al., editors. *Museum Matters: Making and Unmaking Mexico's National Collections*. U of Arizona P, 2021.
Adams, Rachel. *Continental Divides: Remapping the Cultures of North America*. U of Chicago P, 2009.
"Afirma poeta que la literatura indígena está en pleno renacimiento." *El Porvenir*, 22 August 2008, http://www.elporvenir.com.mx/notas.asp?nota_id=243179.
Aguilar Gil, Yásnaya Elena. *Ää: Manifiestos sobre la diversidad lingüística*. Almadía, 2020.
———. "Ëëts, atom: Algunos apuntes sobre la identidad indígena." *Revista de la Universidad de México*, no. 828, September 2017, pp. 17–23.
———. "Jajajatl: ¿Es para reírse?" *Ää: Manifiestos sobre la diversidad lingüística*. Almadía, 2020, pp. 57–61.
———. "La literatura indígena no existe." *Ää: Manifiestos sobre la diversidad lingüística*, Almadía, 2020, pp. 54–56.
———. "La validación como captura." *El País*, 19 April 2020, https://elpais.com/elpais/2020/04/19/opinion/1587329573_401539.html.
———. "Mujeres indígenas, fiesta y participación política." *Revista de la Universidad de México*, no. 854, November 2019, pp. 33–39.
———. "Nosotros sin México: Naciones indígenas y autonomía." *El futuro es hoy: Ideas radicales para México*, Biblioteca Nueva, 2018, pp. 137–58.
———. *¿Nunca más un México sin nosotros?* CIDECI-Unitierra Chiapas, 2018.
———. "Resistencia: Una breve radiografía." *Revista de la Universidad de México*, no. 847, April 2019, pp. 20–27.
Aguirre Beltrán, Gonzalo. *Medicina y magia: El proceso de aculturación en la estructura colonial*. Instituto Nacional Indigenista, 1963.
———. Prologue. *La comunidad indígena*, edited by Sergio Galindo and Alí Chumacero, SEP, 1971, pp. 7–44.
———. *Teoría y práctica de la educación indígena*. SEP, 1973.
Albarrán Solleiro, Aranxa. "La literatura indígena de México: Desigualdad de género y olvido." *La Jornada Semanal*, 6 December 2020, https://semanal.

jornada.com.mx/2020/12/06/la-literatura-indigena-de-mexico-desigualdad-de-genero-y-olvido-2126.html.

Alcoff, Linda Martín. "Epistemologies of Ignorance: Three Types." *Race and Epistemologies of Ignorance*, edited by Shannon Sullivan and Nancy Tuana, State U of New York P, 2007, pp. 39–57.

Allen, Chadwick. *Trans-Indigenous: Methodologies for Global Native Literary Studies*. U of Minnesota P, 2012.

Altamirano-Jiménez, Isabel. "The State Is Not a Saviour: Indigenous Law, Gender and the Neoliberal State in Oaxaca." *Making Space for Indigenous Feminism*, edited by Joyce Green, 2nd ed., Fernwood, 2017, pp. 215–33.

Alvarado Tezozómoc, Fernando. *Crónica Mexicáyotl*. Translated by Adrián León, UNAM, 1998.

Ameyal tlajtolistli / Manantial de palabras: Manual de la lengua náhuatl. Instituto Tlaxcalteca de la Cultura, 2014, https://issuu.com/digital-editorial/docs/manual_nahuatl.

Amith, Jonathan D., editor. *La tradición del amate: Innovación y protesta en el arte mexicano / The Amate Tradition: Innovation and Dissent in Mexican Art*. Mexican Fine Arts Center Museum, 1995.

———. *The Möbius Strip: A Spatial History of Colonial Society in Guerrero, Mexico*. Stanford UP, 2005.

"Ana Gatica Criticizes Rigoberta Menchú." *YouTube*, uploaded by Henry Gales, 4 June 2015, https://www.youtube.com/watch?v=Es9XRM6ogBs.

"Ana Gática irrumpe ante Rigoberta Menchú en Guerrero, México." *YouTube*, uploaded by Bajo Palabra, 29 May 2015, https://www.youtube.com/watch?v=S60YS3JFufA.

Anderson, Benedict. *Imagined Communities: Reflections on the Origin and Spread of Nationalism*. Rev. ed., Verso, 2016.

Anderson, J. O., et al., editors. *Beyond the Codices: The Nahua View of Colonial Mexico*. U of California P, 2021.

Antillón Najlis, Ximena, editor. *Yo sólo quería que amaneciera: Informe de impactos psicosociales del caso Ayotzinapa*. Fundar, 2018, https://fundar.org.mx/mexico/pdf/InformeAyotziFin.pdf.

Anzaldúa, Gloria. *Borderlands / La Frontera: The New Mestiza*. 2nd ed., Aunt Lute Books, 1999.

Aquino Moreschi, Alejandra. "La comunalidad como epistemología del Sur. Aportes y retos." *Cuadernos del Sur*, no. 73, 2013, pp. 7–19.

Arias, Arturo. "Enunciating Alleged Truths: A Response to Ana Forcinito." *Critical Terms in Caribbean and Latin American Thought: Historical and Institutional Trajectories*, edited by Yolanda Martínez-San Miguel et al., Palgrave Macmillan, 2015, pp. 253–59.

———. "Indigenous Literatures? The Anthropocene? Theoretical Equivocations and Conceptual Tangles." *PMLA*, vol. 136, no. 1, 2021, pp. 110–17.

———. "Kotz'ib': The Emergence of a New Maya Literature." *Latin American Indian Literatures Journal*, vol. 5, 2008, pp. 7–28.
———. *Recovering Lost Footprints: Contemporary Maya Narratives, Volume 1*. State U of New York P, 2017.
———. *Recovering Lost Footprints: Contemporary Maya Narratives, Volume 2*. State U of New York P, 2018.
———. *Taking Their Word: Literature and the Signs of Central America*. U of Minnesota P, 2007.
———, editor. *The Rigoberta Menchú Controversy*. U of Minnesota P, 2001.
———. "Tramas y dramas de la descolonización: Un escritor indígena problematiza su otredad indígena." *Precariedades, exclusiones y emergencias: Necropolítica y sociedad civil en América Latina*, edited by Mabel Moraña and José Manuel Valenzuela Arce, Gedisa, 2017, pp. 99–223.
———. "*Tzitzi'n* for the *Poxnai*: Indigenous Women's Discourses on Revolutionary Combat." *Meanings of Violence in Contemporary Latin America*, edited by Gabriela Polit Dueñas and Maria Helena Rueda, Palgrave Macmillan, 2011.
Arroyo, Jossianna. "Transculturation, Syncretism, and Hybridity." *Critical Terms in Caribbean and Latin American Thought: Historical and Institutional Trajectories*, edited by Yolanda Martínez-San Miguel et al., Palgrave Macmillan, 2016, pp. 133–44.
"Artista nahua gana reconocimiento en Inglaterra." *UNAM Global: De la comunidad para la comunidad*, 16 April 2018, https://unamglobal.unam.mx/artista-nahua-gana-reconocimiento-en-inglaterra/.
"Ateri Miyawatl." *Ombligo de Tierra*, directed by Mardonio Carballo, Código Ciudad de México Radio, 30 July 2018.
Ayotzinapa: Una cartografía de la violencia. Plataforma Ayotzinapa, http://www.plataforma-ayotzinapa.org. Accessed 5 January 2021.
Báez-Jorge, Félix. *Entre los naguales y los santos: Religión popular y ejercicio clerical en el México indígena*. Universidad Veracruzana, 1998.
Baronnet, Bruno, et al., editors. *Luchas "muy otras": zapatismo y autonomía en las comunidades indígenas de Chiapas*. CIESAS, 2011.
Bassett, Molly. *The Fate of Earthly Things: Aztec Gods and God-Bodies*. U of Texas P, 2015.
Basso, Keith H. *Wisdom Sits in Places: Landscape and Language Among the Western Apache*. U of New Mexico P, 1996.
Beckett, Samuel. *Happy Days: A Play in Two Acts*. Rpt. ed., Grove P, 2013.
Belausteguigoitia, Marisa. "From Indigenismo to Zapatismo: Scenarios of Construction of the Indigenous Subject." *Critical Terms in Caribbean and Latin American Thought: Historical and Institutional Trajectories*, edited by Yolanda Martínez-San Miguel et al., Palgrave Macmillan, 2016, pp. 23–36.
Bell, Lucy, et al. *Taking Form, Making Worlds: Cartonera Publishers in Latin America*. U of Texas P, 2022.

Bellinghausen, Hermann, editor. *Insurrección de las palabras: Poetas contemporáneas en lenguas mexicanas (en Ojarasca)*. Secretaría de Cultura, La Jornada, and INALI, 2018.

———. "Un viaje por la poesía contemporánea náhuatl." *Ojarasca*, no. 284, December 2020, p. 16.

Blackhawk, Ned. *Violence over the Land: Indians and Empires in the Early American West*. Harvard UP, 2008.

Blackwell, Maylei. "Geographies of Indigeneity: Indigenous Migrant Women's Organizing and Translocal Politics of Place." *Latino Studies*, vol. 15, no. 2, July 2017, pp. 156–81, https://doi.org/10.1057/s41276-017-0060-4.

Bonfil Batalla, Guillermo. *México Profundo: Reclaiming a Civilization*. U of Texas P, 1996.

Bonisch-Brednich, Brigitte, and Catherine Trundle. "Introduction: Local Migrants and the Politics of Being in Place." *Local Lives: Migration and the Politics of Place*, Ashgate Publishing Company, 2010, pp. 17–30.

Brooks, Lisa. *The Common Pot: The Recovery of Native Space in the Northeast*. U of Minnesota P, 2008.

Burdette, Hannah. *Revealing Rebellion in Abiayala: The Insurgent Poetics of Contemporary Indigenous Literature*. U of Arizona P, 2019.

Byrne, Steven. *Identity and Nation in 21st Century Catalonia: El Procés*. Cambridge Scholars, 2021.

Cadena, Marisol de la. *Earth Beings: Ecologies of Practice across Andean Worlds*. Duke UP, 2015.

Cadena, Marisol de la, and Mario Blaser, editors. *A World of Many Worlds*. Duke UP, 2018.

Callaci, Emily. "On Acknowledgments." *The American Historical Review*, vol. 125, no. 1, February 2020, pp. 126–31, https://doi.org/10.1093/ahr/rhz938.

Campos, Haroldo de. *Novas: Selected Writings*. Edited by Antonio Sergio Bessa and Odile Cisneros, 1st ed., Northwestern UP, 2007.

Carballo, Mardonio. *Las Plumas de la Serpiente*. Amoch Libros, 2012.

———. Personal interview. 3 August 2016.

———. Personal interview. 9 June 2013.

———. Personal interview. 31 August 2017.

———. "Pola, o yo le lloro como papan." *Ojarasca*, June 2004, https://www.jornada.com.mx/2004/06/14/oja86-poesia.html.

Carballo, Mardonio, et al. *Las horas perdidas*. CONACULTA, 2014.

Carballo, Mardonio, and Irma Pineda. *Huehuexochitlajtoli / Diidxaguie'yooxho' / Viejos poemas*. Talleres de Impresos MB, 2006.

Cárcamo Huechante, Luis E. "Entre muros y cercados: La auto-ocupación de los cuerpos." *Revista Nomadías*, vol. 12, 2010, pp. 143–47, https://doi.org/10.5354/0719-0905.2010.15264.

———. "Indigenous Interference: Mapuche Use of Radio in Times of Acoustic Colonialism." *Latin American Research Review*, vol. 48, no. Special Issue, 2013, pp. 50–68. *Project MUSE*, https://doi.org/10.1353/lar.2013.0056.

———. "No + *Wingka* Word: Sounds of Mapuche Resurgence in the Poetry of Leonel Lienlaf." *Radical History Review*, vol. 2016, no. 124, January 2016, pp. 102–16, https://doi.org/10.1215/01636545-3159997.

Carlson, Bronwyn, and Jeff Berglund, editors. *Indigenous Peoples Rise Up: The Global Ascendency of Social Media Activism*. Rutgers UP, 2021.

Carrasco, David. "Aztec." *The Oxford Encyclopedia of Mesoamerican Cultures*, Oxford UP, 2006, https://www.oxfordreference.com/view/10.1093/acref/97801 95108156.001.0001/acref-9780195108156-e-34?rskey=3eK2pi&result=34.

Carrillo Tieco, Fabiola. "In tlazinque / La perezosa." *Pensamiento y voz de mujeres indígenas*, edited by Carmen Moreno et al., INALI, 2010.

———. *In xinachtli in tlahtolli: Amoxtli Zazanilli / El semillero de las palabras. Libro de cuentos*. CONACULTA, 2014.

Carro Muñoz, Delfino. *El estigma de los tlaxcaltecas*. Instituto Tlaxcalteca de la Cultura, 2012.

"Cartonera Publishers / Editoriales Cartoneras." *Research Guides: University of Wisconsin-Madison Libraries*, https://researchguides.library.wisc.edu/c.php?g=178157&p=1168976. Accessed 5 January 2022.

Castellanos, M. Bianet. *Indigenous Dispossession: Housing and Maya Indebtedness in Mexico*. 1st ed., Stanford UP, 2021.

Castro-Gómez, Santiago, and Ramón Grosfoguel. "Prólogo. Giro decolonial, teoría crítica y pensamiento heterárquico." *El giro decolonial: Reflexiones para una diversidad epistémica más allá del capitalismo global*, edited by Santiago Castro-Gómez and Ramón Grosfoguel, Siglo del Hombre Editores, 2007, pp. 9–24.

Chacaby, Ma-Nee. *A Two-Spirit Journey: The Autobiography of a Lesbian Ojibwa-Cree Elder*. U of Manitoba P, 2016.

Chacón, Gloria Elizabeth. *Indigenous Cosmolectics: Kab'awil and the Making of Maya and Zapotec Literatures*. U of North Carolina P, 2018.

Chang, David A. *The World and All the Things upon It: Native Hawaiian Geographies of Exploration*. U of Minnesota P, 2016.

"Cómo nos pueden llamar al voto; indígena irrumpe en acto de Menchú en Acapulco." *Vanguardia MX*, 28 September 2015, https://vanguardia.com.mx/noticias/nacional/2967998-como-nos-pueden-llamar-al-voto-indigena-irrumpe-en-acto-de-menchu-en-acapulco-PWVG2967998.

"Constitución Política de la Ciudad de México." *Gaceta Oficial de la Ciudad de México*, 5 February 2017, https://data.consejeria.cdmx.gob.mx/index.php/leyes/constitucion. Accessed 17 November 2023.

Coon, Adam W. "Down the Rabbit Hole and into the Moon: Nahua Perspectives in Mardonio Carballo's *Tlajpiajketl*." *Transmodernity: Journal of Peripheral

Cultural Production of the Luso-Hispanic World, vol. 7, no. 1, 2017, pp. 18–42, https://doi.org/10.5070/T471034114.

———. "*El rescoldo del tlicuil*: Visceral Resistance and Generational Tension among Contemporary Nahua Authors." *Teorizando las literaturas indígenas contemporáneas*, edited by Emilio del Valle Escalante, A Contracorriente, 2015, pp. 205–31.

———. "From Facebook to Ixamoxtli: Nahua Activism through Social Networking." *Indigenous Interfaces: Spaces, Technology, and Social Networks in Mexico and Central America*, edited by Jennifer Gómez Menjívar and Gloria Elizabeth Chacón, U of Arizona P, 2019, pp. 227–52.

———. "Living Languages as the Acoustic Ecologies within the Contemporary Literatures of Anahuac." *LASA Forum*, vol. 50, no. 1, Winter 2019, pp. 25–29.

———. "Los ojos de la cara, la cara de las hojas: Los significados conflictivos de ixtlamatilistli." *Revista de Crítica Latinoamericana*, vol. 46, no. 91, 2020, pp. 79–97.

———. "To *In* or Not to *In*: The Politics Behind the Usage or Disavowal of Classical Nahuatl within Contemporary Nahua Literature." *Revitalizing Endangered Languages*, October 2013, http://www.revitalization.al.uw.edu.pl/eng/Nahuatl/31/studies.

Coppens, Andrew D., et al. "Children's Initiative in Family Household Work in Mexico." *Human Development*, vol. 57, no. 2–3, 2014, pp. 116–30, https://doi.org/10.1159/000356768.

Cornejo Polar, Antonio. "Mestizaje e hibridez: Los riesgos de las metáforas. Apuntes." *Revista Iberoamericana*, vol. 63, no. 180, September 1997, pp. 341–44.

Corte, Myriam. "La indignación y la rabia no se acaban con la acción de votar." *Políticas Media*, 4 June 2015, https://politicasmedia.org/la-indignacion-y-la-rabia-no-se-acaban-con-la-accion-de-votar/.

Cortés, Hernán. *Cartas de relación*. Porrúa, 1967.

Cox, James H., and Daniel Heath Justice, editors. *The Oxford Handbook of Indigenous American Literature*. Oxford UP, 2014.

Cru, Josep. "Language Revitalisation from the Ground Up: Promoting Yucatec Maya on Facebook." *Journal of Multilingual and Multicultural Development*, vol. 36, no. 3, 2015, pp. 284–96.

Cumes, Aura. "Multiculturalismo, género y feminismos: Mujeres diversas, luchas complejas." *Tejiendo de otro modo: Feminismo, epistemología y apuestas descoloniales en Abia Yala*, edited by Yuderkys Espinosa Miñoso et al., Editorial Universidad del Cauca, 2014, pp. 237–52.

Cumes, Aura, and Yásnaya Elena Aguilar Gil. "Entrevista con Aura Cumes: la dualidad complementaria y el *Popol vuj*." *Revista de la Universidad de México*, no. 871, April 2021, pp. 18–25.

Dakin, Karen, et al., editors. *Language Contact and Change in Mesoamerica and Beyond*. John Benjamins, 2017.

de Barrio de Mendoza, Mihaela Radulescu. "El cuerpo ausente en las performances de Emilio Santisteban." *CROMA*, vol. 7, no. 13, June 2019, pp. 29–38.

de la Cruz Cruz, Eduardo. *Cenyahtoc cintli tonacayo: Huahcapatl huan tlen naman*. U of Warsaw P, 2017.

de la Cruz de la Cruz, Abelardo. "The Value of *El Costumbre* and Christianity in the Discourse of Nahua Catechists from the Huasteca Region in Veracruz, Mexico, 1970s–2010s." *Words and Worlds Turned Around: Indigenous Christianities in Colonial Latin America*, edited by David Tavárez, UP of Colorado, 2017, pp. 267–88.

de la Cruz, Eduardo, et al. *Tlahtolxitlauhcayotl: Chicontepec, Veracruz*. Edited by Justyna Olko and John Sullivan, U of Warsaw P, 2016.

de la Cruz, Manuel. "El paralelismo semántico-gramatical en el discurso ceremonial moyankwilliah en la comunidad de Tepecxitla / Semantic-Grammatical Parallelism in moyankwilliah Ceremonial Discourse in Tepecxitla." Native American and Indigenous Studies Association (NAISA) Conference, 20 May 2010, Tucson. Unpublished conference proceedings.

de la Cruz, Víctor. *Guie' sti' diidxazá / La flor de la palabra: Edición bilingüe antología de la literatura zapoteca*. Premià, 1983.

Dehouve, Danièle. *Entre el caimán y el jaguar: Los pueblos indios de Guerrero*. CIESAS, 1994.

"Dejar en paz a los muertos." *YouTube*, uploaded by Jaime Rodrigo Lovera Salazar, 11 June 2014, https://www.youtube.com/watch?v=fBs6LdgyRiY.

Deloria, Philip Joseph. *Indians in Unexpected Places*. UP of Kansas, 2004.

Digital Florentine Codex: An Encyclopedia of 16th-Century Indigenous Mexico. Getty Research Institute, 2023, https://florentinecodex.getty.edu. Accessed 5 November 2023.

"Discriminación México." *Xochikozkatl: Collar de Flores*, directed by Mardonio Carballo, 29, Radio UNAM, 2 August 2021, https://www.radiopodcast.unam.mx/podcast/audio/26408.

Domínguez Ruvalcaba, Héctor. *Modernity and the Nation in Mexican Representations of Masculinity: From Sensuality to Bloodshed*. Palgrave Macmillan, 2007.

Dowling, Sarah. *Translingual Poetics: Writing Personhood Under Settler Colonialism*. U of Iowa P, 2018.

Draper, Susana. *1968 Mexico: Constellations of Freedom and Democracy*. Duke UP, 2018.

Driskill, Qwo-Li. "Doubleweaving Two-Spirit Critiques: Building Alliances between Native and Queer Studies." *GLQ: A Journal of Lesbian and Gay Studies*, vol. 16, no. 1-2, April 2010, pp. 69–92, https://doi.org/10.1215/10642684-2009-013.

———, editor. *Queer Indigenous Studies: Critical Interventions in Theory, Politics, and Literature*. U of Arizona P, 2011.

Echo Hawk, Crystal. "Reflections on Sovereignty: Building Bridges between the North and South." *Indigenous Woman*, vol. 1, no. 3, 1999, pp. 21–22.

Ejército Zapatista de Liberación Nacional. *Cuarta Declaración de la Selva Lacandona.* 1 January 1996, http://palabra.ezln.org.mx/comunicados/1996/1996_01_01_a.htm.

Emre, Merve. "The Repressive Politics of Emotional Intelligence." *The New Yorker*, 19 April 2021, https://www.newyorker.com/magazine/2021/04/19/the-repressive-politics-of-emotional-intelligence?utm_source=twitter&mbid=social_twitter&utm_brand=tny&utm_social-type=owned&utm_medium=social.

Erdrich, Louise. *The Painted Drum.* HarperCollins, 2005.

Escalante Correa, María Luisa, and José Luis Benavides Ledesma. *Utilización de algunos medios de difusión en la educación indígena. El Instituto Nacional Indigenista y la Dirección General de Educación Indígena durante 1976–1983.* UNAM, 1985.

Escritores en Lenguas Indígenas. *Mexico: Diversas lenguas una sola nación. Antología de poesía en lenguas mexicanas.* Edited by Juana Karen, Escritores en Lenguas Indígenas, 2008.

Estrada, Alicia Ivonne. "YouTubing Maya Rock: B'itzma Sobrevivencia's Aural Memory of Survival." *Indigenous Interfaces: Spaces, Technology, and Social Networks in Mexico and Central America*, edited by Jennifer Gómez Menjívar and Gloria Elizabeth Chacón, U of Arizona P, 2019, pp. 99–118.

Farrell, Andrew. "The Rise of Black Rainbow: Queering and Indigenizing Digital Media Strategies, Resistance, and Change." *Indigenous Peoples Rise Up: The Global Ascendency of Social Media Activism*, edited by Bronwyn Carlson and Jeff Berglund, Rutgers UP, 2021.

Faudree, Paja. "What Is an Indigenous Author? Minority Authorship and the Politics of Voice in Mexico." *Anthropological Quarterly*, vol. 88, no. 1, Winter 2015, pp. 5–35.

"Felina Santiago, activista muxe, habla de respeto y diversidad sexual en . . . De Raíz Luna, hoy por Canal 22." *Emeequis*, 20 September 2012, http://www.m-x.com.mx/2012-09-20/felina-santiago-activista-muxe-habla-de-respeto-y-diversidad-sexual-en-de-raiz-luna-hoy-por-canal-22.

Flores Farfán, José Antonio. *Cuatreros somos y toindioma hablamos: Contactos y conflictos entre el náhuatl y el español en el sur de México.* 2nd ed., CIESAS, 2012.

———. "Efectos del contacto náhuatl-español en la región del Balsas, Guerrero. Desplazamiento, mantenimiento y resistencia lingüística." *Estudios de Cultura Náhuatl*, vol. 34, 2003, pp. 331–48.

———. *Variación, ideologías y purismo lingüístico: el caso del mexicano o nahuatl.* 1st ed., CIESAS, 2009.

Flores Martínez, Jesús Alberto. "Resistencia cultural y lingüística a partir de la música tradicional en una comunidad nahua de la Huasteca veracruzana." *La praxis de la documentación del legado lingüístico y cultural*, edited by Zarina Estrada Fernández et al., Universidad de Sonora, 2023, pp. 189–211.

Foucault, Michel. *The Birth of Biopolitics: Lectures at the Collège de France, 1978-1979*. Translated by Graham Burchell, Picador, 2010.
———. *"Society Must Be Defended": Lectures at the Collége de France, 1975-76*. Translated by Arnold I. Davidson, Picador, 2003.
Fregoso Bailón, Raúl Olmo. "Los Normalistas en el pensamiento latinoamericano: de las pedagogías críticas a las decoloniales. De Simón Rodríguez a Ayotzinapa." *América Latina en el orden mundial emergente del siglo XXI*, edited by Alberto Rocha Valencia, Universidad de Guadalajara, 2021, pp. 425-52.
Freire, Paulo. *Pedagogía del oprimido*. 33rd ed., Siglo Veintiuno, 1985.
García, Jaimeduardo. "Textos con pocos lectores: En busca del libro perdido." *Contralínea*, February 2003, http://www.contralinea.com.mx/c11/html/contrass/feb03_textos.html.
García Cook, Ángel, and Raziel Mora López. "Tetepetla: Un sitio fortificado del 'clásico' en Tlaxcala." *Comunicaciones proyecto Puebla-Tlaxcala*, vol. 10, pp. 23-30.
García Moral, Concepción, editor. *Antología de la poesía mejicana*. Editora Nacional, 1975.
Garduño, Roberto, and Enrique Méndez. "En dos años se reducirá 42% el presupuesto de Conaculta." *La Jornada*, 15 November 2013, p. 8.
Garibay K., Ángel María. *Historia de la literatura náhuatl*. Porrúa, 1953.
———. *Poesía Indígena de la Altiplanicie*. UNAM, 2007, www.librosoa.unam.mx, http://www.librosoa.unam.mx/handle/123456789/477.
———. *Poesía náhuatl*. UNAM, 1964-1968.
Gaskins, Suzanne. "Open Attention as a Cultural Tool for Observational Learning." *Semantic Scholar*, 2013, https://web.archive.org/web/20160106054633/http://kellogg.nd.edu/learning/Gaskins.pdf.
Genova, Thomas. *Imperial Educación: Race and Republican Motherhood in the Nineteenth-Century Americas*. U of Virginia P, 2021.
"Gloria Palacios y Gabriela Gonzalez." *Xochikozkatl: Collar de Flores*, directed by Mardonio Carballo, Radio UNAM, 6 December 2021, https://www.radiopodcast.unam.mx/podcast/audio/27485.
Goeman, Mishuana R. "Heteronormative Constructions of Electric Lights and Tourist Sights in Niagara Falls." Native American and Indigenous Studies Association (NAISA) Conference, 7 November 2014, Austin, TX. Unpublished conference proceedings.
Goleman, Daniel. *Emotional Intelligence*. Bantam Books, 1995.
Gómez Correal, Diana. "América Ladina, Abya Yala y Nuestra América: Tejiendo esperanzas realistas." *LASA Forum*, vol. 50, no. 3, Summer 2019, pp. 55-59.
Gómez Martínez, Arturo. *Tlaneltokilli: La espiritualidad de los nahuas chicontepecanos*. Programa de Desarrollo Cultural de la Huasteca, 2002.

Gómez Menjívar, Jennifer. "Indigenous Online." *The Routledge Handbook of Indigenous Development*, edited by Katharina Ruckstuhl et al., 1st ed., Routledge UP, 2022.

Gómez Menjívar, Jennifer, and Gloria Elizabeth Chacón, editors. *Indigenous Interfaces: Spaces, Technology, and Social Networks in Mexico and Central America*. U of Arizona P, 2019.

Gómez Velázquez, Osiris Aníbal. "Tierra: Comunalidad y emancipación en la poesía nahua de Gustavo Zapoteco Sideño y Martín Tonalmeyotl." *Chasqui*, vol. 52, no. 2, November 2023, pp. 9–36.

Gonzales, Sandra M. "Colonial Borders, Native Fences: Building Bridges between Indigenous Communities through the Decolonization of the American Landscape." *Comparative Indigeneities of the Américas: Toward a Hemispheric Approach*, edited by María Bianet Castellanos et al., U of Arizona P, 2012, pp. 307–21.

González, Rocío. *Literatura zapoteca, ¿resistencia o entropía? A modo de respuesta: cuatro escritores binnizá*. UACM, 2013.

Green, Joyce, editor. *Making Space for Indigenous Feminism*. 2nd ed., Fernwood, 2017.

———. "Taking More Account of Indigenous Feminism: An Introduction." *Making Space for Indigenous Feminism*, edited by Joyce Green, 2nd ed., Fernwood, 2017, pp. 1–20.

Guidotti-Hernández, Nicole M. *Archiving Mexican Masculinities in Diaspora*. Duke UP, 2021.

Gundur, R. V. "Negotiating Violence and Protection in Prison and on the Outside: The Organizational Evolution of the Transnational Prison Gang Barrio Azteca." *International Criminal Justice Review*, vol. 30, no. 1, 2020, pp. 30–60, https://doi.org/10.1177/1057567719836466.

Hagler, Anderson. "Exhuming the Nahualli: Shapeshifting, Idolatry, and Orthodoxy in Colonial Mexico." *The Americas*, vol. 78, no. 2, 2021, pp. 197–228.

Haglund, Sue Patricia, editor. *A Selection of Contemporary Gunadale Literature*. Siwar Mayu, 2022, https://siwarmayu.com/wp-content/uploads/2022/05/ENG_Gunadule-2.pdf.

Hale, Charles R. "Between Che Guevara and the Pachamama Mestizos, Indians and Identity Politics in the Anti-Quincentenary Campaign." *Critique of Anthropology*, vol. 14, no. 1, March 1994, pp. 9–39, https://doi.org/10.1177/0308275X9401400102.

———. *Más que un Indio / More than an Indian: Racial Ambivalence and Neoliberal Multiculturalism in Guatemala*. School of American Research P, 2006.

Hale, Charles R., and Rosamel Millaman. "Cultural Agency and Political Struggle in the Era of Indio Permitido." *Cultural Agency in the Americas*, edited by Doris Sommer, Duke UP, 2005, pp. 281–304.

Hall, Lisa Kahaleole. "Navigating Our Own 'Sea of Islands': Remapping a Theoretical Space for Hawaiian Women and Indigenous Feminism." *Wičazo Ša Review*, vol. 24, no. 2, 2009, pp. 15-38. Project MUSE, https://doi.org/10.1353/wic.0.0038.

Hames-García, Michael. "What's After Queer Theory? Queer Ethnic and Indigenous Studies." *Feminist Studies*, vol. 39, no. 2, 2013, pp. 384-404.

Haugen, Jason D. "Borrowed Borrowings: Nahuatl Loan Words in English." *Lexis: Journal in English Lexicology*, vol. 3, 2009, pp. 63-106.

Hernández, Jessica. *Fresh Banana Leaves: Healing Indigenous Landscapes through Indigenous Science*. North Atlantic Books, 2022.

Hernández, Natalio. *Amatlanahuatili tlahtoli tlen Mexicameh Nechicolistli Sentlanahuatiloyan / Constitución política de los Estados Unidos Mexicanos*. Senado de la República, 2010.

———. *De la exclusión al diálogo intercultural con los pueblos indígenas*. Plaza y Valdés, 2009.

———. *De la hispanidad de cinco siglos a la mexicanidad del siglo XXI*. Paralelo 21, 2020.

———. *El despertar de nuestras lenguas / Queman tlachixque totlahtolhuan*. Fondo Editorial de Cultura Indígenas, 2002.

———. *Forjando un nuevo rostro / Yancuic ixtlachihualistli. Orígenes y desarrollo de la educación indígena en México*. 2nd ed., SEP Puebla, 2016.

———. *Ijkon ontlajtoj aueuetl / Así habló el ahuehuete*. Universidad Veracruzana, 1989.

———. *In tlahtolli, in ohtli / La palabra, el camino: Memoria y destino de los pueblos indígenas*. Plaza y Valdés, 1998.

———. *Itoscac ahuehuetl / Las voces del ahuehuete: Homenaje a Miguel León-Portilla*. Trajín, 2021.

———, editor. *Narrativa náhuatl contemporánea: Antología*. CONACULTA, 1992.

———. "Noihqui toaxca caxtilan tlahtoli / El español también es nuestro." *Estudios de Cultura Náhuatl*, vol. 30, 1999, pp. 285-87.

———. *Patlani huitzitzilin / El vuelo del colibrí*. Universidad Veracruzana, 2016.

———. Personal interview. 26 August 2012.

———. Personal interview. 31 August 2012.

———. Personal interview. 22 September 2012.

———. Personal interview. 12 December 2019.

———. "Presencia contemporánea de los nahuas." *Arqueología mexicana*, vol. 19, no. 54, June 2011, pp. 53-57.

———. *Semanca huitzilin / Colibrí de la armonía / Hummingbird of Harmony*. CONACULTA, 2005.

———. *Sempoalxochitl / Veinte flor*. UNAM, 1987.

———. *Tamoanchan: La tierra originaria*. Universidad de Guadalajara, 2017.

———. *Xopantla xochimeh / Flores de primavera: Selección poética para mujeres*. Secretaría de Cultura del Distrito Federal / Fundación Cultural Macuilxochitl, 2012.

———. *Yancuic Anahuac cuicatl / Canto nuevo de Anáhuac*. Diana, 1994.

Hernández, Natalio [José Antonio Xokoyotsin]. *Xochikoskatl / Collar de flores*. Editorial Kalpulli, 1985.

Hernández-Ávila, Inés. "La literatura Indígena y la palabra autónoma de los pueblos originarios: Una perspectiva trans-Indígena y auto-etnográfica." *English Studies in Latin America*, no. 18, January 2020, pp. 1–23.

Hernández Castillo, R. Aída. *Bajo la sombra del guamúchil: Historias de vida de mujeres indígenas y campesinas en prisión*. CIESAS, 2010.

———. *Multiple Injustices: Indigenous Women, Law, and Political Struggle in Latin America*. U of Arizona P, 2018.

Hernández Hernández, Eneida. "Xochiohtli-Xochikoskatl-Xochikali: Camino de flores como práctica para el bienestar." *La Jornada del campo*, 15 October 2016, https://www.jornada.com.mx/2016/10/15/cam-flores.html.

Hernández Reyna, Miriam, and Juan A. Castillo Cocom. "'Ser o no ser indígena': Oscilaciones identitarias dentro de la interculturalidad de Estado en México." *The Journal of Latin American and Caribbean Anthropology*, vol. n/a, no. n/a, March 2021, https://doi.org/10.1111/jlca.12532.

Hill, Jane H., and Kenneth C. Hill. *Speaking Mexicano: Dynamics of Syncretic Language in Central Mexico*. U of Arizona P, 1986.

Hobsbawm, Eric. *The Invention of Tradition*. Cambridge UP, 1992.

hooks, bell. *Feminist Theory: From Margin to Center*. 2nd ed., South End Press, 2000.

INEGI. *Censo de Población y Vivienda 2020*. https://www.inegi.org.mx/programas/ccpv/2020/. Accessed 20 May 2023.

INEGI. *Censo de Población y Vivienda 2020: Marco Conceptual*. INEGI, 2021. *INEGI*. https://www.inegi.org.mx/contenidos/productos/prod_serv/contenidos/espanol/bvinegi/productos/nueva_estruc/702825197520.pdf.

INMUJERES. *Población Indígena*. May 2021, http://estadistica.inmujeres.gob.mx/formas/tarjetas/Poblacion_indigena.pdf.

Instituto Nacional Indigenista, editor. *Acción indigenista: Boletín Mensual del Instituto Nacional Indigenista, 1953–1976*.

———. *Ha fracasado el indigenismo? Reportaje de una controversia (13 de septiembre de 1971)*. SEP, 1971.

"Interrumpen a Rigoberta Menchú." *YouTube*, uploaded by Eduardito Figueroa, 1 June 2015, https://www.youtube.com/watch?v=BE8E5flpkzo.

"Irrumpe indígena de Guerrero en acto de Rigoberta Menchú." *YouTube*, uploaded by 24 horas: El diario sin límites, 29 May 2015, https://www.youtube.com/watch?v=Lbrxuev0t-0&t=13s.

IWGIA. *El mundo indígena 2021: México*. 18 March 2021, https://www.iwgia.org/es/mexico/4149-mi-2021-mexico.html.

Jacinto Meza, Martín [Martín Tonalmeyotl]. *Documentación lingüística de la variante náhuatl de Atzacoaloya, Guerrero*. CIESAS, April 2014.

Jansen, Anne Mai Yee. "Writing *toward* Action: Mapping an Affinity Poetics in Craig Santos Perez's *from unincorporated territory*." *Native American and Indigenous Studies*, vol. 6, no. 2, 2019, pp. 3–29. *JSTOR*, https://doi.org/10.5749/natiindistudj.6.2.0003.

Jiménez, Luz. *Los cuentos en náhuatl de Doña Luz Jiménez*. Edited by Horcasitas Fernando and O. de Ford Sandra, UNAM, 1979.

"Joven cuestiona a Rigoberta Menchú sobre elecciones en Guerrero." Univisión, 2015, https://www.univision.com/shows/noticiero-univision/joven-cuestiona-a-rigoberta-menchu-sobre-elecciones-en-guerrero-video.

"Joven increpa a Rigoberta Menchú y al gobernador de Guerrero." *Proceso*, 30 May 2015, https://www.proceso.com.mx/nacional/2015/5/30/joven-increpa-rigoberta-menchu-al-gobernador-de-guerrero-147738.html.

Justice, Daniel Heath. *Our Fire Survives the Storm: A Cherokee Literary History*. U of Minnesota P, 2006.

———. *Why Indigenous Literatures Matter*. Wilfrid Laurier UP, 2018.

Karttunen, Frances. *An Analytical Dictionary of Nahuatl*. Rev. ed., U of Oklahoma P, 1992.

———. "Indigenous Writing as a Vehicle of Postconquest Continuity and Change in Mesoamerica." *Native Traditions in the Postconquest World: A Symposium at Dumbarton Oaks, 2nd through 4th October 1992*, edited by Elizabeth Hill Boone and Tom Cummins, Dumbarton Oaks, 1998.

———. "Rethinking Malinche." *Indian Women of Early Mexico*, edited by Susan Schroeder et al., U of Oklahoma P, 1997, pp. 291–312.

Kellogg, Susan. *Law and the Transformation of Aztec Culture, 1500–1700*. U of Oklahoma P, 2005.

Keme, Emil'. "For Abiayala to Live, the Americas Must Die: Toward a Transhemispheric Indigeneity." *Native American and Indigenous Studies*, translated by Adam W. Coon, vol. 5, no. 1, 2018, pp. 42–68.

———. *Le Maya Q'atzij / Our Maya World: Poetics of Resistance*. U of Minnesota P, 2021.

Keme, Emil' [Emilio del Valle Escalante]. *Maya Nationalisms and Postcolonial Challenges in Guatemala: Coloniality, Modernity, and Identity Politics*. School for Advanced Research, 2009.

———. *Teorizando las literaturas indígenas contemporáneas*. A Contracorriente, 2015.

Kimmerer, Robin Wall. *Braiding Sweetgrass: Indigenous Wisdom, Scientific Knowledge and the Teachings of Plants*. Milkweed, 2013.

Koch, Alexander, et al. "Earth System Impacts of the European Arrival and Great Dying in the Americas after 1492." *Quaternary Science Reviews*, vol. 207, March 2019, pp. 13–36, https://doi.org/10.1016/j.quascirev.2018.12.004.

Kroskrity, Paul V., editor. *Telling Stories in the Face of Danger: Language Renewal in Native American Communities*. U of Oklahoma P, 2012.

"La escritora y actriz nahua Ateri Miyawatl es premiada en Inglaterra por su libro-arte." *Terceravia.mx*, 3 April 2018, https://terceravia.mx/2018/04/la-escritora-acriz-nahua-ateri-miyawatl-premiada-en-inglaterra-libro-arte/.

Laó-Montes, Agustín. *Contrapunteos Diaspóricos: Cartografías Políticas de Nuestra Afroamérica*. Universidad Externado de Colombia, 2020.

Lara Cisneros, Gerardo. *¿Ignorancia invencible? Superstición e idolatría ante el Provisorato de Indios y Chinos del Arzobispado de México en el siglo XVIII*. UNAM, 2015.

LaRoque, Emma. "The Colonization of a Native Woman Scholar." *Women of the First Nations: Power, Wisdom, and Strength*, U of Manitoba P, 1996.

"Las Hijas de La Malinche #19 Poeta Nahuahablante Ethel Xochitiotzin." *YouTube*, uploaded by Las hijas de la Malinche, 18 February 2022, https://www.youtube.com/watch?v=Z9QMLqvmUVE.

"Las lenguas toman la tribuna (Del 21/02/2019 al 20/02/2020)." *Cámara de Diputados LXV Legislatura*, http://www5.diputados.gob.mx/index.php/camara/Comision-de-Pueblos-Indigenas/Eventos-y-Convocatorias/Las-Lenguas-Toman-la-Tribuna-Del-21-02-2019-al-20-02-2020. Accessed 1 May 2023.

"Las mujeres indígenas: Defensoras de la vida y los territorios, hacia un pensamiento descolonial." *Facebook*, 11 August 2021, https://www.facebook.com/watch/live/?ref=search&v=586828238931823.

Lawrence, D. H. *The Plumed Serpent*. Rpt. ed., William Heinemann, 1955.

Lee, Jongsoo. *The Allure of Nezahualcoyotl: Pre-Hispanic History, Religion, and Nahua Poetics*. U of New Mexico P, 2008.

Leeming, Ben. *Aztec Antichrist: Performing the Apocalypse in Early Colonial Mexico*. UP of Colorado, 2022.

León Portilla, Miguel. *Cantares mexicanos*. UNAM, 2011.

———. *Filosofía náhuatl: Estudiada en sus fuentes, con un nuevo apéndice*. 10th ed., UNAM, 2006.

———. *Literaturas indígenas de México*. 2nd ed., Mapfre / Fondo de Cultura Económica, 2003.

———. *Los antiguos mexicanos a través de sus crónicas y cantares*. 4th ed., Fondo de Cultura Económica, 2012.

———. *Los manifiestos en náhuatl de Emiliano Zapata*. 2nd ed., UNAM, 1996.

———. *Quince poetas del mundo náhuatl*. Diana, 1994.

———. *Trece poetas del mundo azteca*. UNAM, 1984.

———. *Visión de los vencidos*. 1959. 28th ed., UNAM, 2006.

———. "Yancuic tlahtolli: La nueva palabra: Una antología de la literatura náhuatl contemporánea." *Estudios de Cultura Náhuatl*, vol. 18, 1986.

Lepe Lira, Luz María. *Relatos de la diferencia y literatura indígena: Travesías por el sistema mundo*. Grañén Porrúa, 2018.

Lewis, Laura A. *Hall of Mirrors: Power, Witchcraft, and Caste in Colonial Mexico.* Duke UP, 2003.
Link, Adrianna, et al. *Indigenous Languages and the Promise of Archives.* U of Nebraska P, 2021.
Lionnet, Françoise, and Emmanuel Bruno Jean-François. "Literary Routes: Migration, Islands, and the Creative Economy." *PMLA*, vol. 131, no. 5, October 2016, pp. 1222–38.
Lomnitz-Adler, Claudio. "Bordering on Anthropology: The Dialectics of a National Tradition in Mexico." *Revue de Synthèse*, vol. 121, no. 3–4, July 2000, pp. 345–79, https://doi.org/10.1007/BF02970494.
———. *Exits from the Labyrinth: Culture and Ideology in the Mexican National Space.* U of California P, 1992.
López Austin, Alfredo. *The Human Body and Ideology: Concepts of the Ancient Nahuas.* U of Utah P, 1988.
López Bárcenas, Francisco. "¡Y eso no es todo . . . falta Víctor Yodo!" *La Jornada*, 2 February 2021, https://www.jornada.com.mx/notas/2021/02/03/politica/y-eso-no-es-todo-falta-victor-yodo/.
Lucero, José Antonio. "'To Articulate Ourselves': Trans-Indigenous Reflections on Film and Politics in Amazonia." *Native American and Indigenous Studies*, vol. 7, no. 2, 2020, pp. 1–28.
Ludlow, Francis, et al. "The Double Binds of Indigeneity and Indigenous Resistance." *Humanities*, vol. 5, no. 53, 2016, pp. 1–19.
Luna Ruiz, Juan. *Tlaxcala.* CDI, 2006.
Lund, Joshua. *The Mestizo State: Reading Race in Modern Mexico.* U of Minnesota P, 2012.
Lutz, John Sutton. *Makúk: A New History of Aboriginal-White Relations.* UBC, 2009.
Maffie, James. *Aztec Philosophy: Understanding a World in Motion.* U of Colorado P, 2015.
Magaña, Maurice Rafael. *Cartographies of Youth Resistance: Hip-Hop, Punk, and Urban Autonomy in Mexico.* U of California P, 2020.
Manning, Erin. *Politics of Touch: Sense, Movement, Sovereignty.* U of Minnesota P, 2007.
Marcus, George E., et al. *Affective Intelligence and Political Judgment.* U of Chicago P, 2000.
Marimán Quemenado, Pablo. "Los mapuches antes de la conquista militar chileno-argentina." *. . . Escucha, winka . . . !: Cuatro ensayos de Historia Nacional Mapuche y un epílogo sobre el futuro*, edited by José Millalén Paillal et al., LOM Ediciones, 2006, pp. 53–126.
Martínez, Armando. "'¿Cuánta población indígena y afrodescendiente hay en México?'" *Milenio*, 25 January 2021, https://www.milenio.com/politica/comunidad/cuantos-indigenas-y-afrodescendientes-hay-en-mexico-inegi-2021.

Martínez Díaz, Baruc. "Un intelectual indígena del México decimonónico: la vida y la obra de Faustino Chimalpopoca Galicia." *Estudios de Cultura Náhuatl*, vol. 63, June 2022, pp. 103–33.

Martínez González, Roberto. *El nahualismo*. UNAM, 2011.

Mateos Cortés, Laura Selene, and Gunther Dietz. "Universidades interculturales en México: Balance crítico de la primera década." *CPU-e, Revista de investigación educativa*, vol. 21, no. 70, 2016, pp. 683–90, https://doi.org/10.25009/cpue.v0i19.974.

Matías Alonso, Marcos. "Tlayolli: El pan de los indios en Acatlán." *Nuestro maíz. Treinta monografías populares*, edited by Guillermo Bonfil Batalla, vol. 1, SEP, 1982, pp. 92–118.

Matías García, Yolanda. Personal interview. 5 April 2014.

———. *Tonalxochimej / Flores del sol*. Fundación Académica Guerrerense, 2013.

Matías Rendón, Ana. *La discursividad indígena: Caminos de la Palabra escrita*. Kumay, 2019.

———. "Panorama de poesía en lenguas originarias." *Círculo de traductores*, 9 August 2016, http://circulodetraductores.blogspot.com/2016/08/panorama-de-poesia-en-lenguas.html.

Matiúwàa, Hubert. "El día bajo la sombra: Año de los Pueblos Indígenas." *Tlachinollan: Centro de Derechos Humanos de la Montaña*, 9 August 2021, https://www.tlachinollan.org/el-dia-bajo-la-sombra-ano-de-los-pueblos-indigenas/.

———. "Los hombres zanate en *El ritual de los olvidados*." *Trinchera: Política y cultura*, 19 March 2019, p. 15.

Matthew, Laura E. *Memories of Conquest: Becoming Mexicano in Colonial Guatemala*. U of North Carolina P, 2018.

Matthews, Gerald, et al. *Emotional Intelligence: Science and Myth*. MIT, 2002.

McCallum, Pamela. "Painting the Archive: The Art of Jane Ash Poitras." *Indigenous Women and Feminism: Politics, Activism, Culture*, edited by Cheryl Suzack et al., UBC, 2010, pp. 239–57.

McCarty, Teresa L., et al. "Hear Our Languages, Hear Our Voices: Storywork as Theory and Praxis in Indigenous-Language Reclamation." *Daedalus, the Journal of the American Academy of Arts & Sciences*, vol. 147, no. 2, Spring 2018, pp. 160–72.

McDonough, Kelly S. *The Learned Ones: Nahua Intellectuals in Postconquest Mexico*. U of Arizona P, 2014.

———. "Settler Colonial Mexico and Indigenous Primordial Titles." *Allotment Stories: Indigenous Land Relations under Settler Siege*, edited by Daniel Heath Justice and Jean M. O'Brien, U of Minnesota P, 2022, pp. 240–47.

Messing, Jacqueline. "Multiple Ideologies and Competing Discourses: Language Shift in Tlaxcala, Mexico." *Language in Society*, vol. 36, no. 04, 2007, pp. 555–77. *Cambridge Journals Online*, https://doi.org/10.1017/S0047404507070443.

Mestries, Francis, and Enrique Victoria. "Extractivismo, territorio y narcotráfico: Las luchas de resistencia de los pueblos indígenas de Guerrero contra los

megaproyectos." *Territorios neoextractivismo y derechos indígenas en Latinoamérica*, edited by Gabriela Muñoz Meléndez et al., Universidad Juárez del Estado de Durango, 2021, pp. 121–58.
Metztli, Yankuik [Isabel Martínez Nopaltécatl]. "amika nechkaki." *Facebook.com*, 4 May 2013.
Mignolo, Walter. *The Darker Side of Western Modernity*. Duke UP, 2011.
Miller, Tiffany D. Creegan. " 'Kixinto', k'u xa jub'iq' ('I give, but just a little'): Negotiating K'iche' Orality, Self-Translation, and Cultural Agency in "Xalolilo lelele' " by Humberto Ak'abal." *Revista de Estudios Hispánicos*, vol. 54, no. 3, October 2020, pp. 653–77.
———. *The Maya Art of Speaking Writing: Remediating Indigenous Orality in the Digital Age*. U of Arizona P, 2022.
———. "Queering Abiayala: The Persona and Political Cartographies of the Indigenous Americas." *Performances That Change the Americas*, edited by Stuart A. Day, Routledge UP, 2021, pp. 99–115.
Miyawatl, Ateri. "Nahua Poet Ateri Miyawatl Reading from Her Work." *Library of Congress*, 2023, https://lccn.loc.gov/2023702665.
———. *Neijmantototsintle / La tristesa és un ocell / Sadness Is a Bird*. Elies Plana, 2018.
———. Personal interview. 8 November 2019.
———. "Se weyi ostotl notik onka / Hay en mi cuerpo una gran oquedad." *Diario ContraRéplica*, vol. 1, no. 15, 19 October 2018, p. 23.
———. "Tokohkol xonomikileh. Totik noyolicha / Nuestra abuela no ha muerto. Vive dentro nuestro." *Tzam Trece semillas*, May 2022, https://tzamtrecesemillas.org/sitio/tokohkol-xonomikileh-totik-noyolicha-nuestra-abuela-no-ha-muerto-vive-dentro-nuestro/.
———. "Tsintatak." *Strange Horizons*, 30 November 2020, http://strangehorizons.com/issue/30-november-2020/.
———. "Tsintatak (Náhuatl)." *Shilaa'*, no. 01, 2022, pp. 28–31, https://issuu.com/francofelix/docs/shilaa_ed.01-print-issuu.
Miyawatl, Ateri [Anna Gatica], editor. *Atsajtsilistle*. Laboratorio de arte TETL, 2014.
Molina, Alonso de. *Vocabulario en lengua castellana y mexicana y mexicana y castellana*. 1571.
Montaldo, Graciela. "Modernity and Modernization: The Geopolitical Relocation of Latin America." *Critical Terms in Caribbean and Latin American Thought: Historical and Institutional Trajectories*, edited by Yolanda Martínez-San Miguel et al., Palgrave Macmillan, 2016, pp. 153–84.
Montejo, Víctor. *Mayalogue: An Interactionist Theory of Indigenous Cultures*. State U of New York P, 2021.
Montemayor, Carlos, and Donald H. Frischmann, editors. *Words of the True Peoples / Palabras de los seres verdaderos: Anthology of Contemporary Mexican Indigenous-Language Writers*. U of Texas P, 2004.

Mora Bayo, Mariana. "Asesinatos y violencia (neo)colonial contra líderes indígenas en defensa de su territorio en México." *LASA Forum*, vol. 50, no. 4, Fall 2019, pp. 26-30.

———. "Ayotzinapa and the Criminalization of Racialized Poverty in La Montaña, Guerrero, Mexico." *POLAR*, vol. 40, no. 1, May 2017, pp. 67-85, https://doi.org/10.1111/plar.12208.

———. "Desaparición forzada, racismo institucional y pueblos indígenas en el caso Ayotzinapa, México." *LASA Forum*, vol. 48, no. 2, Spring 2017, pp. 29-30.

Moreno, Carmen, et al., editors. *Pensamiento y voz de mujeres indígenas*. INALI, 2010.

Morgensen, Scott Lauria. *Spaces between Us: Queer Settler Colonialism and Indigenous Decolonization*. U of Minnesota P.

Mundy, Barbara E. *The Death of Aztec Tenochtitlan, the Life of Mexico City*. U of Texas P, 2018.

———. "Mesoamerican Cartography." *The History of Cartography: Cartography in the Traditional African, American, Arctic, Australian, and Pacific Societies*, edited by David Woodward and G. Malcolm Lewis, vol. 2, book 3, U of Chicago P, 1998, pp. 183-256.

Muñoz Ramírez, Gloria. *Derecho de réplica. Hablan los pueblos*. https://hablanlospueblos.org/index.html. Accessed 13 January 2022.

———. *EZLN: 20 y 10, el fuego y la palabra*. La Jornada, 2003.

———. "Flores en el desierto: Mujeres del Concejo Indígena de Gobierno." *desInformémonos: Periodismo de abajo*, https://floreseneldesierto.desinformemonos.org/. Accessed 14 October 2021.

Nájar, Alberto. "Los crueles rituales de iniciación del narco en México." *BBC News Mundo*, 10 April 2014, https://www.bbc.com/mundo/noticias/2014/04/140410_mexico_rituales_narcotrafico_templarios_an.

"Nancy Vázquez y Stephanie Delgado." *Xochikozkatl. Collar de Flores*, directed by Mardonio Carballo, Radio UNAM, 11 October 2021, https://www.radiopodcast.unam.mx/podcast/audio/26860.

Nava Vite, Rafael. " 'El costumbre': Ofrendas y música a Chicomexochitl en Ixhuatlán de Madero, Veracruz." *EntreVerAndo*, no. 5, October 2009, pp. 34-52.

———. *La Huasteca / Uextekapan: Los pueblos nahuas en su lucha por la tierra*. CONACULTA, 1996.

Nechikolistli tlen Nauatlajtouaj Maseualtlamachtianej [Organización de Profesionistas Indígenas Nahuas A. C.]. *Neluayotl tekiyotl uan tlajtoltlanauatili / Principios, acciones y estatutos*. OPINAC, 1986.

Negrín, Diana. *Racial Alterity, Wixarika Youth Activism, and the Right to the Mexican City*. U of Arizona P, 2019.

Nelson, Diane M. *A Finger in the Wound: Body Politics in Quincentennial Guatemala*. U of California P, 1999.

"IX Festival de Poesía. Las Lenguas de América. Carlos Montemayor." *YouTube*, uploaded by PUIC UNAM, 13 October 2022, https://www.youtube.com/live/Zo8d4s6dsps?si=seJM-hLf5LLtmPs6.

Nora, Pierre. "Preface to the English Language Edition: From Lieux de Mémoire to Realms of Memory." *Realms of Memory: Rethinking the French Past*, edited by Pierre Nora, Columbia UP, 1996, pp. xv–xxiv.

Nuevos formatos, soportes y cantos en lenguas indígenas. Directed by Mardonio Carballo, 2013, https://mexicana.cultura.gob.mx/en/repositorio/detalle?id=_suri:BV:TransObject:5bce7a787a8a02074f82ff75&word=Soportes,&r=3&t=2728.

Núñez, Rafael E., and Eve Sweetser. "With the Future behind Them: Convergent Evidence from Aymara Language and Gesture in the Crosslinguistic Comparison of Spatial Construals of Time." *Cognitive Science*, vol. 30, no. 3, May 2006, pp. 401–50. *Wiley Online Library*, https://doi.org/10.1207/s15516709cog0000_62.

Nussbaum, Martha C. *Upheavals of Thought: The Intelligence of Emotions*. Cambridge UP, 2001.

Nutini, Hugo Gino. *Todos Santos in Rural Tlaxcala: A Syncretic, Expressive, and Symbolic Analysis of the Cult of the Dead*. Princeton UP, 2014.

O'Brien, Jean M. "Animating Box 331." *The William and Mary Quarterly*, vol. 77, no. 3, 2020, pp. 366–71.

———. "What Does Native American and Indigenous Studies (NAIS) Do?" *American Historical Review*, vol. 125, no. 2, April 2020, pp. 542–45. *EBSCOhost*, https://doi.org/10.1093/ahr/rhaa198.

Olivera, Mercedes. *Pillis y macehuales: Las formaciones sociales y los modos de producción de Tecali del siglo XII al XVI*. CIESAS, 1978.

Olko, Justyna. "Aztec Universalism: Ideology and Status Symbols in the Service of Empire-Building." *Universal Empire: A Comparative Approach to Imperial Culture and Representation in Eurasian History*, edited by Peter Fibiger Bang and Dariusz Kolodziejczyk, Cambridge UP, 2012, pp. 253–79.

———. *Insignia of Rank in the Nahua World: From the Fifteenth to the Seventeenth Century*. UP of Colorado, 2014.

Olko, Justyna, et al. "The Positive Relationship between Indigenous Language Use and Community-Based Well-Being in Four Nahua Ethnic Groups in Mexico." *Cultural Diversity and Ethnic Minority Psychology*, October 2021, pp. 1–12.

Olko, Justyna, et al., editors. *Dialogue with Europe, Dialogue with the Past: Colonial Nahua and Quechua Elites in Their Own Words*. U of Colorado P, 2018.

Olko, Justyna, and Julia Sallabank, editors. *Revitalizing Endangered Languages: A Practical Guide*. Cambridge UP, 2021, https://doi.org/10.1017/9781108641142.

"Open Letter from Indigenous Women Scholars Regarding Discussions of Andrea Smith." *Indian Country Today*, 12 September 2018, https://indiancountry

today.com/archive/open-letter-from-indigenous-women-scholars-regarding-discussions-of-andrea-smith.

Ordóñez-Barba, Gerardo Manuel, and Aída Lilia Silva-Hernández. "Progresa-Oportunidades-Prospera: Avatares, alcances y resultados de un programa paradigmático contra la pobreza." *Papeles de población*, vol. 25, no. 99, March 2019, pp. 77–111, https://doi.org/10.22185/24487147.2019.99.04.

Ordóñez, Samanta. *Mexico Unmanned: The Cultural Politics of Masculinity in Mexican Cinema*. State U of New York P, 2021.

Ortiz, Fernando. *Cuban Counterpoint: Tobacco and Sugar*. Translated by Harriet de Onís, Duke UP, 1995.

Otzoy, Irma. *Maya' b'anikil, maya' tzyaqb' / Identidad y vestuario maya*. Cholsamaj, 1996.

Padilla, Tanalís. *Unintended Lessons of Revolution: Student Teachers and Political Radicalism in Twentieth-Century Mexico*. Duke UP, 2022.

Pastrana, Daniela. "Ayotzinapa, un año después: ¿Qué hemos hecho?" *Magis*, no. 448, November 2015, https://magis.iteso.mx/nota/ayotzinapa-un-ano-despues-que-hemos-hecho/.

Paz, Octavio. *El laberinto de la soledad y otras obras*. Penguin Books, 1997.

"PBI México: Los pueblos indígenas se oponen a la explotación minera en la Costa Chica y la Montaña de Guerrero." *PBI México*, 2 March 2011, https://pbi-mexico.org/es/news/2011-02-03/pbi-m%C3%A9xico-los-pueblos-ind%C3%ADgenas-se-oponen-la-explotaci%C3%B3n-minera-en-la-costa-chica-y.

Peterson, Jeanette Favrot, and Kevin Terraciano, editors. *The Florentine Codex: An Encyclopedia of the Nahua World in Sixteenth-Century Mexico*. U of Texas P, 2019.

Pierce, Joseph M. "In Search of an Authentic Indian: Notes on the Self." *Indian Country Today*, 13 September 2018, https://indiancountrytoday.com/archive/in-search-of-an-authentic-indian-notes-on-the-self.

———. "*Roma* Is a Beautiful Film of Indigenous Erasure." *Indian Country Today*, 28 December 2018, https://indiancountrytoday.com/opinion/roma-is-a-beautiful-film-of-indigenous-erasure-BuOrS3iGSEmLaNZcSHP2Uw.

Pineda, Irma. "Palabra de nube entre flores y piedras." *Caleidoscopio verbal: Lenguas y literaturas originarias*, edited by Osiris Aníbal Gómez, Oro de la Noche, 2020, pp. 81–88, https://issuu.com/visualizaestudio/docs/caleidoscopio/s/13980536.

———. "Xtámbaa / Piel de Tierra de Hubert Matiúwàa." *Latin American Literature Today*, vol. 1, no. 3, July 2017, https://latinamericanliteraturetoday.org/es/reseñas/xtambaa-piel-de-tierra-hubert-matiuwaa-2/.

Porcayo, Omar. "Premian en Inglaterra a indígena mexicana por bello poema escrito en náhuatl." *Barrio*, 27 April 2018, https://esbarrio.com/trending/ateri-miyawatl-premio-inglaterra-neijmantototsintle/.

Powers, Karen Vieira. *Women in the Crucible of Conquest: The Gendered Genesis of Spanish American Society, 1500–1600*. U of New Mexico P, 2005.
Pratt, Mary Louise. "Arts of the Contact Zone." *Profession*, 1991, pp. 33–40.
———. *Imperial Eyes: Travel Writing and Transculturation*. Routledge, 1992.
Quijano, Aníbal. "Coloniality of Power, Eurocentrism, and Latin America." *Nepantla: Views from the South*, translated by Michael Ennis, vol. 1, no. 3, 2000, pp. 533–80.
Raíces a una sola voz: Antología literaria FILIT 2020, edited by Mireya Aguilar et al., 2020.
Rajagopalan, Angela Herren. *Portraying the Aztec Past: The Codices Boturini, Azcatitlan, and Aubin*. U of Texas P, 2018.
Rama, Ángel. *La ciudad letrada*. Universidad Autónoma de Nuevo León, 2009.
———. *Writing across Cultures: Narrative Transculturation in Latin America*. Duke UP, 2012.
Ramazani, Jahan. *A Transnational Poetics*. U of Chicago P, 2009.
Rappaport, Joanne, and Tom Cummins. *Beyond the Lettered City: Indigenous Literacies in the Andes*. Duke UP, 2012.
"Réplica de una joven a Rigoberta Menchú, quien promueve el voto en Guerrero." *YouTube*, Quadratin Guerrero, 2015, https://www.youtube.com/watch?v=o5Gg6-KpDvA&t=3s. Accessed 15 January 2022.
Restall, Matthew. "A History of the New Philology and the New Philology in History." *Latin American Research Review*, vol. 38, no. 1, 2003, pp. 113–34.
Risling-Baldy, Cutcha. *We Are Dancing for You: Native Feminisms and the Revitalization of Women's Coming-of-Age Ceremonies*. U of Washington P, 2018.
Rivera Cusicanqui, Silvia. *Ch'ixinakax utxiwa: Una reflexión sobre prácticas y discursos descolonizadores*. Tinta Limón, 2010.
———. "The Notion of 'Rights' and the Paradoxes of Postcolonial Modernity: Indigenous Peoples and Women in Bolivia." *Qui Parle*, vol. 18, no. 2, Spring/Summer 2010, pp. 29–54.
———. *Pachakuti: Los aymaras de Bolivia frente a medio milenio de colonialismo*. Taller de Historia Oral Andina, 1991.
———. *Violencias (re)cubiertas en Bolivia*. Mirada Salvaje, 2010.
Rocha Vivas, Miguel. *Word Mingas: Oralitegraphies and Mirrored Visions on Oralitures and Indigenous Contemporary Literatures*. Translated by Paul M. Worley and Melissa Birkhofer, U of North Carolina P, 2021.
Rodés, Andrea. "Las lenguas suenan como suenan, porque están vivas." *Al Día*, 25 October 2017, http://aldianews.com/ es/articles/culture/mardonio-carballo-las-lenguas-suenan-como-suenan-porque-est-n-vivas/50394.
Rodríguez, Darinka. "Apapachar: el verdadero significado de una palabra de origen náhuatl." *Verne*, Ediciones El País, 23 July 2020, https://verne.elpais.com/verne/2020/07/23/mexico/1595481612_470684.html.

Rogachevsky, Jorge R. "La voz de la naturaleza en la poesía de Humberto Ak'abal." *Encuentro: Revista del Instituto Guatemalteco de Cultura Hispánica*, vol. 13, 1994, pp. 23–31.
Rogoff, Barbara. "Learning by Observing and Pitching In to Family and Community Endeavors: An Orientation." *Human Development*, vol. 57, no. 2–3, 2014, pp. 69–81, https://doi.org/10.1159/000356757.
Ruiz, Ramón Eduardo. *Mexico: Why a Few Are Rich and the People Poor*. U of California P, 2010.
Rulfo, Juan. *Pedro Páramo*. Fondo de Cultura Económica, 1955.
Sabugal, Eduardo. "Pensar y escribir doble. Conversación con Martín Tonalmeyotl." *Neotraba: From Puebla to the Mundo*, 16 April 2020, https://neotraba.com/pensar-y-escribir-doble-conversacion-con-martin-tonalmeyotl/.
Saldaña-Portillo, María Josefina. *Indian Given: Racial Geographies across Mexico and the United States*. Duke UP, 2016.
———. "Indians Have Always Been Modern: *Roma*, the Settler Colonial Paradigm, and Latinx Temporality." *Aztlán: A Journal of Chicano Studies*, vol. 45, no. 2, Fall 2020, pp. 221–40.
Sánchez, Karla. "Entrevista a Yásnaya Elena A. Gil: 'La lengua tiene una carga política.'" *Letras Libres*, 1 March 2021, https://letraslibres.com/revista/entrevista-a-yasnaya-elena-a-gil-la-lengua-tiene-una-carga-politica/.
Sánchez de la Rosa, Alejandro. "Entre la espada y la pared: la literatura indígena." *La hoja de arena*, March 2014, http://www.lahojadearena.com/entre-la-espada-la-pared-la-literatura-indigena/.
Sandstrom, Alan R. *Corn Is Our Blood: Culture and Ethnic Identity in a Contemporary Aztec Indian Village*. U of Oklahoma P, 1991.
Sandstrom, Alan R., and Pamela Effrein Sandstrom. *Pilgrimage to Broken Mountain: Nahua Sacred Journeys in Mexico's Huasteca Veracruzana*. UP of Colorado, 2023.
Sanjinés C., Javier. *Embers of the Past: Essays in Times of Decolonization*. Duke UP, 2013.
———. *Mestizaje Upside-Down: Aesthetic Politics in Modern Bolivia*. U of Pittsburgh P, 2004.
Santopietro, Judith. "Iguanazul." *The Brooklyn Rail: Critical Perspectives on Arts, Politics, and Culture*, translated by Sixto Cabrera González, April 2015, https://brooklynrail.org/2015/04/criticspage/iguanazul.
———. "Migrantes nahuas celebran a Santiago Apóstol: Un ejercicio de comunalidad en Nueva York." *Transfiguraciones de danzas tradicionales: Ensayos y entrevistas*, Universidad Autónoma de Chiapas, 2017, pp. 176–207.
———. *Palabras de agua*. Praxis, 2010.
———. Personal interview. 10 September 2013.
———. Personal interview. 9 December 2013.
———. *Se incendia la palabra*. Instituto Municipal de Arte y Cultura de Puebla, 2008.

Schroeder, Susan. "The Annals of Chimalpahin." *Sources and Methods for the Study of Postconquest Mesoamerican Ethnohistory*, edited by James Lockhart and Lisa Sousa, University of Oregon Wired Humanities Project, 2008, pp. 1–11.

———. "The Truth about the Crónica Mexicayotl." *Colonial Latin American Review*, vol. 20, no. 2, 2011, pp. 233–47.

Schryer, Frans J. *Ethnicity and Class Conflict in Rural Mexico*. Princeton UP, 1990.

Secretaría de Comunicaciones y Transportes. *Ley Federal de Telecomunicaciones y Radiodifusión*. 14 July 2014, http://www.diputados.gob.mx/LeyesBiblio/ref/lftr/LFTR_orig_14jul14.pdf.

———. *Decreto por el que se reforma el artículo 230 de la Ley Federal de Telecomunicaciones y Radiodifusión*. 1 June 2016, http://www.diputados.gob.mx/LeyesBiblio/ref/lftr/LFTR_ref03_01jun16.pdf.

Secretaría de Educación Pública. *Delegaciones estatales*. SEP, 1982.

———. *Organismos*. SEP, 1982.

———. *Política educativa*. SEP, 1982.

Seefoo, Jennifer. "Escuadrón 421 llega a Cataluña y la bautiza a Cataluña como 'Tierra insumisa.'" *Milenio*, 7 July 2021, https://www.milenio.com/internacional/ezln-escuadron-421-bautiza-cataluna-tierra-insumisa.

Sell, Sean S., and Nicolás Huet Bautista, editors. *Chiapas Maya Awakening: Contemporary Poems and Short Stories*. Translated by Sean S. Sell, U of Oklahoma P, 2017.

Simic, Charles. "Stone." *PBS LearningMedia*, https://www.pbslearningmedia.org/resource/pe11.rla.genre.poetry.simstone/stone-by-charles-simic/. Accessed 1 May 2023.

Simpson, Leanne Betasamosake. *As We Have Always Done: Indigenous Freedom through Radical Resistance*. U of Minnesota P, 2021.

LXIII Legislatura, "Ley Federal de Telecomunicaciones y Radiodifusión." *Cámara de Diputados*, n.d., http://www.diputados.gob.mx/LeyesBiblio/ref/lftr.htm. Accessed 18 November 2023.

Smith, Andrea. "Indigenous Feminism without Apology." *Unsettling Ourselves: Reflections and Resources for Deconstructing Colonial Mentality: A Sourcebook Compiled by Unsettling Minnesota*, edited by UM Collective Members, 2009, pp. 159–61, http://unsettlingminnesota.files.wordpress.com/2009/11/um_sourcebook_jan10_revision.pdf.

Smith, Linda Tuhiwai. *Decolonizing Methodologies: Research and Indigenous Peoples*. 2nd ed., Palgrave Macmillan, 2012.

Smith, Paul Chaat. *Everything You Know about Indians Is Wrong*. U of Minnesota P, 2009.

Solana, Fernando, editor. *Historia de la educación pública en México*. Fondo de Cultura Económica, 1981.

Solís, Patricio, et al. *Por mi raza hablará la desigualdad: Efectos de las características étnico-raciales en la desigualdad de oportunidades en México*. Oxfam México, 2019, https://dds.cepal.org/redesoc/publicacion?id=5051.

Sousa, Lisa. "The Devil and Deviance in Native Criminal Narratives from Early Mexico." *The Americas*, vol. 59, no. 2, October 2002, pp. 161–79, https://doi.org/10.1353/tam.2002.0123.
Speed, Shannon. *Incarcerated Stories: Indigenous Women Migrants and Violence in the Settler-Capitalist State*. U of North Carolina P, 2019.
———. "Structures of Settler Capitalism in Abya Yala." *American Quarterly*, vol. 69, no. 4, December 2017, pp. 783–90.
Spiers, Miriam C. Brown. *Encountering the Sovereign Other: Indigenous Science Fiction*. Michigan State UP, 2021.
Spivak, Gayatri Chakravorty. *Death of a Discipline*. Columbia UP, 2003.
———. "The Politics of Translation." *The Translation Studies Reader*, edited by Lawrence Venuti, 3rd ed., Routledge UP, 2012, pp. 312–30.
Stephen, Lynn. "The Construction of Indigenous Suspects: Militarization and the Gendered and Ethnic Dynamics of Human Rights Abuses in Southern Mexico." *American Ethnologist*, vol. 26, no. 4, 1999, pp. 822–42.
———. *Transborder Lives: Indigenous Oaxacans in Mexico, California, and Oregon*. 2nd ed., Duke UP, 2007.
Suslak, Daniel F. "Ayapan Echoes: Linguistic Persistence and Loss in Tabasco, Mexico." *American Anthropologist*, vol. 113, no. 4, 2011, pp. 569–81.
Suzack, Cheryl, and Shari M. Huhndorf. "Indigenous Feminism: Theorizing the Issues." *Indigenous Women and Feminism: Politics, Activism, Culture*, edited by Cheryl Suzack et al., U of Chicago P, 2011, pp. 1–19.
Tarica, Estelle. *The Inner Life of Mestizo Nationalism*. U of Minnesota P, 2008.
Tavárez, David. *The Invisible War: Indigenous Devotions, Discipline, and Dissent in Colonial Mexico*. Stanford UP, 2011.
Taylor, Diana. *The Archive and the Repertoire: Performing Cultural Memory in the Americas*. Duke UP, 2003.
———. "Dancing with the Zapatistas." *Dancing with the Zapatistas: Twenty Years Later*, edited by Diana Taylor and Lorie Novak, Duke UP, 2015, https://scalar.usc.edu/anvc/dancing-with-the-zapatistas/zapatistas.
Taylor, Diana, and Sarah J. Townsend, editors. *Stages of Conflict: A Critical Anthology of Latin American Theater and Performance*. U of Michigan P, 2008.
Taylor, Melanie Benson. "Indigenous Interruptions in the Anthropocene." *PMLA/Publications of the Modern Language Association of America*, vol. 136, no. 1, 1, 2021, pp. 9–16, https://doi.org/10.1632/S0030812920000139.
Taylor, William B. *Drinking, Homicide, and Rebellion in Colonial Mexican Villages*. Stanford UP, 1979.
Terán, Víctor, and David Shook, editors. *Like a New Sun: New Indigenous Mexican Poetry*. Phoneme Media, 2015.
Tigres en la montaña, petición de lluvia en la montaña de Guerrero. Instituto Nacional de Antropología e Historia, https://www.youtube.com/watch?v=3KutI3eaoXU.

Tlahtolxitlauhquetl tlen Chicontepec, Veracruz. 2012.
Todd, Zoe. "An Indigenous Feminist's Take on the Ontological Turn: 'Ontology' Is Just Another Word for Colonialism." *Journal of Historical Sociology*, vol. 29, no. 1, March 2016, pp. 4–22.
Tonalmeyotl, Martín. "Guerrero: Autores en lenguas originarias." *Ojarasca*, no. 245, September 2017, pp. 14–15.
———. "Literaturas en lengua náhuatl." *Enciclopedia de la Literatura en México de la Fundación para las Letras Mexicanas*, 4 October 2020, http://www.elem.mx/estgrp/datos/1363.
———. *Nosentlalilxochitlajtol / Antología personal*. Colección Colores Primarios, 2017.
———. Personal interview. 6 November 2019.
———. "Poems from Tlalkatsajtsilistle/Ritual of the Forgotten." *Latin American Literature Today*, translated by Whitney DeVos, vol. 1, no. 13, February 2020, http://www.latinamericanliteraturetoday.org/en/2020/february/poems-%C2%A0tlalkatsajtsilistleritual-forgotten-mart%C3%ADn-tonalmeyotl.
———. "Poesía contemporánea en lengua náhuatl." *In xochitl in kuikatl: 24 poetas contemporáneos en lengua náhuatl*, Fundación Universidad de las Américas Puebla, 2020, pp. 12–19.
———. "Poesía indígena sufre de 'inexistencia,' afirma Martín Tonalmeyotl." Interview with Magdiel Olano. *Leviatán*, 2 December 2019, https://leviatan.mx/2019/12/02/poesia-indigena-sufre-de-inexistencia-afirma-martin-tonalmeyotl/.
———. "¿Qué ganamos los pueblos originarios? Ante el triunfo de López Obrador." *Ojarasca*, July 2018, p. 4.
———. *Ritual de los olvidados / Tlalkatsajtsilistle*. Jaguar Ediciones, 2016.
———. "Three Náhuatl Poems from Mexico." *World Literature Today*, translated by Whitney DeVos, 18 November 2020, https://www.worldliteraturetoday.org/blog/poetry/three-nahuatl-poems-mexico-martin-tonalmeyotl.
Tonalmeyotl, Martín, editor. *Flor de siete pétalos: Espina florida de siete poetas mexicanas*. Ediciones del Espejo Somos, 2019.
———, editor. *Xochitlajtoli: Poesía contemporánea en lenguas originarias de México*. Círculo de Poesía, 2019.
Torres, Jacinta Toribio. "Ixtlamatilistli: Las mujeres en la formación de la niñez de Tepenahuac, Veracruz." *La Palabra y el Hombre. Revista de la Universidad Veracruzana*, no. 60, June 2022, pp. 34–38.
Truitt, Jonathan. "Courting Catholicism: Nahua Women and the Catholic Church in Colonial Mexico City." *Ethnohistory*, vol. 57, no. 3, Summer 2010, pp. 415–44, https://doi.org/10.1215/00141801-.
———. *Sustaining the Divine in Mexico Tenochtitlan: Nahuas and Catholicism, 1523–1700*. U of Oklahoma P, 2018.

Trujillo, Javier. "Mujer irrumpe en evento de Rigoberta Menchú en Acapulco." *Milenio*, 29 May 2015, https://www.milenio.com/estados/mujer-irrumpe-evento-rigoberta-menchu-acapulco.

UN DESA. "Protecting Languages, Preserving Cultures." *United Nations*, May 2016, https://www.un.org/en/desa/protecting-languages-preserving-cultures-0.

Vargas, Marcela. "10 poetas en lenguas indígenas que necesitas conocer." *Nodal cultura: Noticias de América Latina y el Caribe*, 7 March 2019, https://www.nodalcultura.am/2019/02/poesia-indigena/?fbclid=IwAR31vCoQqETHHnrZ82eYlOJ-0FcWpW9Pvk0OhEwuDYMNm_jAEfbhXWjDyco.

Varner, Natasha. *La raza cosmética: Beauty, Identity, and Settler Colonialism in Postrevolutionary Mexico*. U of Arizona P, 2020.

Vila, Adrián R. "Ediciones cartoneras latinoamericanas en tiempos de transposición a digital." *Revista chilena de literatura*, no. 94, December 2016, pp. 119–43, http://dx.doi.org/10.4067/S0718-22952016000300007.

Villarreal, Andrés. "Stratification by Skin Color in Contemporary Mexico." *American Sociological Review*, vol. 75, no. 5, October 2010, pp. 652–78.

Villela F., Samuel, editor. *Los pueblos indígenas de Guerrero: Atlas etnográfico*. Secretaría de Cultura, 2021.

Vizenor, Gerald. *Manifest Manners: Narratives on Postindian Survivance*. Bison Books, 1999.

Ward, Thomas. *Decolonizing Indigeneity: New Approaches to Latin American Literature*. Lexington Books, 2017.

Warrior, Robert Allen. "'The Finest Men We Have Ever Seen': Hemispheric Thoughts on Jefferson, Humboldt, and the Osages." Institute for Advanced Study Series, 30 January 2020, University of Minnesota Twin Cities, Minneapolis, MN. Featured speaker presentation.

———. *The People and the Word: Reading Native Nonfiction*. U of Minnesota P, 2005.

———. *Tribal Secrets: Recovering American Indian Intellectual Traditions*. U of Minnesota P, 1995.

Washinawatok, Ingrid. "Sovereignty as a Birthright." *Indigenous Women Address the World: Our Future–Our Responsibility*, North American Indigenous Women's Working Group, 1995, pp. 12–13.

Wilson-Hokowhitu, Nālani, editor. "Introduction: I Ka Wā Mamua, the Past before Us." *The Past before Us: Moʻokūʻauhau as Methodology*, U of Hawaiʻi P, 2019, pp. 1–8.

———, editor. *The Past before Us: Moʻokūʻauhau as Methodology*. U of Hawaii P, 2019.

Wired Humanities Projects. "Cihuatl." *Online Nahuatl Dictionary*, https://nahuatl.wired-humanities.org/content/cihuatl. Accessed 1 May 2023.

Wood, Stephanie. "Gender and Town Guardianship in Mesoamerica: Direction for Future Research." *Journal de la société des américanistes*, vol. 84, no. 2, 1998, pp. 243–76.

Worley, Paul M. "Máseual Excluido/Indio Permitido: Neoliberal Translation in Waldemar Noh Tzec." *Latin American and Caribbean Ethnic Studies*, vol. 12, no. 3, 2017, pp. 290–314.
———. *Telling and Being Told: Storytelling and Cultural Control in Contemporary Yucatec Maya Literatures*. U of Arizona P, 2013.
———. "U páajtalil maaya ko'olel: Briceida Cuevas Cob's Je' Bix K'in and the Rights of Maya Women." *A Contracorriente: Una Revista de Estudios Latinoamericanos*, vol. 10, no. 3, Spring 2013, pp. 141–70.
Worley, Paul M., and Rita M. Palacios. *Des-escribir la literatura maya: Una propuesta desde el ts'íib*. 2019, https://hcommons.org/deposits/item/hc:25525.
———. *Unwriting Maya Literature: Ts'íib as Recorded Knowledge*. U of Arizona P, 2019.
Xochitiotzin Pérez, Ethel. Personal interview. 10 February 2013.
———. *Tlaoxticah in tlahtolli*. U of Warsaw P, 2019.
———. *Tlaoxtika in Tlajtol / Desgranando la palabra: Poesía náhuatl*. 2012.
Yanes, Pablo. "Mexico's Targeted and Conditional Transfers: Between Oportunidades and Rights." *Economic and Political Weekly*, vol. 46, no. 21, 2011, pp. 49–54.
Yasnaya Elena [@YasnayaEG]. "No estoy llorando, es sólo que se me metió al ojo un poema de @mardoniocarbalo sobre la muerte de su madre, Anatolia." *Twitter*, 27 November 2019, https://twitter.com/YasnayaEG/status/1199775457840967680.
Yellow Bird, Michael, et al. "Defunding Mindfulness: While We Sit on Our Cushions, Systemic Racism Runs Rampant." *Zero to Three*, 30 October 2020, https://www.zerotothree.org/resources/3715-perspectives-defunding-mindfulness-while-we-sit-on-our-cushions-systemic-racism-runs-rampant.
Zaid, Gabriel. *Omnibus de poesía mexicana*. 8th ed., Siglo Veintiuno, 1980.
Zamora, Daniel, and Michael C. Behrent, editors. *Foucault and Neoliberalism*. Polity, 2015.
Zapoteco Sideño, Gustavo. *Cantos en el cañaveral / Cuicatl pan tlalliouatlmej*. JM Impresiones, 2004.
———. Personal interview. 20 June 2010.
Zea, Leopoldo. *Positivism in Mexico*. Translated by Josephine H. Schulte, U of Texas P, 1974.

Index

Note: Page numbers in *italic type* refer to illustrative matter.

A^2 + C rock group, 217
Abejas Civil Society, 213
Abram, Philip, 174
Abrams, D. Sam, 232
"Achtlitonaltsin" (Xochitiotzin), 131, 148–51
acoustic ecology, 183–84, 199, 219, 227, 254
"Acteal y futbol, la noticia del día" (Carballo), 213
activism. *See* social activism
affective intelligence, 17, 63–67, 84, 89–98, 119, 231–39, 258. *See also* emotional intelligence
Aguilar Gil, Yásnaya Elena, 84, 88, 100–101, 120, 162, 174, 214, 230, 238
Ak'abal, Humberto, 89, 96, 245
Alianza Nacional de Profesionales Indígenas Bilingües (ANPIBAC), 28
Allen, Chadwick, 71
Alonso, Ana D., 248–49
Altamirano, Ignacio Manuel, 26
Alvarado Tezozomoc, Fernando de, 25
"América invertida" / "Inverted America" (Torres García), 259–60

American Indian boarding schools, 162–63
Amoch Libros, 189
"Amo xchiua" / "Recomendación" (Tonalmeyotl), 110–12
Anderson, Arthur J. O., 25
Ángel Asturias, Miguel, 197–98
anti-coyotialismo, 56–63
ants, 193
Anzaldúa, Gloria, 20, 200, 210
appropriation, 2, 4, 8, 16, 185, 226, 257
Arias, Arturo, 7, 10–11, 38–39
Aristegui, Carmen, 2, 187, 189–90, 222
arte del cuerpo, 240
Así habló el ahuehuete (Hernández), 44–45
assimilationist project, 37–38, 80–81, 177. *See also* colonialism; nationalist project
Association of Indigenous-Language Writers (ELIAC), 30
Australian Aborigines, 162
Ayotzinapa (Escuela Normal Rural Raúl Isidro Burgos), 103–6, 219, 221, 223–24, 234, 235, 263, 297n5

333

Aztec, as term, 6, 22–23
Aztlan, 22

Barlow, Robert, 27
Benjamin Luna, 13
Blackhawk, Ned, 82, 112
Brave New World (Huxley), 44
Broken Spears (León Portilla), 27
The Brooklyn Rail (publication), 163
Brooks, Lisa, 56

Cabañas Barrientos, Lucio, 29
Cabrera González, Sixto, 34, 164, 166, 170
Cadena, Marisol de la, 2
Calderón, Felipe, 85, 263
Cantares mexicanos, 25, 26, 44
Canto nuevo de Anáhuac (Hernández), 45
Carballo, Mardonio: "Acteal y futbol, la noticia del día," 213; "Corazón piedra," 199–202; "¿Cuánto pesa un muerto?," 217; "Ida y vuelta: Jornaleros indígenas," 209; "Las lenguas toman la tribuna," 219–20; "Los idiomas tienen sus secretos," 206; "Maguey Maguaquite, 1980," 214–15; "Manos en armonía," 202–3; metaphor and migration of, 8; Nahuatl language and, 1–2, 10, 83; Nahua women writers and, 127; "La otra campaña," 209; "Otro calor de aliento," 208; "Otro muerto...," 215–17; "Padres de maíz," 197–99; *Las Plumas de la Serpiente* (essay collection), 1, 10, 182–87, 188–222; *Las Plumas de la Serpiente* (radio short series), 2, 5, 183, 186–87; production company of, 5; on Queer studies, 266; on Quetzalcoatl, 4, 20; *La raíz doble*, 22, 186; "El regreso," 197

Cárcamo Huechante, Luis, 182, 183, 184, 227, 254
carnicero, 96
Carrillo Tieco, Fabiola, 124, 126, 127, 128
Casa de la Cultura de Juchitán, 29
Castilian language, 5, 9–10; Aguilar Gil on *we* in, 100–101; Carballo and, 189, 191, 192, 193, 198, 200, 203, 206, 219; Hernández and, 37, 65; Santopietro and, 159, 160, 163, 165, 166, 169, 171, 173, 175–78; Xochitiotzin and, 130
Cata, Victor, 157
Ceh Moo, Marisol, 155
Centro Estatal de Lenguas, Arte y Literatura (CELALI), 30
Chacón, Gloria Elizabeth, 7
Cherokee Nation, 3, 178–79
"Chichetlaltipak" / "Tierra de perros" (Tonalmeyotl), 91–94
chichi, 92, 93
Chikomexochitl, 12, 72
Chimalpahin Quauhtlehuanitzin, Domingo de San Antón Muñón, 24, 25
Chimalpopoca, Faustino Galicia, 26
Círculo de la palabra (publication), 127
Círculo de poesía (publication), 31, 87
city/town binary, 67–68
"Ciudades de arrecife" (Santopietro), 165
CNI (National Indigenous Congress), 161
Coalition of Workers, Peasants, and Students of the Isthmus (COCEI), 28, 29
Codex Chimalpahin, 25
Cohen, Matt, 185
Colección Letras Mayas Contemporáneas, 30

Colectiva Editorial de Mujeres en Prisión Hermanas en la Sombra, 123
"Colonial Borders, Native Fences" (Gonzales), 163
colonialism: as neoliberal multicriminalism, 80–82; population decline due to, 23
colonialismo, 56–63
Comanche, 22
communalism, 7
conjugated, defined, 17
Consejo Nacional para la Cultura y las Artes (CONACULTA), 262, 263
contrapunteo, 185, 205
Contrapunteo del tabaco y el azúcar (Ortiz), 185
"Corazón piedra" (Carballo), 199–202
corn aesthetic, 50–56. *See also* maize
Cortés, Hernán, 58, 93, 120
Cortés Ixtlilxochitl, Fernando de Alva, 25
Creegan Miller, Tiffany D., 245
Crónica Mexicayotl (Alvarado Tezozomoc), 25
Cruz, Zabina, 128
"¿Cuánto pesa un muerto?" (Carballo), 217
cuatrapeado, 14
Cuentos en náhuatl de Doña Luz Jiménez (Jiménez), 27
cultural pluralism, 245
Cumes, Aura, 120
Cusicanqui, Silvia Rivera, 21, 164, 220

Davis, Angela, 258
Day of the Dead, 72, 103, 136–39, 193, 241
Decade of Indigenous Languages (2022–2032), 10
decolonialization, 21
decoyotlization, 61

de la Cruz, Abelardo, 8, 173
de la Cruz, Eduardo, 8
de la Cruz, Sabina, 8
de la Cruz, Victor, 29, 45
Delgado Pop, Adela, 157
Deloria, Philip J., 196
Deloria, Vine, 56
de Molina, Alonso, 23
De Porfirio Díaz a Zapata (Jiménez), 27
deracination, 160, 226
De raíz luna (television program), 22
de Sahagún, Bernardino, 25
descolonialization, 21, 113, 120, 121, 164
Descripción histórica de Tepoztlán (Villamil), 27
dialecto, 2, 13
dispossession, 80–82, 121, 184
"Donde nace el arcoíris" (Xochitiotzin Pérez), 116
Dowling, Sarah, 185, 186
drum, 255

Echo Hawk, Crystal, 121
Ejército Zapatista de Liberación Nacional (EZLN) uprising (1994), 30–31, 85, 164, 165, 174, 205, 209–13
ELIAC, 30, 31, 44–45
Emeequis (publication), 192
emotional intelligence, 7, 94, 284n33. *See also* affective intelligence
Emotional Intelligence (Goleman), 94
epistemicide, 14
Erdrich, Louise, 255
Los escritores indígenas actuales (publication), 30
Escuela Normal Rural Raúl Isidro Burgos. *See* Ayotzinapa
escuelas normales, 223, 297n2. *See also* Ayotzinapa

Espinosa, Miguel Barrios, 27
"Estela de voces" / "Neskayo tlajtoltij" (Santopietro), 164, 166, 167–71
Estudios de Cultura Náhuatl (publication), 27, 28, 75, 117, 156
Ēxcān Tlahtōlōyan, 22–23
extinct Indian trope, 3, 126, 177–79, 271n24, 298n11

face knowledge. *See* ixtlamatilistli
face-text. *See* ixtli
la facultad, 20, 200
Federal Telecommunications Law (Mexico), 184
femicide, 166
feminism, 120–21, 155–56
Festival de Poesía: Las Lenguas de América (biennial), 31
Flor de Noche Buena, 123
Flor de siete pétalos (anthology), 32, 127
The Florentine Codex, 25
Flores de primavera (Hernández), 45
Flores Farfán, José Antonio, 87
flowered songs, 25
Fondo Nacional para la Cultura y las Artes (FONCA), 30
forward observance, 266
Freddy Luna, 13
Freire, Paulo, 14
Frischmann, Donald, 31
Fundación Macuilxochitl, 10

Galeano, Eduardo, 164
García, Fidel, 209–10
García, Jaimeduardo, 262
García Lorca, Federico, 196
Garibay, Ángel María, 40–41
Gatica Matías, Anna Yamel. *See* Miyawatl, Ateri
gender discrimination, 123, 155–56. *See also* Nahua women writers

Glissant, Édouard, 185–86
Goeman, Mishuana, 218
Gonzales, Sandra, 163
Green, Joyce, 120–21
Guchachi' Reza (publication), 29
Guernica (Picasso), 196
Guerrero maize fields, 86–90
Guie' sti' diidxazá / Flor de la palabra (de la Cruz), 29

Hale, Charles, 80
Hall, Lisa Kahaleole, 16
harmony, 75, 80, 85
heart strength. *See* yolchikaualistli
Henestrosa, Andrés, 29
Hernández, Eneida, 13, 16, 19, 21, 260
Hernández, Juan, 265
Hernández, Natalio, 37–77; about, 41–46, 197, 266; *Así habló el ahuehuete*, 44–45; *Canto nuevo de Anáhuac*, 45; civil career of, 43–44, 45; de la Cruz and, 29; *Flores de primavera*, 45; "Iknotlajtoli," 40–41, 47, 50–56; influences of, 44; *Itoscac ahuehuetl*, 45; as leader of Fundación Macuilxochitl, 10, 13, 28; "Na ni indio," 37, 56–63; "Noihqui toaxca caxtilan tlahtoli," 75; *Ohtocani*, 26; *Papalocuicatl*, 45; *Patlani huitzitzilin*, 26, 39–40, 45, 46–50, 67–74, 75–77, 197; *Semanca huitzilin*, 45, 75; "Sempoalxochitl," 45, 47–48, 50, 72–73; *Tlilamatl*, 45; *Universo de las hilanderas*, 19; *Xochikoskatl*, 11, 37, 38–42, 45–50, 71, 75–77, 261
Hernández Castillo, Aída, 124
Hidalgo, Miguel, 26
"Los hijos de la Malinche" (Paz), 115, 116
Historia de la nación chichimeca (Cortés Ixtlilxochitl), 25

Hobsbawm, Eric, 22
Horcasitas, Fernando, 27
Huasteca, as term, 45–46. *See also* knowledge production

I Ching, 164
"Ida y vuelta: Jornaleros indígenas" (Carballo), 209
Iguanazul (publication), 163
Iguanazul publishing house, 10
"Iknotlajtoli" (Hernández), 40–41, 47, 50–56
INALI (Instituto Nacional de Lenguas Indígenas), 161–62, 263
indígena, as term, 24, 84
Indigeneity and language, 162–63. *See also* Nahuatl language
Indigenous agency, 44–45, 49–50
Indigenous feminism, 120
"Indigenous Interruptions in the Anthropocene" (Taylor), 257
"Indigenous literatures," as category, 29, 31, 41–42, 45, 122, 220, 262–63, 265, 302n7
Indigenous methodologies, 16
indio, as term, 24, 61
Institute of Zapotec Language, 29
Instituto de Docencia e Investigación Etnológica de Zacatecas (IDIEZ), 13
Instituto Nacional de Antropología e Historia (INAH), 43
Instituto Nacional Indigenista, 30
"Intajtsitsiuan ayotsitsintin no uelej patlanej" / "Los padres de las tortugas también saben volar" (Tonalmeyotl), 103–4
intellectual, as term, 7
intellectual rights, 15–21
interculturality, 42, 72, 74, 76, 80, 259
intergenerational trauma, 83–84
intersectionality, 2, 7, 8, 185, 220

"In tlazinque" (Carrillo Tieco), 126
"In tonal tomiketsitsi" (Xochitiotzin), 131, 133–36
intuition, 20, 42, 277n10
invented tradition, 22
In xinachtli in tlahtolli: Amoxtli Zazanilli (Carrillo Tieco), 127
"Itlan tlayouisyotl" / "Bajo la noche" (Tonalmeyotl), 96–97
Itoscac ahuehuetl (Hernández), 45
ixtlamatilistli, 2, 3, 15, 38, 117
ixtli, 17
"Ixtololotsin tlen kitsakuilia ixayak tonantsi intlali" (Xochitiotzin), 131, 141–44
"Izcaltitla" (Santopietro), 159, 165, 166, 171–76

Jansen, Anne Mai Yee, 39
Jean-François, Emmanuel Bruno, 221–22
Jiménez González, Julia (Doña Luz), 10, 27, 117, 156
La Journada (publication), 31–32, 87, 90, 127
La Journada Semanal (publication), 128
"Jueves kuak nokua posojle" / "Jueves de pozole" (Tonalmeyotl), 105–6
Justice, Daniel Heath, 3

"Kanik tlakati in kosemalotl" (Xochitiotzin), 131, 136–39
Karttunen, Frances, 116, 117, 156
"Kaxtiltecakah in Tenochtitlan ihuan Tlacoltica Yohualli" (Rojas), 27
Keme, Emil', 258
knowledge production, 3, 6–7, 12–13, 21, 39, 50–56
"Kuak nikneke ninokuikatis" / "Intento de melodía" (Tonalmeyotl), 79, 109–10

kuali iyolo, 17
kuikakali, 52–53

El laberinto de la soledad (Paz), 196
land theft, 81, 121, 184. *See also* dispossession; violence over the land
language and Indigeneity, 162–63. *See also* Nahuatl language
Laó-Montes, Agustín, 185
Latin American Studies Association (LASA), 7–8
The Learned Ones (McDonough), 9, 10
"Las lenguas toman la tribuna" campaign, 219–20
León Portilla, Miguel, 17, 25, 40
LGBTQ Nahuas, 156–57, 188, 266
linguicide, 14
López Austin, Alfredo, 190
López Obrador, Andrés Manuel, 263
Los de abajo (Azuela), 26
"Los idiomas tienen sus secretos" (Carballo), 206
Lucero, José Antonio, 71

Macuilxochitl Cultural Foundation, 13
Maguaquite, 5
"Maguey Maguaquite, 1980" (Carballo), 214–15
maize, 4, 21, 120, 139–51, 176, 198–99. *See also* corn aesthetic
male dominance, 115–18, 121, 155–56
"Malinalli" (Xochitiotzin), 131
Malinche, 120
Malintzin, 116, 117, 137, 138–39, 142, 143
Manning, Erin, 66
"Manos en armonía" (Carballo), 202–3
manual labor, 17, 57, 81, 182, 188
mapache, 174–79

"Maquiztli" (Rojas), 27
Marcus, George E., 94
Martín Alcoff, Linda, 201
Martínez, Bety, 8
Martínez Nopaltécatl, Isabel. *See* Metztli Nopaltecatl, Yankuik
Matías García, Yolanda, 124
Matiúwàa, Hubert, 88, 94, 177
Matthews, Gerald, 94
May, Miguel Ángel, 29–30
Maya, Ildefonso, 10
Le Maya Q'atzij / Our Maya World (Keme), 11
Maya Yucatec, 30
McCallum, Pamela, 255
McDonough, Kelly S., 7, 9, 10, 24
media colonialism, 184
media sensationalism, 229–30
Menchú, Rigoberta, 223–25, 226, 229
Messing, Jacqueline, 129, 149
mestizaje, 81, 160, 169
Metztli Nopaltecatl, Yankuik, 124–26
Mexican Constitution, 62
Mexican language, as term, 61
mexicanoh/mejikanoj, 23, 37, 38, 61
Mexican Republic, 6
Mexican Revolution (1910–), 26
Mexican War of Independence (1810–1821), 26
Mexicas, 5, 22
Mexica Tenochca, 25
Mexico, as term, 216
México: Diversas lenguas, una sola nación (ELIAC), 31, 124
Mexihcatl itonalama (publication), 27
Mexihcayotl (publication), 27
Mexihco-Tenochtitlan, 5, 47–48
Mexijko, 22
Meyer, Manulani Aluli, 18–19
Mezcala-Solidaridad Bridge, 257
Mijkailuitl, 72

Miyawatl, Ateri, 127, 155, 224;
  *Neijmantototsintle / La tristesa és
  un ocell / Sadness Is a Bird,* 225–45;
  Tsintatak, 226–28, 244–56
Modernity project, 3, 161, 260
moikxipejpena, 18, 218
Montemayor, Carlos, 30, 31
mo'okū'auhau, 18
Morelitos, 123
multicriminalism, 80
Muñoz Corona, Calixta, 128
"Músicas" (Carballo), 205
muxe, 266

NAFTA (North American Free Trade
  Agreement), 30
Nahua, as term, 23–24
Nahua identity: Santopietro on,
  167–79; Xochitiotzin on, 151–54.
  See also Nahuas, overview; Nahuatl
  language
nahuales, 159, 160, 163, 173, 174,
  175, 176–79
Nahua methodologies, 15–21
Nahuas, overview, 5–6, 22–32, 188.
  See also Nahua identity; Nahuatl
  language
Nahua Studies, 9–12
Nahuatl language, 5, 9–10; language
  family of, 254–55; as lingua franca,
  23–24; Miyawatl's work and,
  254–56; prevalence of speakers in,
  116; racial discrimination by the
  state and, 123; romanticization
  of, 1–2; Santopietro's work and,
  159–63, 177–79. *See also* language
  and Indigeneity; Nahua identity
Nahuatl-Spanish xochitlajtoli. *See*
  xochitlajtoli
Nahua women writers, 115–18,
  123–28, 154–57
Nahuaxochimilli (Valenzuela), 27

"Na ni indio" (Hernández), 37, 56–63
Narrativa náhuatl contemporánea
  (publication), 30
National Electoral Institute (INE), 224
National Indigenista Institute (INI),
  76
nationalist project, 3, 6, 40, 74, 112–
  13, 177–78. *See also* assimilationist
  project
nation-state independence
  movements, 24, 61, 121. *See also*
  Tlaoxtika in tlajtoli (Xochitiotzin
  Pérez)
Native Studies, 9–12
nauyaca, 5
Nauyaca Producciones, 5
Nechicoliztli Zohuatlahtolxochitl, 128
Nechikolistli tlen Nauatlajtouaj
  Maseualtlamachtiane, 28
*Neijmantototsintle / La tristesa és un
  ocell / Sadness Is a Bird* (Miyawatl),
  225–45
nemilistli, 16
neoliberal multicriminalism, 80, 82,
  102–7
neoliberal multiculturalism, 80, 109
"Nestora Salgado" (Tonalmeyotl), 104–5
Neza (publication), 29
"Niknekiskia" (Xochitiotzin), 131,
  139–41
"Nipeua nixtentlapoue" / "Primeros
  párpados" (Tonalmeyotl), 98–100
Nishnaabeg, Michi Saagiig, 121
"Noihqui toaxca caxtilan tlahtoli"
  (Hernández), 75
noixmatkauaj, 18
nokuamekayo, 18
"Nonauatlajtol" / "Mi lengua náhuatl"
  (Tonalmeyotl), 107–12
noneluayo, 18
*Nosentlalilxochitlajtol / Antología
  personal* (Tonalmeyotl), 87

notlaltipak, 91–92
"Notlaltsin" / "Mi tierra" (Tonalmeyotl), 101
notsonyo, 18
Nueva York Poetry (publication), 31
Nussbaum, Martha, 65

Ohtocani (Hernández), 26
Ombligo de tierra (radio program), 22, 87
One Hundred Years of Solitude (García Márquez), 193
onomatopoeia, 207, 244, 245, 248
Oportunidades welfare program, 122–23
Organization of Nahua Indigenous Professionals Civil Association (OPINAC), 28, 43
Originaria, 127, 155, 231
Ortiz, Fernando, 185
Osorio Cruz, José Guadalupe, 26, 71
"La otra campaña" (Carballo), 209
"Otro calor de aliento" (Carballo), 208
"Otro muerto..." (Carballo), 215–17
Otros Saberes Congress, 7–8
Our Fire Survives the Storm (Justice), 3

"Padres de maíz" (Carballo), 197–99
The Painted Drum (Erdrich), 255
"Painting the Archive" (McCallum), 255
Palabras de agua (Santopietro), 127, 159–79; about publication, 163–67; "Estela de voces" / "Neskayo tlajtoltij," 164, 166, 167–71; "Izcaltitla," 159, 165, 166, 171–76; on Nahua identity, 167–79; "Proética," 166–67; "Raíz de vuelo," 164
Palacios, Rita M., 4, 185
Papalocuicatl (Hernández), 45

Partido de los Pobres, 29
The Past before Us (Meyer), 18–19
Patlani (Hernández), 165
Patlani, Araceli, 127
Patlani huitzitzilin (Hernández), 26, 38, 39–40, 45, 46–50, 67–74, 75–77, 197
patriarchy, 121–22
Patricio Martínez, María de Jesús (Marichuy), 161, 162
patrimonio, 199
Paz, Octavio, 115, 116, 196
Pedagogy of the Oppressed (Freire), 14
Peña Nieto, Enrique, 263
Pérez López, Enrique, 30
Pessoa, Fernando, 211
Pierce, Joseph, 178
Pineda, Irma, 29, 80
Pineda Henestrosa, Victor, 29
Plana, Elies, 229
pluma, 5
Las Plumas de la Serpiente (essay collection by Carballo), 1, 10, 182–87, 188–222
Las Plumas de la Serpiente (radio short series), 2, 5, 183, 186–87
poesía insurrecta, 80
poesía resurrecta, 80
Poeta en Nueva York (García Lorca), 196
population decline, 23
Por mi raza hablará la desigualdad (Solís), 81
Portilla, Miguel León, 27–28
Premio de Literaturas Indígenas de América (PLIA), 155
Primer Encuentro Nacional de Escritores en Lenguas Indígenas, 30
"Proética" (Santopietro), 166–67
Programa Universitario México Nación Multicultural de la UNAM, 31

Q'atzij, 11
Queer studies, 266
"Quenin ka in yolli" (Rojas), 27
Quetzalcoatl, 4, 187
Quijano, Aníbal, 57

raccoons. *See* nahuales
racial discrimination, 123, 160–61
racist antiracism, 81
radio short series, 2
"Raíz de vuelo" (Santopietro), 164
La raíz doble (documentary series), 22, 186
Rama, Ángel, 44
Ramírez, Enrique, 15
Ramírez Castañeda, Isabel, 117, 156
readership, 262–64
Recovering Footprints (Arias), 10–11
reeducation programs, 37–38
Regino, Juan Gregorio, 45, 122
"El regreso" (Carballo), 197
Reina Sofía, 196
"The Revolution Will Not Be Televised" (Scott-Heron), 217, 218
Reynoso, Alejandra, 123–24
Risling-Baldy, Cutcha, 5
ritual, as term, 83–84
Ritual de los olvidados (Tonalmeyotl), 18, 89
Rodríguez Reyna, Ignacio, 189–90
Rojas, Jacobo, 27
romanticization of Nahuatl, 1–2
Ruiz, Samuel, 29
Rumi, 210

sacred landscapes, 50–56
Saldaña-Portillo, María Josefina, 220
San Andrés Accords, 30
Sanjinés, Javier, 90
Santiago, Felina, 266
Santisteban, Emilio, 240

Santopietro, Judith, 10, 127, 159–63. See also *Palabras de agua* (Santopietro)
Scanlon, Arlene Patricia, 44
Schroeder, Susan, 25
Scott-Heron, Gil, 217, 218
Second Mexican Empire, 26
Secretaría de Educación Pública, 26–27, 28, 42, 67
Secretariat of Culture, 263
Semanauakuikatl / Canto al Universo (Matías García), 124
Semanca huitzilin (Hernández), 45, 75
"Sempoalxochitl" (Hernández), 45, 47–48, 50, 72
Serpent's Plumes, as metaphor, 4, 5, 8
settler colonialism, as term, 80. *See also* colonialism
Shoshoni, 22
Sideño, Gustavo Zapoteco, 7
Simic, Charles, 200, 201
Simpson, Leanne Betasamohsake, 121, 155
Sisters in the Shadow Editorial Collective are Perla Negra, 123
Situación actual y perspectivas de la literatura en lenguas indígenas, 30
Smith, Linda Tuhiwai, 5
"Soatsin" (Xochitiotzin), 131–33
social activism, 156–57, 188–89, 224–26, 229, 257–58, 266. *See also* Ayotzinapa
sovereignty, 121
Spanish invasion (1521), 23
Speed, Shannon, 21, 80–81, 82, 97–98, 112–13, 205
Spivak, Gayatri Chakravorty, 12
state-sponsored violence, 102–7
"Stone" (Simic), 201
Strange Horizons (publication), 244, 245
surveillance, 90–91

Taller de Historias de Vida, 123
Taller de Literature Maya, 30
Taylor, Diana, 173, 240
Taylor, Melanie Benson, 257, 258
Teacher's College, Ayotzinapa. *See* Ayotzinapa
Tehono O'odham, 212
tekipamitl, 13
tekolotl, 125
Tepetolo, José Antonio, 70
"Teskatl" (Xochitiotzin), 131, 152–53
Tetepetla, 116, 136, 137, 138, 286n4, 290n39
Tezozomoc, 24
tierra morena, 138, 143
"Tijxochiyotisej tlajtoli" / "Hacer florecer la palabra," 16
tlachialistli, 17
tlachianij, 53–54
tlaixpan, 2, 3, 15, 19, 119
tlajlamikilistli, 17
tlajtol/tlajtoli, as term, 120
Tlalkatsajtsilistle / Ritual de los olvidados (Tonalmeyotl), 79–113; "Amo xchiua" / "Recomendación," 110–12; "Chichetlaltipak" / "Tierra de perros," 91–94; "Intajtsitsiuan ayotsitsintin no uelej patlanej" / "Los padres de las tortugas también saben volar," 103–4; "Itlan tlayouisyotl" / "Bajo la noche," 96–97; "Jueves kuak nokua posojle" / "Jueves de pozole," 105–6; "Kuak nikneke ninokuikatis" / "Intento de melodía," 79, 109–10; "Nestora Salgado," 104–5; "Nipeua nixtentlapoue" / "Primeros párpados," 98–100; "Nonauatlajtol" / "Mi lengua náhuatl," 107–12; *Nosentlalilxochitlajtol / Antología personal*, 87; "Notlaltsin" / "Mi tierra," 101–2; "Tlamiktijketl" / "Carnicero," 95–96; "Tokatsitsintin" / "Las arañas," 100–102; "Under the Night," 105
tlamiktijketl (concept), 96
"Tlamiktijketl" / "Carnicero" (Tonalmeyotl), 95–96
Tlaoxtika in tlajtoli (Xochitiotzin Pérez), 33, 115–57; about publication, 127; maize metaphors in, 139–51; Nahua identity in, 151–54; past and remembrance in, 130–39; theoretical framework for analysis of, 119–23
Tlaxcaltecans, 23
Tlilamatl (Hernández), 45
"Tokatsitsintin" / "Las arañas" (Tonalmeyotl), 100–102
"Tokohkol xonomikileh" (Miyawatl), 249
Toledo, Francisco, 29
Toledo, Natalia, 29, 155
tonal, 69, 72
Tonalmeyotl, Martín, 10, 18, 32, 86–90, 261. *See also Tlalkatsajtsilistle / Ritual de los olvidados* (Tonalmeyotl)
Tonalxochimeh / Flores del sol (Matías García), 124
Torres García, Joaquín, 259–60
Totlalnantsij, 9
toxic positivity, 83
Trece semillas (publication), 249
tributary knowledge, 7
Triple Alliance, 22–23
ts'íib, 4
Tsintatak (Miyawatl), 226–28, 244–56
24 poetas contemporáneas en lengua náhuatl (publication), 32
tziktli, 205
Tzoc, Manuel, 157

"Uanxaka techita" / "Invisibles" (Tonalmeyotl), 102–3
ueuejtlajtoli, 17

Ueuejtlajtoli (Carballo), 182
ueuejtlakamej, 17
ueuetl, 119
UNAM, 12, 31, 45, 117, 204
"Under the Night" (Tonalmeyotl), 105
UNESCO, 10
Universo de las hilanderas (Hernández), 19, 260
Unwriting Maya Literature (Worley and Palacios), 5, 11
urdimbre, 138
Utes, 22
Uto-Nahua, 22
utopianism, 40, 164
U yajal maya wiiniko'ob (publication), 30

Valenzuela, Pedro Barra, 27
vanquished Indians trope, 3, 126, 177–79, 271n24, 298n11
Varner, Natasha, 177–78
Veracruzana, Huasteca, 27
Villa, Francisco, 231, *233, 241, 242*
Villamil, Enrique, 27
violence over the land, 91, 98–102. *See also* land theft
Violence over the Land (Blackhawk), 112
Visión de los vencidos (León Portilla), 27
La voz profunda (publication), 31
vulnerability, 82

Warrior, Robert, 16
Washinawatok, Ingrid, 121
we, as term, 100–101
"When I Want to Sing" (Tonalmeyotl), 79–80
Wilson-Hokowhitu, Nālani, 18–19
Words of the True Peoples (publication), 31
World Literature Today (publication), 31

Worley, Paul M., 4, 185

Xochikali, 71–72
Xochikoskatl (book by Hernández), 11, 37, 38–42, 45–50, 71, 75–77, 261
xochikoskatl (concept), 11–12, 39
xochikuikatl, 12
xochitekitl/xochitlachijchiualistli, 12
Xochitiotzin Pérez, Ethel, 10, 116, 118–19, 128–30. See also *Tlaoxtika in tlajtoli* (Xochitiotzin Pérez)
xochitl, 4
Xochitlahtol ika moyollot / Palabra florida para tu corazón (Matías García), 124
xochitlajkuiloani, 12
xochitlajtoli (concept), 2, 3–9, 17, 73, 83, 89, 193
Xochitlajtoli: Poesía contemporánea en lenguas originarias de México (anthology), 32, 87, 89, 127
xochitlajtsontli, 12
"Xochitlaoltsin" (Xochitiotzin), 131, 144–47
xochitlatsotsontli, 51
Xokoyotsin, José Antonio, 42, 47, 50, 63–64
"Xolko temiktl" / "Surco de sueños" (Xochitiotzin), 153–54

Year of the Indigenous Languages (2019), 10
yolchikaualistli, 17, 39, 54
yolotl, 17, 63–67, 119
yolotl, 200
yoltlajlamikilistli: connectivity of, 15, 17–18, 19, 35; Hernández's work and, 39; as term, 2; Tonalmeyotl and, 80, 86, 94, 98, 113; Xochitiotzin and, 119

Zapata, Emiliano, 26

Zapatista movement, 26, 28–29, 30–31, 173, 174
Zapotec language, 29
Zapotecs, 29
Zongolica (band), 125
Zoque, 30

www.ingramcontent.com/pod-product-compliance
Lightning Source LLC
Chambersburg PA
CBHW051556230426
43668CB00013B/1877